A SHORT HISTORY OF AMERICAN LITERATURE

Other Books in the Series

A Short History of African American Literature

A Short History of Australian Literature

A SHORT HISTORY OF AMERICAN LITERATURE

Krishna Sen & Ashok Sengupta

Orient BlackSwan

A SHORT HISTORY OF AMERICAN LITERATURE

ORIENT BLACKSWAN PRIVATE LIMITED

Registered Office
3-6-752 Himayatnagar, Hyderabad 500 029, Telangana, India
e-mail: centraloffice@orientblackswan.com

Other Offices
Bengaluru, Chennai, Guwahati, Hyderabad,
Kolkata, Mumbai, New Delhi, Noida, Patna

First published 2017
Reprinted 2019, 2020, 2022, 2024, 2026

042713

ISBN 978 93 86392 72 5

Typeset in Simoncini Garamond Std. 10.5/13.5 *by*
PrePSol Enterprises Pvt. Ltd., Haryana

Printed and bound at
SS Colour Impression Pvt Ltd, Chennai 600 106

Published by
Orient Blackswan Private Limited
3-6-752 Himayatnagar, Hyderabad 500 029, Telangana, India
e-mail: info@orientblackswan.com

CONTENTS

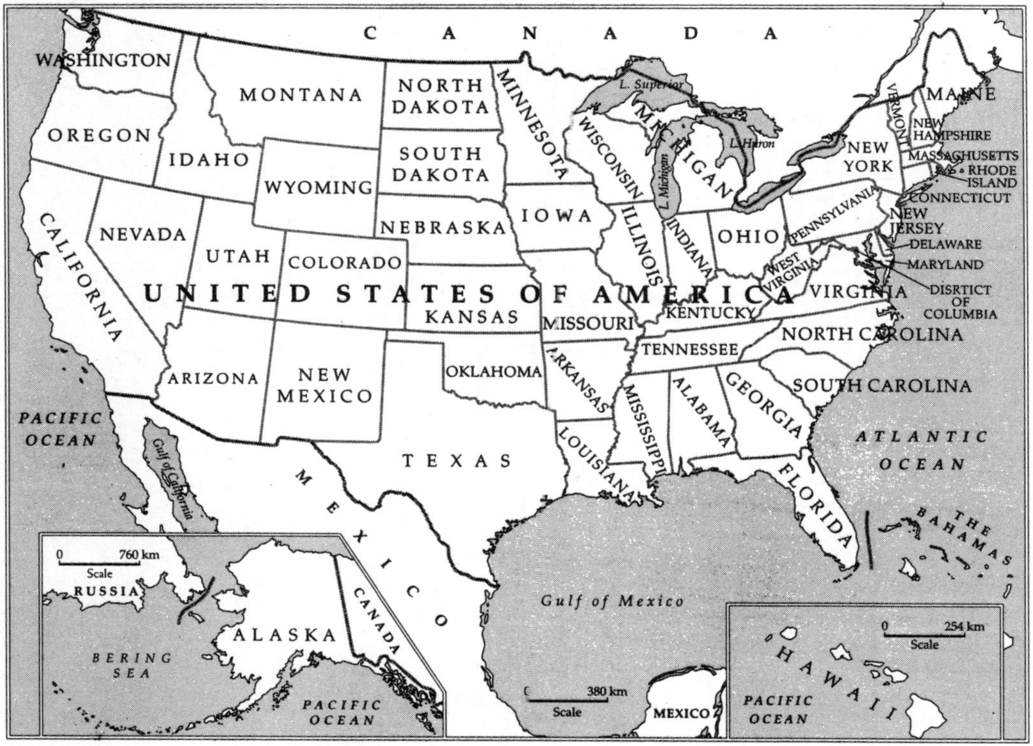

Political Map of the United States of America

A Note on References

Unless otherwise stated, and apart from references to individual novels, all primary references and data have been taken from the following books/anthologies/websites:

Chapter 1

Bode, Carl, ed. *American Perspectives: The United States in the Modern Age.* Washington DC: United States Information Agency (USIA), 1992. Print.

Daniels, Roger. *Coming to America: A History of Immigration and Ethnicity in American Life.* New York: HarperCollins, 1990. Indian edition; New Delhi: East-West Press, 1992. Print.

Jenkins, Philip. *History of the United States.* New York: St Martin's Press, 1997. Print.

Ludtke, Luther S., ed. *Making America: The Society and Culture of the United States.* Washington DC: United States Information Agency (USIA), 1988. Print.

Schuck, Peter H. *Diversity in America.* Indian edition; Noida: Frank Brothers, 2005. Print.

Chapter 2

Gray, Richard. *A Brief History of American Literature.* New York: Wiley-Blackwell, 2014. Print.

Lauter, Paul, gen. ed. *The Heath Anthology of American Literature, Vol. I* (Colonial Period to 1865). Lexington, Mass.: DC Heath & Co., 1990. Print.

Lemay, J. A. Leo, ed. *An Early American Reader.* Washington DC: USIA, 1992. Print.

Chapter 3

Inge, M. Thomas, ed. *A Nineteenth-Century American Reader.* Washington DC: USIA, 1989. Print.

Lauter, Paul, gen. ed. *The Heath Anthology of American Literature, Vol. I* (Colonial Period to 1865). Lexington, Mass.: DC Heath & Co., 1990. Print.

Miller, Perry, ed. *The Transcendentalists: An Anthology*. Cambridge, Mass.: Harvard UP, 1950, rpt. 1978. Print.

Chapter 4

Botting, Fred. *Gothic*. London and New York: Routledge, 2014. Print.

King, R. H. *Southern Renaissance: The Cultural Awakening of the American South, 1930–1955*. Oxford: Oxford UP, 1980. Print.

Lane, Jack, and Maurice O'Sullivan, eds. *A Twentieth-century American Reader, Vol. I* (1900–1945). Washington DC: USIA, 1999. Print.

Michael, George, and Frederick Crews, eds. *Anthology of American Literature: Realism to the Present*. New York: Macmillan, 1989. Print.

Rubin, Louis D., Jr., ed. *The American South: Portrait of a Culture*. Washington DC: USIA, 1991. Print.

Chapter 5

Chamelzky, Jules, ed. *Jewish American Literature: A Norton Anthology*. New York: Norton, 2001. Print.

Lauter, Paul, gen. ed. *The Heath Anthology of American Literature, Vol. II* (1865 to the Present). Lexington, Mass.: DC Heath & Co., 1990. Print.

Putz, Manfred, and Peter Freese, eds. *Postmodernism in American Literature: A Critical Anthology*. Ann Arbor: U of Michigan P, 1981. Print.

Waldman, Anne, ed. *The Beat Book: Writings from the Beat Generation*. Boston: Shambala Publications, 2007. Print.

Chapter 6

Chapman, Abraham, ed. *Black Voices: An Anthology of African American Literary Narratives*. New York: Signet Classics, 2001. Print.

Gates, Henry Louis, Jr., and Nellie McKay, eds. *The Norton Anthology of African American Literature*. New York: Norton, 1997. Print.

Locke, Alain. *The New Negro* (1925). Available in several editions. Print.

Nanda, Aparajita, ed. *Black California*. Santa Clara, CA: Heyday and Santa Clara University, 2011. Print.

Smith, Rochelle, and Sharon Lynette Jones, eds. *The Prentice-Hall Anthology of African American Literature*. Upper Saddle River, NJ: Prentice-Hall, 2000. Print.

Chapter 7

Native American Literature

Native American Authors. Web. www.ipl.org/div/natam/

NativeWeb. Web. www.nativeweb.org/

Trout, Lawana. *Native American Literature: An Anthology*. New York: McGraw Hill, 1998. Print.

Mexican American Literature

A Selection of Chicano Studies Resources on the Web. Web. http://homework.sdmesa.edu/libinstr/docs/chicano_web.pdf

Aranda, José F., Jr. *When We Arrive: A New Literary History of Mexican America*. Tucson: U of Arizona P, 2005. Print.

Valdez, Luis, and Stan Steiner, eds. *Aztlan: An Anthology of Mexican American Literature*. New York: Random House, 1972. Print.

Multicultural American Literatures

2010 US Census – current demographic break-up through maps and charts. Web. http://www.buzzfeed.com/mjs538/interesting-us-census-maps-and-charts#.ia40G2wk5

Banerjee, Neelanjana, Summi Kaipa, and Pireeni Sundaralingam, eds. *Indivisible: An Anthology of Contemporary South Asian American Poetry*. Fayetteville: U of Arkansas P, 2010. Print.

Chan, Jeffrey P., ed. *The Big Aiiieeee!: An Anthology of Chinese American and Japanese American Writers.* New York: Meridian Books, 1991. Print.

Chan, Jeffrey P., and Frank Chin, eds. *Aiiieeee!: An Anthology of Asian American Writers.* New York: Meridian Books, 1997. Print.

Choi, Yearn Hong, and Haeng Ja Kim, eds. *Surfacing Sadness: A Centennial of Korean-American Literature, 1903–2003.* Dumont, NJ: Homa & Sekey Books, 2003. Print.

Gillan, Maria Mazziotti, and Jennifer Gillan, eds. *Unsettling America: An Anthology of Contemporary Multicultural Poetry.* New York: Penguin Books, 1994. Print.

Chapter 8

Inge, M. Thomas, ed. *Handbook of Popular American Culture*. New York: Arnold, 1981. Print.

———, ed. *Handbook of American Popular Literature.* New York: Dayton, 1988. Print.

Landrum, Larry N. *American Mystery and Detective Novels: A Reference Guide*. Westport, CT: Greenwood, 1999. Print.

Maltby, Richard, and Ian Craven. *Hollywood Cinema.* Oxford: Blackwell, 1995. Print.

CHAPTER 1

The History and Culture of the United States of America

Krishna Sen

THE NARRATIVE OF AMERICAN LITERATURE

North America was sporadically settled by Europeans in the sixteenth century, and by large numbers of English settlers, many of them fleeing from religious or political persecution, from the early seventeenth century onwards. Written texts in English date only from this period – prior to this, the continent was densely populated by indigenous tribes who possessed rich oral cultures but no written literature. It is surprising that American literature, that has produced so many Nobel laureates, has such a short history. England, for instance, had already transited through the Old English, Middle English and Elizabethan periods by the time the first English writings appeared in America.

The English settlers wrested independence from England in 1776 and established the United States of America. From the seventeenth to the nineteenth century, however, American writing was marginalised both at home and abroad as a minor offshoot of English literature since it was written in the language of another country (England) and lacked an aesthetic heritage of its own. Several scholars from premier American universities (from Harvard, established in 1636, to

Cornell, founded in 1865) dismissed American texts as unworthy of being taught in literature classrooms. British critics were particularly patronising, at least till the recent advent of British Americanists like Paul Giles. Reviewing an American publication in *The Edinburgh Review* (No. 33, 1820), Reverend Sydney Smith rhetorically queried: "In the four quarters of the globe, who reads an American book? Or goes to an American play?" A century later, F. R. Leavis (who had identified Henry James as an "English novelist" in *The Great Tradition* by virtue of James's acquiring British citizenship the year before his death) magisterially proclaimed in an article in *Commentary* (1 November 1952) that American literature had neither "examinable content" nor "memorable books". Even the oracular American critic Harold Bloom highlights only two American authors in his voluminous *The Western Canon* (1994) – Walt Whitman and Emily Dickinson.

Nevertheless, oppositional voices emerged quite early, very much along the lines of D. H. Lawrence's perceptive observation, in *Studies in Classic American Literature* (1923), that there is a uniqueness that "belongs to the American continent and to nowhere else. . . . It is the shifting over from the old psyche to something new, a displacement." Lawrence was ahead of his time in recognising this quality in American colonial authors writing between 1620 and 1776, for all that they lacked the literary excellence of their English counterparts. The leitmotif of these colonial texts that chronicled the adventure and the agony of fashioning a new civilisation was the *difference* between the intrepid New World of America and the tradition-bound Old World of Europe. Colonial writers sought to compensate for the absence of American history by creating through their sermons and exploration narratives, a virtual metahistory in which the settlers were portrayed as God's chosen people elected to civilise what William Bradford termed in *Of Plymouth Plantation* (1826–47) as "this hideous and desolate wilderness". Like the Israelites in the Bible, they were to create a New Jerusalem in that wilderness, a new "City upon a Hill". They were inspired by the evocative European dream of a land of fabulous possibilities beyond the oceans that dated back to Plato, and that gained immense currency through the Utopian writings of the European Renaissance. The great contribution of these colonial writers was to invest their adopted country with a sense of destiny.

The post–1776 nationalist writing continued the work of constructing a new cultural identity. The prose of J. Hector St. John de Crèvecœur, Benjamin Franklin and Thomas Jefferson, and the fiction of Charles Brockden Brown, Washington Irving and James Fenimore Cooper projected this new entity, the American, as an ardent Republican who was individualistic, enterprising, industrious and innovative. Pre-nineteenth-century texts collectively formulated the notion of "Americanness". In his seminal *Main Currents in American Thought* (1927), Vernon L. Parrington hails these "germinal ideas that have come to be reckoned as traditionally American . . . determining . . . our characteristic ideals and institutions."

American self-fashioning continued in the nineteenth century. The identitarian politics of Ralph Waldo Emerson's essays (notably "The American Scholar" [1837] that carefully distinguished between American and English literary themes and forms) and Walt Whitman's celebration of democratic America (versus monarchical Europe) were supplemented by important non-literary works. For example, Noah Webster, whose pioneering *American Spelling Book* (1783) had replaced "English" with "American" spelling ("color" for "colour"; "realize" for "realise"), confirmed the autonomy of American English in his provocatively titled *American Dictionary of the English Language* (1828) that contained over ten thousand words unknown in England (prairie, maize, tomahawk, okra, coyote, rattlesnake, etc.). In 1829, Samuel Knapp countered Reverend Sydney Smith's derogatory remarks in *The Edinburgh Review* with the earliest history of American literature, *Lectures on American Literature, with Remarks on Some Passages of American History*. Knapp focused the singular contribution, not only of colonial and nationalist literary texts, but also of early American oratory, painting, music and even scientific treatises such as those by Franklin, in crafting the narrative of an emerging culture. Knapp's conflation of literature, history, science and the arts in defining America is now considered the precursor of the contemporary interdisciplinary field known as American Studies.

The nineteenth century also witnessed a literary efflorescence – the prose of Emerson and Henry David Thoreau, the poetry of Whitman and Emily Dickinson, and the fiction of Edgar Allan Poe, Nathaniel Hawthorne, Herman Melville and Mark Twain. Other authors, like Henry Wadsworth Longfellow, Louisa May Alcott, William Dean Howells and Bret Harte, enhanced the range of this corpus. F. O. Matthiessen famously described this period as the "American Renaissance" in his 1941 book of the same name. Matthiessen's influential contention that American literature properly began only with Emerson impacted several well-regarded literary histories of that time, such as Robert E. Spiller's *The Cycle of American Literature* (1955).

However, a different literary history had been highlighted in the first three-volume edition of *The Cambridge History of American Literature* (1917), where the Emerson era appeared only midway through the second volume. While not claiming literary importance for all the early writers, the contributors followed Knapp in appreciating their nation-building discourses. They argued against using English literary categories like "Renaissance" and "Romanticism" for assessing American literature, since the two histories and cultures were so dissimilar. This is underscored in James Truslow Adams's *The Epic of America* (1931), Henry Nash Smith's *The Virgin Land: The American West as Symbol and Myth* (1950) and Perry Miller's *Errand into the Wilderness* (1956). These major socio-cultural studies foreground the non-European myths and values that inform the American imaginary, such as the Frontier, Manifest Destiny and the American Dream.

Another significant factor that has shaped the American ethos is a degree of racial and ethnic diversity unimaginable in Europe. Besides the existing native tribes, the importing of African slaves, and the entry of a Hispanic population after the annexation of Mexican territory in the 1840s, the US has witnessed extensive Asian immigration. Following the successful African American and other minority Civil Rights movements in the 1960s, multiculturalism has emerged as a compelling aspect of American life and letters. The pioneer in going beyond Anglocentrism was the 3000-page *Heath Anthology of American Literature* (1998), edited by Paul Lauter, that begins with tribal oral narratives, focuses on colonial and nationalist writing, and features every ethnic community in the US. A Norton anthology soon followed suit. The literary histories that are currently the most acclaimed, *The Columbia Literary History of the United States* and the six-volume *Cambridge History of American Literature*, not only emphasise cultural history and its colonial and nationalist articulations, but give equal weight to both Anglocentric and multicultural literary productions.

Within its limited compass this *Short History* follows the same paradigm. In place of the usual chronological commentary, its distinctive approach is to investigate the vital interface between American literature and the culture that nurtured it. Hence the first chapter offers a comprehensive account of the histories (such as the struggle for independence and the Civil War), values (the Puritan inheritance) and the myths (like Manifest Destiny, the Frontier, and the American Dream) that irradiate American literature and make it so different from English literature (as can be seen from the comparative timeline at the end of this book). The *Short History* then moves from colonial and nationalist writing, through the Emerson era, to American modernism and postmodernism. It also gives equal importance to non-Anglocentric and non-mainstream writing by devoting two detailed chapters to ethnic and multicultural literatures, and by including a special section on American literature and popular culture. This is important because, without the presence of ethnic and popular literary modes like the slave narrative and the Western, American literature would not have produced the kind of work unknown in English literature – such as Toni Morrison's *Beloved* and Cormac McCarthy's *Blood Meridian*, both of which are among the great novels of the twentieth century. The *Short History* thus aims to be both inclusive and contemporary, and to foster an informed appreciation of American literature.

American Civilisation: European Settlers in a New Continent

The Early History

The land mass that we associate with the United States of America – extending from the Atlantic Ocean in the east to the Pacific Ocean in the west, and from the Canadian border in the north to the Gulf of Mexico in the south, an area almost three times the size of

India – has witnessed continuous human habitation from at least 8000 BC. But the country we know as the United States of America began to evolve as recently as the seventeenth century and emerged as an independent nation only in 1776. The original inhabitants of the area were Asiatic nomads clustered in several tribes. Their stirring and tragic history will be summarised in the section on Native American literature (in Chapter Seven of this book). Here we shall briefly survey how white, Western Christian civilisation took root in America, and especially how it developed through historical experiences so different from Europe's that it ultimately diverged radically from its European origins.

Long before Europeans set foot in America, a legend had circulated about a fabulous land far to the west of Europe, somewhere in the vast reaches of the Atlantic. The great Greek philosopher Plato (c.428–348 BC) was one of the first to imagine this mythical country which he called "Atlantis". In *Timaeus* (c.360 BC) it appears as an ideal state, and in *Critias* (c.360 BC) it is bountifully stocked with crops and minerals. With the revival of classical learning during the European Renaissance, Plato's dream blossomed into a rich tradition of Utopian writing revolving around this imaginary site – in England, Thomas More, Philip Sidney, Francis Bacon and James Harington called it "Utopia", "Arcadia", "The New Atlantis" and "Oceania", respectively; in Italy, it was Francesco Patrizi's "The Happy City" and Tommaso Campanella's "The City of the Sun"; and in German, Johannes Andreae named it "Christianopolis". These Christian writers enhanced Plato's Elysian fantasy with biblical images recalling the Christian Paradise before the Fall of Man. Thus, though concrete political and socio-economic reasons spurred the European engagement with North and South America, the aura of the Americas for Europe surely stemmed from this long cultural connection with Plato's *Atlantis* and the biblical Garden of Eden.

The first European foray into North America dates to around AD 1000, when Icelandic Vikings led by Leif Eriksson landed in present-day eastern Canada, according to available archaeological evidence. But this did not develop into full-fledged settlement. In the fifteenth century, ambitious monarchs, especially in England, France, Spain and Portugal, sought to establish overseas empires and vied with one another to sponsor voyages of exploration to conquer new territories. Another major objective of these voyages was to facilitate the lucrative Asian trade by discovering shorter sea routes that would bypass the arduous land routes to Asia.

This was exactly what the Italian mariner Christopher Columbus, liberally funded by King Philip II and Queen Isabella of Spain, was attempting to do, when in 1492, he landed on an island in the Caribbean Sea. Columbus mistook it for an island in the Indian Ocean and dubbed the islanders "Indians" (American Indians, now known as Native Americans). History records that Columbus "discovered" America in 1492, but this was only a European "discovery" since those places had been inhabited for centuries by indigenous peoples.

Recording his impressions in his *Journal*, Columbus slipped easily into the Utopia/Paradise discourse – "This island and all others are fertile to a limitless degree . . . and fruits in great diversity." The *Journal*, which circulated widely in translation in Western Europe, created the same kind of fascination for the Americas as the biblical Promised Land or "New World" that Marco Polo's *Travels* (1298) had done for India and China as fabled Eldorados in the thirteenth century. Mexico's Spanish bishop, Vasco de Quiroga, makes an early reference to the Americas as the "New World" (later applied exclusively to the US) in *Information on Rights* (1535) – "For not in vain . . . is this called the New World, not because it is newly found, but because it is like . . . the first and golden age." French explorer Jean de Léry's *History of a Voyage to the Land of Brazil* (1578) contains another reference – "This land of America . . . is so unlike what we have in Europe, Asia and Africa that it may well be called a 'New World' with respect to us." Among English poets, Michael Drayton (1563–1631) hailed "Earth's only Paradise" in "To The Virginia Voyage"; John Donne (1572–1631), in "An Anatomy of the World" imagined the New World emerging from the carcass of the Old; while Andrew Marvell (1621–78) evoked the pleasures of the Garden of Eden in "Bermudas" ("He makes the figs our mouths to meet / And throws the melons at our feet").

The immense natural and mineral wealth of the two continents attracted numerous explorers and conquering armies; Spain and Portugal quickly divided Central and South America between themselves, while England and France looked to North America and the Caribbean islands. Spaniards also settled the entire southern belt of North America, from Texas to California, and the second language there even today is Spanish. For England, John Cabot made the first voyage to North America in 1498. Very soon, England chartered several "trading" (actually, colonising) companies to establish sugar, cotton and tobacco plantations along the Atlantic seaboard. The acute demand for unskilled labour in the plantation economy was met by shipments of convicts from Britain and slaves from West Africa. (The history of Black people in the US, now known as African Americans, will preface Chapter Six which is on African American literature.) Despite the lure of huge profits, settlement was perilous and quite unlike Paradise with thousands perishing from disease, tornados and Native American onslaughts.

Another compelling motive for braving these hazards was to escape religious and political persecution by the increasingly autocratic European monarchs. Anti-Royalist liberals and anti-Roman Catholic Huguenots fled from France to the Gulf of Mexico and Canada, but the largest influx of religious refugees to North America was from the anti-monarchical Puritan community in England. Along with freedom of worship, they also sought to serve their God by converting the Native Americans to Christianity. For both these reasons, the early Puritan migrants zealously characterised their project in North America as a holy mission, and identified themselves as "pilgrims" (later revered as the "Pilgrim Fathers" or founders of the new nation) rather than as adventurers for economic gain. "They know they are pilgrims," wrote William Bradford (1590–1637), the first governor of the Puritan settlement at Plymouth, Massachusetts, in his journal *Of Plymouth Plantation*.

Colonial America: The Thirteen English Colonies

The first permanent English settlement in North America was Jamestown, founded in 1603 by settlers recruited by a London company. The Puritan "pilgrims" came in 1620 in the *Mayflower* and founded Plymouth. Between 1623 and 1733, thirteen colonies were founded along the Atlantic seaboard with mainly British, but also some liberal-minded German, Dutch and Swedish settlers.

While the settlers owed their allegiance to England, they had separate legislatures and regarded themselves as administratively autonomous. The hardy and industrious settlers prospered against all odds and soon their republican tendencies riled the mother country. In 1765, the British Parliament imposed exorbitant taxes on the colonists and forbade prospecting for free land west of the Appalachian Mountains. Tensions escalated enormously through incidents such as the British army's "Boston Massacre" of protesting civilians in 1770. In April 1775, the thirteen colonies proclaimed open rebellion against the British Crown.

The Revolutionary War and the Declaration of Independence

Following Benjamin Franklin's exhortation to "Join or Die", the thirteen colonies united in a Congress, boycotted trade with England and fought a six-year Revolutionary War (also called the War of American Independence) under the leadership of George Washington. Washington was a superb tactician, and despite initial losses to Britain's four invading armies, he succeeded in separating and defeating them individually. On 4 July 1776 (now America's "National Day"), even as the war raged, the thirteen colonies signed the "Declaration of Independence" drafted by Thomas Jefferson and proclaimed themselves the United States of America. The Declaration opened with the ringing affirmation:

> We hold these truths to be self-evident, that all men are created equal, that they are endowed by their Creator with certain unalienable Rights, that among these are Life, Liberty and the Pursuit of Happiness. That to secure these Rights, Governments are instituted among Men, deriving their just powers from the consent of the governed.

The Revolutionary War ended in October 1781 with a decisive American victory over the British commander Charles Cornwallis (who later became Governor General of India and defeated Tipu Sultan). In 1783, the Treaty of Paris officially ended British colonial rule in North America and recognised the United States (still only the thirteen colonies) as a sovereign nation under its first President, George Washington. The US, thus, became the first British colony to successfully terminate British rule. The shock felt in England at the loss of its American colonies was graphically recorded by William Blake in his long apocalyptic poem, *America, A Prophecy* (1793).

The Civil War and the Emancipation Proclamation for Slaves

Within a century of independence, Americans had spread right across the continent from the Atlantic to the Pacific coast, exploring new territories for white settlement and creating new states and new wealth for the Union – plantations in the Southwest, fertile prairies in the Midwest and gold in California. This was the great era of pioneers, entrepreneurs and cowboys. By the mid-nineteenth century, the country had extensive road, rail and river transportation, a flourishing merchant navy and nation-wide communications using the telegraph invented in 1832 by the American inventor Samuel Morse.

However, there was a dark underside to this triumphant saga of progress and prosperity – the inhuman blot of slavery in the plantations, and the indiscriminate massacre of Native Americans vainly fighting the colonists' guns with bows and arrows to redeem their ancestral lands. Of these, slavery became the more acrimonious issue because it directly impacted the equations between the "slave states" of the "Deep South" (the original pre-Revolutionary War Southern colonies) and the manufacturing and trading states of the North. The plantation barons derived enormous profits by brutally exploiting free slave labour; they then leveraged their wealth to establish new "slave plantations" in the Southwest, tipping the balance of national power in their favour. The Northern Abolitionists (those who wished to abolish slavery), led by the Republican Party, sought to curtail Southern affluence through bitterly fought legal and political anti-slavery battles in the courts and the US Congress (the bicameral legislature consisting of two houses – the Senate and the House of Representatives). The shocking disclosures about slavery in Harriet Beecher Stowe's bestselling novel *Uncle Tom's Cabin* (1852) greatly assisted the cause of Abolition. Pro- and anti-slavery violence escalated and slaves began fleeing to the North.

The last straw was the Republican Abraham Lincoln's election to a four-year term as President in November 1860. South Carolina seceded from the Union in December 1860. Six more slave states followed and together formed the anti-North Confederacy. The Civil War started on 12 April 1861, when Confederates bombarded a Union-held fort in South Carolina. When Lincoln retaliated with naval blockades of all Southern ports, four more slave states seceded, taking the total to eleven. Twenty-three states, from California through the Midwest to the Northeast, remained loyal to the Union.

The hard-fought Civil War between the Northern Union and the Southern Confederacy was marked by the frequency and ferocity of the battles and lasted from April 1861 to June 1865. The terrible carnage was vividly recorded in the Civil War poems by the great American poet from the North, Walt Whitman (1819–92), such as "A Sight in Camp in the Daybreak Gray and Dim" which eulogised slain Union soldiers: "Young man, I think I know you – I think this face is the face of the Christ himself, / Dead and divine and brother of all, and here again he lies." Even while the war continued, Lincoln proclaimed freedom for all slaves from 1 January 1863. The "Emancipation Proclamation" declared:

> That on the first day of January, in the year of our Lord one thousand eight hundred and sixty-three, all persons held as slaves within any State or designated part of a State . . . shall be then, thenceforward, and forever free; and the Executive Government of the United States . . . will recognize and maintain the freedom of such persons, and will do no act or acts to repress such persons, or any of them, in any efforts they may make for their actual freedom.

That this was no mere vengeful anti-Confederacy measure but part of Lincoln's larger vision of a democratic polity was memorably enunciated in his Gettysburg Address commemorating the Union dead on 19 November 1863:

> Four score and seven years ago our fathers brought forth on this continent a new nation, conceived in Liberty, and dedicated to the proposition that all men are created equal. . . . from these honored dead we take increased devotion to that

> cause for which they gave the last full measure of devotion – that we here highly resolve that these dead shall not have died in vain – that this nation, under God, shall have a new birth of freedom – and that government of the people, by the people, for the people, shall not perish from the earth.

Lincoln's words inspired Whitman's 1867 ode, "For You, O Democracy":

> Come, I will make the continent indissoluble,
> I will make the most splendid race the sun ever shone upon . . .
> I will plant companionship thick as trees along all the rivers of America,
> and along the shores of the great lakes and all over the prairies . . .

Meanwhile, Lincoln was re-elected for a second term in November 1864. By early 1865, Union armies (that now included freed Blacks or "freedmen") and its navy had surrounded the South from all sides, and the war ended with decisive Northern victories by June. On 11 April 1865, Lincoln had proposed voting rights for former Black male slaves. This incensed both Southerners and Northern conservatives. On 14 April 1865, Lincoln, one of America's greatest Presidents, was assassinated by a Northern Confederate sympathiser, John Wilkes Booth.

The American Civil War preserved the integrity of the nation and achieved the goal of abolishing slavery, but it shattered the Southern plantation economy. In his *Absalom, Absalom!* (1936), the powerful Southern novelist William Faulkner described "the Deep South dead since 1865 and peopled with garrulous outraged baffled ghosts." To this day, except for Texas, where large petroleum deposits were discovered in 1901, the American South is less affluent than the rest of the country.

The Era of Reconstruction

Even before the war ended Lincoln had set up a Reconstruction Plan with two objectives – to re-stabilise the stricken South and to rehabilitate the freed but unskilled slaves. The Plan prevailed till

1877, when widespread grievance surfaced against the high taxes imposed for paying for it. Under its first objective, the restoration of damaged towns, ports and transport infrastructure in the South was initiated. Under its second objective, a Freedom Bureau was constituted to protect the legal rights of Blacks and establish educational institutions to promote their employable skills. Thousands of Northerners (derisively dubbed "carpetbaggers" by Southerners) were encouraged to settle in the South to skew the cultural balance. An 1867 law granting franchise to Black males sparked immense turbulence and proved ineffectual. Slavery was gone but racism was still rampant throughout the country. Yet, though Reconstruction failed to achieve all its goals, it was an important first step in rebuilding a nation devastated by civil war, and also in offering the Black community their first glimmers of opportunity.

A Nation of Immigrants

A Nation of Immigrants is the title of a book by President John F. Kennedy that was published posthumously in 1964. It is a graphic description of the uncommonly composite demography of the US. Right from independence, American governments actively encouraged white European immigration to increase the population and settle the vast territory stretching to the Pacific. The first US census of 1790, when many of the Pacific states had not yet been founded, showed a population of just under four million – of this over half was English, around 75000 were slaves of African origin, and the rest were French, German, Dutch, Swedish, Scottish and Irish. With the advent of larger and faster steam-powered ships in the 1880s, the waves of Western immigrants swelled into floods with migrants now also arriving from Italy, Sicily and Russia.

Most of these immigrants were poverty-stricken or persecuted. The Irish influx, for instance, tripled during the Irish Potato Famine (1845). America was the dream destination because of the free and good life promised by cheap and plentiful farmlands in the South and West and burgeoning manufacturing jobs in the North during the Industrial Revolution. The fitting symbol for these aspirations was the colossal Statue of Liberty (305 feet/93 metres high), unveiled on Liberty Island in New York harbour on 28 October 1886, which became the first glimpse of America for incoming immigrant ships. The contemporary poet Emma Lazarus's poem "The New Colossus" (engraved on the pedestal of the statue) images America as a refuge for the down-trodden:

> . . . Give me your tired, your poor,
> Your huddled masses yearning to breathe free,
> The wretched refuse of your teeming shore . . .
> I lift my lamp beside the golden door!

But this golden door was no easy passport to prosperity. In the uncharted territory beyond the thirteen colonies, wealth had to be wrested from the land through self-reliance and hard work.

Non-European immigration (apart from African slaves) began in earnest in the nineteenth century with cheap Asian male labour shipped in by labour contractors. By 1852, about 25,000 unskilled Chinese men were helping to build several major railroad systems in the US. Northern manufacturers preferred skilled Japanese workers who accepted lower wages than what was offered to Europeans. Additionally, many liberal-minded Japanese fled to Hawaii after the restoration of the absolutist Meiji dynasty in Japan in 1868. South Asians were latecomers to this labour market – Indian Sikhs settled along the Pacific coast as farm and railroad workers only in the early twentieth century.

The American response to non-white immigration was varied, and has been surveyed later in this chapter under "American Multiculturalism". The reactions ranged from outright opposition to accommodation of diversity. To cite some early laws, the Chinese Exclusion Act (1882) debarred further Chinese immigration; a 1917 Act barred immigration from most Asian countries and colonies, while a 1924 Act modified this to permit limited quotas. By contrast, the mid-twentieth-century surge of qualified non-white immigrants was facilitated by President Lyndon B. Johnson's liberal Immigration Act of 1965. From time to time laws enabling immigrants to access American citizenship have also been passed.

The 2010 US Census data showed that as of 1 April 2010, there were 308.7 million American citizens, of whom 72 per cent identified themselves on their census forms as racially "white". But they could have originated in any "white" country from Austria to Australia. The remaining 28 per cent comprised Black African Americans, Asian Americans from various Asian countries, Spanish-speaking Hispanic Americans from Cuba and South America, Arab Americans and indigenous peoples such as Mexican-origin Chicanos, Native Americans, Pacific Islanders from Hawaii and native tribes in Alaska.

The common thread binding all phases and categories of immigration, from the Pilgrim Fathers to the present-day computer engineers, is the hope for greater prospects and a better life. But this also creates an extremely unusual demographic profile. In the normal course of things most citizens of a country come from that country. In the case of the United States, instead of coming from America, Americans come from all over the world.

The Myths that Shape American Culture and Literature

The New World

The cultural issue predicated by this eclectic diversity obviously is: how then do we define "Americanness"? Part of the answer has to do with a distinctive strain in the national character. As the historical and demographic overview of the US clearly demonstrates, only a particular kind of person chose to settle there. These were risk-takers who relied on their tenacity, industry and enterprise to carve out their own destinies in a new place.

America still draws such people because of its privileging of adventure, inventiveness, achievement and success. Today, more than two hundred years after its founding in 1776, the US has lost none of its glamour as the iconic "New World" of limitless opportunity. This is the celebrated "myth of America". The French cultural theorist Jean Baudrillard explains this enduring, transcultural allure in his *America* (1996; English translation in 1998):

> Still, there is a violent contrast here, in this country, between the growing abstraction of a nuclear universe and a primary,

> visceral, unbounded vitality, springing not from rootedness, but from the lack of roots, a metabolic vitality . . ., the US . . . [is the] society of the future, a society of complexity, hybridity, and the greatest intermingling [of peoples]. . . .

For Baudrillard, the strength of America lies in its lack of an ancient history and traditions that would have weighed it down with rituals and formalities. The constant churning of immigrant influx with its bewildering array of languages, religions and heritages infuses the social fabric with the dynamism of change. America is a nation that continually reinvents itself through new configurations of desire and power, enabling it to set the pace for modern lifestyles.

The credit for fashioning a unique American worldview that all later migrants inherit goes to the early settlers. The Pilgrim Fathers not only settled a new country but literally crafted a new civilisation. In *Regeneration through Violence* (1973), cultural historian Richard Slotkin highlights "this artificially created American nation – the self-baptized American people . . .". The highly individualistic orientation of the "New World" settlers was diametrically opposed to the feudal mindset of "Old World" Europe. Their revisionist ideal was "Life, Liberty and the Pursuit of Happiness", and they fought a Revolutionary War and a Civil War to uphold it. The values articulated by the Pilgrim Fathers and their immediate successors constitute the bedrock of American culture till today. The critic Susan Faludi calls them "America's Guardian Myths". Not that these myths have gone unchallenged. Marginalised minorities like the Blacks and the indigenous peoples have questioned why this egalitarian democracy does not accommodate them. Literary works such as Arthur Miller's play *Death of a Salesman* (1949) have exposed the vulnerabilities of a society glorifying youth and success beyond all. Yet, the myths continue to ground and inspire Americans, rendering American culture significantly different from other Eurocentric cultures.

"A City upon a Hill": The Foundational Puritan Myth

American popular culture, Hollywood and Wall Street so extensively propagate the notion of a materialistic and hedonistic society that the centrality of religion and a rigorous work ethic, especially in the vast expanse of Middle America, is often obscured. Freedom of worship motivated the early settlements – Puritans in Massachusetts, Roman Catholics in Maryland, Quakers in Pennsylvania, and so on. With the settlers resolving to erase their past and begin anew, the Puritans proved most adept at deploying biblical narratives to conceptualise and contextualise this new-born civilisation with no history or traditions. The motifs of the sacred mission and the pilgrimage effectively legitimised their forcible occupation of Native American territory as an offering to their Lord. Anticipating later imperial discourses, Captain John Smith observed in *A Description of New England* (1616), the first English book to be written in America: "What so truly suits with honour and honesty as the discovery of things unknown . . . peopling countries, informing the ignorant . . . teaching virtue. . . ."

Life was dangerous and fraught with terrifying Native attacks. Settlers needed reassurance and Puritan leaders provided it by appropriating the Bible to signify their hallowed status allegorically. If this was the Promised Land, then they were the new Israelites, the new chosen people of God elected to this onerous task of glorifying His name. The paradigmatic motivational rhetoric is John Winthrop's sermon, "A Model of Christian Charity", aboard the Pilgrim ship *Arbella* (April 1630):

> The Lord will . . . dwell among us as His own people . . . the God of Israel is among us. For we must consider that we shall be as a city upon a hill [Jerusalem]. The eyes of all people are upon us. . . . And to shut this discourse with the exhortation of Moses . . . that the Lord our God may bless us in this land whither we go to possess it.

Indeed, it was a firm conviction that "possessing" the New World was a "Covenant" between these new Israelites and their God, based on His "Ordinances". John Cotton wrote in "God's Promise to his Plantations" (1630):

> . . . here is meant some more special appointment, because God tells them it by his own mouth. . . . He gives them the land by promise. . . . And that is when He giveth them . . . His Ordinances. It is a land of promise where they have provision for soul as well as for body.

This imagined analogy between the Pilgrims and the Israelites exiting a decadent Egypt (symbolising the Old World) for Palestine (the New World) in the Old Testament in effect co-opted the Bible as the ultimate provenance for the new nation.

Ironically, such enthusiastic piety promoted a kind of religious fundamentalism as to who exactly were "chosen" and fomented fissures in the Puritan ranks. Rhode Island colony was formed by freethinking Puritans expelled from Massachusetts. Again, later settlers proved more materialistic, "striving only to increase their stocks" (Bradford, *Of Plymouth Plantation*), thus reneging on their sacramental ordinance to build a New Jerusalem in the New World. No longer were they models of Christian charity. The fiery Cotton Mather, grandson of John Cotton, admonished in his sermon "A Christian and His Calling" (1701) that apart from serving God, "every Christian also hath a personal calling . . . by which his usefulness to his neighbourhood is distinguished."

However, there was a sinister aspect to this millennial zeal that sought to unite, inspire and sustain the settlers. For if this was Eden, then there had to be Satan too. The serpent in the Garden was obviously the Native American who swooped in on the settlements to burn and kill. In *Wonders of the Invisible World* (1693), Cotton Mather prefigures the later imperialist demonising of the racial Other while recalling one such raid: "The New Englanders are a people of God settled in those which were once the devil's territories. . . . An army of devils is horribly broke in upon the place. . . ." Similarly *A Narrative of Colonel Ethan Allen's Captivity written by Himself* (1779) describes a Native "savage": ". . . the wrath of devils and of damned spirits are the emblems of his countenance." The settlers retaliated by devastating Native villages. In *News from America*, Captain John Underhill defends the methodical extermination of the Pequot Indians (1636–37): "It may be demanded, Why should you be so furious? Should not Christians have more mercy and compassion? Sometimes the Scripture declareth women and children must perish with their parents. Sometimes the case alters, but we will not dispute it now. We had sufficient light from the word of God for our proceedings." This culturally constructed binary, apparently with biblical sanction, of the righteous colonist versus the diabolical Native shaped their conjoined histories for the next two centuries.

Excessive Puritan austerity and its crippling effect on emotional spontaneity have been critiqued by Americans themselves. Perhaps the most famous instance of such censure is Nathaniel Hawthorne's *The Scarlet Letter*. William Carlos Williams derides "the niggardliness of the damning Puritan tradition . . . that spiritually withering plague" in his *In the American Grain* (1925). Eugene O'Neill flays Puritan religiosity in *Mourning Becomes Electra* (1931). Nevertheless, core Puritan values have subtended America's philosophical development. This relates not just to the primacy of religion, whether Judaism or Protestant Christianity, for most white Americans. Politically and socially too, the US still prioritises liberty and democracy, individualism and innovation, aspirational discourses, the right to free enterprise and the Puritan work ethic.

Yet, perhaps the most crucial contribution of the Pilgrim Fathers and their successors was to fashion, in place of the usual markers of nationhood (a usable historical past, embedded cultural traditions and a geographically located national identity), a set of myths that would constitute "Americanness". As Cotton Mather wrote in *Magnalia Christi Americana* (1702), "Geography must now find work for a Christiano-graphy, in the history of a New English Israel . . . to anticipate the state of a New Jerusalem."

The Potent Myth of American Exceptionalism

A nation that believes itself to be ordained by the "Word of God" and fashioned as His chosen "Elect" is bound to enjoy a special sense of destiny as being qualitatively different from other nations and, in some way, exceptional. The evangelical fervour of American "exceptionalism" is an enduring Pilgrim legacy. The term "exceptional" was probably first used by the French historian Alexis de Tocqueville who, in his two-volume *Democracy in America* (1835 and 1840), marvelled at how, unlike Europe, America had evolved a non-hierarchical polity: "The position of the Americans is therefore quite exceptional, and it may be believed that no democratic people will ever be placed in a similar one." The next notable use was in the early twentieth century when the minority American Marxist Party contended that the absence of class struggle in their highly industrialised society was due to American exceptionalism, an observation that incensed Stalin.

The idea greatly inspired some early American writers. Philip Freneau imagined America as "Destiny's child" in "On the Rising Glory of America" (1772):

> And such America at last shall have
> When ages, yet to come, have run their round
> And future years of bliss alone remain.

Walt Whitman saluted America's uniqueness in "America" (1888):

> Strong, ample, fair, enduring, capable, rich,
> Perennial with the Earth, with Freedom, Law and Love,
> A grand, sane, towering, seated Mother,
> Chair'd in the adamant of Time.

Even the Black poet Phillis Wheatley, who was sold into slavery and freed by the "Emancipation Proclamation", celebrated America and her (forced) conversion to Christianity in "On Being Brought from Africa to America" (1768) – "'Twas mercy brought me from my Pagan land. . . ."

Far more than literature, it is American public and political life that is pervaded by the ideology of exceptionalism. On 25 December 1780, Thomas Jefferson declared that the newly-created nation was destined to establish a worldwide "Empire of Liberty"; in his annual message to the US Congress on 1 December 1862, President Lincoln designated America as "the last best hope of man on earth"; in his oft-quoted farewell speech as President, Ronald Reagan extolled America as the "shining city [upon a hill]"; and President Barack Obama announced in his "State of the Union Address" (28 January 2014), ". . . the United States is better positioned for the twenty-first century than any other nation on earth." The most contentious repercussions of this ideology are in American foreign policy. While other countries chafe at America playing the "policeman to the world", America genuinely considers itself the natural guardian of the globe. An archetypal reaction can be found in Republican politician Mitt Romney's speech of 7 October 2011: "America must lead the world. . . . I believe we are an exceptional country with a unique role and destiny in the world." America's prosperity and advancement help to perpetuate this assumption that chimes well with the Puritan conviction of a sacred mission.

The monological discourse of American exceptionalism has been challenged most resonantly in some of its literature. From the novels of Washington Irving on the American West to Herman Melville's *Moby-Dick* (1851), and especially in the powerful works of African American authors, white America's delusions of superiority have been scathingly subverted. But perhaps the greatest blow to the exceptionalist narrative was the destruction of the "Twin Towers" in New York by the al-Qaeda on 9 September 2001 ("9/11"). It certainly has not quelled the notion; yet, it did provoke much anger, but also much soul-searching among Americans.

Manifest Destiny and the Myth of the Frontier

A direct corollary of the exceptionalist ideology is America's curious belief in the righteousness of its expansionist policies. With the pressure of a population burgeoning through migration, land for settlement was at a premium, and throughout the nineteenth century expansionism involved occupation of the continental land mass up to the Pacific. This meant lengthy wars with the Mexican kingdom in the southwest and with Native Americans everywhere else, with the better-armed Americans always emerging victorious.

Expansionism gained an eloquent new name redolent of Puritan exceptionalism and the new spirit of romantic nationalism when American journalist John L. O'Sullivan coined the phrase "Manifest Destiny" in 1845. He had used the concept but not the term in an earlier 1839 article in the *United States Magazine and Democratic Review* when he spoke of America's "blessed mission to the nations of the world" to teach them "the natural rights of man". This was a kind of political evangelicalism without territorial gain. But his August 1845 article in the same journal, written just before the Mexican–American War and the conquest of Texas, and titled "Annexation", declared, "... our manifest destiny [is] to overspread the continent allotted by Providence for the free development of our multiplying millions. . . . It is a right such as that of a tree to the space of air. . . ." This right to others' territory was deemed natural because of the assumed superiority of the white race. Native Americans and Chicanos (conquered Mexicans) were either killed or displaced from their ancestral lands and locked up in large fenced compounds called "reservations". Native American author Gerald Vizenor writes in *Manifest Manners: Postindian Warriors of Survivance* (1994), "Manifest Destiny would cause the deaths of millions of tribal people from massacres, diseases and the loneliness of reservations. Entire cultures have been terminated in the course of nationalism." If the classic Western novels and Hollywood films celebrated the machismo of the frontiersman and the cowboy, the later "dark Westerns" like Cormac McCarthy's *Blood Meridian* (1985) focus on Vizenor's nightmare.

Expansionism had its opponents even in O'Sullivan's time. Preacher William Channing wrote in 1837 of the need for America's "laying an immediate curb on its passion for extended territory. . . . We are a restless people, prone to encroachmen. . . ." But the myth of Manifest Destiny caught the public imagination and powered the westward drive to California. Here this myth intersected with another forceful myth, that of the Frontier or the 'frontierist' identity of America.

Till 1890, the decennial US Census had named the westernmost point of white settlement as America's "western frontier". In 1890, the Census Bureau announced the "closing of the frontier" since white settlers had reached the Pacific. This announcement sparked the celebrated "Frontier Thesis" of American historian Frederick Jackson Turner. In his speech at the 1893 conference of the American Historical Association, titled "The Significance of the Frontier in American History", Turner maintained that "the colonization of the Great West" and its immense "area of free land . . . explains American development." Like O'Sullivan, for Turner too, non-white people are invisible and their centuries-old land holdings are "free land". The Frontier Thesis contends that America is what it is *because* it took up the challenge of taming a wilderness, that the Frontier developed America's "stalwart and rugged qualities", and that without such a challenge the American spirit would suffocate. In 1920, Turner expanded and nuanced these arguments into a book, *The Frontier in American History*. The important new dimension here, in view of the fact that physical frontiers no longer existed on the continent, is the concept of the "figurative frontier" – "In place of old frontiers of wilderness there are new frontiers of unwon fields of science, fruitful for the needs of the race. . . ."

Manifest Destiny and the (figurative) Frontier remain enormously resilient in America's imagination. Perhaps their most compelling modern articulation is President Kennedy's 1962 speech urging support for his ambitious space programme – "Yet the vows of this Nation can only be fulfilled if we in this Nation are first, and, therefore, we intend to be first. . . . What was once the furthest outpost on the old frontier of the West will be the furthest outpost on the new frontier of science and space."

The Myth of Success: The American Dream

American exceptionalism materialises in individual lives in terms of the "American Dream" – the conviction that in this Promised Land happiness and success are every American's birthright. The title of Barack Obama's 2006 autobiography is *The Audacity of Hope: Thoughts on Reclaiming the American Dream.* As the first two-term African American President of a nation with a history of slavery and racism, Obama is a vibrant emblem of the American success myth. Benjamin Franklin and Abraham Lincoln, too, had surmounted extreme poverty through their own efforts. America prides itself on its meritocracy and the possibility of upward mobility for every deserving American.

The emotive phrase, "American Dream", was coined by American historian James Truslow Adams in *The Epic of America*

(1931). Written just after the massive American economic depression of 1929 (commonly known as the "Great Depression"), it was intended to edify and encourage by recalling America's providential history. Among the advantages Adams listed was "the *American Dream*, that dream of a land in which life should be better and richer and fuller for every man, with opportunity for each according to his ability or achievement" (italics in the original). Yet, Adams also problematised the Dream – "It is easy to say a better and richer life for all men, but what *is* better and what *is* richer?"

Adams was obviously thinking of values, but with the economic uncertainties at the turn of the century, too many Americans interpreted the Dream in material terms. In his 1999 book *American Dreams in Mississippi*, sociologist Ted Ownby sketches four typical "Dreams" – "Dream of Abundance", "Dream of a Democracy of Goods", "Dream of Freedom of Choice", and the very American "Dream of Novelty". But the closing of the Frontier, excessive immigration and over-rapid industrialisation led to unavailability of "free" land, increasing competition, inflation and unemployment, and corruption in big business – and the Dream soured for some.

Contemporary writers insistently exposed the fallacies of the Dream with its inherent intolerance of failure. One thinks of novels such as William Dean Howells's *The Rise of Silas Lapham* (1885), Frank Norris's *McTeague* (1899), Theodore Dreiser's *The Financier* (1912), F. Scott Fitzgerald's *The Great Gatsby* (1925) and John Steinbeck's *Of Mice and Men* (1937), and Arthur Miller's play *Death of a Salesman* (1949). Minorities, for their part, protested their exclusion from the American Dream that left them second-class citizens. Native American novelist Sherman Alexie, who grew up in a fenced reservation, recounts the poverty and violence experienced by his community, and his *Indian Killer* (1996) is a horrific story of retaliatory vengeance. Chicano author Gloria Anzaldúa depicts her community inhabiting the periphery of the Dream in *Borderlands/La Frontera* (1987). Well before Obama's rise, Toni Morrison vented the Black community's anger in *Playing in the Dark* (1990) and narrated its tragic history in all her novels, notably *Beloved* (1987).

Yet, against all odds, the Dream persists and inspires. It was memorably leveraged by the African American leader Martin

Luther King Jr. to launch the Black Civil Rights Movement in a racially segregated society on 28 August 1963:

> I still have a dream, a dream deeply rooted in the American Dream – one day this nation will rise up and live up to its creed. . . . I have a dream that one day . . . injustice and oppression will be transformed into an oasis of freedom. I have a dream that my four children will live in a nation where they will not be judged by the color of their skin but by the content of their character. I have a dream today.

King was assassinated by white conservatives on 4 April 1968 but not before he realised his dream, beginning with President Lyndon Johnson's promulgation of the Civil Rights Act of 1964.

The Myth of the Garden: American Pastoralism

The Pilgrim Fathers battled a "hideous" wilderness in the New World while fervently believing that they had been providentially conferred a new Garden of Eden. Transforming the wilderness into a garden was as central to early American history as conquering the Frontier was to the nineteenth century. But the ideology of America as a garden (of Eden) existed in ambivalent tension with the ideology of America as a city (upon a hill). The French immigrant Hector St. John de Crèvecoeur's *Letters from an American Farmer* (1782) viewed the land as a metaphor for virtue and claimed that "the simple cultivation of land purifies them [i.e., migrants from decadent Europe]." Thomas Jefferson was another strong proponent of what he considered the morally superior "agrarian ideology". In his *Notes on the State of Virginia* (published 1785) he declared, ". . . those who labor in the earth are the chosen people of God. . . . let us never wish to see our citizens occupied at a workbench."

But by the early nineteenth century, urbanisation and industrialisation could no longer be ignored. As social historian Louis Marx observes in *The Machine in the Garden* (1964), the period between 1820 and 1860 was the "Machine Age" of industrial production, with steam-powered freight trains hurtling across the continent from 1830. Transcendentalist philosopher Ralph Waldo Emerson was troubled by the power of technology over both the human intellect and nature as his essays – such as "The American Scholar" (1837), "Nature" (1837), "American Civilization" (1862) and "Farming" (1870) – demonstrate. His acolyte Henry David Thoreau famously retired from the machine civilisation for over two years to live close to nature by Walden Pond in Massachusetts, recording his experiences in *Walden* (1854).

The ideological tussle between the Garden and the City continued into the early twentieth century with American realist fiction both censuring and celebrating the City – poets like Robert Frost memorialising human involvement with nature, novelists like John Steinbeck and Willa Cather focalising both the promise and the harshness of nature, and Eugene O'Neill writing a play named *Dynamo* (1929) in which a crazed worshipper of technology immolates himself by plunging upon this new machine-god. This contest still remains an issue in American literature. Yet, though technology appears to have won the battle, American pastoralism resurfaces paradoxically as a science with *Silent Spring* (1962) by American biologist and conservationist Rachel Carson. This pioneering work alerted not just America but the world to endangered nature and heralded the science of ecology. While not using the Puritan moral rhetoric, Carson's epigraph from Albert Schweitzer carries the same equation of the loss of vitality with the loss of nature – "Man has lost the capacity to foresee and to forestall. He will end by destroying the earth."

American Multiculturalism: Melting Pot or Salad Bowl?

Multiculturalism is the one major strand in America's culture that is not of Puritan ancestry but emanates from its being a nation of immigrants. Its radical dimensions in a society without class or ethnic barriers is vivid in President Barack Obama's "rainbow" family (to use a popular term) – a Kenyan-origin father, a white American mother, an adopted half-Indonesian sister and a Chinese-American brother-in-law. Obama commends America's ability to forge a national identity from such heterogeneous elements. But this accommodation was not easy and passed through several phases.

The US was in fact multicultural from its very beginnings. Western Europeans settled a land already inhabited by thirty thousand native tribes, and within a century, African slaves and conquered Chicanos entered the population. But when Crèvecoeur queried in "Letter III" of his *Letters*, "What then is an American, this new man . . . [with] that strange mixture of blood," he discounted the "tawny" people and insisted that white settlers forget their origins since, "Here individuals of all nations are melted into a new race of men." The observant Alexis de Tocqueville completely ignored non-Europeans in his voluminous tomes on American democracy. In his Frontier Thesis, Turner envisaged white settlers being "Americanized, liberated and fused into a mixed race [in the] crucible of the frontier."

The problem of accommodation surfaced not with non-white people, who were invisible anyway, but with non-Western European white immigrants who flooded America in the "steamship era" at the turn of the century. In May 1916, journalist Randolph Bourne (of British descent) published a controversial article titled "Trans-National America" where he warned against conservative demands that "the alien shall be forcibly assimilated to that Anglo-Saxon tradition which they unquestionably label 'American'." This assimilationist metaphor of melting down differences into a monolithic Anglicist Americanness had been etched into America's consciousness by Israel Zangwill's 1908 play *The Melting Pot*, where a character says, "America is God's Crucible, the great Melting Pot."

South and East European migrants vehemently opposed the "melting pot theory". Yugoslav-born journalist Louis Adamic's polemical 1932 article, "Thirty Million New Americans", alleged that the new (white) arrivals were "oppressed" by the ethnic prejudice of the "old stock". Non-white immigrants faced worse discrimination, and all Japanese-American citizens were forcibly interned during the Second World War when Japan bombed America's Pearl Harbour. The plight of marginalised Asian immigrants is the theme of innumerable diasporic novels such as Korean-American Chang-rae Lee's *Native Speaker* (1995).

Two events altered the situation somewhat – the success of the Black Civil Rights movement in 1964 that spurred Native Americans and Chicanos to also campaign for their privileges, and President Lyndon Johnson's relaxed foreign immigration policy in 1965. The terms "multicultiralism" and "pluralism" came into popular use around this time to signify recognition, if not total acceptance, of diversity as a marker of the nation. Conservatives have always opposed non-Anglocentric immigration, just as forcefully as they opposed Black and indigenous rights. To cite some instances, in 1891, *The Nation* targeted migrants "not related to us in race or language"; in a 1924 speech Senator Ellison DuRant Smith feared that too many foreigners "would melt the pot in place of us being the melting pot"; as recently as 2006, the screaming rhetoric of Senator Patrick J. Buchanan's book, *State of Emergency: Third World Invasion and Conquest of America,* was most disturbingly rated by the *New York Times* as a best-seller. The xenophobic trend is particularly noticeable after the 9/11 attacks.

Nevertheless, as Randolph Bourne had predicted, diasporic communities gradually became more influential in American society, which perforce had to settle for a more complex model of social acculturation than the uniformity of assimilation. The old melting pot had to be discarded. Many emblems were suggested for the present many-hued American populace – from "multicoloured mosaic" to "Martini cocktail" to a "braid of many-colored ribbons". But the most popular image is that of the "salad bowl" in which each ingredient retains its distinctive identity and yet blends into a multi-flavoured whole. Multiculturalism is but the latest instance of Baudrillard's contention that the United States continually reinvents itself.

Chapter 2

From the Early Narratives to the Colonial Era

Ashok Sengupta

"America" had been conceived in the European imagination before it was recorded as a written fact in its literature. In fact, America was an invention of Europe, created in historical memories, fantastic tales, classical references, religious aspirations and travel writing such as those of Richard Hakluyt in his *Voyages and Discoveries* (1598–1600) and Samuel Purchas in *Hakluytus Posthumus or Purchas His Pilgrims* (1625). This myth of an Edenic and Arcadian America was also invoked in several English works beginning with Sir Thomas More's *Utopia* (1516) and Sir Philip Sydney's *Arcadia* (1590, 1593). It was a recurring image in Edmund Spenser's *Faerie Queene, Book VI* (1590, 1596) and William Shakespeare's *The Tempest* (1611). A similar hyperbolic idealisation is implicit in John Donne addressing his mistress as "O My America! My new-found land" in his *Elegies* (1665); whereas, George Herbert's *The Temple* (1633) mentions the religious immigration that followed the Reformation and became foundational for the colonies established in the newly discovered continent: "Religion stands on tip-toe in our land / Ready to pass to the American strand".

The first permanent English settlement was Jamestown, established in Virginia in 1607. John Smith's history, *A True Relation* (1608), mentions that it had been commissioned by the

Virginia Company to explore the region farther north, adding, in his *A Description of New England* (1616), that it was finally named "New England". Another group of about a hundred Puritans with a title charter from the Plymouth Company sailed on the *Mayflower* for Virginia but accidentally landed in a region west of Cape Cod in 1620. This colony was thus named "Plymouth" and it formulated its own charter, the "Mayflower Compact". The Plymouth Colony finally joined the New England Federation in 1643. A larger group of Congregationalists, under the leadership of John Winthrop (1588–1649), sailed on the *Arbella* to found, in 1630, a colony that became Boston, with its own charter designating it as the "Massachusetts Bay Colony".

Puritan Literature of the Colonial Era

The Puritans came to settle in America as an act of faith. They saw themselves, like the Israelites, as God's chosen people committed to the divine task of establishing Christianity and justifying the ways of God to "men" in the New World. Thus, the founding of the colonies was part of a religious mission which had been ordained by the Lord and was now becoming manifest as history. As Cotton Mather (1663–1728), one of its notable apologists, stated,

> The *Church* of our Lord Jesus Christ, well compared unto a *Ship*, is now *victoriously* sailing around the Globe . . . [carrying] some thousands of *Reformers* into . . . an *American Desart* on purpose that . . . He might there, *To* them first, and then *By* them, give a *Specimen*of many Good Things, which He would have His Churches elsewhere aspire and arise unto . . . *Geography* must now find work for a *Christiano-graphy* in . . . the HISTORY OF A NEW-ENGLISH ISRAEL . . . and to anticipate the state of the *New Jerusalem*.

Thus, the Puritans formulated a Christian myth and a prophetic literature for America much before they arrived in the colonies. Winthrop's sermon delivered on the *Arbella* testified to this when he proposed that there was a covenant between God and the Puritans. In his "Model of Christian Charity", Winthrop advocated the creation of an exemplary society in the New World: "The God of Israel . . . has set up this people that we shall be as a city on a hill—. The eyes of all people are upon us." The Puritan colonists therefore saw themselves as part of a sacred drama enacted on the stage of this New Jerusalem – America. This new settlement was thus rewritten as a re-enactment of the Old Testament tale of the exodus of the Jews in search of their "Chosen Land". The Puritans' journey across the Atlantic was compared to the earlier crossing of the Red Sea, and the founding of New England was seen as paralleling the formation of a New Zion, initiating the New Millennium with its implicit prophecy of Christ's Second Coming. The Puritans arrived in America with a divine sense of history based on a fully developed teleology in which the discovery of America was considered to be a vindication of Protestantism. John Cotton (1584–1652), another important divine to record this process, wrote in 1630: "Other peoples have their land by providence; we have it by promise." Puritan writing during the colonial period is thus characterised by this typological and analogical emphasis, as is evident in Edward Johnson's (1598–1672) *Wonder-Working Providence of Sion's Saviour in New England* (1654); in the annals and histories such as William Bradford's (1663–1752) *Of Plymouth Plantation* (1630) and John Winthrop's *History of New England from 1630 to 1649* (1825–26); in the numerous autobiographies, journals and biographies; and in the poetry of Anne Bradstreet (1612–72) and Edward Taylor (1644–1729).

Histories and Journals

Puritan writing during this phase of discovery and settlement had little that could be called the imaginative or literary. The forms which had a reasonable dominance at this time were histories, journals and diaries. These histories, beginning with John Smith's *The Generall Historie of Virginia, New England and the Summer Isles* [Bermuda] (1624) to Cotton Mather's monumental *Magnalia Christi Americana* (1702), became works which used the historical in service of religious interpretation and prophecy. It is probably in this tendency towards religious signification that the histories approach the element of the imaginative. For instance, in *Of Plymouth Plantation*, after recording the slaughter of four hundred members of the Native Pequot tribe, Bradford considered the massacre a part of a providential plan and admitted that the victors ought to give "the praise thereof to God, who had wrought so wonderfully for them". This is also the usual resolution in Increase Mather's (1639–1723) *A Brief History of the War with the Indians* (1676) and William Hubbard's (1621–1704) *Narrative of the Troubles with the Indians* (1677). Bradford's *Of Plimoth Plantation*, later titled *History of Plymouth Plantation*, written in two separate phases and published in 1856, described the arrival of the colonists in 1630 and reminded the children of the settlers "what difficulties their fathers wrastled in going through these things in their first beginnings". The second book of the *History* regretted the loss of the settlements' identity and attempted to explain this undoing. The *Journal* Winthrop had begun on board the *Arbella* became the *History of New England from 1630 to 1649*. Unlike Bradford, who remained outside his account, Winthrop depicts himself as a character in his *History*, summarising and extrapolating his own opinions and views, and justifying his decisions and actions as governor of the colony.

Though better known by its original title, *Wonder-Working Providence . . .* (given above), Edward Johnson's *A History of New England* (1654) is clearly a defence of what he calls the "New England Way". It was an attempt to see the history of the colony as part of a providential design – as "the place where the Lord will create a new Heaven and a new Earth". This mythicising of history is a recurrent aspect of these chronicles, evident in Cotton Mather's encyclopaedic *Magnalia Christi Americana* or *The Great American Works of Christ*. Mather's account is an attempt to recreate the history of America as a Christian epic, to authorise fiction as historical fact: "But whether *New-England* may *Live* anywhere else or no, it must *Live* in our History!"

Another account of the formation of the Plymouth Colony was Nathaniel Morton's (1613–85) *New England Memorial* (1669), which was considered to be the only version of the story till Bradford's *History* was discovered in the nineteenth century. However, two objective accounts of the colony – Thomas Prince's *Chronological*

History of New England in the Form of Annals (1736) and Thomas Hutchinson's three-volume *History of the Colony* (1764) – were published in the eighteenth century, while William Hubbard's *General History of New England*, though completed in 1680, had to await publication till 1815. Along with these chronicles, several others documented the lives of the Native tribes: Increase Mather's *A Brief History of the War with the Indians in New England* (1676), Hubbard's *A Relation of the Troubles which Happened in New England, By Reason of the Indians There* (1677) and Cadwallader Colden's *The History of Five Indian Nations* (1727). It is, however, important to note that the concept of the South as having a separate historical identity also made its presence at this time, in Robert Beverley's *The History and Present State of Virginia* (1705), John Lawson's *A New Voyage to Carolina* (1709), William Byrd II's *The History of the Dividing Line betwixt Virginia and North Carolina Run in the Year of Our Lord 1728*, and Patrick Tailfer's *A true and Historical Narrative of the Colony of Georgia* (1741).

Biographies, Autobiographies and Conversion Narratives

Since there were instances of the personal narrative and the journal becoming the basis of New England's history, the forms of autobiography and biography also made a major contribution to New England literature. In fact, they seem to anticipate Ralph Waldo Emerson's observation that "there is properly no history; only biography". One of the earliest examples of such personal narratives was *The Autobiography of Thomas Shepard*, which was probably composed in 1640 but was published in 1832. A record of Shepard's struggles towards salvation, this became a dominant form of Puritan writing – the conversion narrative or the spiritual autobiography. Though these genres of the autobiography and the biography primarily deal with the individual self as subject, the Puritan versions used the personal tale as religious exemplum and a reflection of dominant ideological concerns. Shepard thus records the spiritual conflict that he undergoes through the "daily meditation about the evil of sin and my own ways . . . my hypocrisy and self and secret sins", and finally turns to the Lord and decides to become a minister. Shepard defines this conversion as a process which involves his priestly duties in New England where he admits to have experienced "renewed conversions" through which he recognises that his weaknesses are the source of his strength: "When I was most empty, then by faith I was most full". A similar purpose and structure shapes *The Diary* of the poet Michael Wigglesworth (published in 1965), *The Diary of Cotton Mather for the Years 1681–1708* (published 1911–12), the *Diary of Samuel Sewall* and the *Autobiography of Increase Mather* (published 1962) which also began as a diary. In these autobiographies and diaries, the life of the individual became the story of the community. This tendency to merge the private with the public is the basis of another important genre of Puritan writing – the biography. The earliest American Puritan biography was John Norton's *Abel Being Dead Yet Speaketh* (1658) on the life of John Cotton. As is evident in the title, the analogies with the Bible confer on this record a figural significance as the story of a saint, thereby introducing the element of hagiography into this form of writing. This pattern is reiterated in Increase Mather's biography of his father, *The Life and Death of That Reverend Man of God, Mr. Richard Mather* (1670), and Cotton Mather's biography of Increase, *Parentator* (1724).

Sermons

The literature that was thus authorised and sanctified by the Puritan colonists had a clear didactic subject and purpose. To bless the departure of the *Arbella* from Southampton, John Cotton delivered a famous sermon, "God's Promise to His Plantations". The predilection towards preaching is evident in the sermon Winthrop delivered on the same ship, "A Model of Christian Charity", before the immigrants had landed on the promised shores. Based on the models in the Bible, the preacher was given a position of honour and responsibility in New England society where the sermon became an indispensable feature of both the religious and political life of the community, as was evident in the importance given to the Election Day sermon. The first sermon to be published was Alexander Whitaker's *Good News from Virginia* (1611). The other notable New England sermons include, Peter Bulkeley's *The Gospel Covenant* (1646) and versions of Cotton's *Treatise of the Covenant of Grace* (1659). The theme of many of these sermons was a reassertion of the conversion model as the path towards redemption. Thus, in *The Preacher* (1656), William Chappell included the exemplary sermons of three New England sermon writers in the chapter titled "On True Conversion" – Shepard's *The Sound Believer* (1645) and *The Sincere Convert* (1646), Cotton's *The Way of Life* (1641) and Thomas Hooker's *The Soul's Preparation* (1632), *The Soul's Imitation* (1637), *The Soul's Vocation* (1637), *The Soul's Implantation* (1637) and *The Soul's Exaltation* (1638), a series of sermons that Hooker later revised and enlarged in two volumes titled *The Application of Redemption* (1656). Along with these noted preachers, the contribution of John Eliot was equally significant. He was credited with translating the Bible into the Algonquian tongue and thus bringing the gospel to Native Americans as the "apostle to the Indians". Together with the Bible, Eliot's *Indian Grammar Begun* (1666) and *Indian Primer* (1669) are considered significant contributions to the growing literature on the Native Americans represented in Roger Williams's *A Key into the Language of America* (1643) and Daniel Gookin's *An Historical Account of the Doings and Sufferings of the Christian Indians* (1836). A similar plea for greater tolerance is evident in the writings of Roger Williams – *The Bloudy Tenent of Persecution, for the Cause of Conscience* (1644) and *The Bloudy Tenent, Yet More Bloudy* (1652).

Jeremiads and Captivity Narratives

From the late 1660s and 70s there was a darkening of the Puritan covenant that had blessed the New England enterprise. Doubts regarding the commitment of the faithful, over the possible links between tragic occurrences and this disbelief, and the consequent anxiety regarding God's abandonment of His people found expression in a distinctive sermon form – the jeremiad. Though Thomas Shepard's *Wine for Gospel Wantons* (1645) was an earlier instance, Samuel Danforth's *A Brief Recognition of New England's*

Errand into the Wilderness (1670) is usually seen as the prototype of this convention. Referring to several occasions in biblical history when the Jews strayed from faith, Danforth invokes the prophet Jeremiah "that he may reduce the people from their backslidings, cries in the ears of Jerusalem". During the 1670s and 80s, preachers used the jeremiad on funerals, fast-days, executions and Election Days to bring the disbeliever back to the path of the Lord. Increase Mather and his son Cotton Mather were leading exponents of this form with *Day of Trouble is Near* (1674), *A Renewal of Covenant the Great Duty Incumbent on Decaying and Distressed Churches* (1677), *Pray for the Rising Generations* (1677) and *A Call from Heaven to the Present and Succeeding Generations* (1679); while Cotton preached on witchcraft in *Memorable Providences, Relating to Witchcraft and Possessions* (1689) and *The Wonders of the Invisible World.* Other such notable examples include, Thomas Walley's *Balm in Gilead to Heal Zion's Wound* (1669), Jonathan Mitchell's *Nehemiah on the Wall in Troubled Times* (1671), Urian Oakes's *New England Pleaded With* (1673), Samuel Hooker's *Righteousness Rained from Above* (1677) and William Adams's *The Necessity of Pouring Out of the Spirit from on High Upon a Sinning Apostating People* (1679).

The Indian captivity narrative, a characteristic writing of this period, was a significant supplement to the jeremiads. In aim and design, the captivity narrative is similar to these sermons, as the incarcerated protagonist undergoes a period of spiritual anxiety resulting in a revival of faith. The most celebrated example of this type of narrative is that of Mary White Rowlandson who was kidnapped by a Wampanoag raiding party during the First Indian War, also known as King Philip's War (1675–78). Her story, *The Sovereignty and Goodness of God, Together With the Faithfulness of His Promises Displayed: Being a Narrative of the Captivity and Restoration of Mrs. Mary Rowlandson. . .*(1682), despite its emotional rhetoric, seems to have a didactic function suggested in the preface by Cotton Mather.

Poetry

Puritanism discouraged imaginative writing, particularly poetry. In spite of this, there is clear evidence of the enthusiasm for poetry in New England since the 1640s. Understandably, poetry was also used as a form of preaching, and therefore, a common tendency towards the anagram, acrostics, epitaphs and elegies marked the writing of the period. Thus, in 1640, *The Whole Book of Psalms Faithfully Translated into English Meter*, called *The Bay Psalm Book*, was endorsed by John Cotton because it was a "faithful endeavor to keep close to the original text" though "the verses are not always so smooth and elegant as some desire or expect; (yet) let them consider that God's Altar needs not our polishing". Nevertheless, in 1651, a revised translation of this psalter was undertaken by Henry Dunster of Harvard and Richard Lyon with "a special eye" for the "sweetness of the verse", which Cotton finally accepted as "it was thought that a little more of Art was to be employed upon the verses". In fact, several Puritan writers found the language of the Bible and the typology that permeated their writing to be essentially metaphoric and poetic – an argument that was used by Richard Baxter to justify his use of invention and figurative language in *The Saint's Everlasting Rest* (1650), and by Roger Williams, when using poetic images to illustrate religious and moral precepts, in the poems he interspersed between chapters in *A Key into the Language of America* (1643). As in most other forms of Puritan writing, the dominant investment was religious, though there were isolated instances of secular poetry, such as those of William Wood in his *New England Prospect* (1634) and John Josselyn in his *An Account of Two Voyages to New England* (1674). Another remarkable collection of poems is that by John Saffin, *John Saffin, His Book* (1665–1708, published in 1928), which includes scientific notes, philosophical observations, personal experiences, summaries of his reading, satires and love poems. In fact, Saffin is credited for the first valentine poem, "On Presenting a Rare Book to Madame Hull Senior: His Vallintine".

However, it is important to note that a tradition of poetry existed in colonial New England in the frequent composition of elegies, used not only to lament the death but also to assert the communal bond between the deceased saint and his people. The most notable elegy was by Urian Oakes on the occasion of the death of Thomas Shepard, *An Elegie upon . . . Thomas Shepard* (1677). Benjamin Tompson, who was designated "the renowned poet of

New England" in the epitaph on his gravestone, uses his poem "New England's Crisis" (1676) as a jeremiad to explain the cause of the Indian wars as God's punishment to the people who had "quickly sinned away for love of gold". Therefore, the elegy was meant to use death as a form of introspection for the community which, it was assumed, had strayed from its commitment to the Lord. This emphasis is evident in Samuel Torrey's "Upon the Death of Mr. William Tompson" (1666) and in an untitled epitaph written the same year by Benjamin Tompson for his deceased father. Tompson also produced a short mock-epic, "On a Fortification at Boston Begun by Women" (1676), about the barricade built by the women of Boston as a defence against native attacks. Though it is usually considered irreverent to associate the comic with Puritan writing, there are several examples of satire and the mock heroic in the poetry of this period. Thomas Morton's *New English Canaan* (1637) criticises the disbelieving Puritans, and Nathaniel Ward's *The Simple Cobler of Aggawam in America* (1647) is a similar commentary on the religious and political problems during the reign of Charles I.

Literary historians are of the common opinion that the three most important poets of this period were Anne Bradstreet (1612–72), Michael Wigglesworth (1631–1705) and Edward Taylor (1644–1729).

Bradstreet was probably the first woman poet writing in the English language in America. Cotton Mather remarked in 1712 that Bradstreet "wrote such things as have been very valuable; especially relating to their own experiences". She had sailed to the Massachusetts Bay Colony with her father and husband (who later became its governors) and composed long poems titled, "The Four Elements", "The Four Humors of Man", "The Four Ages of Man", "The Four Seasons", and a few shorter lyrics. They were published by her brother-in-law, John Woodbridge, in 1650 in London as *The Tenth Muse Lately Sprung Up in America* (1650). Bradstreet's poetry was influenced by Edmund Spenser, Philip Sidney and the French poet Guillaume du Bartas; and after attempting historical themes, she depended on the personal and the domestic, admitting that her poems are made of "home-spun cloth". However, she is equally aware that her efforts would be dismissed as "stolen, or else it was by chance", and thus attacks those who think "I am obnoxious to each carping tongue / Who says my hand a needle better fits" , in "The Prologue". Thus, in the 1642 poem on Queen Elizabeth, "In Honor of that High and Mighty Princess Queen Elizabeth", she attempts to disprove male assumptions about women: "She has wip'd off th' aspersion of her Sex, / That women wisdom lack to play the Rex". In *Several Poems* (1678), a second edition of her works, Bradstreet assumes the position of a mother to her poems in "The Author to her Book". This volume contains verses dealing with family illnesses, elegies on the death of her grandchildren and daughter-in-law, love poems to her husband and a poem on the fire which destroyed her house:

> Here stood that Trunk, and there that chest;
> There that store I counted best:
> My pleasant things in ashes lye,
> And them behold no more shall I.

Though she finally reconciles herself to the loss with the consolation that "My hope and Treasure lyes Above", she is also aware that it is only the knowledge of death, rather than religion, which prompts people to accept the notion of eternity, "for were earthly comforts permanent, who would look for heavenly".

Michael Wigglesworth's *Day of Doom* (1662) is considered to be one of the most popular verse sermons on the apocalyptic doctrines of the Day of Judgment. Written, therefore, in terms of the jeremiad, the poem was described by Cotton Mather, in "The Praise of Eloquence", as a "verse catechism", and its utility as religious instruction was the main justification of the poem. As Mather further stated, "How sweetly doth eloquence even inforce the trueth upon the understanding, and subtly convay knowledge into the minde be it never so dulle of conceiving and sluggish in yielding its assente." However, the passion in Wigglesworth's descriptions of impending doom and God's wrath gives it a genuine religious and poetic fervor:

> For at midnight brake forth a Light
> which turned the night to day,
> And speedily a hideous cry
> did all the world dismay.

A similar warning is central to Wigglesworth's second verse jeremiad, *God's Controversy with New England* (1662), which warns its readers of the dire consequences of the slackening of their faith. In 1670, Wigglesworth published his last work, *Meat Out of the Eater*, which offers consolation to the faithful for submitting to Christ's saving grace.

In contrast to the bleak picture drawn in Wigglesworth's poetry, there were others who tried to depict the beauty and tranquility of nature in New England – poets such as William Wood in his *New England Prospect* (1634) and George Alsop in *A Character of the Province of Maryland* (1666).

Edward Taylor's poetry was largely unknown till the discovery, in 1937, of a manuscript in the Yale University Library where it had been deposited by his grandson Ezra Stiles, then president of the university, in 1883. Like Bradstreet, Taylor had also emigrated from England in 1668 and worked as the pastor and physician of Westfield, a remote village in New England. In comparison with the other poets of this period, Taylor's poetry is distinctive for the conscious literary and aesthetic sense that marks his writing. Thus, his poems display a strong influence of the English Metaphysical poets of the seventeenth century. Though the poetry is based on Puritan devotional and didactic objectives, it contains Platonic ideas and, surprisingly, even reveals baroque elements; thereby, it attests to a Puritan sensibility nourished by the culture of Renaissance England. Taylor's poems are, therefore, poems of meditation which are often part of sermons and pastoral preaching. He draws his images and metaphors from nature and ordinary rural life, and tends to find mystical and emblematic meanings in nature: "Natural things are not unsuitable to illustrate supernaturals by. For Christ in his parables doth illustrate supernatural things by natural, and if it were not thus, we could arrive at no knowledge of supernatural things, for we are not able to see above naturals."

Taylor's *God's Determination Touching His Elect* (1682) has the structure of a spiritual meditation on the theme of conversion and salvation. It emphasises the need of the faithful to fight temptation, pray to Christ and be worthy of God's grace and deliverance. However, the element of the comic, uncharacteristic in a Puritan poem, which Taylor uses to comment on the various ways in which people imagine the figure of God, suggests that the necessary metaphors that are used to conceive God ultimately prove to be inadequate. Thus, the universe is seen as an infinity of nothingness: "Infinity when all things it beheld / In Nothing, and of Nothing all did build". This conjunction of opposites, similar to that of a metaphysical conceit where nothingness is refigured as the source of something, is a definitive aspect of Taylor's verse. The poems written between 1682 and 1725 are collected in *Preparatory Meditations*. Continuing the form of the spiritual exercise, these lyrics seem to involve a more secular treatment of the Lord in the use of sensual metaphors of food and satiety, which seem to echo those in Donne's *Holy Sonnets*. In "Huswifery",Taylor thus weaves domestic images into an appeal for salvation:

> Make me, O Lord, thy Spinning Wheel complete.
> Thy Holy Word my Distaff make for me.
> Make my Affections thy Swift Flyers neat
> And make my Soul thy holy Spool to be.

Though Anne Bradstreet is considered the most notable woman writer of this period, recent research has been able to rediscover other women poets such as, Anna Hayden (1648–1720) with two elegies; Sarah Kemble Knight (1666–1727) whose *Journal* contains six poems; an acrostic poem written by a certain Mary English (1652–94) in her own name; Sarah Goodhue (1641–81) whose *Valedictory and Monitory Writing* (1681) contains one important poem; Grace Smith's (1685–1740) *The Dying Mother's Legacy* (1712) which includes some of her poems; Mercy Wheeler's (1706–96) *An Address to Young People, Or . . . Warning from the Death* (1733) where some of her experiences are given in verse; and Jane Colman Turell (1708–35), some of whose substantial work were selectively published in *Memoirs of the Life and Death of . . . Mrs. Jane Turell* (1735).

Literature of the Eighteenth Century

As the eighteenth century began, there was a distinct change in the spirit and literature of New England. As the colonies became more economically stable, socially heterogeneous and more expansive, there was an increasing tendency to be receptive to new ideas from Europe and the other colonies, and this prompted a movement away from the earlier theological dominance of the Reformation towards the rational and secular mentality of an American Enlightenment. This is first evident in the "Great Awakening", the religious revival which swept the colonies in the 1730s. It was basically an attempt to accommodate the sons and daughters of the original settlers within the religious denomination and thus increase the membership of the Puritan Church. Thereby, what was originally a sectarian movement, limited to the select membership of the "Pilgrim saints", was extended to include those not necessarily a part of this religious practice. Thus in 1662 the New England churches proposed a "Halfway Covenant" which allowed baptism for the children of those who had not undergone religious conversion. As the term suggests, this was both a revival and a compromise, for what it implied was that the Congregationalists were making a transition from their status as an elect sect to that of a "church" with more general and hereditary membership.

Jonathan Edwards (1703–58), who was the pastor of Northampton, Massachusetts, asserted his commitment to this revival in his *Personal Narrative* (1743) by stating that "the appearance of everything was altered" as "there seemed to be . . . a calm sweet cast, or appearance of divine glory, in almost everything". Shocked by the dilution of the Halfway Covenant, Edwards assumed the responsibility of restoring some of the traditional Puritan seriousness by becoming one of its major apologists. He thus adapted Puritanism to the changing mentality of the eighteenth century. Without reducing the importance of human faith and agency in the conception of the divine, Edwards emphasised the need for a systematic and even scientific contemplation in religious experience. His *Treatise Concerning Religious Affections* (1746) was an attempt to understand the role of emotions in the development of faith. For Edwards, emotion and intuition were important affective impulses which shaped any religious awakening. Thus, in works such as *Two Dissertations* (1756) and *The Great Christian Doctrine of Original Sin Defended* (1758), Edwards used a reasoned argument to reassert a surrender to God's retribution and consequent grace by investing in ideas from Descartes, Shaftesbury and other Enlightenment thinkers. An example of his inclination to employ science in the service of typological reasoning is stated in *Images or Shadows of Divine Things*: "The late invention of telescopes, whereby heavenly objects are brought so much nearer and made so much plainer to sight and such wonderful discoveries have been made in the heavens, is a type and forerunner of the great increase in the knowledge of heavenly things. . . ." Notwithstanding the jeremiads he delivered to strengthen the programme of conversion, a sermon like "Sinners in the Hands of an Angry God" (1741) also uses rhetorical figures and imagery which clearly reveal his tendency to read natural signs in terms of "the emotions of the sweet benevolence of Jesus Christ". Edwards believed that since the world of nature is the Lord's hieroglyph, it is logically spiritual and moral, and therefore, the human endeavour directed towards its service is implicitly a recognition of God: "The Son of God created the world for this very end to communicate Himself in an image of His own excellency."

If Edwards represented the traditional Puritan interests reaffirming itself in a changing America, his contemporary, Benjamin Franklin (1706–90) became an advocate of the freedom of the individual and an example of the self-created American. In this he not only responded to the Enlightenment but contributed to the formation of one of the nation's dominant myths of self-identity, as J. Hector St. Jean de Crèvecoeur, the French traveller, was to define in his *Letters from an American Farmer* (1782): "The American is a new man, who acts upon new principles; he must therefore entertain new ideas, and form new opinions." It was in his famous *Autobiography* (published 1791 and 1818) that Franklin expressed most of the opinions that would distinguish him as an exemplary American. Divided into three sections, it enumerates the principles adopted to achieve a moral perception that ultimately ensures his wealth and success as a scientist, politician and philanthropist, after his humble beginnings in Philadelphia where he had fled from Boston to set up a print shop. In the second edition of the *Autobiography* (1784), Franklin suggests that he undertook "a course complete" in moral education involving "moral virtues" such as "temperance", "order", "silence", "resolution" and "frugality". Tracing a graph of such virtues, he suggested that "four courses in a year" would enable the individual to achieve not only self-reliance but also a distinct self-identity through reason, common sense and hard work. This probably became the first formulation of the American myth of the self in the quest of the American Dream that was to be emulated and bemoaned in major American works of the nineteenth and twentieth centuries.

The Puritan debate regarding the comparative importance of prayer and meditation, and that of works and moral practice, was clearly weighed in favour of the latter in Franklin's life and letters. From 1733, he started publishing an almanac of practical and topical advice called *Poor Richard.* Though almanacs meant to provide farmers with relevant information about the weather and the market were popular during this period, Franklin supplemented the regular features with short essays and proverbs which provided both useful and moral instructions: "Plough deep, while sluggards sleep and you shall have corn to sell and keep." *The Way to Wealth* (1758), a collection of Franklin's proverbs,, became a national bestseller and was reprinted several times. These works not only advocate his moral and economic principles of diligence, thrift, independence and discipline, but also reflect his sense of humour and wit. These features define the style of his writing which also emphasised clarity and economy of expression that marked the Puritan preference for the "plain style" – a style derived from William Langland and the English medieval poets, which avoided the eloquent and the ornate and recommended the direct expression of simple truths, good conscience and moral rectitude. This is evident throughout Franklin's career as a writer, from his early series of satirical essays titled the "Silence Dogood" papers to the treatises promoting his philanthropic and political ideas, *A Proposal for Promoting Useful Knowledge* (1743) and *Proposals Relating to the Education of Youth in Pennsylvania* (1749).

Franklin's involvement in scientific study and experiment was inspired equally by his practical and philanthropic preoccupations. First to identify lightning as a form of electricity, he was able to suggest several practical uses for this energy in his *Experiments and Observations on Electricity, Made at Philadelphia* (1751). While Cotton Mather and Jonathan Edwards viewed science in typological and religious terms, Franklin was to promote it as an independent field of useful knowledge by founding the American Philosophical Society in 1743. It was devoted to the study of science and its development, particularly in areas such as botany and medicine. Franklin's commitment to America, and his contribution to the formation of a national identity, is clear in the pamphlet "Information to Those Who Would Remove to America" (1784). Though aware of "the almost general Mediocrity of Fortune that prevails in America", Franklin felt that this very reason obliged all "healthy young Laboring men" in the country "to follow some business in America" and thereby to "easily establish themselves", for here "those Vices that arise usually from Idleness, are in great measure prevented"; therefore, "Industry and Employment" became the "great preservatives of Morals and Virtue", which made the nation a land of opportunity, tolerance and independence. These ideas and values went on to define the Constitution of the United States and the Declaration of Independence, in whose drafting Franklin had been chosen to participate.

Though Franklin devoted most of his energies and his writing to create an independent national identity for America, he was also aware of the oft repeated complaint that "good poetry is not to be expected in New England". Ironically, much of eighteenth-century American literature depended on an imitation of English models. In "On the Prospect of Planting Arts and Learning in America" (1726), Bishop George Berkeley, the British theologian and philosopher, expressed the hope that "There shall be sung another golden age / The rise of empire and of arts". However, even in 1782, Franklin was to regret that "the natural Geniuses that have arisen in America with such Talents, have uniformly quitted the country for Europe, where they can be more suitably rewarded". This anxiety shadows the careers of several American writers in subsequent generations. Nevertheless, it is this narrative of exile and return which became dominant in defining the development of American writing in the nineteenth and twentieth centuries.

However, in London that same year, 1782, a Frenchman, St. Jean de Crèvecoeur (1735–1813), published his *Letters from an American Farmer* which, in its celebration of the new republic, attempted to restore this declining faith. Comprising twelve letters by the fictional James Hector St. John, an American-born farmer of English descent, written to "F.B.", an English gentleman, it combines autobiography, philosophical reflection and essayistic commentary on the emergence of a new nation in an epistolary form. In fact, the literature developing around the American Revolution was invested with a deep concern about this definition of the American identity, as is evident in Crèvecoeur's opening question, "What is an American?" Primarily addressed as an answer to this, *Letters* emphasises the superiority of the American self by contrasting it with that of Europe:

> He is arrived on a new continent; a modern society offers itself for contemplation, different from what he had hitherto seen. It is not composed as in Europe of great lords who possess everything and of a herd of people who have nothing. . . . The rich and the poor are not so far removed from each other as in Europe.

This belief in an agrarian democracy is one of the central assertions in the epistolary chronicle. The narrator declares it "the most perfect society now existing in the world" because "we are all tillers of the earth . . . all animated with the spirit of an industry which is unfettered and unrestrained, because each person works for himself". Thus, the American emerges as the "new man" for "here individuals of all nations are melted into a new race of men, whose labors and posterity will one day cause great changes in the world". Thus, some of the foundational tropes that were to define this nation – America as the "melting pot" of various races and identities, the notion of the American as Adam inheriting a Rousseauian Utopia, the individualistic nature of American identity and the commitment to a belief in American exceptionalism – were clearly formulated in the *Letters*.

Many Americans – George Washington being one of them – considered Crèvecoeur's exuberant praise of the new nation "embellished" and "rather too flattering"; more a confirmation of the idealism of a Jeffersonian generation, it ignored the realities of colonial rule. However, the early optimism of the *Letters* soon gives way to doubt and disillusionment in the ninth epistle describing a visit to Charles Town in South Carolina where James is a witness to the evils of slavery: "Here the horrors of slavery, the hardship of incessant toil, are unseen; and no one thinks with compassion of these showers of sweat and tears, which from the bodies of the Africans, daily drop and moisten the ground they till." The note of irony and ambiguity is clearly evident when this tendency is considered basic to humanity: "We certainly are not that class of beings which we vainly think ourselves to be; man an animal of prey, seems to have rapine and the love of bloodshed in his heart." Thus, when Crèvecoeur, owing to his Tory opposition to the Revolution, falls foul of the Republicans, he decides to take refuge with the Native Indians whom he considers to be more tolerant and peaceable:

> Without temples, without priests, without kings, and without laws, they are in many instances superior to us; and the proofs of what I advance, are that they live without care, sleep without inquietude, take life as it comes . . . and die without any kind of apprehension for what they have done, or for what they expect to meet with hereafter.

Crèvecoeur, it has often been suggested, saw the American colonies as a testing ground for Enlightenment principles. The *Letters*, nevertheless, represents one of the earliest attempts to formulate a belief in society as the guardian of the natural rights of man, a preoccupation that dominated the writings of his American contemporaries and also some of the Romantic writers in Europe.

Thomas Paine's (1737–1809) life and writing were, in fact, literally dedicated to championing and defending the social and political rights of man which, for him, was most adequately represented in his involvement in the American Revolution. Born in Norfolk in England on 29 January 1737, Paine was a pamphleteer and an international revolutionary whose *Common Sense* (1776) became a foundational treatise of the American demand for independence from Britain. Paine declared, "The world is my country, all mankind are my brethren, and to do good is my religion." Having secured letters of introduction from Benjamin Franklin, whom he had met in London, Paine arrived in Philadelphia in November 1774. Employed by Robert Aitkin to edit the *Pennsylvania Magazine*, he soon emerged as a political pamphleteer arguing, in *Common Sense*, for the defeat and overthrow of the corrupt British administration and the establishment of a republican government in America. Paine's polemical writing was characterised by a rhetoric and style whose clarity and directness implied its contemporary faith in reason and in secular values and institutions. This tendency is further evident in *The American Crisis* (subsequently referred to as *The Crisis*), a series of sixteen essays written between 1776 and 1883 to revive and strengthen the declining hopes of the Continental Army after their initial defeats at the hands of the British. Hence, the pieces included in *The Crisis* had the effectiveness of maxims and slogans: "These are the times that try men's souls. The summer soldier and the sunshine patriot will, in this crisis, shrink from the service of the country. But he that stands it *now*, deserves the love and thanks of man and woman." Paine defended Washington's retreat as a strategic withdrawal needed for another concerted attempt to achieve victory. Confident of this end, he appealed for a greater effort from "those who expect to reap the blessings of freedom" for they "must like men, undergo the fatigues of supporting it". Paine was attached to the Continental Army as a civilian aide. In *The Crisis,* he appealed for the formation and recruitment of a regular army and federal taxation for the war effort. As a member of the Congress and the Pennsylvania Assembly, Paine called for the institution of a Bank of America to raise money for the nationalist enterprise.

Paine returned to England and soon became involved in the events which announced the beginnings of the French Revolution. Therefore, when Burke published his *Reflections on the Revolution in France* (1790), Paine responded with his *Rights of Man* (1791), a virulent attack on hereditary monarchy and justifying the need for parliamentary reform in Britain:

> Every age and generation must be as free to act for itself in all cases as the age and generation which preceded it. The vanity and presumption of governing beyond the grave is the most

> ridiculous and insolent of all tyrannies. Man has no property in man; neither has any generation a property in the generations which are to follow.

Paine's advocacy of the natural rights of man, his support of republicanism and his proposals for social welfare made his treatise distinctively different from other reformist tracts which had appeared during the period. Accused of sedition, Paine had to flee to France. In France, Paine was included in the committee to draft a republican constitution, but his plea for the life of Louis XVI led to his falling foul of the Jacobin faction. He was arrested on 27 December 1793 and narrowly escaped the guillotine through the intervention of James Monroe, the American consul. He returned to America in 1803. Paine's last publication, *The Age of Reason* (1794–95), attacked religion, particularly Christianity, as it often went against "religious duties [which] consist in doing justice, loving mercy, and endeavoring to make our fellow creatures happy". Denounced for his radical views, Paine became increasingly isolated and died almost forgotten by the nation which he had helped to found.

Literature and the Revolution

Though the Declaration of Independence was adopted by the Continental Congress in Philadelphia on 4 July 1776, the colonies had started demanding autonomy around 1773 by refusing to accept British taxation laws and boycotting goods manufactured in England and Ireland. The year 1773 is famous for the "Boston Tea Party" when the rebels destroyed a cargo of East India tea in the city's harbour. This was followed by intermittent clashes between the British army and American rebels. The first battles resulted in an American defeat in June 1775 at Bunker Hill in Charlestown, Massachusetts; but, by that time, the Congress had announced the formation of a rebel government with George Washington as the commander of its army. The protracted war which followed ultimately ended with the surrender of Lord Cornwallis's troops in October 1781. Though the British continued their naval attacks for the next two years, the Treaty of Paris in 1783 finally declared the emergence of the United States – a territory that stretched from the Atlantic to the Mississippi.

However, the nationalist self-assertion of the colonies was not simply a consequence of their quest for a political and economic identity. This was also a result of their material and commercial growth which became the basis of the development of a more secular, liberal and cultured mentality evident in the growth of literacy, publishing and the demand for a more indigenous literature. A significant affirmation of this is in the rise of the reading public, suggested by the unprecedented increase in the number of newspapers and magazines and the popularity of the lecture circuits. Thus, writing and authorship assumed a professional viability which intimated the possiblility of a literary market. This possibility is hinted at in the fact that Susan Warren's *The Wide, Wide World* (1850) became the first American novel to sell more than a million copies.

Washington Irving (1783–1859) began his career by exploring his readers' tastes by publishing a literary miscellany, *Salmagundi; or The Whim-Whams and Opinions of Launcelot Langstaff, Esq., and Others* (1807–08). This collection of satirical and comic essays was influenced by Joseph Addison and Oliver Goldsmith, and these pieces, as the title suggests, covered various subjects ranging from literary criticism, fashion and contemporary social mores and morals. It also included essays written by Irving's brothers and James Kirke Paulding, all members of a group known as the "Nine Worthies" or "Lads of Kilkenny" of "Cockloft Hall". Irving's essay, "Of the Chronicles of the Renowned and Ancient City of Gotham", had the distinction of supplying New York city its enduring nickname, Gotham. Irving's reputation, in fact, was to a large extent created by his comic history of the city, *History of New York from the Creation of the World to the End of the Dutch Dynasty, by Diedrich Knickerbocker* (1809). Linked by their common interest in the city, Irving, Paulding, Fitz-Greene Halleck, Gulian Verplanck, John Howard Payne and Lydia Maria Child, formed the "Knickerbocker School" of writers associated with the *Knickerbocker Magazine* (1832). The *History*, with its comments on contemporary politics and its satirical portraits of public figures, marks an important attempt to write on American subjects and issues. However, in 1815, Irving immigrated to England where he became involved with the Romantic writers Walter Scott and

Thomas Campbell, and produced a series of stories and sketches in *The Sketchbook of Geoffrey Crayon, Gent.* (1819, 1820), *Bracebridge Hall* (1822) and *Tales of a Traveller* (1824). Though most of the pieces in these books deal with English life, two of them are notable for their contribution to the development of the American short story – namely "Rip Van Winkle" and "The Legend of Sleepy Hollow". The origins of these stories, Irving admits, were in German folktales, but their real debt to Romanticism is evident in the use of the Gothic and the interweaving of the real and the illusory. The story of the lazy, henpecked Rip Van Winkle is a significant example of Irving treating history in terms of fiction. On his return from the Catskill Mountains in New York State after a twenty-year period of slumber there, the protagonist finds that "instead of being a subject of His Majesty George the Third, he is now a free citizen of the United States". A similar preoccupation with time and change marks the subtly comic treatment of a quaint, pastoral and superstitious community in "Sleepy Hollow". The community's resistance to change is ironically suggested in the failure of Ichabod Crane to defeat his rival, the bumpkin Brom Bones, in a contest for the fair Katrina Van Tassel. Distinctive to Irving's narrative style is the sense of detail which is reminiscent of Dutch miniature paintings used to depict this traditional society; yet, the story also involves an awareness of a threat to this rural idyll, implied in the manner in which it parodies tall tales, ghost stories and the epic. In this, it not only anticipates Irving's later work but also the fictional works of Mark Twain and Bret Harte. After returning to the United States in 1832, Irving characteristically set out to travel over the American West, an experience that produced *A Tour on the Prairies* (1835), *Astoria* (1836) and *The Adventures of Captain Bonneville* (1837). Irving was aware of the political implications of this westward expansion, and tried to explore the cultural aspects of this region, thereby preparing the context for the development of the myth of the Frontier in the novels of James Fenimore Cooper.

Emergence of the American Novel

The development of the American novel, however, was slow and belated. This is explained by several reasons – the Calvinist disapproval of imaginative fiction; the dominance of English works and European translations in the colonies; and a belief that the general equality and homogenous nature of its society, which had no "intrinsic" cultural traditions, discouraged fiction. There is now a consensus regarding William Hill Brown's *The Power of Sympathy; or, The Triumph of Nature* (1789) as being the first American novel. A Richardsonian cautionary tale of seduction and female sexual indiscretion, the tale testifies to the first of the two basic categories into which these early American novels could be classified – sentimental romances and political allegories. The sentimental tales dealt mainly with the domestic world of women who were limited to their worries about careless husbands, the perils of repeated childbirths, grief for dead children, religious duties and the danger of the perennial seducer. Thus, similar to Hill's tale were Susannah Hanswell Rowson's *Charlotte* (1794) and Hannah Webster Forster's *The Coquette* (1797). The latter was based on the tragic career of Elizabeth Whitman who, having flirted with the Rev. Joseph Buckminster, was seduced by a mysterious rake, believed to be Pierpont, the son of Jonathan Edward, and finally died in misery in Denver, Massachusetts. Another novel, different in theme but identical in treatment, was Royall Tyler's *The Algerine Captive* (1797).

These novels seem to suggest that romance was generic to American fiction, which tends to derive its features more from Romanticism rather than the social and rational values of neoclassicism. Though indebted to English and European writers, the American novel is distinctively different from their works. Thus, while the English novel begins in social conflict and disunity, there is always a restoration of a sense of order with a narrative resolution that is generally comic. In American fiction, the protagonist is usually in conflict with society, but this conflict involves not merely social issues but metaphysical and spiritual questions which tend to alienate the protagonist, who ultimately affirms his or her individual values and identity. Thus, American fiction tends to deal with contradictions and disunities and is inclined towards tragedy.

In the list of political allegories can be included Francis Hopkinson's *A Pretty Story* (1774), which was a satire on contemporary historical developments in the relationship between

England and its colonies. Complementing this theme, Jeremy Belknap, the historian of New Hampshire, wrote *The Foresters* (1792) which was a comic history of the colonists from the days of the settlement to the establishment of the Republic. The most important writer in this category was Hugh Henry Brackenridge (1748–1816) whose satirical novel, *Modern Chivalry* (written between 1792 and 1815), became one of the most significant fictional works of this period. Brackenridge was influenced by the writings of Miguel Cervantes, Alexander Pope and Jonathan Swift; and following the model of Swift's *Tale of a Tub* (1704), he alternated narrative sections of his novel with satirical essays on various contemporary subjects. His hero, Captain Farrago, is almost an American version of Don Quixote. Farrago decides to "ride about the world a little, with his man Teague at his heels, to see how things were going on here and there and to observe human nature". A notable representation of the manners of the early days of the Republic, this picaresque novel takes the two travellers around the "lubberlands" of Pennsylvania into the cultured society of Philadelphia. Moreover, in the misadventures of Teague O'Reagan, the coarse Irish servant who is the Sancho Panza of this romance, Brackenridge criticises the political upstarts of his time, portrays certain political events such as the Whisky Rebellion, and reflects on the work of universities and philosophical societies. Thus, the second part, which is a burlesque history of the United States after the Revolution, reiterates the original purpose of the novel.

Another important novelist among these pioneers of the genre in America was Charles Brockden Brown (1770–1810) of Philadelphia, who is often considered America's first professional writer. Influenced by the ideas of the English and French radical philosophers, particularly William Godwin, Brown's ambition was to be a philosophical novelist and to produce something similar to the former's *Caleb Williams* (1794). Brown wrote a remarkable series of novels, notable among which are *Wieland* (1798), *Ormond* (1799), *Arthur Mervyn* (1799, 1800) and *Edgar Huntly* (1799). Many of them follow the basic pattern of Gothic fiction – exploring the tensions between desire and fear, psychological anxieties and instabilities, a Faustian aspiration for new scientific knowledge and the despair of weakening faith and authority. By dealing with these aspects of the mind, Brown traced the contours of a major tradition of American fiction, which was to mature in the writings of Edgar Allan Poe (1809–49) and Nathaniel Hawthorne (1804–64). Thus, in the preface to *Edgar Huntly*, Brown tries to consider an American form of the novel:

> America has opened new views to the naturalist and politician, but has seldom furnished themes to the moral painter. That new springs of action and new motives to curiosity should operate; that the field of investigation opened to us by our own country should differ essentially from those which exist in Europe, may be readily conceived.

James Fenimore Cooper and the Myth of the Frontier

James Fenimore Cooper (1789–1851) is credited with the creation of the myth of the Frontier, which became a pervasive feature in American literature and culture. He was the first to popularise this theme in his Leatherstocking novels and was, therefore, responsible for setting the terms and forms of this fiction in the early nineteenth century. However, there were other writers, both contemporary to Cooper and writing after his time, who continued to deal with this theme in their novels – novelists like Robert Montgomery Bird (1806–54) and William Gilmore Simms (1806–70). Significantly, the Frontier developed into a legend permeating the American popular consciousness, initially expressed in the repeated use of its metaphors and imagery in the dime novels of Ned Buntline and Prentiss Ingraham, till it contributed to the formation of a dominant genre of American cinema – the Western. The "Frontier" denotes a phase in American history, which is also termed the era of settlement after the colonial period and the Declaration of Independence in 1776. It also represents a period of American emigration and expansion during the late eighteenth and nineteenth centuries. Thus the Frontier referred to a geographical location, a pastoral Utopia and an imperialist aspiration. In 1862, the Homestead Act was passed; and in 1889, the Oklahoma territory – the last of the unoccupied regions in the West – was opened to homesteaders. By 1890, a census announced that the Frontier had been officially closed. In 1893, Frederick Jackson Turner delivered his famous lecture, "The Significance of the Frontier in American History", later published as *The Frontier in American History* (1920), where he established it as the defining identity of the American nation – its manifest destiny. Thus, America became representative of this quest for new frontiers, not limited only to the terrestrial but ultimately justifying the conquering of outer space.

Cooper's depiction of the Frontier was evidently influenced by his childhood memories of Cooperstown, a frontier settlement founded by his father, William Cooper. Therefore, as the Frontier was a matter of personal history, its narrative has a sense of graphic immediacy, which explains much of the success of his fiction. *The Pioneers* (1823) was the first novel to deal with this theme – though there were two other works, *Precaution* (1820) and *The Spy* (1821), which preceded it. The depiction of the Frontier is complex: on the one hand, there are rich and detailed descriptions of the wilderness and the community with a suggestion of a pastoral Paradise; and on the other, an incipient recognition that the human settlement poses a threat to the natural resources as a potential source of destructive change. Apart from its warning about ecological destruction, which this and most of Cooper's other novels reiterate, *The Pioneers* also introduces characters of narrow self-interest – such as, Richard Jones and Hiram Doolittle – who constitute Cooper's criticism of democracy, because the acquisitiveness of such individuals and their descendants ultimately lead to the destruction of the community. Natty Bumppo – the aged Leatherstocking, pioneer and guide in the wilderness, who is the generic hero of these tales – forms a contrast to these avaricious characters. Natty kills only what he needs; he is, therefore, opposed to the settlements and their communities for they cause the displacement and destruction of the original owners of the land, the Indians or Native Americans represented by Indian John, Natty's companion and one of the members of his diminishing tribe. These constitute the conflicts and anxieties of his fiction. However, unlike the tendency in his later fiction, in *The Pioneers*, Cooper attempts to arrive at a symbolic resolution of the tensions through the marriage of Oliver Effingham, who is of Indian descent, and the Governor's daughter, Elizabeth.

The Last of the Mohicans (1826), which has become an American classic, established Cooper's international reputation and is central to the Leatherstocking series of five novels. The novel attempts to trace the historical ancestry of the Americas, developing this genealogical account by showing how a civilisation was built on the ruins of a primitive idyll. Cooper's view of history is, therefore, romantic and tragic, and assigns to American history an intrinsic element of violence and instability. The novel, in two volumes, traces the vicissitudes of the "old French war". The narrative follows the journey of the rescue team which travels from Fort Edward to Fort William Henry, in 1757. While recording this journey and other subsequent adventures, the first volume provides details of the geographical setting, the historical background and the ethnological history of the Native tribes. The second volume deals with the careers of the fictional characters, charting the changes in their courses of action and ending with the ceremonial paean to Cora and Uncas, whose deaths mark the passing away of the last of the Mohicans. Cooper thus portrays colonial America as a fallen world whose natural purity has been defiled by the violent struggles in the eighteenth century for the possession of its territories, overwhelmed by forces beyond the control of the contestants.

Though written after *The Last of the Mohicans*, *The Prairie* (1827) was probably the first episode of the five Leatherstocking novels. Emerging almost as a mythic figure, Natty plays a central role in this tale of the westward movement of the nation, from the forests of New York State to the great prairies of the Midwest. The treatment is more romantic, emphasising the legendary nature of this journey and foundational myths which evolved from this experience, which is given an epical elevation by the death of Natty. Cooper returned to the theme of the Frontier in the Littlepage trilogy in the 1840s with *Satanstoe* (1845), *The Chainbearer* (1845) and *The Redskin* (1846).

As a response to popular demand, Natty was resurrected in *The Pathfinder* (1840) and *The Deerslayer* (1841), thirteen years after the publication of *The Prairie*. Unlike the earlier novels, in these two works, the wild landscape is less rugged or resistant; neither are these novels preoccupied with contemporary social problems. In fact, a return to a pastoral idyll is also suggested in the uncharacteristic first romantic involvement of Natty, and this love theme is used to reconcile the generic opposition between the freedom of the wilderness and the compromises of a peaceful domesticity. However, this turns out to be an impossible dream; Natty returns to the wild, implying that the nation's Edenic past can never be retained in a complex and urban present. Natty is not just a representative of the American as Adam, nor are these tales a simple recreation of America's paradisal past before the Fall, but historical narratives which reflect and evaluate the developments in a nation's growth and its destiny.

Cooper's importance lies in the fact that he was able to convert autobiography into myth. In *The Deerslayer*, he was able to identify the archetypal patterns of consciousness which gave the country its self-presence as "nature's nation". In the Leatherstocking tales, he was able to define the terms of this myth and also explore its contradictions, thereby emerging as probably the most successful historical novelist of his time. Cooper's significance, therefore, lies in the tradition he initiates for the American novel, which finally distinguishes itself by becoming a representative narrative of the nation.

One of the defining characteristics of the Frontier theme in Cooper's fiction is the conflict over the possession of the land. This, again, may have been prompted by the novelist's troubles in preventing the loss of his own paternal estate as a result of complicated legal entailments, though the more relevant historical source of this issue was the obvious consequences of the westward white dispersion, which led to the dispossession of traditional Native settlements. In *The Spy: A Tale of the Neutral Ground*, set during the time of the American Revolution, Cooper uses a narrative device borrowed from Walter Scott to deal with this conflict: the creation of a character who mediates between the warring groups. In most novels, the hero Natty serves this function by expressing the collision in personal and social terms and by negotiating this crisis to bring about an honorable and moral solution.

A more direct treatment of the Revolution is found in *Lionel Lincoln* (1823), whose attempt to give it an epic dimension in thirteen parts devoted to different periods of the struggle had to be finally abandoned. In some of his other works – such as *The Pilot* (1824), *The Red Rover* (1827) and *The Water Witch* (1830) – Cooper attempted to experiment with nautical tales, thus revealing the diversity of his writing which included the novel of manners, the political satire, allegory and the dynastic novel spread over several generations. This clearly indicates his intentions to attempt an epical portrayal of the nation.

The formula of what can be termed the settlement novel, formed of this dynastic theme, is repeated by Cooper in *The Wept of Wish-ton-Wish* (1829), *Wyandote* (1843) and *The Crater* (1847). However, the treatment of this theme is not always uniform: while in *The Wept* Cooper offers the hope of regeneration after a fire destroys the settlement, in *Wyandote* this hope is undermined when it is revealed that the white settlers, disguised as Natives, destroy the settlement. This awareness of an internal threat also shapes *The Crater*, where the settlement is shifted to a Pacific Ocean island. What is significant about these novels is that they constitute Cooper's historical critique of America. The novelist thus attacks Calvinism for the narrow acquisitiveness of the nation; moreover, *The Crater* exposes and condemns political factionalism, abuses of democratic practice, irresponsible journalism and educational experiments, and hold them accountable for the country's decline. Cooper's criticism of America is also evident in the didactic strain that marks three novels which follow: *Jack Tier* (1848), *The Sea Lions* (1849) and *The Oak Openings* (1848).

The importance of Cooper's fiction lay in the fact that it was able to transform history into myth. He was able to formulate the terms of the Frontier vision by tracing the epical westward movement of the nation from the forests of New York to the great prairies of the Midwest. In this, his fiction marks the culmination of the American foundational myth which had begun with the first settlements in the New World. This tendency of transfiguring history into myth thus became definitive not only of the American novel but also of the nation.

CHAPTER 3

From Emerson to Twain

The American Renaissance

Ashok Sengupta

CONSOLIDATING THE NATIONALIST DISCOURSE: TOCQUEVILLE

Alexis de Tocqueville (1805–49), political scientist and historian, in *Democracy in America* (1835–40), admitted that "the inhabitants of the United States have, then, at present, properly speaking no literature". Rather, he observed, "Not only do the Americans constantly draw upon the treasure of English literature, but it may be said with truth that they find the literature of England growing on their own soil." Though Tocqueville did not ascribe this only to the development of the "democratic principle", he felt that the lack of an aristocracy, usually associated with literary and cultural activities in Europe, was greatly responsible for such a condition in America. This opinion was to be echoed by several writers and historians of the Republic in the nineteenth and twentieth centuries.

Along with his friend, Gustave de Beaumont, Tocqueville arrived in America on 11 May 1831, ostensibly to study prison reforms in the country. During the nine months they spent there, they travelled widely over the United States and Canada to produce not only *The Penitentiary System in the United States and Its Application in France* (1833) and Beaumont's novel, *Marie, Or, Slavery in the United States* (1835), but also Tocqueville's *Democracy in America, Part I* (1835). This treatise, finally published in four volumes in France in 1840, is a study of the social and political system in America in the nineteenth century: "There is one country in the world where the great social revolution that I am speaking of seems to have nearly reached its natural limits. . . . This country is reaping the fruits of the democratic revolution which we are undergoing, without having had the revolution itself." A comprehensive account of the American government in the 1830s, the document is also a reflection and commentary on the guarantees and dangers of liberty and equality as social and philosophical ideas. The first part deals with specific institutional aspects of government and politics with Tocqueville exploring such basic questions as the advantages and pitfalls of universal suffrage; the idea and practice of the rule of law; the nature of majority rule and its possible dangers; the effects of centralised administration; the relationship of religion and democracy; and the future of the three principal races of this new nation. In the second part, Tocqueville considers such issues as the position of women; the influence of the Frontier on manners and morals; the spread of education and culture; the armed services in a democracy; and the tendency to form "associations" and promote an "aristocracy of manufacturers". Compared to the former, the second part tends towards generalisations, which makes *Democracy* an important contribution to the social philosophy of liberal reform.

Tocqueville's notion of democracy shows signs of undergoing changes in the process of writing the treatise. While in 1830 he viewed it as a dynamic and inevitable development involving an "equality of conditions", in the later volumes, he recognises a more homogenising tendency, reducing intellectual and individual distinctions to the "tyranny of the masses". He thus proposes a system of restrictions and balances which not only ensures the defence of individual liberty against authority but also justifies the use of authority against libertarian excesses. Tocqueville is aware of the fact that the wide readership of a flourishing democracy demands a variety of books, and that this would encourage a "trading spirit in literature": "Democratic literature is always infested with a tribe of writers who look upon letters as a mere trade; and for some few great authors who adorn it, you may reckon thousands of idea-mongers." In an important sense, therefore, Tocqueville was anticipating Hawthorne's complaint against the "tribe of scribbling women" who were cornering the literary market in the nineteenth century with their sentimental romances. For Tocqueville, these not only implied a trivialisation of literature and culture in the United States, but also, paradoxically, an extreme form of literary self-consciousness evident in the "inflated" language which distinguished the writing "as soon as they attempt a more poetical diction". This rhetorical extravagance also explained the American tendency towards the abstract and the universal – "to search below the external surface which is palpable to the senses, in order to read the inner soul" for "they are led to acknowledge a trace of that universal and eternal plan on which God rules our race." Thus, by identifying some of the basic features of American writing, *Democracy* fulfils an important function of defining the terms and aims of the literature that was defining the nation in the nineteenth century.

THE "FIRESIDE" OR "SCHOOLROOM" POETS

At the beginning of the nineteenth century, therefore, two contrary tendencies seemed to define American literary aspirations. There was, on the one hand, a growing awareness that literature was severely limited in a democratic and a dominantly commercial society. Moreover, as Samuel Miller observed in his *A Brief Retrospect of the Eighteenth Century* (1803), Americans were still associated by "language, manners and taste" to Britain, a fact which made British literature popular and easily available to its readers. This prompted indigenous writers to depend on British models. As William Tudor, the editor of the November 1815 issue of *The North American Review*, complained, American poets were inclined to emulate the "classical poets" and their British followers, ignoring the literary possibilities of exploring their own landscapes, it's "romantick past" and the life of the native "Aborigines". Consequent to this recognition, on the other hand, was a positive appeal and assertion for a national literature in New England in the nineteenth century. In fact, at this time, New England became the centre of significant reform movements such as feminism and the anti-slavery movement, which made Tocqueville consider Boston the "Hub of the Universe". Though Edgar Allan Poe dismissed its literary activities as those of the "Boston Frogpondium", New England was able to produce writers such as William Cullen Bryant (1794–1878), Henry Wadsworth Longfellow (1807–82), John Greenleaf Whittier (1807–92), Oliver Wendell Holmes (1809–94) and James Russell Lowell (1819–91). They constituted an important group of American poets also known as the "Fireside" or "Schoolroom" poets, who represented these dual tendencies in the literature of the period.

Though William Cullen Bryant spent most of his life as a newspaper editor in New York, his poem "The Prairies" (1834) was evidence enough to justify the honour, given to him by his contemporaries, of being the founding father of American poetry. In fact in "Thanatopsis" (1817), Bryant had already marked American poetry with the terms and tropes of a European Romanticism. Often considered "the American Wordsworth", Bryant viewed nature and the American landscape as a reflection of the divine in poems such as "To a Waterfowl" (1818), "A Forest Hymn" (1825), "To the Fringed Gentian" (1832), "Earth" (1835), "Oh Mother of a Mighty Race" (1847) and "The Flood of Years" (1876). Thus, while he finds in the movements of the waterfowl ". . . a Power, whose care / Teaches thy way along that pathless coast—", the fringed gentians stand as symbols of hope and salvation when the

> hour of death draw near to me,
> Hope, blossoming within my heart,
> May look to heaven as I depart.

In spite of a competent sense of form and rhythm, Bryant's verse is rarely profound. In fact, he distinguished poetry from prose precisely in these terms – the former as "excluding all that disgusts, all that tasks and fatigues the understanding, and all matters which are too trivial and common to excite any emotion whatsoever". Most of Bryant's best verse was completed by the time he was forty and published in two volumes – both the volumes carried the simple title *Poems* (1821, 1832). However, he remained active as a translator of the *Iliad* (1870) and the *Odyssey* (1871–72) till the end of his life.

More celebrated than the others in this group of poets, Longfellow was born in Maine and distinguished himself as a professor of modern languages at the Bowdoin College and then as Smith Professor at Harvard University. Deeply influenced by German Romanticism, his travels on the continent yielded his first prose work, *Outre-Mer: A Pilgrimage Beyond the Sea* (1833–35), a travel account modelled on Washington Irving's *The Sketch-Book* (1819). This was followed by *Hyperion* (1839), a romance based on Goethe's *Wilhelm Meister* (1795–96), and his first book of poems, *Voices of the Night* (1839). Longfellow's verse is marked by a genteel optimism and moral assurance – clarity and simplicity of expression, celebrating the domestic values of the homestead and the hearth, thus became their own guarantees of right thinking and good poetry. In fact, like Bryant, Longfellow believed in a poetry that would "fill up the interludes of life with a song, that shall soothe our worldly passions and inspire us with a love of heaven and virtue". This becomes clear in *Ballads and Other Poems* (1841), whose "The Village Blacksmith" and "The Wreck of the Hesperus" became standard elocution exercises for many schoolboys. Longfellow's ambitions to write an American epic was evident in his attempt to give indigenous legends a classical form in *Evangeline* (1847), *The Song of Hiawatha* (1855) and *The Courtship of Miles Standish* (1856). In fact, in a lecture at Bowdoin, he had spoken of poetry being inspired by "the spirit of the nation"; yet, these narratives of the nation were embodied not in their historical changes but, rather, as he stated in "The Jewish Cemetery at Newport" (1852), in the permanent values of human nature enshrined in the harmonious relations of home and community:

> Gone are the living, but the dead remain,
> And not neglected; for a hand unseen,
> Scattering its bounty, like a summer rain,
> Still keeps their graves and their remembrance green.

Longfellow's translation of Dante's *Divine Comedy* (1865–67) involved a lifetime of scholarly commitment; the sixty-three sonnets which he wrote while dedicated to this project (and posthumously published in 1907) affirm not only his formal skill but reveal, like in "Mezzo Cammin" (1842), a deeper understanding of life's disappointments:

Not indolence, nor pleasure, nor the fret
Of restless passions that would not be stilled,
But sorrow, and care that almost killed,
Kept me from what I may accomplish yet.

The eponymous implication of this group of poets is best suggested in Whittier's notion of poetry as being one of "simplicity, and genuine, unaffected sympathy with the common joys and sorrows of daily life. It is a home-taught, household melody. . . . It is the poetry of home, of nature, and the affections." Whittier began by writing political allegories inspired by his involvement in the Abolitionist movement in works such as, *Poems Written during the Progress of the Abolition Question* (1837) and *Voices of Freedom* (1846). In fact, in "Proem" (1847), he admitted to his lack of artistic learning owing to his rural beginnings in Haverhill, Massachusetts:

The rigor of a frozen clime,
The harshness of an untaught ear,
The jarring words of one whose rhyme
Beat often Labor's hurried time.

Whittier thus saw himself more as a popular balladeer whose work is best represented in *Home Ballads* (1860), *In War Time* (1864), *The Tent on the Beach* (1867) and *Among the Hills* (1869).

As the dean of the Harvard Medical School, Holmes naturally dismissed poetry as insignificant to the struggles of existence: "How small a matter literature is to the great seething, toiling, struggling, love-making, bread-winning, child-rearing, death-waiting men and women who fill this huge, palpitating world of ours!" In his novel, *Elsie Venner* (1861), Holmes identified himself with "the Brahmin caste of New England", and confirmed his aristocratic Boston lineage in *The Autocrat of the Breakfast Table* (1858), a witty, Augustan satire which had two more sequels – *The Professor at the Breakfast Table* (1860) and *The Poet at the Breakfast Table* (1872). Though much of Holmes's poetry was written to mark public events and inaugurations, his verse has a comic energy which served as a moral reflection on the times, as in this satire of the Transcendentalists, from "An After-Dinner Poem":

> And oh, what questions asked in club-foot rhyme
> Of Earth the tongueless and the deaf-mute Time!
> Here babbling 'Insight' shouts in Nature's ears
> His last conundrums on the orbs and spheres.

Holmes's writing reflects his humanitarian beliefs, a logical outcome of his scientific reasoning which is revealed in two more "medicated novels" – *The Guardian Angel* (1867) and *A Mortal Antipathy* (1885) – where he explores psychological complexities, anticipating many of the concerns of the future American novel.

Like Holmes, Lowell was also a member of one of the foremost Boston families and, after Longfellow, became a professor of French and Spanish at Harvard. Together with Holmes, he founded *The Atlantic Monthly*, and was its editor between 1857 and 1861. With Charles Norton Eliot, an eminent scholar and critic, Lowell also edited *The North American Review.* Lowell published his first volume of poetry, *A Year's Life*, in 1841. It was followed by *Poems* in 1844. The year 1848 witnessed a prolific output of his writing, starting with *Poems: Second Series*, *A Fable for Critics*, *The Vision for Sir Launfal* and the first series of the *The Biglow Papers.* While the *Fable for Critics* was a verse satire on the contemporary literary world, *The Vision* was a romance inspired by the Grail legend. *The Biglow Papers* used a Yankee dialect to attack both slavery in the South and the American Mexican War which was seen by many as a ploy to extend slavery into these regions. Similarly, the second series of *The Biglow Papers* (1867) revealed Lowell's continued involvement with the social and political issues of his day such as the Civil War.

The genteel tradition of the Fireside poets inevitably lost its energy and grace in postbellum America. Their work was representative in the sense that it was able to voice some of the patrician values and aspirations of the early nineteenth century, which was negotiating its literary nationalism through a recognition of the best in other literatures and cultures. Lowell, therefore, seems to express this common faith when he observes, "Surely the highest office of a great poet is to show us how much variety, freshness, and opportunity abides in the obvious and familiar. He invents nothing, but seems rather to *re*-discover the world about him."

Emerson, Thoreau and American Transcendentalism

Transcendentalism can be considered the first important philosophical and literary movement in nineteenth-century America. It began as a religious reform movement in the Unitarian Church around 1836 and continued to exert its influence till the 1850s. In fact, the movement began as a discussion group of four Unitarian clerics – Ralph Waldo Emerson (1803–82), George Ripley (1802–80), Frederic Henry Hedge (1805–90) and William Henry Channing (1810–84). This developed into what later came to be known as the Transcendental Club, which met regularly at Harvard to discuss issues relating to American life and letters, and also to publish the journals which represented the aims and ideas of the movement – *The Boston Quarterly Review*, *The Dial* and *The Spirit of the Age*, among many others.

Religious Reform

The reform movement that was the precursor to Transcendentalism began towards the middle of the eighteenth century, when a few dissenting ministers rejected the views of the dominant Calvinistic Congregational Church – that man was corrupt and, therefore, beyond the hope of redemption. This dissatisfaction with the Calvinist religious doctrine led to a more liberal and positive view of human nature and an emphasis on individual piety and ethical practice as a way to salvation. This development was called the Unitarian Controversy, which finally resulted in a split in the older Puritan churches and the formation of the American Unitarian

Association in 1825. William Ellery Channing (1780–1842), one of its leaders, stated: "It is plain that a doctrine, which contradicts our best ideas of goodness and justice, cannot come from the just and good God, or be a true representation of his character." Thus, Channing's emphasis on the spiritual quality of the self, which was based on the notion of a "likeness to God", became the cornerstone of the Transcendentalist faith. The Transcendentalists, therefore, accepted the Unitarian claim that human nature could be improved through nurture and culture. However, they extended this optimism by reacting against the principles of the British philosopher John Locke's (1632–1704) theory of knowledge on which Unitarianism was based. The Transcendentalists felt that Lockean empiricism, with its stress on the senses as the sources of all experience, seemed to deny direct spiritual perception, therefore alienating man from God. They proposed a conception of human nature that was inherently divine, and a belief of divinity as immanent in human nature. Emerson called this "the infinitude of the private man".

Romantic Influences

This rejection of the rationalist principles of the eighteenth-century intellectual movement – the Enlightenment – gives Transcendentalism its kinship with European Romanticism. American Romantic ideas were generally mediated through this movement, which was also indebted to Immanuel Kant (1724–1804) and German Idealist philosophy. In fact, the designation, "transcendental", may have been derived from Kant's *Critique of Practical Reason* (1788) where it was stated, "I call all knowledge transcendental which is concerned not with objects but with our mode of knowing objects so far as this is possible *a priori*." The movement was also influenced by the Swedish scientist and philosopher Emanuel Swedenborg (1688–1772) and his doctrine of the correspondence between nature and the human mind. In his essay, "The American Scholar", Emerson considered Swedenborg's importance to be evident in the fact that the latter was able to show "the connexion between nature and the affections of the soul". Emerson also acknowledges the influence of William Wordsworth, Thomas Carlyle and Samuel Taylor Coleridge, and particularly of

Wordsworth's monistic theory of God and nature and the Romantic conception of the poet as prophet.

Transcendentalism is Romantic in the sense that it proposed an indomitable capacity for wonder and an infinite sense of hope. In an essay titled "The Transcendentalist" (1841), Emerson suggested that the Transcendentalist "believes in miracle, in the perpetual openness of the human mind to new influx of light and power; he believes in inspiration, and in ecstasy". Thus, the movement is defined in terms of an idealism which is neo-Platonic. Emerson thus specifies, "What is popularly called transcendentalism among us is Idealism as it appears in 1842." Moreover, the eclectic character of Transcendentalism is also evident in its borrowings from the teachings of Confucius and Hindu philosophy.

Ralph Waldo Emerson

For Emerson, Transcendentalism suggested the essential connectedness of spiritual doctrine as it is expressed in the natural world and in individual experience. This was based on the monistic principle which believed in the unity of the world and God and the immanence of God in nature and in man. In his first book, *Nature* (1836), Emerson proposed that the natural world was God's scripture which was more directly accessible than the usual religious texts. This belief in the indwelling of divinity implied that the soul of the individual was identical with the soul of nature and, therefore, contains in itself all that the world contains. Emerson termed this radical confidence in the individual "Self-Reliance"; and he called the benevolent and pervasive God-principle in both nature and man "Over Soul". In *Essays: First Series* (1841), Emerson thus advocates that the individual should acquire a state of spiritual vision. In "Spiritual Laws", he speaks of man as the "unobstructed channel" of divine energy. "The Over Soul" explores this source of the divine in terms of a mystical apprehension or, otherwise, through an experience of truth, beauty and goodness embodied in nature. In "The Transcendentalist", Emerson suggests that the essential meanings of the world were derived from "spiritual laws" which "transcended" received dogma and institutional norms and imbibed by men through intuitive faculties. In both "Self

Reliance" and "The American Scholar" (1837), Emerson thus announced an individualist ethic which was based on a strong sense of independence from earlier traditions of thought and feeling. In fact, he considers society to be a hindrance to self-reliance as it often denies intuitive perceptions. Emerson thus calls for a kind of philosophical anarchism when he states, "Who so would be a man must be a non-conformist."

In one important sense, therefore, Transcendentalism became a form of spiritual revivalism. It attempted to find a private and unmediated relation between the self and the universe. It also sought a spiritual experience of the natural world. This individualised experience of the world is the main concern not only in much of Emerson's writing, but also forms the basis of Henry David Thoreau's (1817–62) *Walden* (1854).

Henry David Thoreau and *Walden*

Walden describes Thoreau's experiment in living in a cabin he had built near Walden Pond, close to Concord, on an estate owned by Emerson. However, the actual terms of building a home and the common business of living is an elaborate allegory for social and metaphysical meditations: "I went to the woods because I wished to live deliberately, to front only the essential facts of life, and see if I could not learn what it had to teach, and not, when I came to die, discover that I had not lived." The narrative in *Walden* thus goes beyond the topical and the particular, in order to trace the historical origins of a place and that of the individual and also signal future directions. *Walden* finally involves, as Thoreau described it in the last chapter, building a "home cosmography" – a phrase which can be simplified to suggest the idea of the home and its relation with the world. In fact, this description is basic to the Transcendentalist attempt to define an American self-identity in the nineteenth century.

However, to consider Thoreau an ascetic using this experiment in solitude to comment on the trivial diversions of society would be a partial portrayal of his commitments. Though he did not join in the communitarian projects of the Transcendentalists, Thoreau was an Abolitionist strongly opposed to the Fugitive Slave Law and America's Mexican War. Thus, Thoreau, who had earlier withdrawn from society in *Walden* because, he believed, he had come "into this world, not chiefly to make this a good place to live in, but to live in it", now became involved in duties that forced him to be "harsh, and stubborn, and unconciliatory". This is the basis of his essay "Resistance to Civil Government" (1849), which later became famous under the title "Civil Disobedience", published in *A Yankee in Canada with Anti-Slavery and Reform Papers* (1866). This essay later influenced Mahatma Gandhi's *Satyagraha* or non-cooperation movement against the British as a strategy to achieve India's independence. Thoreau, therefore, emphasises that this moral duty actually constitutes an individual's self-definition – any assertion of the self, whether active or passive, implicitly confirms a social and political action: "If *one* HONEST man, in this State of Massachusetts, *ceasing to hold slaves*, were actually to withdraw from this co-partnership, and be locked up in the country jail therefore, it would be the abolition of slavery in America."

Cultural and Literary Influences of Transcendentalism

Thus, Transcendentalism, which began as a movement for church reform, went on to influence different spheres of American writing and culture in the nineteenth century. These can be classified under separate categories such as: (1) theological and philosophical; (2) educational reforms and Utopian communitarianism; (3) literary and cultural.

Theological and Philosophical Writing

The theological ideas of Transcendentalism are mainly found in Emerson's "Address" to the Harvard Divinity School graduates in 1838 and in Theodore Parker's *A Discourse of Matters Pertaining to Religions* (1842). The Transcendentalist theory of knowledge, on which its philosophical and spiritual discourse was based, is expressed in Emerson's *Nature* (1836) and in his posthumously published *Natural History of the Intellect* (1893). Together with these, Frederic Hedge's essays on Coleridge and German philosophy and George Ripley's *Discourse on the Philosophy of*

Religion (1836) were consistent attempts to establish the Kantian origins of Transcendentalist thought.

Educational Reforms and Community Living

Fundamental to the Transcendentalist movement were the educational reforms undertaken by Amos Bronson Alcott (Louisa Alcott's father, 1799–1888), Margaret Fuller (1810–50) and Elizabeth Peabody (1804–94). Alcott and Peabody started an experimental school in Boston and their experiences were documented in Peabody's *Record of a School* (1835) and Alcott's *Conversations with Children on the Gospel* (1836). Peabody became involved in promoting the kindergarten movement, while Alcott advocated adult education. Between 1839 and 1844, Fuller organised discussion groups for women in Boston, which combined educational training with propagating an awareness of women's rights. This formed the basis of what can be considered America's first feminist treatise, *Women in the Nineteenth Century* (1854).

The Transcendentalists undertook two significant experiments in community living – Brook Farm in West Roxbury, Massachusetts, and Fruitlands near Harvard in Massachusetts. The first was an attempt to develop agrarian communes based on the vision of the French political theorist Charles Fourier (1772–1837). George Ripley, who encouraged many of the others to join this organisation, saw it as a means to combine manual and intellectual labour and, thereby, live a more unified and harmonious existence. Though satirised by Nathaniel Hawthorne in his *The Blithedale Romance* (1852), Brook Farm achieved a measure of success till a disastrous fire closed it permanently. Fruitlands, however, lasted less than a year. Both these experiments attested to the fact that the Transcendentalists were actively concerned with social, economic and political issues.

Literary Writing

The most significant and abiding influence of Transcendentalism was to shape the literature of the time. This is evident in the production of a substantial number of literary classics which included, Emerson's

Nature and his series of *Essays* (1841, 1844), Thoreau's *Walden* and Walt Whitman's (1819–92) *Leaves of Grass* (1855). In fact, from its very inception, the movement had an aesthetic emphasis. Emerson resigned from his position as a Unitarian cleric in order to pursue his vocation as a writer. His essay on the American Scholar actually is an appeal for a distinctive literary and cultural nationalism. In his essay "The Poet", Emerson considers the necessity of promoting a poetic imagination to give expression to the diverse experiences of the nation: "Yet America is a poem in our eyes; its ample geography dazzles the imagination, and it will not wait long for meters." Emerson saw himself as "more of a poet than anything else", and his volume of *Poems* (1846) gives evidence of his versatile use of the tetrameter couplet over a wide range of subjects such as nature ("The Humble Bee"), moral treatises ("The Visit"), parables ("The Sphinx") and myths ("Bacchus", "Merlin"). Apart from Emerson and Whitman, the other poets of the movement included Theodore Parker, Jones Very, Amos Alcott and William Ellery Channing. Margaret Fuller, who was the first editor of the Transcendentalist journal, *The Dial*, was involved in literary criticism and travel writing.

Transcendentalism, as a movement, however, did not continue beyond the 1850s. Therefore, it seems rather surprising that a parochial New England reform movement should have such an influence on American literature and culture. This is probably because Transcendentalism was able to address several important social and cultural issues which contributed to the formation of the American self-identity. Though it did not evolve into a consistent philosophical system, Transcendentalism was able to initiate a literary reawakening which has been termed the "American Renaissance". This reawakening set the terms and forms which went on to define American writing not only in the nineteenth but also in the twentieth century.

The Fiction of the American Renaissance

Nathaniel Hawthorne

In the prefatory essay to his second novel, *The Scarlet Letter* (1850), titled "The Custom House", Nathaniel Hawthorne (1804–64) admits that his Puritan ancestors would not have approved of his becoming a novelist. Nevertheless, Hawthorne had expressed his desire to choose the vocation of a writer quite early, in a letter to his mother written as a student from Bowdoin College in 1821: "What do you think of my becoming an Author, and relying for support upon my pen. Indeed I think the illegibility of my handwriting is very authorlike. How proud you would feel to see my works praised by the reviewers. . . . But Authors are always poor Devils, and so Satan may take them."

Hawthorne's anxiety regarding the indigence of a writer was prompted by the fact that within a few years of his birth in 1804, he had lost his sea-captain father and the family, reduced to genteel penury, had to depend on the assistance of his maternal relations. With their support, he was able to acquire a college education with classmates among whom were Henry Wadsworth Longfellow, who would become one of the leading American poets of the period, and Franklin Pierce, who became the President of the United States (1853–57) and was also responsible in helping Hawthorne overcome an author's insolvency. Unfortunately, Hawthorne's mother died in 1849 and the novelist was unable to show her the praise in the reviews of his most notable work, *The Scarlet Letter.* Herman Melville's celebratory essay, "Hawthorne and his Mosses" (1850), placed Hawthorne beside Shakespeare: "Some may start to read Shakespeare and Hawthorne on the same page. . . . But Shakespeare has been approached. There are minds that have gone as far as Shakespeare into the universe. . . . Believe me, my friends, that men, not very much inferior to Shakespeare, are this day being born on the banks of the Ohio."

Hawthorne's early writings, consisting mostly of sketches and tales, were published anonymously during the 1830s, in a Boston journal called *The Token*. These included, "Sights from a Steeple", "The Gentle Boy", "Roger Malvin's Burial", "My Kinsman, Major Molineux", "The May-Pole of Merry Mount" and "The Minister's Black Veil" – many of which appeared in the collection of stories, *Twice Told Tales* (1837). It is quite evident that these pieces became the writer's means of "scribbling for a living" that also included producing several books for children, such as *Peter Parley's Universal History on the Basis of Geography* (1836), *Grandfather's*

Chair (1841), *Famous Old People* (1841), *Liberty Tree* (1841), *Biographical Stories for Children* (1842) and *Wonder Book for Boys and Girls* (1851).

When the Democrats were elected to form the United States government, Hawthorne's financial straits were considerably lessened, as he received patronage assignments as the Surveyor of the Boston Custom House and later, of the Salem Custom House, between 1836–41 and 1846–49, respectively. After his marriage to Sophia Peabody in 1842, the Hawthornes settled in the Old Manse in Concord, Massachusetts. In fact, the years between 1842 and 1852 turned out to be one of the most productive periods of Hawthorne's career. A second edition with additional tales of *Twice Told Tales* appeared in 1842; this was followed by *Mosses from the Old Manse* (1846) comprising the stories written after his marriage. The novels, or the "romances" as he termed them, appeared in quick succession: *The Scarlet Letter* in 1850, *The House of the Seven Gables* in 1851 and *The Blithedale Romance* in 1852. Another series of stories were published as *The Snow Image* (1851) and *The Tanglewood Tales* (1853). In 1853, after his friend Franklin Pierce became the President, Hawthorne was appointed the Consul at Liverpool and then at Manchester in England, where he lived till 1857. After spending another two years in Italy, the Hawthornes returned to Concord. *The Marble Faun* (1860) is considered to have been inspired by this European sojourn. Except for selections from his *English Notebooks*, titled *Our Old Home* (1863), no other notable publication appeared before Hawthorne's death in 1864. His unfinished manuscripts were published posthumously as *Septimus Felton* (1872), *The Dolliver Romance* (1876) and *Dr Grimshawe's Secret* (1883).

Though much of Hawthorne's writing is based on specific historical sources, the writer consistently describes his fiction as "romances": *The Scarlet Letter, A Romance; The House of the Seven Gables, A Romance; The Blithedale Romance;* and *The Marble Faun Or The Romance of Monte Beni.* This dichotomy between fact and fiction, realism and romance, is implicit in his definition of the romance mode of writing, given in the preface to *The House of the Seven Gables*:

> When a writer calls his work a Romance, it need hardly be observed that he wishes to claim a certain latitude both as to its fashion and material, which he would not have felt himself entitled to assume, had he professed to be writing a Novel. The latter form of composition [novel] is presumed to aim at a very minute fidelity, not merely to the possible, but to the probable and ordinary course of man's experience. The former [romance] – while as work of art it must subject itself to laws and, while it sins unpardonably, so far as it may swerve aside from the truth of the human heart – has fairly a right to present that truth under circumstances, to a great extent, of the writer's own choosing or creation.

The Scarlet Letter is, on the one hand, a faithful recreation of America's Puritan past; yet, on the other, there are several important deviations from history which give the tale an ironical and complex implication. The tale deals with the punishment given to an adulteress in seventeenth-century Puritan New England. However, comparison with historical records reveal that one of the judges, entrusted with sentencing the heroine in the tale, was also guilty of a sexual misdemeanor. Though this Puritan governor was subsequently removed from office, Hawthorne's deliberate inclusion of this patriarch during Hester's trial is an ironical criticism of the Puritan society of colonial America. For Hawthorne, therefore, the "latitude" offered by the Romance mode becomes a means to bring out the contradictions of the religious and moral rectitude that defined this society and its laws. Romance, thus, becomes a transgressive form whose imaginative freedom is used to fuse fact with fiction, to enable a powerful critique of the time. This, in fact, becomes a justification for the preference for this form of writing in American literature of the nineteenth century.

"*The Scarlet Letter* is a hell-fired story", Hawthorne had written to his publisher after completing the manuscript, "it will weary very many people and disgust some." Hawthorne's preoccupation with the Puritan past also resulted in his use of allegory which, in fact, is definitive of his view of life. This is evident in many of his tales, such as "Young Goodman Brown", "The Minister's Black Veil", "The Bosom Serpent", "The Birthmark" and "The Celestial Railroad". Thus, Hawthorne has been considered a moral allegorist whose chief thematic concern is the Calvinist anxiety regarding the Fall and the consequent sense of Original Sin and Innate Depravity. However, the ostensibly allegorical emphases in *The Scarlet Letter* tend to become ambiguous and indeterminate with the mutations in the meaning of the "scarlet letter", from "Adulteress" to "Able" and even "Admirable", in the course of the narrative. This ambiguity suggests a conflation of allegory with symbolism, which gives a complex significance to this novel. For Melville, therefore, there was a "black conceit" in Hawthorne that "pervades him through and through". Hawthorne's awareness of evil and his obsession with guilt were as "deep as Dante" and gave to his fiction a "blackness ten times black". In "Hawthorne and his Mosses", Melville thus acknowledges an influence which went on to shape his own *Moby-Dick* (1851). The profound tragic sense that characterises two of the greatest American novels of the nineteenth century seems, thus, to transgress the self-reliant optimism that was proposed in the writings of Emerson and, thereby, indicates a sense of alienation which forms a major theme in their fiction.

Many of Hawthorne's stories – "Egotism; or, The Bosom Serpent", "Young Goodman Brown", "The Birthmark", "The Artist of the Beautiful" and "Rappaccini's Daughter" – examine the consequences of obsessive passions which ultimately lead to isolation. Hawthorne terms this a form of "insulation" which puts one outside the "magic circle" or the "magnetic chain" of humanity: "There is no fate in the world so horrible as to have no share in its joys or sorrows," Hawthorne had once written to Longfellow. Goodman Brown, Ethan Brand Rappaccini and Roger Chillingworth are some of those who are destroyed by this loss of community. In fact, *The House of the Seven Gables* and *The Blithedale Romance* also explore the decline and loss of a family lineage, a tradition and history. While the former traces the slow decline of Salem, the latter is a satire based on his experience of the experiment in Utopian living at Brook Farm in Concord. In *The House of the Seven Gables*, "Maule's Curse" is, in an important sense, the Puritan past of the family; Phoebe and Holgrave must escape this fateful history of the house and find redemption through love and marriage. This optimism is, however, missing in *The Blithedale Romance*, in spite of the recreation of an Edenic enterprise. A romance of a socialist colony, Blithedale is an attempt at community living. However, it soon becomes evident that most of its important members are caught within their own self-regarding prejudices. Miles Coverdale, the sceptical narrator, realises that this is an "exploded scheme for beginning the life of Paradise anew". Therefore, Coverdale's role as the narrator becomes unreliable owing to its impressionability and uncertain attitude displayed towards the project. Hawthorne's treatment of this figure of the artist implicitly expresses his own doubts about the artist and writer.

Edgar Allan Poe

American Romanticism did not coincide with the Romantic movement which was born and developed in England and Europe in the late eighteenth and early nineteenth centuries. If the Transcendentalist movement of the 1830s and 40s is seen as the chief mediator of Romanticism in the United States, then the major phase of the movement east across the Atlantic had already ended. Though Emerson is often considered the official spokesman of the movement, Edgar Allan Poe (1809–49) is identified as an important representative, expressing in his writing some of the characteristic American themes and concerns of the movement. This relationship is mainly based on Poe's use of the Gothic in his *Tales of the Grotesque and Arabesque* (1839, 1840), a mode of writing almost generic to Romanticism and a form usually accepted as definitive of the American version of this movement. However, Poe's association with Romanticism is not limited merely to his use of the Gothic. Though Poe invoked the work of Samuel Taylor Coleridge, Thomas De Quincey and the German Romantics, he went on to point out that "terror is not of Germany, it is of the soul". In fact, the Gothic actually becomes the means with which Poe is able to revise some of the Romantic assumptions about nature, individual identity, the role of the mind in our understanding of reality, and ideas about poetry and language. Thus, Poe's association with Romanticism is ambiguous and contradictory, often reversing the very notions that he derives from it.

Deserted by his father and born of an itinerant actress mother in Boston on 7 October 1809, Poe found foster parents in Richmond,

Virginia, after his mother's sudden death. He grew up in the family of John and Frances Allan. After a discreditable time at the University of Virginia and the military academy at West Point, the fact that Poe refused to join John's mercantile firm confirmed his desire to be a writer and a poet. He published his first book, *Tamerlane and Other Poems*, in 1827, while still at university. In 1829, a second edition with additional poems, *Al Aaraaf, Tamerlane and Minor Poems*, followed. When John Allan disowned Poe's literary ambitions, the latter got the cadets of West Point to sponsor his third volume, *Poems* (1831). Ironically, barring a few notable exceptions, the South is hardly represented in Poe's writing; though many of his tales did subscribe to African-American stereotypes, it is clear now that Poe was not the author of the pro-slavery "Paulding-Drayton Review" which appeared in the *Southern Literary Messenger* in April 1836. Nevertheless, many of his tales contained the indigenous sense of decadence, desolation and oppressive gloom that became a signature of Southern literature.

For Poe, the biggest hurdle he had to overcome was not a defined talent or opportunity, but poverty. Receiving no recognition for his poetry, Poe acquired some notoriety as a reviewer for his virulent attacks on contemporary novels and poetry, in the *Southern Literary Messenger*, *Burton's Gentlemen's Magazine* and *Graham's Magazine*, earning him the epithet, "Tomahawk Man". The *Narrative of Arthur Gordon Pym*, a fictional account of a journey to Antarctica, attracted considerable attention and was published in the *Messenger* and as a separate short novel in 1838. Many of Poe's tales had already started appearing in these journals, which encouraged the current taste for the Gothic and the sensational. The two-volume *Tales of the Grotesque and Arabesque* was rejected by *Harpers* and was finally published by Lea and Blanchard. Economic difficulties prompted Poe to unsuccessfully seek alternative employment in government administration. His bitterness against hostile publishers and deep distress at the death of his wife, Virginia, in 1847, led to an alcoholic and melancholic phase which contributed to the image typically ascribed to Poe – that of an obsessively depressed and psychotic individual with a raven on one shoulder and a black cat on the other. Yet, in 1848, Poe was to publish *Eureka: A Prose Poem*, a unique science-fictional meditation on the nature of the universe.

Poe died in mysterious circumstances in Baltimore, coincidentally on 7 October 1849. The words of Thingum, a character from a late comic tale, "The Literary Life of Thingum Bob Esq.", could just have been his own: "Look at *me*! – how I labored – how I toiled – how I wrote ! Ye Gods did I *not* write? I knew not the word 'ease'."

Beginning his career as a poet, Poe believed that, since poems depend on an intensity of effect, a long poem was a contradiction in terms. Defining the poetics of his writing in his "Philosophy of Composition" (1846), he suggested that, ideally, a poem should be read within the "limit of a single sitting" and thus its "proper" length should be, as in his "The Raven", "about one hundred lines". This would evidently imply his Romantic preference for the lyric and the basic theme of his poetry to be dependent on subjective experiences. As in his tales, Poe's poetry is concerned with emotional disturbances and profoundly distraught mental states which often imply derangement. In this sense, Poe's Romantic inclination was not towards an Emersonian optimism and sense of affirmation, but involved an awareness of human anguish, hurt and alienation. Therefore, Poe could not be included with the New England School of Poets as he himself admitted that, unlike them, he did not accept the "heresy of *The Didactic*", by which literature, in general, and poetry, in particular, was usually given the duty to express truth: "It has been assumed, tacitly and avowedly, directly and indirectly, that the ultimate object of all Poetry is Truth. Every poem, it is said, should inculcate a moral; and by this moral is the poetical merit of the work to be adjudged." In his posthumous essay, "The Poetic Principle" (1850), Poe offers a theory of poetry which anticipates modernist and symbolist ideas:

> We have taken into our heads that to write a poem simply for the poem's sake, and to acknowledge such to have been our design, would be to confess ourselves radically wanting in the true Poetic dignity and force:—but the simple fact is, that, would we but permit ourselves to look into our souls, we should immediately there discover that under the sun there neither exists nor *can* exist any work thoroughly dignified—more supremely noble than this very poem—this poem *per se*—this poem which is a poem and nothing more—this poem written solely for the poems' sake.

One important element, which contributed to this autonomous idea of poetry, is Poe's insistence on musicality and rhythm as formative of a poem. Though this earned him Emerson's derision as the "jingle man", Poe considered poetry to be an expression of beauty, and beauty, since it is a non-didactic pleasure, transcended definition and was, in fact, "*in*definite sensations—to which end music is essential, since the comprehension of sweet sound is our most indefinite conception". Therefore, Poe's definition of poetry affirms the Romantic quest for beauty but undermines its verbal and imaginative significance to emphasise a musicality which is essentially self-referential: "We would define in brief the Poetry of words as the *Rhythmical Creation of Beauty*. Beyond the limits of Beauty its province does not extend. Its sole arbiter is Taste. With the Intellect or with the Conscience it has only collateral relations. It has no dependence, unless incidentally, upon either Duty or Truth." The supernatural effect in "The Raven", the much anthologised poem from *The Raven and Other Poems* (1845), is created by its conscious musical quality. The repetitive element becomes a rhythmic invocation of an otherworldly presence which takes the form of the raven. Overcome by grief, the speaker of the poem seeks diversion in "forgotten lore", which fails to offer the desired consolation when he is visited by "this ebony bird" whose singular and enigmatic utterance leads to the profound awareness of the transience of desires and hopes, and thus induces a lasting sense of melancholy:

> Startled at the stillness broken by reply so aptly spoken
> 'Doubtless,' said I, 'what it utters is its only stock and store,
> Caught from some unhappy master whom unmerciful Disaster
> Followed last and followed faster till his songs one burden
> bore—
> Till the dirges of his Hope that melancholy burden bore
> Of "Never—nevermore."'

Anguished by the death of his beloved, Lenore, the narrator contemplates "that species of despair which delights in self torture" and indulges in the "luxury of sorrow" which finds its poignant approval in the bird's refrain, "Nevermore". It soon becomes evident that the experience is part of the speaker's "sad fancy";

that the incantatory rhythms induce a psychological condition which leads to a sense of immobility and silence suggested by the repetition of the word "still" at the end, which clearly implies a metaphoric death.

Poe's writing tends to be preoccupied with this sense of despair and melancholy – often the result of insularity, transience, loss and guilt. As Poe admitted, "Melancholy is thus the most legitimate of all poetic tones." Poe considered the "most melancholy of topics most poetical . . . when it most closely allies itself to *Beauty*: the death, then, of a beautiful woman is, unquestionably, the most poetical topic of the world." Death then becomes one of the dominant themes in Poe's writing, envisaging morbid variations in conception and treatment. "The Sleeper", "Ulalume", "Lenore" and "Annabel Lee" can be included in this category. While "Eldorado", "The City in the Sea", and "The Valley of Nis" attempt the Romantic recreation of the Oriental and exotic, "To Helen" explores the ephemeral nature of the beautiful which defies legible conceptions and can only be given idealised forms in poetry and art. Thus, the narrator in "Dreamland" speaks of a strange land, "out of Space – out of Time": Poe's poetry involves this quest for an elusive reality that can only be glimpsed in dreams or, sometimes, as suggested in his tales, in trance-like states accompanying madness.

It is ironic that though Poe's ambitions had been a desire for recognition as a poet, he achieved most of his fame and success from his tales. An anonymous 1845 review of the *Tales of the Grotesque and Arabesque,* probably written by Poe himself, commended their style as being "strictly earnest", thereby suggesting the writer's "belief in his statements" actually derived from a "power of simulation" which revealed the "high genius" involved in the "exercise of the loftiest of talent . . . afforded by the wide domains of mere prose". Defending the *Tales* as having a "unity of design", in the "Preface", Poe dismissed their common reception as mere "German" or Gothic sensationalism. This suggested a complex modification of the typical devices of terror stories and a continuous experimentation with the themes and forms of the tale derived from indigenous traditions, responding to the contemporary popularity of magazine fiction. In fact, Poe described himself as a "magazinist" and went on to defend this practice by observing that the "history of

Magazines" had achieved success with stories where "the ludicrous (was) heightened into the grotesque: the fearful coloured into the horrible: the witty exaggerated into the burlesque: the singular wrought out into the strange and mystical." Poe believed that "... every work of art should contain within itself all that is requisite for its own comprehension"; in his *Eureka*, he thus emphasised the principles of truth and consistency which ensured this sense of meaning: "A thing is consistent in the ratio of its truth—true in the ratio of its consistency. *A perfect consistency, I repeat, can be nothing but absolute truth*" (italics in original).

The seventy tales Poe published between 1832 and 1849 are remarkable for their variety: they included horror stories such as the "The Murders in the Rue Morgue", "The Pit and the Pendulum" and "The Black Cat" (to name a few); pseudo-science fiction – "Metzengerstein", "The Balloon Hoax" and "The System of Dr. Tarr and Professor Fether"; exotic adventures, as in "MS. Found in a Bottle", "A Descent into the Maelstrom" and "A Narrative of Arthur Gordon Pym"; comedy and satiric tales such as "Three Sundays of a Week", "Loss of Breath", "The Duc de L'Omelette" and many more. In fact, Poe's tales can be divided into three distinct groups: "grotesque", "arabesque" and "ratiocinative". The first group mostly consists of his early sensational tales characterised by their Gothicism, such as "King Pest", "The Assignation", "A Slight Predicament" and "How to Write a Blackwood Article" which was, in fact, a parody of this Romantic form of writing. The arabesques comprise the most notable examples of Poe's tales. Deriving the term from the German, he gave them a romance form yet with a serious meaning. These tales actually involve psychological adventures, as in "Ligeia", "The Fall of the House of Usher" and "The Tell-Tale Heart" which, in exploring the interior landscapes of the mind, inverts the realms of the real and the unreal, sanity and insanity, the mystical and the speculative, the truth and the lie. The later "ratiocinative" tales, written between 1841 and 1845, consist of the stories dealing with the crime-solving adventures of Monsieur C. Auguste Dupin, an early version of the literary detective. These tales contribute to Poe's inclusion in the history of crime fiction in America. "The Purloined Letter" and "The Murders in the Rue Morgue" fall clearly into this category, and "The Mystery of

Marie Roget" may also be included, though it does not feature the activities of Dupin.

In his "The Philosophy of Composition", Poe announced his basic method in the tales: "I prefer commencing with the consideration of an *effect*." By "effect" he was evidently suggesting the importance of the tale's impact upon the reader; but he was also echoing what he had stated to be the basis of his poetry when he suggested that "brevity is in direct ratio [to] the intensity of the intended effect". Thus, a rigorous sense of structure became central to Poe's aesthetics of narrative: "In the whole composition there should be no word written, of which the tendency, direct or indirect, is not to the one pre-established design." In spite of Poe's association with Romanticism, there was an equal concern with neoclassical notions of formal order and unity which ensured the proper effect of the tales:

> Nothing is more clear than that every plot, worth the name, must be elaborated to its 'denouement' before anything be attempted with the pen. It is only with the denouement constantly in view that we can give a plot its indispensable air of consequence or causation, by making the incidents and especially the tone at all points, tend to the development of the intention.

"The Fall of the House of Usher", therefore, has a circularity of structure where the house, with its two windows, itself is a metaphor of a head and the narrator's visit to his friend is his entrance into the mind. The tale thus becomes the narrator's journey not only into Usher's agonised mind but also his own unconscious self, the descent into which is a traumatic experience, resulting in his disintegration implied by the final destruction of the house. In fact, Poe's transformation of Gothicism involves his use of the narrator to internalise terror and, thereby, to implicate the reader in this psychological scrutiny. Many of Poe's tales actually deal with unreliable narrators who are either involved in manipulating the facts of the event or, evidently, falsifying them. For instance, in "The Tell-Tale Heart" and in "The Black Cat", the narrators attempt to hide their crimes with ingenious strategies. By pleading sanity, the narrator in "The Tell-Tale Heart" actually reveals his lunacy – the sound of the beating heart becomes his own; it suggests the return of a buried guilt which forces his confession. The tale, therefore, is also concerned with the act of its telling. Poe's preoccupation with the narrative function and his complex experiments with shifting points of view seem to anticipate similar developments in the modern novel, particularly in the fiction of Henry James and William Faulkner.

The grotesque and gratuitous violence that characterises many of Poe's tales thus becomes a metaphor of an interior landscape of the mind tormented by spectres of hidden guilt and an inversion of the boundaries of sanity and insanity. Though born and brought up in Boston, in one important sense, Poe defines the "Southern Gothic", not merely as a literary mode borrowed from German Romanticism, but generic to the geography of its society and culture. The decadent Romanticism that these sensational aspects in Poe's writing invoke can be traced to the frontier stories of the Southwest and the novels of Charles Brockden Brown. Dismissing what he called the "heresy of the Didactic", Poe denied giving to his tales and poems a moral reference. He thus preferred to consider art as having autonomous value and significance, as he stated in his posthumous treatise, "The Poetic Principle". Poe's treatment of nature is, thus, intimidating and ambiguous: it is neither the idyll that traditional Romanticism eulogises, nor does it encourage a correspondence between mind and matter, rather, actively resisting the mind's ability to understand its inexorable caprices and fatalities. The supernatural in Poe is thus evoked in the very nature of things – terror is a state of the mind constantly grappling with unconscious demons of desire and doom, as in "The Fall of the House of Usher", "Ligeia", "The Cask of Amontillado" and "The Pit and the Pendulum", to name just a few such instances.

Similarly, art, for Poe, often becomes a verbal puzzle, a play of meanings where the reader often has to assume the role of the detective, like Dupin. By advocating a self-referential form of writing, Poe was anticipating certain significant developments that would mark American modernism. Poe's appreciation and critical revaluation had thus to wait till the twentieth century – for T. S. Eliot and for the French poet Charles Baudelaire and the Symbolists.

This seems to give credibility to Evert Duyckinck's observation that, "Our most neglected and best (sic) abused authors are generally our best authors."

Herman Melville

Herman Melville (1819–91) was born in a traditional and distinguished family – the Calvinist Melvilles of Boston on his father's and the Dutch Reformed Gansevoorts of Albany on his mother's side. Unlike Hawthorne, Melville had no ambitions of becoming a writer. The early death of his father, after a period of economic hardship, ended his formal school education when he was twelve. The need to support his family led to his becoming first a bank clerk, then a teacher, a farm hand, a salesman and, finally, a cabin boy on a ship to Liverpool. The family attraction for the sea seemed to prompt him again to join a whaling ship, the *Acushnet*, in 1841 on a Pacific voyage along the coast of South America to the Galapagos and Marquesas islands. Here he abandoned ship and lived among primitive tribes in the valley of the Typees. Rescued by an Australian whaler and after further travels in the Hawaiian islands, Melville finally returned to Boston aboard the *United States*, a government frigate, in 1844. Ishmael, the narrator in *Moby-Dick; or, The Whale* (1851), considered the whale-ship as the only Yale and Harvard he ever had; this was true of his creator. Melville's writing grew out of, or was based on, these sea voyages. In fact, Melville was supposed to have told Hawthorne: "Until I was twenty-five, I had no development."

Melville's *Typee: A Peep at Polynesian Life* (1846) and *Omoo: A Narrative of Adventures in the South Seas* (1847) marked him as a writer of fictionalised travel and adventure narratives. However, by imaginatively embellishing his experiences with his wide reading, Melville was able to give these exotic and Edenic tales a social and moral emphasis, particularly in his criticism of the destructive influence of missionary activities in these islands.

Mardi: And a Voyage Thither (1849), Melville's next novel, with its allegorical structure and its preoccupation with metaphysical questions, anticipates the themes which would characterise his later fiction. Though, at the center of *Mardi*, there is a romantic relationship between the narrator, Taji, and the mysterious Yillah, the narrative also addresses issues of history, religion and philosophy, particularly in Babbalanja's quest for an ideal way of life. Moreover, when completing the novel, Melville was stirred by the revolutionary developments in Europe in 1848, which motivated him to widen the scope of the narrative to include chapters of political allegory. Melville's insight into the implications and results of contemporary events is revealed in his observations on the closing of the American Frontier.

However, the failure of *Mardi* made Melville revert to the formula of his earlier autobiographical romances. *Redburn: His First Voyage* (1849) is thus based on his trip to Liverpool as a young sailor. The novel deals with the career of a generic American hero – the innocent and romantic individual whose confrontation with the harsh realities of a sailor's life and the English slums finally leads to his disenchanted maturity. The significance of Redburn's experiences thus extends beyond his personal education into a commentary on the condition of the laboring poor. Hence, Melville's writing acquires a sense of realism which would become definitive of his later fiction.

This element, in fact, is distinctive of *The White Jacket* (1850), which is based on Melville's brief career on a warship of the US Navy. The novel reiterates the conflict between naiveté and maturity, where the hero's white jacket is a metaphoric rallying point of his innocence trying to withstand derision and persecution. The regimented, dehumanising world of the man-of-war, the naval ship *USS Neversink,* anticipates the destructive determinism which defines the industrial and naturalist novel at the turn of the century. In the rigid hierarchy of the ship's crew, Melville finds gross injustice and cruelty, which undermines the values of the very nation the warship aims to defend. This sense of irony characterises Melville's interrogation of the American self-conception and the tragic consequences of its belief in a Manifest Destiny.

Melville described *Moby-Dick* as "a romance of adventure founded upon certain wild legends in the Southern Sperm Whale Fisheries and illustrated by the author's own personal experience as a harpooner". The novel, however, extends far beyond this simple account, for it is considered a classic of nineteenth-century

American fiction, owing to its ability to attain the significance of a national epic. Melville fused the traditional heroic literature of Europe with aspects of essentially American experience, including its individualist values and moral idealism, to create a representative work of fiction.

Moby-Dick is a Faustian tragedy. In fact, Melville's deep involvement with Shakespeare's plays at the time he planned and wrote the novel, suggest that Captain Ahab, that "grand, ungodly, God-like man", was modelled on some notable Shakespearean heroes. Ahab's tragedy is not the result of his malignity against the white whale responsible for "dismembering" him. His vengeance seeks to pierce the inscrutable "pasteboard" surfaces of meaning represented by nature, the whale and the material world, and thus to confront the dark forces that lurk behind them. The novel has the conceptual economy of a classical tragedy where Ahab sees himself as a victim of malevolent Fate, caught in a metaphysical struggle against traditional forces of evil. Thus, a characteristic allegorical implication is basic to the romance in which fallen man, abandoned in the world, tries to regain a sense of identity and dignity. In fact, Ahab once observes that ". . . dramatically regarded . . . all men tragically great are made so by a certain morbidness." There is an evident self-regarding obsession which makes Melville refer repeatedly to the myth of Narcissus. So, Ahab's morbidity involves his attempt to struggle with the contradictory impulses in his own self, and his tragedy recalls that of Shakespeare's Brutus "at war with oneself".

However, the structure of the tragic feeling and its development would not have been effective without the narrator Ishmael, through whose point of view Ahab's desire and despair is mediated. Ishmael performs the important function of understanding the contrary turns of the narrative. For it is Ishmael who recognises the fact that Ahab's tragic greatness is actually defined by a white whale, strangely tattooed with codes, but who remains absent for the most part of the novel. The absence of the whale thus forms a mystery which seems to suggest a fundamental indifference and emptiness which is central to Ahab's universe. This is implicit in the ambiguous whiteness of the whale which, for Ishmael, being "a colorless all-color" seems to suggest an "indefiniteness" that "shadows forth the heartless voids and immensities of the universe . . ." By reducing the vast and variable universe to the unitary meanings of his emblematic Puritan consciousness, Ahab sees the whale both as an image and object, a sign and an idea. In this sense, his tragedy is a consequence of his inability to separate the world from one's conception of self. This examination of Emersonian idealism and the American self-definition in terms of the nation, is thus at the centre of this complex novel. "I've written a wicked book," Melville had told Hawthorne, "and I feel spotless as a lamb."

Melville's playing with these binaries in theme and structure continued into his next novel, *Pierre or, The Ambiguities* (1852), where what Melville described as a "rural bowl of milk" becomes a dark exploration of psychological aberrations involving incest and isolation. *Pierre* was admittedly written to raise the "bill for the baker", but the antagonism it generated in its readers, inevitably, prevented this aim. In 1855, Melville published *Israel Potter: His Fifty Years of Exile*, a historical romance depicting the course of the Revolution, which was equally unsuccessful. However, his venture into shorter fiction –*The Piazza Tales* (1856) – was more rewarding, particularly, "Bartleby, the Scrivener: A Story of Wall Street" and "Benito Cereno". *The Confidence Man: His Masquerade* (1857), while dealing with the traditional figure of the trickster, is an incisive satire of the moral trickery and degeneration of American society.

In the late 1850s, Melville turned towards poetry to record his travels in Egypt and Palestine. *Clarel: A Poem and Pilgrimage in the Holy Land* (1876) was an exploration of the crisis of modern civilisation and a young man's search for religious faith. This quest is expressed through the discourses of a remarkable group of characters, many of whom seemed to have been resurrected from his earlier fiction. *Battlepieces and Aspects of War* (1866), which grew from Melville's reflections on the Civil War, considers this conflict as a betrayal of the democratic values of the nation and appeals for a reassertion of fraternal ideals derived from an acceptance of a common tragedy. Most of his later poetry is collected in *John Marr and Other Sailors* (1888) and *Timoleon* (1891), which actually create the context for Melville's return to prose fiction in *Billy Budd* (published posthumously in 1924). Conceived initially as an allegory, the novel examines questions of individual agency and justice; questions which remain relevant even today.

Mark Twain

Mark Twain (1835–1910) was born Samuel Langhorne Clemens on 30 November, in a small village called Florida, in Missouri. The pseudonym by which he became famous was probably adopted after he became a steam-boat pilot on the Mississippi river in 1859, and actually referred to the leadsmen's cry to the pilot when some peril was sighted in the river water ahead. As a boy, Samuel grew up in Hannibal, a town on the banks of the Mississippi, absorbing the sights and life on the river and on its banks. These experiences and memories were to become the material of his fiction till the end of his career as a writer. Samuel's involvement in writing began after his father died in 1847, when he became a printer's assistant and compositor in the press from where his brother, Orion, used to publish a local newspaper. The youthful and humorous features, which appeared as "Our Assistant's Column", soon became a regular series of travel pieces for the *Evening Post* with the by-line "Thomas Jefferson Snodgrass".

With the outbreak of the Civil War in 1861, when traffic on the Mississippi was severely reduced, Clemens, like his celebrated hero Huckleberry Finn, "lighted out" for the West. At Angel's Camp in the Sierras he heard the tale which became the basis for "The Celebrated Jumping Frog of Calaveras County", which was subsequently published in the *New York Evening Post.* It later became the titular story of Twain's first book, *The Celebrated Jumping Frog of Calaveras County and Other Sketches* (1866). One important source of Twain's early writing is, evidently, his travels over the Americas and Europe between 1861 and 1865. The experiences produced *Innocents Abroad* (1869) and *Roughing It* (1872). The first dealt with a staple theme in American writing – the naïve and idealistic American's encounter with the traditions of an older European culture. However, Twain approached this issue in his characteristic iconoclastic manner. Unlike Hawthorne earlier and Henry James later, he sees Europe in terms of a "splendor of gay immorality" which suggests that American innocence could be a form of sceptical realism; an interpretation that would become definitive of Twain's comic assessment of human society. *Roughing It* deals with his journey across the Midwest and Nevada. In fact, many of the adventures recounted in this work contribute to the image of "Mark Twain" that the writer constructed in his writing: a careless, shambling man with unruly hair who moved through Frontier towns investing and losing money in silver mines and poker. Much of Twain's writing developed out of an oral tradition of the American tall tale,* whose itinerant variations were more justified than its authenticity – attested by what Huck Finn, on another occasion, observes, "Mr. Mark Twain . . . he told the truth, mainly."

In *The Gilded Age* (1873), written in collaboration with Charles Dudley Warner, Twain attempted to portray the changing history of his times which, in fact, imbibed the epithet of the novel's title. More than the consequences of the American Civil War, the Reconstruction and Abolitionism, Twain was preoccupied with what came to be termed "boomtimes" and "boomtowns" reaping the prosperity from the dramatic technological growth which spanned the continent with electricity, steamboats, railroads and the motor car. Twain's satire of this bubble and burst of an American success story is epitomised in the character of the comic huckster, Colonel Sellers, drawn with some inspiration from Charles Dickens's *Martin Chuzzlewit*. Significantly, this figure of the huckster was to become ubiquitous in Twain's later novels and testified to the formation of an American stereotype in the fiction of nineteenth and twentieth centuries. Thus *The Gilded Age* anticipates the dualism that defines Twain's fiction – a simultaneous fascination and irreverence for social and moral certainties.

In 1875, Twain started a series (in seven installments) for the *Atlantic Monthly – Old Times on the Mississippi*. These were added

---

* A tall tale is a narrative or yarn which deals with an unlikely and exaggerated adventure of a folk hero in hyperbolic and pretentious language, such as those associated with the legendary heroes of the American Frontier like Paul Bunyan, the giant lumberjack of the Northwest; Mike Fink, the Mississippi keel boatman; and David Crockett, the backwoods Tennessee marksman.

to a further thirty-nine chapters forming *Life on the Mississippi* (1883). Not only does the river return to these pages as a way of life but also becomes a metaphor of initiation and education. As in the case of Ishmael in *Moby-Dick*, the steamboat and the river are the school where Twain admits being "... personally and familiarly acquainted with about all the types of human nature to be found in fiction, biography, or history". Moreover, for Twain, the river was also a symbol of freedom, a theme which he would relentlessly pursue in his next two novels: "... a (steam-boat) pilot in those days was the only unfettered and entirely independent human being that lived on the earth."

The Adventures of Tom Sawyer (1876) is probably one of the most enduring novels of American literature. Ostensibly meant for the young, its popularity was ensured by the fact that it was also meant to "remind adults of what they once were themselves". As its title suggests, it is a loose collection of stories surrounding a murder, its detection by Tom Sawyer and Huck Finn, and the final arrest of the real criminal. The boys' games thus frequently confront the world of adults and, in the course of these adventures, involve their own growth and the implicit loss of innocence. Though structured as a *bildungsroman*, Twain often gives his narrative an ambiguous turn in which the adults are revealed as incompetent and irresponsible. Thus, the value of a simple and youthful innocence – a theme to which Twain would repeatedly return in his writing – is reasserted at the end of the novel.

The Adventures of Huckleberry Finn (1885) is sometimes considered a sequel to *Tom Sawyer*, and Tom, in fact, has a brief but important role in the tale. Yet, it marks Twain's return to what is termed "the matter of Hannibal", a romance cycle of myths of the Mississippi which had shaped his identity as a novelist. Thereby, the novel fulfils a representative function by embodying the aspirations, beliefs and values of the nation. *Huckleberry Finn* is the story of a boy whose desire for freedom from the codes and conventions of society makes him dissimulate his own death. This pattern of death and rebirth is a dominant structure of the narrative, which also explores other thematic oppositions such as the wilderness and community, nature and culture, and illusion and reality.

Huckleberry Finn is distinctive for the fact that Mark Twain is not the narrator in the novel – by usurping this role from his creator at the very beginning of the novel, the young hero not only subscribes to the functions of an autobiographical mode, but the first-person narration here literally becomes Huck's spontaneous and unlettered voice with its misspelt and mispronounced words and dialectal inflections. Huck's revolt, thus, involves not only a rejection of the false words of "sivilization" but also the language which both expresses and authorises them. In fact, Twain describes *Huckleberry Finn* as "a book of mine where a sound heart & a deformed conscience come into collision & conscience suffers defeat". In the course of Huck's journey on a raft down the Mississippi, with the runaway slave Jim, this conflict is manifested in his indecision about returning his companion to slavery: ". . . what's the use you learning to do right when it's troublesome to do right and aint no trouble to do wrong and the wages is just the same?" This inversion of moral standards, evidently a consequence of slavery, is challenged here, not with religious or social precepts, but with a natural innocence which remains bewildered about the rationale of social values. Unable to formulate and express the basis of his decision, Huck takes recourse to a comic conspiracy to expose the elaborate deceit of civilisation. Thus, he validates his doing the "right" only by accepting his transgression into that which is "wrong", admitting, "All right then, I'll *go* to hell."

The narrative moves between the river and the towns on its banks, encountering different types of people representing various forms of human venality and hypocrisy – all trying to grab the most from the "gilded times". The river thus becomes a refuge and also a stage on which a moral drama is rehearsed and reenacted. In this sense, the river acquires a mythic significance, not only by suggesting an Edenic harmony with nature, but also by reasserting the individual desire for freedom, basic to the spirit of the nation. However, for Huck, the problem of freedom ironically involves a withdrawal from the very society which valorises it. James T. Farrell, therefore, considers Huck and Tom to be "two accusing fingers pointing down the decades of American history". Twain's humour and satire in *Huckleberry Finn* thus become the means by which the novelist examines the issues of individual autonomy and political control, which became important concerns of the evolving democracy in nineteenth-century America.

Twain's comic realism is a legacy of the American Frontier – a hybrid, dialectal and idiosyncratic tradition whose primary aim is the debunking of romantic notions – notions which he criticises in Walter Scott and James Fenimore Cooper: "It is a restful chapter in any book of his when somebody doesn't step on a twig and alarm all the reds and whites for two hundred yards around. . . . In fact, the Leather-Stocking Series ought to have been called the Broken Twig Series." In *A Connecticut Yankee in King Arthur's Court* (1889), Twain's primary focus is thus to contrast Yankee practical sense and ingenuity with Medieval English injustice, poverty and the tendency towards superstition. Making a notable use of the formula of time-travel, Twain's Yankee finds himself, after a blow to his head, in Camelot, "as lovely as a dream and as lonesome as Sunday." The novel is thus a remarkable blend of satire, the tall tale, the picaresque and comedy, all of which contribute to a celebration of American ideals and values.

In the early 1890s, Twain faced a series of personal failures and tragedies. The considerable money and hope that he had invested in a publishing project with the Paige typesetting machine collapsed. This was followed by the deaths of his wife and two daughters. The resultant despair and derision for human kind is reflected in *The Tragedy of Pudd'nhead Wilson* (1894) which, he admitted, "changed itself from a farce to tragedy while I was going along with it". Thus, underneath the burlesque, the novel is a bitter criticism of social evils, which seems to justify an observation made in a later posthumous work called *The Mysterious Stranger* (1916): "No man can be happy for, to him, life is real, and he sees what a fearful thing it is." Twain's later writing is thus overcast with a growing pessimism regarding human dishonesty and stupidity. In *The Man that Corrupted Hadleyburg* (1900) and *The Mysterious Stranger*, Twain voices his most cynical and trenchant criticism of human and social evils: "I think I can make it tell what I think of Man . . . and what a shabby, poor, ridiculous thing he is and how mistaken he is in his estimate of . . . his place among the animals."

Therefore, in *What is Man?* (1917), a characteristic Social Darwinism is used as an answer: for man, "by the law of his nature . . . takes on the color of the place of his resort. The influences about him create his preferences, his aversions, his politics, his taste, his morality, his religion." A dual vision, characteristic of American literature, also marks Twain's fiction. With a pervasive ironic sense, the humourist repeatedly emphasises the absurdity of human illusions which actually conceal self-deception and desolation. Twain's humour thus imbricates the smile with the tear, for, as he confessed, "The secret source of Humor itself is not joy but sorrow. There is no humor in heaven."

To see Mark Twain as a writer of boys' adventures, or merely a regional humourist of the American Frontier, would be a limited assessment of the novelist. In fact, he was able to shape an American tradition of fiction whose contours can be traced through the realists and naturalists to that of William Faulkner. Twain, thus, seems to conform to Emerson's figure of "a humorist who in a good deal of rattle had a grain or two of sense. He shocked the company by maintaining that the attributes of God were two – power and risibility, and that it was the duty of every man to keep up the comedy."

The Poetry of the American Renaissance

Walt Whitman

The nineteenth century holds a significant place in the history of American literature, not only because it has produced some of its literary classics but also because it has the rare privilege of witnessing this literature contributing to the definition of the nation. In the 1867 edition of *Leaves of Grass* (1855), Walt Whitman (1819–92) declared the distinctive American theme and aim of the poem: "One's self I sing, a simple, separate person; / Yet utter the word Democratic, the word *En-Masse*." Thereby, Whitman was able to fulfil the appeal for a literary nationalism that Emerson had made in his essay "The American Scholar" (1837). Enunciating his purpose in *Leaves of Grass*, Whitman states that it was

> . . . a feeling or ambition to articulate and faithfully express in literary or poetic form and uncompromisingly, my own physical, emotional, moral, intellectual and aesthetic Personality, in the midst of, and tallying, the momentous spirit and facts of its immediate days and of current America – and to exploit that Personality, identified with place and date, in a far candid and comprehensive sense than any hitherto poem or book.

Whitman's desire for self-definition is, therefore, linked to finding an American identity. This fashioning of a representative self makes *Leaves of Grass* an epic of the democratic America emerging in the nineteenth century. It also involves a mythic dramatisation of the poet as a representative American, thereby echoing Emerson's belief about America being a poem, by reasserting that "The United States themselves are essentially the greatest poem."

Whitman's life, however, does not indicate any signs of his poetic vocation or his ambitions to produce an American epic. Born in a modest, working-class family of eight brothers and sisters on Long Island, Massachusetts, in 1819, Whitman received merely five or six years of formal education. After working with his carpenter father for a few years, he joined a printing press as an apprentice compositor. After serving as an itinerant school teacher, Whitman eventually turned to journalism becoming the editor of the *Brooklyn Daily Eagle* in 1846. *Leaves of Grass*, which first appeared in 1855 and went through several revisions and additions during his lifetime, hardly afforded the poet financial security. The final edition of the collection appeared in 1891, a year before the poet's death. Whitman served as a male nurse during the Civil War, a record of which is collected in the prose pieces of *Democratic Vistas* (1871) and in *Memoranda During the War* (1875), and also in the poems published in *Drum Taps* (1865) and *Sequel to Drum Taps* (1865–66) which includes the famous elegy to President Abraham Lincoln, "When Lilacs Last in the Dooryard Bloom'd". In 1871, Whitman attempted to explore a vision of the spiritual regeneration of the human race in "Passage to India". He suffered a paralytic stroke in 1873, which confined him to a wheelchair for the next twenty years. His later writings are included in *Two Rivulets* (1876) and *Specimen Days* (1882), while his newspaper poems have been collected in *November Boughs* (1888).

Whitman's poetry attests to the multiplicity of his experiences:

Walt Whitman, a kosmos, of Manhattan the son,
Turbulent, fleshy, sensual, eating, drinking and breeding,
No sentimentalist, no stander above men and women or apart
    from them,
No more modest than immodest. ("Song of Myself")

Yet, it is this myriad and diverse nation – "Chants of the prairies, / Chants of the long running Mississippi, and down to the Mexican sea" – which shapes his choice of a vocation as a poet:

Now in a moment I know what I am for—I awake,
And already a thousand singers—a thousand songs, clearer,
    louder and more sorrowful than yours,
A thousand warbling echoes have started to life within me,
Never to die. ("Out of the Cradle Endlessly Rocking")

In an important sense, the celebration of the self as the nation, which *Leaves of Grass* proclaims, marks the apotheosis of the American Renaissance. For Whitman, the self is emblematic of the "divine inside out" – a complex but complete expression of the union of body and soul, intellect and emotion, form and feeling, announced in the epigraph of the 1855 edition of the poem:

Come, said my Soul,
Such verses for my Body to write, (for we are one,)
That should I after death invisibly return,
Or long, long hence, in other spheres,
There to some group of mates the chants resuming.

Whitman's poetry has, therefore, been considered representative of some of the major tenets of the Transcendentalists. He was thus the first to receive Emerson's approval, "greetings . . . at the beginning of a great career". In his role as the poet and prophet of America, Whitman substantiated the notions of the poet and poetry elucidated in Emerson's essays such as "Self Reliance" and "The Poet", by proclaiming, "I am the acme of things accomplished, and I an encloser of things to be." However, Whitman's poetry simultaneously resists the Emersonian separation of the body from the soul. While the Transcendentalists, like the English Romantics, saw the body as a vestment of the soul, Whitman considered the body to be the hieroglyph of the soul:

> I am the poet of the Body and I am the poet of the Soul,
> The pleasures of heaven are with me and the pains of hell are with me
> The first, I graft and increase upon myself, the latter I translate into a new tongue. ("Song of Myself")

In a sense, this was a defence of the "libidinous joy" often revealed in his poems, particularly in "Calamus" and "Children of Adam", which had been frowned upon both by Emerson and the American establishment. Whitman lost a position as a clerk in the Department of Interior owing to the sexual references in his poetry. Nevertheless, this is one of the central arguments used to develop the theme of spiritual rebirth as the poet wonders in "I Sing the Body Electric":

> And if those who defile the living are as bad as they who defile the dead?
> And if the body does not do fully as much as the soul?
> And if the body were not the soul, what is the soul?

Leaves of Grass begins with the poem "One's Self I Sing", which announces the central idea and aim of the poem:

> I celebrate myself and sing myself,
> And what I assume you shall assume,
> For every atom belonging to me as good belongs to you.

Thus, the self here is both the individual Walt Whitman and the general, the representative American. The first person used as an address in the poem denotes both an experiencing self and an archetypal figure; it is also the poetic persona mediating the discourse of the self as American. This metonymic definition of the self is basic to the thematic focus of the poem. This is implicit in the symbolism of the "grass" that constitutes the "uniform hieroglyphic" which articulates a pervasive sense of life that springs and spreads and aspires for the sun:

They are alive and well somewhere,
The smallest sprout shows that there is really no death,
And if ever there was it led forward life, and does not wait at
the end to arrest it

The definition of the self in *Leaves of Grass* has a three-fold structure. In the first, which includes poems such as "Song of Myself", "Children of Adam" and "Calamus", the self is related to other individuals – men and women – through whom the poet discovers physical and spiritual love. Next, in the "song" section of the poem (including poems such as "Crossing Brooklyn Ferry", "Song of the Answerer", "Song of the Broad Axe" and "Song of the Rolling Earth"), Whitman tries to integrate the self to the nation and its history. Finally, the third group of poems (including "Birds of Passage", "Sea Drift", "By the Roadside" and "A Broadway Pageant") tries to explore the relationship of the self not only to history but also to metaphysical and spiritual experiences, and apprehensions of visionary meanings.

The most important poem belonging to Whitman's Civil War writing is his elegy on Abraham Lincoln, "When Lilac Last in the Dooryard Bloom'd", published in the *Sequel to Drum Taps*. Though he wrote his elegy in the tradition of Milton's *Lycidas* or Shelley's *Adonais*, Whitman was not personally acquainted with his subject, the slain President. The poet uses this elegy to ponder over the irreconcilable association of love and death, which is a major preoccupation of many of his poems – particularly, "Out of the Cradle Endlessly Rocking". However, Whitman refuses to resolve the conflict by choosing the "open road" of life as a reassertion against the dominion of death:

Dances for thee I propose saluting thee, adornments and
feastings for thee,
And the sights of the open landscape and the high-spread sky
are fitting,
And life and the fields, and the huge and thoughtful night.

A similar sense of future promise is central to the poem "Passage to India", whose composition was prompted by the completion of the Suez Canal, the Union Pacific Railway and the laying of the Atlantic Cable. Yet, the poem was not only a celebration of technological achievements but also found in these marvels, the hope of a potential world community, a brotherhood of man:

> Passage to India!
> Lo, soul! seest thou not God's purpose from the first?
> The earth to be spann'd, connected by net-work,
> The people to become brothers and sisters,
> The races, neighbors, to marry and be given in marriage,
> The oceans to be cross'd, the distant brought near,
> The lands to be welded together.

Whitman attempted to create a distinctive American rhetoric for his poetry by using a vernacular idiom and style, which he derived from the language of common men and women and the vast diversity of the nation:

> Chants of the prairies,
> Chants of the long-running Mississippi, and down to the Mexican sea,
> Chants of Ohio, Indiana, Illinois, Iowa, Wisconsin and Minnesota,
> Chants going forth from the centre from Kansas, and thence equidistant,
> Shooting in pulses of fire ceaseless to vivify all.
> ("Starting from Paumanok")

It is, thus, a poetry of the spoken tongue, resonant as a song of the spirit of discovery and of immersion in the sensuous paean to earth and sky. Thus, the usual conventions of lyric restraint and form are openly abandoned in favour of a heroic and hyperbolic abundance, which becomes the index of the epic amplification and seriousness of the verse. Describing himself as "An American bard at last", Whitman considered his poetry to be the voice of the nation, its language and the discourse of American self-expression, in "Starting from Paumanok":

Take my leaves America, take them South and take them
North,
Make welcome for them everywhere, for they are your own
off-spring,
Surround them East and West, for they would surround you,
And you precedents, connect lovingly with them, for they
connect lovingly with you.

Ironically, Whitman did not receive as much critical acclaim in the country he celebrated in his poetry as he did in Europe. This was partly due to his explicit treatment of the sexual in an America still contending with Puritanical values, and also because of a tendency towards abstraction and obscurity in his later poetry. Nevertheless, *Leaves of Grass*, which wrote the nation as it developed through the conflicts and changes of the later nineteenth century, remains a seminal text of the American literary tradition, precisely because it attains this sense of identity by denying a European lineage. In fact, William Carlos Williams acknowledges this curious paradox when he writes: "There is no art of poetry save by the grace of other poetry. So Dante to me can only be another way of saying Whitman. Yet, without a Whitman there can be for me no Dante." Whitman's poetry is, thus, representative of his age and anticipatory of the transformations which would soon overcome American poetry, as he observed in "A Backward Glance O'er Travell'd Roads": "It is certainly time for America, above all, to begin the readjustment in the scope and basic point of view of verse; for everything else has changed."

Emily Dickinson

Emerson once described the period known as the American Renaissance in the nineteenth century as "The age of the first person singular". This statement is one the most apt descriptions of the poetry of Walt Whitman and Emily Dickinson (1830–86). The first expresses this awareness in a celebration of the self as a representative American; the latter, however, is more reclusive and contemplative in the exploration of her identity as a woman and a poet.

Emily Dickinson, born in 1830 in Amherst, Massachusetts, was the daughter of a prominent lawyer, Edward Dickinson. She was educated in Amherst Academy and at the Mount Holyoke Female Seminary; but Emily Dickinson did not complete her term at the seminary because her father indulgently felt that too many books would be detrimental to her health, and also because she was needed at home to nurse her ailing mother. Thus, most of her life was spent within the calm confines of home. She never married, though she had several enriching intellectual relationships with men like Benjamin Newton, her father's assistant, and the Reverend Charles Wadsworth. In fact, in the last twenty-five years of her life, she led a completely secluded existence except for meeting her most intimate friends and close relatives. She wrote her poems behind the closed doors of her room, guarding them even from the knowledge of her family. Only six of her poems appeared in print during her lifetime, and the rest of her work was discovered and published posthumously.

Emily Dickinson's life, therefore, was proof of her poetry that dealt primarily with subjective desires and experiences. The poems are an exploration of emotional and spiritual conflicts and, thus, are attempts to write the self as an experience of art. This is not to suggest that she was preoccupied with herself – that the writing was an egotistical self-contemplation leading to a solipsistic alienation from the real. Her reclusive life was a measure of her self-possession which was, at the same time, intensely conscious of the life around her. This is evident in her definition of poetry: "If I read a book [and] it makes my whole body so cold no fire can ever warm me, I know *that* is poetry. If I feel physically as if the top of my head were taken off, I know *that* is poetry. These are the only way [sic] I know it. Is there any other way?" In one important sense, she was able to turn her retreat and confinement into a space which gave birth to her poetry.

However, in spite of this reclusive and subjective emphasis in her life, her poems do not display a tendency towards personal and emotional indulgence. She mocks at self-regarding individualism in Poem 288:

> How dreary – to be –
> Somebody!
> How public – like a Frog –
> To tell one's name – the livelong June –
> To an admiring Bog!

In fact, one of the major themes which preoccupied her writing is the simple desire of being alive: "I find ecstasy in living – the mere sense of living is joy enough", she had told her literary friend, T. W. Higginson. This sense of joy is expressed in Poem 214, titled "I Taste a Liquor Never Brewed":

> Inebriate of air am I,
> And debauchee of dew,
> Reeling through endless summer days,
> From inns of molten blue.

Emily Dickinson's celebratory response to life strongly influences her attitude to nature, which is characterised by a confident and sensitive bonding (Poem 986):

> Several of Nature's People
> I know, and they know me –
> I feel for them a transport
> Of Cordiality –

Thus, these poems are marked by an awareness of nature's distinctiveness, its "otherness", as is evident in the poem on a snake:

> His notice sudden is –
> The Grass divides as with a Comb –
> A spotted shaft is seen –
> And then it closes at your feet
> And opens further on –

This sense of detail, which is basic to her poetry, implies a sensuous apprehension of the natural, suggested in the manner in which she merges disparate sensory experiences in her images: "the lawn is full of south and the odors tangle, and I hear today for the first the river in the tree". Emily Dickinson's poetry does not simply involve an externalisation of her thoughts and emotions in natural themes and images, it implies a recognition – evident in the Transcendentalist writings of Thoreau – that the human includes the non-human world. Together with this awareness, there is the realisation that nature, ultimately, remains inscrutable and beyond the expressive forms of language, as in Poem 668: "Nature is what we know – / Yet have no art to say –"

Nevertheless, this physical, almost tactile and sensuous, response to nature and the world of the living seems to explain her scepticism towards orthodox religion and conventional notions of faith. "I know not why," she wrote to her friend Abiah Root, "I feel that the world holds a predominant place in my affections. I do not feel I could give up all for Christ, were I called to die." Though she later admitted to feelings of guilt after such confessions, Emily Dickinson never responded to contemporary theological controversies, nor did she subscribe to the Emersonian ideas of salvation. Therefore, a latent agnosticism seems to be the basis of her interrogating conventional religious and secular values, contributing to a credible psychological realism in her poetry.

Ironically, this strong sense of lived experience, asserted through a consciousness of the self in the world, is countered by an equal, if not dominant, awareness of death. Emily Dickinson's poetry thus oscillates between the antinomies of life and death (Poem 286): "The Cordiality of Death – / Who drills his Welcome in."

The same sensuous apprehension of nature now seems to define her treatment of death, as evident in such lyrics as "I Heard a Fly Buzz – When I Died", "Because I Could Not Stop for Death", "It was not Death, for I Stood Up" and"I Felt a Funeral, in My Brain". What distinguishes her poetry is her ability to fuse the opposing states of death and life within a verbal and conceptual economy, giving her poetry the intellectual and emotional subtlety of Metaphysical wit.

Like the works of the Metaphysical poets of seventeenth-century England, Emily Dickinson's poetry also explored the interconnections and similarities between disparate and contradictory experiences and things. This is evident in her repeated use of the oxymoron to dramatise ambivalent and paradoxical ideas and conditions such as, "numb Alarm", "Confident Despair", "Heavenly Hurt" and "a piercing Comfort", to list a few. Though Emily Dickinson's language and imagery are drawn from ordinary life and vocabulary, she frequently draws her ideas, images and terms from geography, geology, natural sciences and the literature of exploration. She attempts to combine these into simple verse forms, predominantly lyrical structures, which often constitute experiments in unusual metaphors and poetic styles. For instance, the month of November is described in terms of a Metaphysical conceit (Poem 1140): "November hung his Granite Hat / Upon a nail of Plush –" Thus, her poetic language and style is characterised by a verbal restraint and semantic concentration which is reflected in the nuances of rhythm and half-rhyme, and also in her distinctive use of dashes instead of orthodox punctuation. These have the effect of undermining accepted syntactical rules with their fixed periods and definitions of form and meaning, and suggesting the immediacy of the poetic experience as a configuration of language, thought and feeling. Emily Dickinson's disrupted phrases, inverted syntax and metrical variations express a sense of uncertainty and ambiguity involving her provisional conception of the world – a world both multiple and relational, exploring the boundaries between the familiar and the unknown, the concrete and the abstract, the mortal and the eternal, best expressed in her poem, "Forever – is Composed of Now –": "The Finite – furnished / With the Infinite –"

Emily Dickinson's contribution to American poetry – particularly, that of the twentieth century – is clearly confirmed in William Carlos Williams acknowledging her as his "patron saint". In fact, her creative experiments in poetic language and rhythm went on to influence the poetry of Ezra Pound, Marianne Moore and Adrienne Rich. Though her reclusive nature kept many aspects of life away from her poetry, she was able to use her isolation to delve deep into the existential and emotional conflicts which defined her selfhood as a woman and a poet. Moreover, her ability to confront questions of faith and doubt makes her poetry representative of similar intellectual concerns of her age.

◆ ◆ ◆

While acknowledging its lineage in British and European traditions, American literature in the nineteenth century was an important assertion of its separate and distinctive identity. Therefore, this period is not only marked by a significant growth in all the major areas of writing, but also anticipates some of the major developments that went on to define its literature in the twentieth century. Though drawing on ideas and formal experiments, American modernism is, thus, distinguished by its individual difference from that of the Continent. This reaffirmation of the nation's diverse yet singular status assumes a considerable significance in the literature of the next century.

CHAPTER 4

From Howells to Miller

Realism, Naturalism, Regionalism and Modernism

Ashok Sengupta

REALISM IN AMERICAN LITERATURE

"The arts must become democratic," wrote William Dean Howells (1837–1920) in *Criticism and Fiction* (1891), "and then we shall have the expression of American art." In spite of its echoing what Whitman had proclaimed three decades ago, Howells's statement was actually expressing his involvement with realism, a literary movement which developed in the final decades of the nineteenth century. For Howells, this democratic element was evident in the "life of small things", as he wrote in *A Modern Instance* (1882): "Don't despise the day of small things." Fiction, for Howells, had to be "true to the motives, the impulses, the principles that shape the life of actual men and women". Yet, this realism did not imply the pessimistic negation that characterised the writing of naturalism, another literary movement that was to follow it: "Realism at its best is not tendencious," Howells added. "It does not seek to grapple with human problems, but is richly content with portraying human experiences." In fact, as the novelist was to explain, realism in the United States was the assertion of a type of optimism involving "the talent that is robust enough to front the everyday world" which, according to him, made "our novelists concern themselves with the more smiling aspects of life, which are more American."

The immediate causes behind the growth of realism were the unprecedented changes that occurred in America owing to the rapid industrial progress, expansion of communication and material growth in the nineteenth century. This transformed the earlier predominantly agrarian society and, consequently, forced it to accept the values of urbanisation and modernisation, which undermined the moral certainties of the traditional community by establishing the power of capital as the controlling impulse of the human endeavour for success. Together with a considerable influx of immigrants from Europe, this period saw a significant population movement from rural to urban centres, making the rise of the city a determining influence on literature and culture. Another notable development which went on to influence the realist movement in the United States was the growth of newspapers, magazines, advertising and photography, which made an important contribution in defining the terms of this fictional method. Therefore, realism not only involved a preoccupation with the city, but was also an attempt to understand and portray modern life in its various aspects, occupations, class divisions and manners.

However, this tendency towards a realistic form of narrative had emerged in the 1860s. In an essay titled "The Great American Novel" (1868), John William De Forest had appealed for a novel which would be a "picture of the ordinary emotions and manners of American existence". This was also a reaction against a contemporary denial of American subjects as being commonplace and unfit for attention; it also intended to overcome the dominance of the East in American fiction. Edward Eggleston, thus, became an advocate of the Midwest, and in the 1892 Preface to his *Hoosier Schoolmaster* (1871), a dialect novel of the "Middle Border" of America, observed,

> It used to be a matter of little jealousy for us, I remember, that the manners, customs, thoughts and feelings of New England country people filled so large a place in books, while our life, not less interesting, not less romantic, and certainly not less

> filled with humorous and grotesque material, had no place in literature. It was as though we were shut out of good society.

In fact, this regional – or, what was often termed "local color" – fiction had been anticipated in the novels of Harriet Beecher Stowe (1811–96), Louisa May Alcott (1832–88) and Horatio Alger (1832–99), and in Bret Harte's (1836–1902) *The Luck of Roaring Camp* (1870) and Joel Chandler Harris's (1848–1908) Uncle Remus stories. This type of fiction attempted to capture the distinctive landscape and character of regions and districts, dialects and customs. However, by depicting the life of the Frontier, it was also able to introduce American fiction not only to a whole new geography and people, but also their language and values, drawing upon the comic resources of popular narratives such as the tall tale and immigrant folk stories.

Early Examples of Regional Fiction: Stowe, Alcott, Alger, Harte and Howells

Though Harriet Beecher Stowe began her career as a regionalist writer with "A New England Sketch" (1834) in James Hall's *Western Magazine*, she was able to overcome this circumscription with the phenomenal success of *Uncle Tom's Cabin* (1851–52). The novel sold 10,000 copies in a few days, becoming an international bestseller with an annual sale of 30,000 copies in the US and another one-and-a-half million worldwide. In fact, Stowe admitted to divine intervention: "God wrote the book", she said, adding, "I took His dictation." A significant moral attack against slavery, the novel traces the sufferings of Uncle Tom, a faithful and saintly slave sold by his original owner to another tyrannical master who has him flogged to death for not revealing the names of two runaway slaves. When "Mas'r George" Shelby, the son of his previous owner, arrives, it is too late to save Tom. However, Shelby vows to fight for Abolition and begins by freeing all the slaves on his own plantation. Woven around this central plot are several subsidiary stories which give the novel a comprehensive range of human experience and emotions, attesting to its wide appeal. Though melodramatic, sentimental and didactic, the novel reveals Stowe's keen awareness of the various prevalent arguments in favour of slavery and often includes a theological reasoning to refute them. The work also shows Stowe's skill in assimilating several contemporary narrative forms, such as that of plantation fiction, the allegorical tale, slave narratives and the tall tale of Southwestern humour.

Together with its emphasis on Black equality and empowerment, an important aspect of *Uncle Tom's Cabin* is its serious recognition of the role of women in family and society. Thus, the Quaker community in which George and Eliza Harris, a fugitive slave couple, take shelter, is managed by women implementing matriarchal and communal values – "so sociably, so quietly, so harmoniously". Consequently, the "feminine" principles of sympathy, supportiveness and creativity are reaffirmed as more worthy than "masculine" tendencies of aggression and oppression. However, in spite of the protagonist's fortitude and silent martyrdom, Stowe has often been criticised for using the stereotypes of servility and passivity, with which she has depicted the Blacks, in order to give her work a Christian conclusion. Stowe, in fact, was not closely familiar with Black life; therefore, after *Dred: A Tale of the Dismal Swamp* (1854), dealing with a slave uprising, she returned to regional and realistic portraits of New England domestic life and those of Native Americans in *The Minister's Wooing* (1859), *Oldtown Folks* (1869) and *Poganuc People* (1878).

Like Stowe, Louisa M. Alcott, daughter of one of the minor Transcendentalists, Bronson Alcott, achieved publishing success with her *Little Women* (1869), which can be called an early example of teen fiction. Autobiographical in its origins, the novel portrays the struggles of the March family to cope with their genteel poverty. Much of the realism is thus reflected in domestic tensions as "Marmee" toils to guide her daughters into a difficult adulthood and maturity which, ironically, unmakes the family that Jo, the eldest, so resolutely attempts to keep together. *Little Women* expresses the growing awareness that women's fate was largely determined by patriarchal assumptions; and, thus, a desire for independence, that was defining women in America during this period, became the focus of Alcott's next novel, *Work: A Story of Experience* (1873). Christie, its heroine, is resolved "not to be a slave to anybody" and thus takes on several jobs. Inspired by the stories of her fellow women workers, she finally joins a "loving league of sisters" devoted to the cause of women's right to their choice of work as a step towards economic liberation and individual identity.

Another important contribution to the development of fiction between 1860 and 1890 was the steam press which allowed the inexpensive mass production of books. This went on to motivate the growth of the popular "Dime Novel Series" promoted by Erastus and Irwin Beadle in 1860. Taking its name from the affordable pricing of these ten-cent novels, these actually influenced a major expansion of popular writing, particularly in the form of Westerns, sentimental romances, tales of adventure meant for children and lurid tales of crime and desire. One such writer who achieved remarkable success was Horatio Alger, Jr. whose stories for adolescent boys, *Ragged Dick; or, Street Life in New York*, was first serialised in *Student and Schoolmate* in 1867 and published as a novel in 1868. Alger went on to write more than a hundred such novels. These novels had a set formula, that of a fairytale rags-to-riches story of an orphaned street urchin who struggles against poverty and uses his moral integrity and hard work to finally gain economic and social recognition. In spite of a strong sense of social Darwinism in these tales, this formula, in fact, became a national myth, drawing on similar examples, such as those recounted by Benjamin Franklin in his *Autobiography,* emphasising honesty of character and self-improvement as qualities ensuring a gospel of success.

Another writer who was an important influence in the developing literature of realism was Bret Harte, a journalist who worked in the West as editor of *The Californian* and, subsequently in 1868, the *Overland Monthly*, where he published most of his poems and stories collected in *The Luck of Roaring Camp and Other Stories*. These stories, located in Frontier settings, deal with examples of human innocence and goodness among the miners and gamblers who struggle for survival in mining camps and border towns.

Howells, who was himself a Midwesterner, considered realism the "only literary movement of our times that seems to have vitality in it" as it was committed "to assert that fidelity of experience and probability of motive . . . are the essential conditions of a great imaginative literature." *A Modern Instance* (1882) develops themes which Howells explored in his early novels – *A Chance Acquaintance*

(1873), *A Foregone Conclusion* (1875) and *A Fearful Responsibility* (1881). It deals with the tragic career of his New England heroine, Marcia Gaylord, whose desire for social and sexual freedom is ultimately sacrificed to the demands of her dissolute husband and the diffidence of her conservative lover. However, in his *The Rise of Silas Lapham* (1885), Howells is able to focus on a recurrent theme in realist fiction – the financial fall and commensurate moral rise of the self-made businessman. Similarly, in *Annie Kilburn* (1888) and *A Hazard of New Fortunes* (1890), Howells examines the new terrain of labour unrest which was to dominate American fiction in the late nineteenth and the early twentieth centuries.

Narratives of Loss and Recovery: Garland, Anderson and Lewis

The regional novel was defined primarily in terms of certain common concerns such as the contrast between the country and the city, with the consequent conflicts between familial and community values and the desires of an individualist and corporate world. Thus, the sense of a detailed recreation of a decaying society and its remote life became, for the "local colour" novelists, both a means of bemoaning a loss of traditional values and a resistance against the imminent crisis and breakdown of these communities. These novels became narratives of memory whose nostalgia implied a self-assertion of their identity and a tragic awareness of both recovery and loss, as is evident in Hamlin Garland's *Main-Travelled Roads* (1891), Mary Wilkins Freeman's *A New England Nun* (1891), Sarah Orne Jewett's *The Country of the Pointed Firs* (1896), Kate Chopin's *The Awakening* (1899) and Willa Cather's *My Antonia* (1920). In fact, the South was a major representative in the development of regional fiction. Howells considered John William De Forest's *Miss Ravenel's Conversion from Secession to Loyalty* (1867) to be one of the most "realistic" treatments of the Civil War. Albion W. Tourgée, a Northern lawyer who became involved in Reconstruction politics, used a tragic love story between a Confederate soldier and a mulatto servant in his *A Royal Gentleman* (1881) to criticise the caste pride on which slavery was based. Consequently, the contribution of Black writers to American realism adds a complex element to the original democratic principles on which realism was based. While Charles Chesnutt's *The Conjure Woman* (1891) and Laurence Dunbar's *Folks from Dixie* (1898) are attempts to offer an authentic version of folk tales derived from indigenous Black experiences, W. E. B. Du Bois's novel *The Quest of the Silver Fleece* (1911), in its portrayal of the conflict of Blacks with the cotton economy of the Reconstructed South, anticipates industrial labour novels which constituted a major aspect of both literary realism and naturalism. This transition of the Old into the New South became a recurrent theme with Ellen Glasgow, whose *The Voice of the People* (1900) is a sensitive study of the different emergent classes in post-war Virginia.

Hamlin Garland (1860–1940) saw himself as a "veritist" whose method involved "the truthful statement of an individual expression corrected by reference to fact". This adherence to empirical facts, which was definitive of naturalism, also implied an assertion of present realities and the hope of a reformed future: "The veritist sees life in terms of what might be, as well as in terms of what is, but he writes of what is, and, at his best, suggests what is to be, by contrast." This is true of Garland's most notable work, *Main-Travelled Roads* (1891). The autobiographical *A Son of the Middle Border* (1917) and *A Daughter of the Middle Border* (1921) drew on his experience of Frontier life while, at the same time, recognising the fact that the "free land was receding at railroad speed". Garland's notion of realism, with its investment in a hopeful future, also implies a faith in human will and its desire for social change, and points to a significant category of fiction which accompanied the growth of realism – Utopian fiction, such as Edward Bellamy's *Looking Backward* (1888), Ignatius Donnelly's *Caesar's Column* (1890), Isaac K. Friedman's *By Bread Alone* (1901) and Winston Churchill's *The Dwelling-Place of Light* (1917).

Significantly, therefore, regionalism not only shaped realist fiction but also went on to define many of the terms and themes of American fiction in the twentieth century. This is evident in the fiction of Sherwood Anderson (1876–1941) and Sinclair Lewis (1885–1951), whose satire of provincial American life and its values become initiative of a literary modernism. Anderson's *Winesburg, Ohio* (1919), a linked series of short stories, reveals the diminutive lives of the Midwest middle class in the titular town. In the Preface,

Anderson describes it as "The Book of the Grotesque", where the grotesque is paradoxically linked to the beliefs that the characters have created about themselves and their existence: "It was the truths that made the people grotesques. . . .The moment one of the people took one of the truths to himself, called it his truth, and tried to live his life by it, he became a grotesque and the truth he embraced became a falsehood." These sensitive psychological portraits also imply an experiment with the linear narrative where the fragmentary structure is held together not only by the single narrator but also by the imbricated nature of truth and falsehood in the meanings and implications of the stories. Anderson's *Poor White* (1920), another Midwestern tale, employs specific naturalist elements in its close attention to surface realities; nevertheless, in its treatment of the lapses between language and meaning, it is able to hint at deeper realisations and disappointments. Anderson's later fiction – *Many Marriages* (1923) and *Dark Laughter* (1925) – did not achieve the same subtlety of form and meaning, though the stories in *The Triumph of the Egg* (1921) and *Death in the Woods* (1933) had some notable pieces of writing.

Sinclair Lewis's *Main Street* (1920) is a tale of the mediocrity of American provincialism represented by the small town of Gopher Prairie. Carol, the wife of the local doctor, rebels against the deadening existence of the town and escapes to Washington, only to return and compromise with the restrictions of class and security. Lewis's second novel, *Babbit* (1922), continues his critique of provincial America, now in the form of middle-class boosterism and vulgarity which assumes that the small town is the centre of civilisation. Yet, Lewis displays an ambiguous attitude by betraying a sympathy for the society he mocks. Though Lewis's later fiction suggests an awareness of social and political change, as in *Asa Vickers* (1933) and *It Can't Happen Here* (1935), towards the end of his career he tends to defend the very provincial values that he had begun by satirising.

The Realist Drama of Clifford Odets

The Theatre Guild of New York was the leading drama company of the 1920s. Between 1931 and 1941, in spite of constant financial constraints, it was able to produce twenty-two new plays. Among these was *Golden Boy* (1937) by Clifford Odets (1906–63), a young actor and playwright, and it turned out to be a rare commercial success. The Group Theatre, which actually grew out of the Guild, though never espousing a doctrinaire political theatre, remained involved with the drama of social commitment. Of all the dramatists associated with the Group, Odets was the most representative of this trend. Therefore, seven of Odets plays were staged, of which *Waiting for Lefty* (1935) still remains the most notable. Characteristically dealing with a taxi strike, it became an important work of contemporary "Proletarian Realism" and "agitprop" theatre. The play has a documentary structure of six scenes which attempt to explain the actual causes behind the strike and reveal the corrupt practices and demoralised ethics of big business and the taxi syndicates. In the final scene, the news of Lefty's murder arrives and it rouses the men to march for the strike – with the actors leading the audience to join in support, in an early example of performance theatre. *Awake and Sing!* (1935), Odets's next play, involves his criticism of the illusions of bourgeois respectability of the Bergers, a poor Jewish family which struggles through poverty and misfortune to come to a realisation of the need for radical and collective protest to assert their identity. *Till the Day I Die* (1935), a one-act play, recounts the activities of the German Communists in the early years of Hitler's reign. *Paradise Lost* (1935) and *Golden Boy* bring out the tragic consequences of pursuing the American success myth. However, Odets's plays always reaffirm a faith and hope in human endeavour, as attested in the words of two young men in *Night Music* (1940): "Where there is life there is hope," observes one, adding, "Only the living can cry out against life." To this the other responds with what seems to be a representative slogan of the times: "*Make this America for us!*"

Odets continued to produce plays even after the dissolution of The Group Theatre. His later plays include *The Big Knife* (1948), about an idealistic actor's compromise with the wealth from the movies; *The Country Girl* (1950); and *The Flowering Peach* (1954), a rewriting of the Noah tale. Nevertheless, the plays written for the Group remain his major achievements. This is mainly because of their distinctive use of language, which is marked by the rhythms of a tough urban dialect mixed with exaggerated, topical metaphors

– as in, "I wouldn't trade you for two pitchers and an outfielder." Evidently a stylised language, it serves its purpose of recreating the cynical humour and fatalism that feature in the everyday struggles of the urban lower-middle-class people who are the heroes of Odets's plays.

Naturalism in American Literature

However, this belief in human agency gradually waned by the end of the century as the wheels of industry accelerated to bring about radical technological changes and material advancement. These developments created a corresponding social crisis involving wide differences between the rich and the poor, industrial conflict and fragmentation of the community. Big businesses grew bigger, spawning legendary millionaires like Charles Gould, Andrew Carnegie and John D. Rockefeller. By assuming monopoly status, these corporate empires precipitated an industrial crisis with increasing labour conflicts and violence. Agrarian discontent gave rise to a populist movement and led to some reforms, but these were rather inadequate in comparison with the distress created by these developments. The nation also faced a series of political scandals involving corruption and graft, which induced a general disenchantment and despair that was reflected in the literary movement called "naturalism". This movement went on to influence American fiction in the closing years of the nineteenth century and the early decades of the twentieth.

Naturalism was characterised by a scientific awareness that was strengthened by the new developments in anthropology proposed in the writings of Georges Cuvier, Sir Charles Lyell and, finally, in Charles Darwin's theory of evolution which completely transformed earlier notions of nature and man. These notions also seriously destabilised the traditional faith in religion and related moral values. Herbert Spencer applied Darwin's ideas to society and offéred a pessimistic explanation for the contemporary social crises by coining the phrase, "survival of the fittest". Social Darwinism, therefore, was used to justify inequality by accepting it as a logical precondition for social progress. Moreover, distinctive to the American naturalist movement was the contribution made by "muckraking" journalism whose patronage by Joseph Pulitzer and William Randolf Hearst, noted newspaper barons, became an incentive for fictional disclosures of social wrongs.

Few American novelists actually described themselves as naturalists, in spite of displaying some of the characteristic concerns of the movement. There is little evidence to show that the major novelists had adhered to the main tenets of Emile Zola's "Naturalist Manifesto" or, particularly, those in his essay, "The Experimental Novel" (1880). Of the four major naturalist novelists, only Frank Norris (1870–1902) had read Zola; Stephen Crane (1871–1900) admitted not to have read him; and Jack London (1876–1916) and Theodore Dreiser (1875–1945) turned to Darwin and Marx only in their later fiction.

Naturalism differed from realism by denying the autonomy of individual will and the freedom of moral choice by its commitment to an "absolute determinism" by social and material circumstance. "Determinism", in fact, was a new term appearing in print around 1846. It was used to refer to economic and psychological influences which conditioned human action and existence. Thus, individuals were no longer independent actors in a moral universe; rather, they were irrevocably controlled by forces of environment and heredity in dramas of coercion and defeat. In this sense, naturalism was often termed "pessimistic determinism". Consequently, this concept motivated new methods of narrative and the conception and depiction of characters. Ironically, however, in his "A Plan for Romantic Fiction" (1903), Norris returned to calling this new form of fiction "Romance", by arguing that "realism" "notes only the surface of things", while "Romance" deals with "the wide world for range, and the unplumbed depths of the human heart, and the mystery of sex, and the problems of life, and the black unsearched penetralia of the soul of man".

Stephen Crane

Stephen Crane's early stories – such as "The Open Boat" (1897), "The Blue Hotel" (1898) and "The Bridge Comes to Yellow Sky" (1898) – seem to suggest that, for him, naturalist writing was a project he had chosen to pursue when he decided to be a novelist. His small corpus of fiction, which included two significant novels, *Maggie: A Girl of the Streets* (1893) and *The Red Badge of Courage* (1895), present a picture of an almost nihilistic universe in which Crane dramatises the futility of deliberation and choice. *Maggie*, which is probably one of the earliest naturalist American novels, is a harrowing tale of a poor sensitive girl driven to prostitution and suicide by her environment and circumstances. *The Red Badge of Courage*, which is set in the Civil War period, attempts a portrait of heroism by paradoxically undermining the romantic ideas of heroism as irrelevant in the contingencies of war. Crane's naturalistic method is also evident in his parody of fictional forms – the Horatio Alger slum tale in *Maggie*; the war novel in *The Red Badge of Courage*; the sea story in "The Open Boat" and the Western in "The Bridge Comes to Yellow Sky". Crane avoids giving his characters names, thereby repudiating the conventional labels by which an individual is identified. In fact, he questions the very concept of the self by making the belief in a unified personality seem to be an illusion. Finally, by disrupting accepted syntax and forms of narrative expression, Crane gives a sense of ambiguity to the use of language and the act of communication, thereby creating a complex meaning in the nature of experience.

Frank Norris

Unlike Crane, Frank Norris was influenced by the theory of Social Darwinism. Though his characters are denied the element of choice and moral responsibility, they ultimately contribute to a general social development. Beginning his career with *McTeague* (1899), Norris aimed to write fiction dealing with economic conditions. He thus planned a trilogy devoted to the "Epic of Wheat" and completed two parts before his death. *The Octopus* (1901), the first of the three, dealt with the production of the grain and the economic forces which were controlled by the Southern Pacific Railroad, the octopus of the title. *The Pit*, which was posthumously published in 1903, examined wheat distribution and marketing in Chicago. The third part of the trilogy, which was to be called *The Wolf* and was supposed to be dealing with the consumption of the grain and a wheat famine in Europe, was never written. Norris's novels bring out the inexorable nature of economic forces in which human and national destinies become meshed. Impersonal forces control and often sacrifice individuals to the irrevocable march of social progress.

In spite of the unrelenting determinism in the fiction of Crane and Norris, naturalist writing was also characterised by an implicit faith in the possibility of reforming the environment and social institutions, and thus improving the human condition. This reformist tendency is evident in the fiction of Upton Sinclair (1878–1968) and Jack London (1876–1916).

Jack London

Though London achieved remarkable early success with his short stories, his novels – based on his experiences in the Klondike during the Alaska goldrush – were representative of his view of the future of human society. Significantly, in *The Son of Wolf* (1900), *The Call of the Wild* (1903), *The Sea-Wolf* (1904) and *White Fang* (1906), London used animals, particularly dogs, as central figures, thus avoiding the question of human agency and emphasising heredity and circumstance as the basis of existence. In London's fiction, therefore, natural forces overpower the individual and survival depends on forces beyond human control. In the autobiographical *Martin Eden* (1908), London is critical of romantic individualism, as opposed to a faith in the class struggle. This commitment to collective action testifies to the influence of Marx and Socialist ideas on London's later fiction. Thus, in *The Iron Heel* (1907), he conceives of a Utopian socialist future following a revolt against fascist forces in America.

Theodore Dreiser

The fiction of Theodore Dreiser (1871–1945) presents a contrary tendency: there is an emphatic assertion of a deterministic philosophy, together with an intrinsic sense of idealism affirming the human ability to surmount tragic defeat. Describing "man", Dreiser thus observed, ". . . his feet are in the trap of circumstance; his eyes are on an illusion." This seems to explain the nature of his thinking and writing, which seem to be less the product of his reading of Huxley, Spencer and Darwin, than that of his difficult childhood and journalism. The novels, therefore, express hope in human progress (towards the end of his career he did support reformist causes); and yet, this hope is soon undermined by a picture of relentless futility. For instance, in *Sister Carrie* (1900), Dreiser traces the career of Carrie Meeber, from her beginnings as a farm girl to that of a star on the New York stage. This success is largely achieved through Carrie living out of wedlock with two men, Charles Drouet and George Hurstwood. What makes this significant is not so much Carrie's defiance but her amoral indifference towards the implications of her act: she neither feels a sense of guilt nor considers herself a fallen woman. In fact, Dreiser broke with a literary tradition by allowing a fallen woman to survive and even prosper as a financially successful sex symbol and celebrated actress. In Dreiser's fiction, consumerist – and not ethical – considerations influence decisions. Thus, Carrie's success ironically expresses society's expectations and aspirations – its seduction by materialism and money. This alliance of chance and environment, evident in *Sister Carrie*, is repeated in *Jennie Gerhardt* (1911) and *An American Tragedy* (1925).

In his "Trilogy of Desire" comprising *The Financier* (1912), *The Titan* (1914) and *The Stoic* (1947), Dreiser explores stories of failure. The novels chart the tragic curve of business baron Frank Algernon Cowperwood, whose simple motto is: "I satisfy myself." After his ruthless success in high finance, Cowperwood recognises that "things live on each other"; but this social parasitism is the order of the world: "That's the way it has to be." In Dreiser's novels, therefore, impersonal forces always engulf desire, because success and failure are two sides of the same coin. Circumstances and the urban setting do not curb desire but dramatise it, though, at the end, that desire remains unfulfilled. By situating the theatre of these stories of desire and defeat in Chicago and New York, Dreiser is probably one of the first American writers to make the city a character in his novels. Distinctive to his fiction is his narrative style, which substitutes the coherent plot for a series of often disconnected situations. These are in turn depicted through an accretion of concrete physical details which reflect and often overwhelm sight and understanding. Dreiser's aesthetic, thus, combines the documentary and the artful, claiming that, "True Art Speaks Plainly . . . with a bitter brutal insistence on their so-ness."

Literature of Social and Political Critique and Commitment

Dreiser's aesthetics of the documentary, in fact, remained dominant in the fiction of the turn of the century, which was increasingly directed towards a criticism of contemporary economic and social evils such as monopoly and political corruption. The "muckraking" tendency in journalism thus attracted several important writers, such as Thorstein Veblen whose *Theory of the Leisure Class* (1899) was an influential attack against the "pecuniary" ideology of the nation. Similarly, Lincoln Steffens, who had himself exposed municipal mismanagement in *McClure's Magazine* in 1897, published an indictment of urban ghettoisation in *The Shame of the Cities* (1904). Upton Sinclair (1878–1968), after spending seven weeks studying the dehumanising conditions of immigrant workers in the Chicago stockyards, published *The Jungle* (1906). In the novel, Jurgis, the Lithuanian peasant who had come seeking the American Dream, discovers another America: "Here in this huge city, with its stores of heaped-up wealth, human creatures might be hunted down and destroyed by the wild-beast powers of nature." Sinclair, who had joined the Socialist Party of America in 1904, remains committed to the political aim of the novel when he uses a relentless accumulation of details to dramatise the remorseless suffering of the workers. Though melodramatic, this is basically the method of naturalist fiction which emphasises a sense of authenticity in order to draw on the readers' empathy. The end of the novel, thus, has a sense of hope when Jurgis turns to socialism, which delivers him "from the thralldom of despair" and holds out the promise of the liberation of the workers. In fact, Sinclair's novel ultimately brought about major reforms in the food-packing industry.

The naturalist novel, therefore, contributed to the development of a literature of political commitment and radical ideology that found its expression in the Depression era of the late 1920s and 30s.

Writers as varied as John Reed, Michael Gold, John Dos Passos, Nathaniel West, John Steinbeck and Richard Wright were drawn to the literary Left as Malcolm Cowley later recalled: "Thousands were convinced and hundreds were half-persuaded that no simple operation would save us.... There had to be the complete renovation of society that Marx had prophesied in 1848. Unemployment would be ended; war and fascism would vanish from the earth, but only after the revolution." Mike Gold (1893–1967) thus joined the Communist Party of the United States and campaigned for a proletarian literature in an article in *The Masses*, titled "Toward Proletarian Art". His efforts received encouragement from the success of another such documentary novel by John Reed (1887–1920), a journalist and an activist who had given an eyewitness account of the Russian Revolution in *Ten Days that Shook the World* (1919). Gold's *Jews Without Money* (1930) was a fictionalised autobiography; yet it gave rise, during this period, to a subgenre called the "proletarian" novel. The notable examples of this writing include, Mary Heaton Vorse's *Strike!* (1930), Dos Passos's *The 42nd Parallel* (1930), Jack Conroy's *The Disinherited* (1933), Robert Cantwell's *Land Of Plenty* (1934), Josephine Herbst's *Rope of Gold* (1934) and John Steinbeck's *In Dubious Battle* (1936).

John Steinbeck

John Steinbeck's (1902–68) study of marine biology had possibly influenced his deterministic view of humanity as a biological system shaped by collective movements as a condition of its survival: "The fascinating thing to me is the way a group has a soul, a drive, an intent, an end, a method, a reaction and a set of tropisms which in no way resembles the same things possessed by the men who make up the group." This notion of the "herd mentality", the very theory that was to support the sociology of modern organisations and human movements, is evident in his *Tortilla Flats* (1935) and *In Dubious Battle*, a novel dealing with a strike called by the fruit workers in California. Steinbeck's *Of Mice and Men* (1937), the tale of two itinerant farm workers, achieves a tragic grace in the innocence and helplessness of Lennie Small. *The Grapes of Wrath* (1939), his most celebrated novel, began as a series of newspaper reports on migratory workers searching for work in California during the Depression. In the expatriation of the Joad family from the Oklahoma "dust bowl" to the fruit farms in California, Steinbeck recreates not only a contemporary rural and human disaster, but also a mythic, biblical journey which was to become his model of an American epic reiterated in *East of Eden* (1952). Later, Steinbeck denied that *The Grapes of Wrath* was merely a social document or a novel of protest; rather, it was a testament to archetypal human values of courage, compassion and resignation, eloquent in the scene where Rose of Sharon suckles a dying man back to life.

◆◆◆

Naturalism developed as a result of specific historical conditions which had, by the time of the First World War, been assimilated and naturalised. Though Dreiser's fiction went on to influence many of the major American novelists of the 1920s and 30s, the movement itself was brief. American literary naturalism, thus, was the expression of a particular historical and ideological necessity which nevertheless shaped a vision of human struggle and defeat, of enduring power and value.

American Regional Literature

The Literature of the American South

The attempt to give the American South a separate identity was as much a consequence of history as it was a myth created by its literature and culture. Unlike the myth of the West, the debate regarding that of the South began in the eighteenth century, intensified during the Civil War (1861–65) and the national crisis in the nineteenth, and still recurs variously even today. Thus, the eleven Confederate states, together, marginally with Kentucky, which comprised the South were generally assimilated in terms of a common climate and an agricultural and feudal economy which politically justified that "peculiar institution" – slavery. In fact, during the antebellum period, Southern rhetoric increasingly involved a self-assertion which appeared to confirm the observation made by one historian: "The South is not quite a nation within a nation, but the next thing to it." Though the Old South, with its regional legends such as those of Davy Crockett (1786–1836) and Mike Fink (c.1770—c.1823), had its indigenous literature of tall tales, frontier adventure, country humour and native wit, much of what is considered as the literature of the South was actually written by Northerners. For instance, Harriet Beecher Stowe's much acclaimed version of the South, *Uncle Tom's Cabin* (1852), was written in Maine and based on a derivative knowledge of the region. Similarly, Stephen Foster and Charles Harris, who wrote the popular songs about the South, "My Old Kentucky Home" and "Mid the Green Fields of Virginia" respectively, admitted that their views of plantation society was entirely imaginative and not the product of actual experience or observation, thereby, lending credence to what William Styron wrote in *Sophie's Choice* (1979): ". . . at least Southerners have ventured North, have come to see what the North is like, while very few Northerners have troubled themselves to travel to the South." Owing to the romantic nostalgia associated with it, the society and culture of the South, therefore, was inclined to remain rather enigmatic, as evident in Shreve McCannon, in William Faulkner's (1897–1962) *Absalom,Absalom!* (1936), urging Quentin Compson to, "Tell about the South! What do they do there? Why do they live there? Why do they live at all?"

The Writers of the South

Ironically, the defeat of the South in the Civil War was greatly responsible for a reassertion of its distinctive identity. The failure of the Reconstruction in 1877 that followed this defeat added insult to injury, for neither did it assuage the wounds of the war, nor fulfil the expectations of economic and social development that was promised by the Union. In fact, the crisis revealed the backward nature of the region, for, by pursuing agriculture rather than industry, and adopting feudal and landed values instead of democratic progress, the region had been reduced to conditions reminiscent of the Depression that was to beleaguer, in the next century, one of the richest nations of the world. Postbellum Southern writing, thus, involved an attempt to recover and celebrate a society and culture that was fast disappearing. Hence, the myth of the South was being given its elegiac commemoration by Henry Timrod (1828–67) and Sidney Lanier (1842–81) in their poetry. Timrod's poem, "Ode: Sung on the Occasion of Decorating the Graves of the Confederate Dead, at Magnolia Cemetery, Charleston, S.C., 1867" (1872), and Lanier's polemical and dialect pieces, "Thar's More in the Man Than Thar is in the Land" (1877) and "Jones's Private Argument" (1877), are notable examples. Romantic recreations of the antebellum South comprise an important aspect of the stories of Joel Chandler Harris (1848–1908). For instance, *Told by Uncle Remus: New Stories of the Old Plantation* (1905) describes the Old South as, "Dem wuz laughin times . . . an' it looks like dey ain't never comin' back". Harris, whose tales draw on African American folk traditions, thus adapts them to Southern conditions in trickster characters such as Brer Rabbit, who uses his humility and apparent gullibility to deceive and overcome the stronger Brer Fox and Brer Wolfe in *Uncle Remus: His Songs and Sayings* (1880) and *Nights with Uncle Remus* (1883).

Among the writers who came into prominence in the postbellum turn of the century was George Washington Cable (1844–1925) whose fiction depicted the life of his home town, New Orleans. Cable focuses on the romance, desire and deceit of an old Creole society, exploring its violent racial conflicts and dark history of miscegenation in his novel, *Grandissimes: A Story of Creole Life* (1800). A tale of a family feud between two proud Creole families, the novel displays Cable's distinctive skill in using the dialect of the community and its history to explore the rich diversity of the cultures and traditions of old Louisiana. However, the examination of the Creole society also becomes a criticism of the South of his times which extends into a treatise, *The Silent South* (1885), suggesting racial reform. Another novelist who was equally concerned with the racial and sexual assumptions of nineteenth-century Louisiana was Kate Chopin (1851–1904). Chopin's fiction tries to represent the various classes of this town in her first two collections, *Bayou Folk* (1894) and *A Night in Acadie* (1897); yet, her deep involvement with questions of racial and sexual liberty is evident in her short stories, "Wiser than a God" (1889), "A Point at Issue", "Desiree's Baby"

(1892) and "The Storm" (1898). Her novel, *The Awakening* (1899), denouncing "marriages which masquerade as decrees of Fate" and satirising "women who idolized their children, worshipped their husbands, and esteemed it a holy privilege to efface themselves as individuals and grow wings as ministering angels", thus provoked strong criticism and was banned in St Louis. It deals with the self-assertion of its protagonist, Edna Pontellier, who in realising that she had been in a "life-long, stupid dream" of a conventional marriage, decides, after the death of her husband, to choose to commit suicide rather than surrender her independence.

Women Writers of the South

Significantly, a major consequence of the Civil War was the questioning of racial and gender inequality and a resistance to Southern patriarchal codes. This trend saw the advent of several women writers announcing the ethos of a new, self-conscious woman who seemed to anticipate modern developments in literature. In fact, it is often argued that the Civil War marked the beginnings of a burgeoning industrial modernism both for the South and the North in America.

Ellen Glasgow (1873–1945) is considered to have initiated the movement called the Southern Renaissance, which was responsible for that notable development of fiction and poetry in writers such as William Faulkner, Robert Penn Warren (1905–90), Eudora Welty (1909–2001), Carson McCullers (1917–67) and Flannery O'Connor (1925–64). Glasgow divided her attention between satiric portraits of white women characters in her early novel *Virginia* (1913), and accounts of stoical and heroic endurance and labour suffered by them to survive on a sterile earth, in novels such as *Barren Ground* (1925) and *Vein of Iron* (1930). Glasgow called the first type "novels of history" or "novels of the town" to which *Life of Gabriella* (1913), *The Romantic Comedians* (1926) and *The Sheltered Life* (1932) belong; while the second was designated as "novels of the country", comprising*The Voice of the People* (1900), *The Romance of a Plain Man* (1909) and *One Man in His Time* (1922). In *Virginia,* Glasgow, ironically, allows her heroine to "let her mother slave over her because she had been born into a world where the slaving of mothers was part of the natural order, and she had not as yet become independent enough to question the morality of the commonplace". Thus, in dealing with women redefining themselves, Glasgow tries to explore the possibilities of a female *bildungsroman*, tracing in the character of Virginia Dorinda Oakley, in *Virginia*, a woman's rise to the position of a social leader through her strength of will, managerial skills and the ability for diligent labour.

Though Willa Cather (1873–1947), like Glasgow, was born in Virginia, only her last novel, *Sapphira and the Slave Girl* (1940), is given a Southern locale; but *O Pioneers!* (1913) and *Song of the Lark* (1915) have a strong sense of pre-industrial America and the still wild and untamed land of the West. The last two novels present her attempt to develop an alternative woman's perspective opposing the male, industrial urban nation which was growing at a rapid pace in the early decades of the new century. Characteristically, her novels are also peopled with strong heroines – the "Amazonian" Alexandra Bergson of *O Pioneers!*, Thea Kronberg of *Song of the Lark*, and Antonia Shimerda of *My Antonia* (1918). Juxtaposing American history and myth with an exploration of gender, *My Antonia* is Cather's attempt to record the contribution of women to the myth of the West. It also explores the conflicts between the "natives" and the "immigrants", and the gradual commercial transformation of the landscape, in a style that balances romance with realism. Her later novels – *A Lost Lady* (1923), *The Professor's Wife* (1923), *Death Comes for the Archbishop* (1927) and *Shadows on the Rock* (1931) – recreate the historical memories of New Mexico and of the conflicts on the French–Canadian borders in the seventeenth century, through the careers of the characters in these novels.

Katherine Anne Porter (1890–1980), whose fiction is committed to the theme of a woman's search for independence despite the security offered by a conventional home and family, is another important woman writer of the South. In the beginning of the twentieth century, her work contributed to developments which acknowledged a woman's right to choose the terms of her sexual freedom. That theme was first explored in her collection of short stories, *Flowering Judas and Other Stories* (1930), and in *Pale Horse, Pale Rider: Three Short Novels* (1939). Miranda Rhea, the protagonist, whose rites of passage when growing up in the Old

South is first charted in *Pale Horse, Pale Rider* and then in "The Old Order", included in *Collected Stories* (1965), has to negotiate between the responsibilities of society and family and her desire for personal development. Adulthood, thus, implies her forsaking many of the codes and ceremonies of the old plantation society. Porter's fiction, which includes the novel *Ship of Fools* (1962), is, therefore, primarily concerned with the study of her heroines' acquiring a sense of independent self-awareness. The psychological symbolism in her narrative style becomes the form which appropriately expresses the account of this journey along, what she terms, "the downward path to wisdom".

In her essay, "Place in Fiction" (1962), Eudora Welty insisted that "Feelings are bound up in place. . . . It is by knowing where you started that you grow able to judge where you are." Though some of Welty's stories are set in Europe, most of those collected in *A Curtain of Green* (1941), *The Golden Apples* (1949) and *The Bride of Innisfallen* (1955) are situated in the South. This is also true of her major novels such as *The Robber Bridegroom* (1942), *Delta Wedding* (1946), *Losing Battles* (1970) and *The Optimist's Daughter* (1972). This sense of place is also evident in Welty's work as a photographer of the Works Progress Administration, documenting images of the South during the Great Depression. It is similar to the work of the photographer Arthur Rothstein, and that of James Agee and Walker Evans, another photographer, in *Let Us Now Praise Famous Men* (1941). Many of Welty's stories have comic and dramatic elements, as in "Why I Live at the P.O.", and these imply her use of the Gothic and grotesque in "The Petrified Man", which also verge on the tragic in "The Travelling Salesman" and is sometimes redeemed in the lyricism of "A Still Moment". As with Cable, Welty's tales emphasise a pervasive use of the nuances of Southern speech, which supports her belief that language is basic to the individual's sense of identity and community. Thus, Welty's preoccupation with place involves the dialectic of a struggle against community and/or a compromise of one's separate identity. Moreover, Welty's fiction also has the characteristic Southern sense of ambiguity where, "All things are double", as the reader is informed in *The Robber Bridegroom*. In fact, the detailed realism of her stories, like her photographs, always seems to elude the truth as she admitted, "never the essence, only a sum of parts". Welty's fiction often has a profound complexity of meaning, as suggested by her observation: "Ours is the century of unreason; the stamp of our behavior is violence and isolation: non-meaning is looked upon with some solemnity."

Towards the end of her life, Carson McCullers declared: "I have my own reality of language and voices and foliage." Her fiction is almost a literal expression of this admission, as in her stories collected in *The Mortgaged Heart* (1971), her novella, *The Ballad of the Sad Café* (1951), and her four novels, *The Heart is a Lonely Hunter* (1940), *Reflections in a Golden Eye* (1941), *The Member of the Wedding* (1946) and *Clock Without Hands* (1951). Nevertheless, the South which formed her fictional world was both a geographical location and an imaginative setting created out of her childhood memories, feelings and experiences in Georgia: "Everything that happens in my fiction has happened to me", she stated in her unfinished autobiography, *Illumination and Night Glare* (2000). Simultaneously a self-exploration as they are a reflection on the strange and marginal existence of her characters, McCullers's works seem to disclose a common and contemporary human predicament – being "surrounded by a zone of loneliness". Frankie Adams, the young protagonist of *The Member of the Wedding*, is thus initiated into this reality when she is made to realise that she is "a member of nothing". At the centre of *The Heart is a Lonely Hunter* is John Singer, a deaf-mute depressed for being separated from Spiros Antonapoulos, another mute with whom he is able to communicate. Ironically, all the other "isolatees" in this small Georgia town come to Frankie to confess their deepest desires and fears, representing him "as he wished him to be". However, Singer's own suicide robs these people of the consolation and peace they found in him, leaving them to face the "radiance and darkness" of the unknown on their own.

In her collection of essays, *Mystery and Manners* (1969), Flannery O'Connor wrote: "The two circumstances that have given character to my writing have been those of being Southern and being Catholic." O'Connor's religious beliefs in a predominantly Puritan Georgia gave her an "outsider's" view of human fallibility, which she portrayed with a brutal and farcical realism that did not "excuse all human weakness" because "human weakness is human". Her novels, *Wise Blood* (1952) and *The Violent Bear it Away* (1960), together with her stories in *A Good Man is Hard to Find* (1955) and *Everything That Rises Must Converge* (1965), thus depict a world forsaken by God, and victims of evil like Haze Motes, in *Wise Blood*, who preaches, "Nothing matters but that Jesus is a liar". However, this blasphemy hides his need of the faith he so perversely denies. The characters that O'Connor creates are deliberately distorted; but she believed that readers would find such distortions "natural" to bring out their spiritual poverty and guilt, for, as she wrote, "To the hard of hearing you shout and for the almost-blind you draw large and startling figures." The grotesques that people her fiction, thus, portray a spiritual and cultural primitivism whose unnaturalness presumes its redemption through the restoration of God's grace. In this allegorical nature of her writing, she draws on the traditions of seventeenth-century Puritan writing which went on to influence Hawthorne and Gothic writing both in the nineteenth and the twentieth centuries, and thus shaped a major development of American literature. O'Connor was not a simple moralist; neither was she merely a regional writer. This is equally true in the case of all the other women who wrote of the South, including Harper Lee (1926–2016).

Lee – who is mainly known for her 1960 success, *To Kill a Mocking Bird* – considers herself as a "chronicler of something that I think is going down the drain very swiftly, and that is small town, middle class Southern life. There is something universal in it. There is something decent to be said for it, and there is something to lament when it goes, and its going, its passing." Based on the Scottsboro Trials of 1931, *To Kill a Mocking Bird* is a strong moral indictment of racial inequality; with the character of Atticus Finch, it also remains a tribute to the courage and decency of many forgotten people of the South. Another novel, *Go Set a Watchman*, which Lee had written in the 1950s as a sequel to her first novel, was discovered and published in July 2015. However, irrespective of the usual elements that characterise the fiction of the South, Lee admitted that her novels were basically a record of the manners of the region: "In other words, all I want is to be the Jane Austen of South Alabama." Nevertheless, despite such modest aims, the fiction of these regional writers was able to impress a deeper meaning and wider resonance to the literature and culture of their times. For, as always, the place or the region only became for them the imaginative site for examining complex social, moral and often philosophical issues which transcend the fixities of time or place.

Modernism in American Literature

As is evident from its writing, *fin de siècle* America involved a continuous critical attempt to understand the tumultuous industrial and technological changes that was transforming its economy, society and culture. American modernism was thus distinctively characterised by its attempt to overcome parochial national concerns and the regional limitations of its literature and culture, and turn towards a global aspiration. Ironically, this initially took the form of an expatriate rejection of its cultural backwardness; the quest for the new and the modern still ranged across the Atlantic, taking many of the notable writers to London and Paris. Yet, these very cultural immigrants from America were also aware of the artistic needs of a country poised on the threshold of its international role and were able to contribute to the development of a distinctly American tradition of modernism.

Overawed by the giant electromagnetic dynamos displayed in the Great Exposition of 1900 in Paris, Henry Adams, a professor of medieval history at Harvard, defined the "modern" as characterised by "Multiplicity, Diversity, Complexity, Anarchy, Chaos". In fact, these five terms are often considered definitive of American modernism, whose heterogeneous nature became clearly evident in the International Exhibition of Modern Art, popularly called the Armory Show, in New York in 1913. American modernist poets like William Carlos Williams who visited the Show were shocked and delighted by its break with earlier conventions and traditions. However, this rupture, generic to modernism, acquired an American dimension when the same poet would see in it nativist vernacular elements – the "rediscovery of a primary impetus" in the "local conditions" of regional America. Thus, American modernism is distinguished by conflicting tendencies such as those between the international and the native, the experimental avant-garde and the commercially popular, involving, according to Matthew Josephson, "the frenetic passions of baseball crowds, and skyscrapers ris[ing] lyrically to the exotic rhythms of jazz bands which upon waking up we find to be nothing but the drilling of pneumatic hammers on steel girders". Turning away from a "high modernism", this "heterodox modernism", thus, seems both to celebrate and decry the effects of industrial change; to recognise the need to seek innovative forms of expression, only to understand its own history and traditions. Finally, dominated as it was by a proliferating visual culture of the cinema and the billboard, American modernism also redefined the relationship between the artist and his work, aesthetic form and literary conventions. America thus emerges as one of the most significant contributors to the modernist movement which encompasses all areas of literature and culture.

Modernist Fiction

Henry James

The major fiction of Henry James (1843–1916) can be described as America's rediscovery of Europe. His novels deal with the expatriate's experience of Europe, reversing the romance of the earlier quest into a tragicomic encounter with the older civilisation and culture, which came to be termed the "international theme": "My choice is the Old World–my choice, my need, my life." This theme was the consequence of James's own childhood and youth, when his father, Henry James Sr., having inherited a considerable fortune, decided to give his children a cosmopolitan, liberal and "sensuous education" by travelling extensively over the continent, absorbing its art, literature and music. The novelist thus abandoned the Harvard Law School and resolved his vocation to be a writer: "I shall immortalise myself", he wrote to his sister from Florence while working on the first chapters of *Roderick Hudson* (1875). Thus, James repeatedly returned to Europe between 1869 and 1875, finally settling in London at the end of 1876, thereby exploring the double landscape that would become definitive of his fiction. In 1888, he was to tell his brother, William James, the philosopher and psychologist,

> I aspire to write in such a way that it would be impossible to the outsider to say whether I am at a given moment an American writing about England or an Englishman writing about America (dealing as I do with both countries), and so far from being ashamed of such ambiguity I should be exceedingly proud of it, for it would be highly civilized.

Therefore, in *Roderick Hudson*, James deals with an American sculptor's sense of disenchantment with the cultural poverty of his own country and his desire to experience the rich variety of life in Europe as an inspiration for his art. A theme pervasive in his fiction, this tension and anxiety regarding the paucity of an "old civilization" in the United States can be traced to James's own *Notebooks* and his short critical study, *Hawthorne* (1879). In a letter to his friend W. D. Howells in 1880, he reiterated, ". . . it takes an old civilization to set a novelist in motion. . . . It is on manners, customs, usages, habits, forms upon all these things, matured and established, that a novelist lives – they are the very stuff that his work is made of; . . . which, I enumerate, as wanting in American society . . .". In fact, this is translated into a conflict of cultures and the interplay of traditions which forms the basis of James's "international theme", first evident in the tale, "The Passionate Pilgrim" (1875), a collection of sketches and travel articles called *Transatlantic Sketches* (1875) and in *The American* (1877). In the novel, the titular Christopher Newman, who echoes the name of the nation's progenitor, thus represents the type of "young innocent" from the New World, who has strayed among the tainted nobility of the Old. In search of a cultured wife in Paris, Newman is exploited for his wealth and then contemptuously rejected by the young woman's aristocratic family. Though capable of avenging himself, Newman desists, thereby attesting to a true sense of honour missing in the older civilisation. Aware that this romance of the New World had caught the interest of the reading public, James termed it his "Americano-European legend", which would dominate many of his novels in the first phase of his literary career between 1865 and 1882.

In *The Europeans* (1878), however, James inverses the situation by bringing two American expatriates back to Boston, with comic and satiric consequences. Though the Bostonians were not amused with this version, James's international romance actually examined the "complex fate [of] being an American". Thus, he added, "Conscious of so few things in the world, these unprecedented creatures were least of all conscious of deficiencies and dangers; so that the grace of youth and innocence and freshness aiding, their negatives were converted and became in certain relations lively positives and values." The tragedy with which *Daisy Miller* (1879) ends brings out the "stranded helplessness" of these Americans abroad; and though James seems to imply that the malaria to which Daisy succumbs is a metaphor for the Old World's corruption, he is paradoxically aware that she is also the victim of her own innocence.

James's *The Portrait of a Lady* (1880–81) is considered to be one of the most notable treatments of the international theme and also proof of his consummate success in the depiction of women characters. James described the novel as a story of "a certain young woman confronting her destiny". Isabel Archer, the attractive young girl from Albany, New York, is given the wealth and freedom by her aunt and her cousin, Ralph Touchett, to choose her destiny. She is courted by an American tycoon, an English lord and an expatriate American art connoisseur. She marries the third, Gilbert Osmond, with disastrous results. In spite of her realisation that she had been tricked by Gilbert and his mistress, Madame Merle, who had merely used her wealth and idealism to imprison her in a union of convenience, she declines the alternative offered by Caspar Goodwood, her earlier American suitor. Renouncing her happiness, Isabel returns to her house in Italy, where she tries to reconcile herself with her fate in a silent soliloquy:

> It was a house of darkness, the house of dumbness, the house of suffocation. Osmond's beautiful mind gave it neither light nor air; Osmond's beautiful mind, indeed, seemed to peep down from a small high window and mock at her. . . . It was her scorn for his assumptions – it was that that made him draw himself up. He had plenty of contempt, and it was proper that his wife should be as well furnished; but that she should turn the hot light of her disdain upon his own conception of things – this was a danger he had not allowed for.

In fact, James had announced the central tenet of fictional practice in the preface to the novel by emphasising, "Place the center of the subject in the young woman's consciousness . . . and you get as interesting and as beautiful a difficulty as you could wish. Stick to *that* – for the center, put the heaviest weight into *that* scale which will be so largely the scale of her relationship to herself." In *The Portrait*, therefore, the drama of contesting cultures found a theatre of the consciousness which was used as a narrative mode. James, thus, reformulated the poetics of the novel by mediating the narrative in and through the consciousness of the protagonist. This relocation of the narratorial perspective had complex implications. First, it emphasised the dramatic importance of showing the action rather than authorial telling and summary. Second, the method of implicating the protagonist or the characters in the narration involved the ironies and uncertainties of a limited and, often, unreliable narrator. In *The Art of Fiction* (1884), therefore, James acknowledges the contribution of Gustave Flaubert and Emile Zola in making the novel "discutable" – the focus of theoretical discussion.

Influenced by the ideas of his illustrious brother, the psychologist William James, Henry James believed that the human consciousness did not follow a linear development. In the case of Isabel, the moment of recognition of her tragic destiny suggests that a character's growth was not merely dependent on the acquisition of knowledge but, rather, a self-realisation which involved moments of epiphanic discovery. Thus, for James, it became necessary to formulate a nuanced treatment of character, which included the use of metaphor, repetition and a detailed scenic method of narration. This consisted of the use of the Jamesian theory of "point of view", where the story was presented from several and, often, alternating perspectives. Consequently, his fiction also involved the frequent use of oblique signs and suggestions and the use of free indirect speech, contributing to a dramatic irony which anticipated a modernist tendency to implicate the reader in the recovery of meaning. Moreover, this self-conscious preoccupation with the means of fictional representation, particularly evident in his essays on French novelists and the prefaces to the New York edition of his novels, clearly foreshadowed another feature of modernism.

The Bostonians (1886) and *The Princess Casamassima* (1886), which followed *The Portrait of a Lady*, mark the beginning of the second phase of James's literary career. While the former dealt with the reform movement of the Bostonian suffragettes, the latter was an ironical exploration of the world of the London anarchists in the late nineteenth century. "I am quite a Naturalist", James had told a friend when collecting notes for *The Princess*. This emphasis on social details distinguishes the two novels, making them, in an important sense, tales of two cities – Boston and London. However, both the novels, "from which I expected so much and derived so little," as James wrote to Howells, "reduced the desire and the demand for my production to zero." Nevertheless, the issues, such as the emerging feminist movement and an engagement with political issues, drew the attention of twentieth-century readers. Therefore, in *The Tragic Muse* (1890), James used his growing interest in drama to depict the conflicts of an actress and a politician-painter attempting to overcome a hostile environment and achieve their aspirations. Discernibly, between 1890 and 1895, James immersed himself in the theatre, writing seven plays, two of which were staged – a dramatisation of *The American* and *Guy Domville* (1895), a comedy of manners which was summarily rejected by its audience.

James's failure in the theatre, however, found a fresh avenue of expression in a series of short stories and novels which were written in the form of dramatic scenarios: *The Spoils of Poynton* (1897), *What Maisie Knew* (1897), *The Turn of the Screw* (1898), *The Awkward Age* (1899) and *The Sacred Fount* (1901). These works focus on three important themes – that of childhood in a corrupt adult world, the psychology of the supernatural tendency and the paradox of literary success. Some of these themes recur in the short stories written during this period –"The Figure in the Carpet", "The Lesson of the Master", "The Death of the Lion" and "The Aspern Papers". These short novels and tales are also significant for James's experiments with fictional techniques. Many of these works explored childhood consciousness in terms of its own sense of innocence and its gullibility. His adolescent protagonists tend to be more passive and vulnerable, and their suffering is therefore expressed through the use of alternating points of view structured according to the "successive Acts of a Play". In *What Maisie Knew*, this method is effective in comically revealing the adult world to be emotionally empty and morally bankrupt.

The final phase of James's career is marked by a return to the international theme in three notable works – *The Wings of the Dove* (1902), *The Ambassadors* (1903) and *The Golden Bowl* (1904). In *The Ambassadors*, Lambert Strether, the ambassador sent to Paris to bring another compatriot back to Massachusetts, is himself seduced by the culture and charms of Europe into a denial of his original mission. This denial is prompted by his own awareness of a wasted youth and a realisation that nothing could compensate for this loss: "Live all you can; it is mistake not to. It doesn't so much matter what you do in particular, so long as you have your life. If you haven't had that, what *have* you had? . . . What one loses one loses, make no mistake about that." Adopting the method of alternating points of view, James structured the novel into four major scenes set in an evidently mythical garden, thereby implicating the characters within a generic conception of the American as Adam before and after the Fall. Thus, *The Ambassadors*, like James's earlier novels, deals with the education and growth of the hero, which also involves a reconciliation with a sense of loss.

James's concern with fictional techniques is evident in *The Wings of the Dove,* the tale of Milly Theale, a young American heiress whose fatal illness makes her the victim of the treachery of an English couple. James concentrates on developing the characters around Milly and employs this oblique method to develop a tragic allegory of wilful manipulation succumbing to goodness and grace. James's insistence on the "organic" relationship between form and subject is reaffirmed in *The Golden Bowl*, which tries to rewrite the international theme with an ironic reversal of the earlier preoccupation with the innocent and exploited American. Adam Verver and his daughter Maggie are, thus, on the one hand, depicted as acquisitive Americans collecting European art works, with mutual indifference, and, on the other, as compassionate saviours of Prince Amerigo and Charlotte Stant. The novel is characterised by an ambiguity that tends to undermine its ostensible meaning. In fact, the thematic and formal complexity of these novels also testify to a *fin de siècle* aestheticism which, in the case of James, seemed to be a consideration of art as a type of religion.

Nevertheless, James's importance as a historian of the society of his times was finally attested by *The American Scene* (1907), which remains one of his most poetic commentaries on his native land. The writer's last years were devoted to organising the New York Edition of his novels and two autobiographical volumes, *A Small Boy and Others* (1913) and *Notes of a Son and Brother* (1914), while the third, *The Middle Years,* was posthumously published in 1917.

James's cosmopolitanism was a continuation of Whitman's call, in his poem "Passage to India", which saw the American destiny as a mission of establishing connections with the outside world, and the marriage of nations and cultures. In his fiction, James's investment in this myth actually became his quest to define an American identity. Thus, in spite of his expatriate alienation, James was able to contribute to the formation of a national literature. Together with this, his experiments with fictional methods and his development of a theory of the novel anticipated and gave authority to the growth of the modernist novel.

F. Scott Fitzgerald

F. Scott Fitzgerald's (1896–1940) career as a novelist is something of a paradox. Though immensely successful as a writer, towards the end of his life, he increasingly felt that he had wasted his talents and sacrificed his art in the pursuit of wealth. Thus, he later stated in his autobiographical collection of essays, *Crack Up* (1945), that he had gained popularity but failed as an artist. In fact, in an earlier "Notebook" entry, Fitzgerald had also admitted: "I write with the authority of failure. Ernest [Hemingway] with the authority of success. We could never sit across the same table." Thus, Fitzgerald was often dismissed during his time as a "seasonal" writer featured in popular magazines, as he wrote stories of wealthy people in palatial houses, beautiful girls and the riotous lifestyles of the fashionable rich of the American 1920s, often called the Jazz Age.

In the fourth chapter of *The Great Gatsby* (1925), the narrator, Nick, records the names of the famous people who attended

Gatsby's parties in the blank spaces of a train time-table: "This schedule in effect, July 5, 1922." This fact not only situates the novel in the 1920s, but also emphasises Fitzgerald's importance as a chronicler of the 20s. This was a distinctive period of American history because it is marked by a post-war economic boom which brought a tremendous sense of freedom and optimism in American society and culture. Moreover, this economic growth and sense of renewed hope became the basis of the myth of success which defines America as a nation and a culture. Recounting this period, Fitzgerald later observed that it was the time when America was growing out of its traditional, provincial limitations and redefining itself as a young, adventurous and confident society: ". . . it seemed only a question of a few years before the older people would step aside and let the world be run by those who saw things as they were – and it seemed rosy and romantic to us who were young then . . .". It is this "extraordinary gift of hope", a "romantic readiness" and a "heightened sensitivity to the promises of life" which was definitive of Gatsby's personality and the Jazz Age which he represented.

Most of Fitzgerald's fiction deals with these basic preoccupations: *This Side of Paradise* (1920), his first novel, and *The Beautiful and Damned* (1922), which followed it, were both attempts to represent and examine the age. In this sense, all his novels have an autobiographical basis, as he once confirmed: "Sometimes I don't know whether I'm real or whether I'm a character in one of my novels." Amory Blaine (in *This Side of Paradise*) and Anthony Patch (in *The Beautiful and Damned*) are, thus, the typical "cynical idealists" of the 20s, while Gloria Gilbert of *The Beautiful and Damned* is representative of the sexually liberated women of the age – termed, the Flappers – who also become the model for Daisy Buchanan in *The Great Gatsby* and Nicole Warren in *Tender is the Night* (1934). In an important sense, however, Fitzgerald also attempts to depict the decadence and decline of this affluent and expatriate society whose expectations are easily satiated and usually end in despair and disillusion. Therefore, this recreation of a specific time and place also evokes an emotion associated with a transitory moment of romantic wonder which Fitzgerald was to later admit: "After all any given moment has its value; it can be questioned in the light of after-events, but the moment remains." There is, therefore, a strong sense of time in Fitzgerald's writing, which made his friend Malcolm Cowley once observe that his fiction gave one the impression that he was living in a room surrounded by clocks.

The Great Gatsby is saturated by this sense of time: beginning with the striking image of Tom Buchanan's lawns "jumping over sun dials", it uses the metaphor of a defunct mantelpiece clock at the static centre of the novel, immortalising the reunion of the lovers, and, finally, ends with the coda involving an ode to the historical origins of the nation: "And as the moon rose higher the inessential houses began to melt away until gradually I became aware of the old island here that flowered once for Dutch sailors' eyes – a fresh, green breast of the new world." The basic love story, which constitutes the plot of the novel, involves a rather sentimental attempt to reverse time, which seems to resonate in the traditions of American writing, in Emerson and Melville: "'Can't repeat the past?' he cried incredulously. 'Why of course you can!'", Gatsby tells Nick when he decides to win back Daisy, his beloved now married to Tom. This desire for the past, manifested in Gatsby's impossible love story, re-enacts the discovery of a prelapsarian America and the quest for plenitude and fulfilment that was basic to the American Dream, a paean to which ends the novel. *The Great Gatsby* is not merely about the Jazz Age; the optimism and quest for success of the 20s expresses the historical consciousness of the nation. The novel, thus, explores the mythic implications of this age by dramatising the romantic imagination in the New World and also by tracing the corruption of this promise in urban America: "That's the whole burden of the novel –" explained Fitzgerald, "the loss of those illusions that give such color to the world that you don't care whether things are true or false as long as they partake of the magical glory." Thus, the novel becomes a criticism of the travesty of the American Dream in contemporary America, ironically expressed through the antithetical symbolism of the "Ash Heap" and the "Eyes of Dr T. J. Eckleburg", suggesting American disillusionment.

T. S. Eliot considered *The Great Gatsby* a modern American classic – "the first step that American fiction had taken since Henry James". Significantly, the modernist aspect of the novel is evident in the experimental treatment of a modified, first-person point of view of Nick, whose narration is characterised by a dualism involving a contrast between romance and realism, fact and fiction: "I was within and without, simultaneously enchanted and repelled by the inexhaustible variety of life." In an interview in 1924, Fitzgerald said that ". . . the writer, if he has any aspiration toward art, should try to convey the feel of his scenes, places and people directly – as Conrad does; and as few Americans (notably Willa Cather) are already trying to do". In *The Great Gatsby*, the novelist, like Conrad, consciously uses a dramatic and poetic narrative method using several rhetorical devices to communicate the immediacy of emotion and experience, as in the elaborate party scenes at Gatsby's mansion and also during the confrontation between Tom and his mistress, Myrtle, in a New York hotel. However, Fitzgerald's treatment of the character of Gatsby remains enigmatic and ambiguous. He remains alienated, never clearly revealed except during certain moments of crises and tension when the narrator gets a transitory glimpse of his authentic identity. This distancing of the hero is deliberate, because Gatsby, as a representative of the American Dream, is given a mythic significance. In fact, in the treatment of Gatsby, Fitzgerald also follows Conrad in his use of impressionism. There is, thus, a play of several viewpoints, of facts and fiction, which are made necessary to reconstruct the truth of Gatsby's story. This is further complemented by the shifts in narrative time by which the tale is fragmented and shifts between the past and the present to create a plurality of meanings that is characteristic of a modernist novel.

Though it remained incomplete, *The Last Tycoon*, published posthumously in 1941, is considered one of the best Hollywood novels. Monroe Stahr, the last of the great producers, is finally destroyed by the changes which overcome the film industry where art is sacrificed to commerce. Continuing Fitzgerald's examination of the American Dream, the novel presents Hollywood with its "cardboard and tinsel", as one of the most appropriate configurations of its wondrous and meretricious seductions. The writing of the novel coincided with a crisis in the writer's personal life, and is imbued with a tragic awareness of the novelist's own compromises between art and commerce, his romantic dream and moral decadence. A note appended to the unfinished manuscript of the novel seems to stand almost as an epitaph, both for the novelist and for the protagonists of his fiction: "ACTION IS CHARACTER". Nevertheless, Fitzgerald's writing continuously reaffirms that, though the ideal remains perpetually beyond our reach, it is necessary, as he asserts in "The Crack-Up" essay, that "one should . . . be able to see that things are hopeless and yet be determined to make them otherwise".

The Lost Generation

The First World War marked an important watershed between the nineteenth and twentieth centuries in America and influenced significant changes in its society, its values and literature. Not only does the event feature notably in poetry and novels, but it became the occasion which prompted many writers to consider it the beginning of modernism in American literature. Though America refrained from active involvement in the war, it contributed to the war effort and reaped its commercial benefits, which resulted in the unprecedented economic prosperity of the 1920s. However, the young American writers who had seen the war as journalists and medical workers, returned from the continent with a profound sense of disenchantment that made Gertrude Stein (1874–1936), the elderly poet and novelist, term them a "lost generation". Though F. Scott Fitzgerald's *This Side of Paradise* (1920) did not directly deal with the war, it was probably the earliest American novel to portray the disillusion and rebelliousness of the post-war generation. John Dos Passos (1896–1970) and E. E. Cummings (1894–1962), who had served in the Norton–Harjes Ambulance Corps, contributed two important war novels – *Three Soldiers* (1921) and *The Enormous Room* (1922), respectively. William Faulkner (1897–1962), who had trained in the Royal Air Force, satirised the illusions of heroism in his first novel, *Soldier's Pay* (1926); and, as a reporter, Ernest Hemingway (1899–1961), in his *A Farewell to Arms* (1929), made the war a stage on which a tragedy of love and commitment is enacted.

One important consequence of this disillusion was an evident break with the anachronistic nature of the American past and its traditions. A common reaction against this was that of the expatriate writer, a tendency which went back to James, Pound and Eliot, and whose centre, during the post-war years, became Stein's salon in Paris where many notable American writers gathered for ideas and encouragement. In *The Making of Americans* (1925), Stein had noted, "It has always seemed to me a rare privilege, this, of being an American, a real American, one whose tradition it has taken scarcely sixty years to create." A significant aspect of the creation of what is considered the tradition of American modernism involved the emulation of the avant-garde and experimental principles of modernist literature developed in the European art movements of cubism, expressionism and surrealism, and also proposed by Pound in his injunction of novelty and freedom, which was to be definitive of the period he termed as the "Risorgimento". In her *Lectures in America* (1935), Stein felt that American writers were capable of representing the modern because of their ability "to completely express that actual present", because of their awareness of "the simplicity of something always happening". Thus, in her *Narration* (1935), Stein added, "If you are an American gradually you find that really it is not necessary . . . that anything and everything has a beginning, a middle, and an ending."

Yet, this sense of an apparently eternal present ironically involves a repeating of the past. In spite of the tragic consequences of this desire in Fitzgerald's *The Great Gatsby*, in confirming that the American present implies an inexorable regression into the past, the end of the novel emphasises a duality basic to the sense of time expressed in the American novel: "So we beat on, boats against the current borne back ceaselessly into the past." Thus, the American historian Lawrence Levine identifies "a web of ambivalence", characteristic of the first three decades of the twentieth century, which, he says, involves "the central paradox of American history: a belief in progress coupled with a dream of change, an urge towards the inevitable future combined with a longing for the irretrievable past; a deeply ingrained belief in America's unfolding destiny and a haunting conviction that the nation was in a state of decline."

William Faulkner

William Faulkner seems to represent this paradox: though considered one of the foremost modernists of American fiction, his identity in the "actual present" entails a continuous rewriting of his past – the history of the antebellum South and its period of Reconstruction that followed the Civil War between 1861 and 1865.

Faulkner was, therefore, essentially a Southern novelist investigating and attempting to understand its historical crisis by remembering and imaginatively reconstructing that history in the lives of the individuals in the fictional town of Jefferson in Yoknapatawpha County: "Beginning with *Sartoris* I discovered that my own little postage stamp of native soil was worth writing about, and, that by sublimating the actual into the apocryphal, I would have complete liberty to use whatever talent I might have to its absolute top." After *Sartoris* (1929), Faulkner repeatedly returned to this history in *The Sound and the Fury* (1929), *As I Lay Dying* (1930), *Sanctuary* (1931), *Light in August* (1932) and *Absalom, Absalom!* (1936). In fact, he once admitted, "I am telling the same story over and over." This repetition thus became a form of rediscovery of the lost meanings of his past, necessary for an apprehension of, "myself and the world". A similar reclamation of the past is evident in his later novels such as *Go Down Moses* (1942), *Intruder in the Dust* (1948), and in the Snopes trilogy which included *The Hamlet* (1940), *The Town* (1957) and *The Mansion* (1959).

Faulkner's mythic Yoknapatawpha County, "a cosmos of my own", is evidently based on the region around his own home in New Albany, Mississippi. Therefore, it is an imagined community whose genealogical history becomes the subject of the novels. In fact, the Yoknapatawpha series comprises a historical chronicle covering more than a century, from the early nineteenth to the middle of the twentieth. However, Faulkner is not a historical novelist; his is not a factual recreation of the Southern past but a commentary on its decline, as dramatised and recounted in the lives and fates of the Compson family in *The Sound and the Fury.* Hence, Faulkner's historical sense implies a continuous interweaving of private and public histories where the present is framed and judged in terms of the past. The narrative, divided into four sections, is assigned to the members of the Compson family – Benjy, Jason, Quentin and, finally, the Black American cook Dilsey – whose separate monologues attempt an explanation for their absent sister, Caddy, and, thereby, reconstitute a condensed history of the family and the region. This obsession with the past, and the need to confront and comprehend its conflicts and dislocations, form the moral and psychological imperatives of the characters in the novel. Caddy, the novel's absent centre, is a metaphor of this disruption which exposes instances of corruption and repression, whose inexorable knowledge ultimately leads to Quentin's suicide. Ironically, it is in the story of the autistic Benjy that a basic notion of humanity tentatively emerges. Though Dilsey's Christian assumptions, in the conclusive section of the novel, offers the hope of redemption from the prison-house of this past, her faith is unable to explain the decline of the Compsons or that of the South.

Faulkner's epic of Yoknapatawpha continued in the novels that followed: *As I Lay Dying*, *Sanctuary*, *Light in August* and *Absalom, Absalom!*. However, in these novels, the vagaries of Southern history become intertwined with issues of race and gender, which had a considerable bearing on its defeat and decline. Though they usually remain absent or silent, the women in Faulkner's novels not only determine the action but also advance the promise of a sense of order in this irrevocable process of loss and disintegration. Addie, in *As I Lay Dying*, had made her husband, Anse, promise that, when she died, he would bury her in Jefferson, because she had realised "the reason for living was to get ready to stay dead a long time". The novel is a grotesque prolongation of this ritual by the members of the Bundren family, each with separate agendas for accompanying the dead across incidents of flood and fire. Like many others, this novel introduces the tragicomic and Gothic elements in Faulkner's fiction. In this, Faulkner was retaining his links with the major traditions of Southern literature such as oral, folk and vernacular narratives.

Light in August deals with the attempt by Joe Christmas to recover the origins of his mulatto identity. He resists the simplified racial divisions of white and black, which he finds demeaning to his self-respect; and yet, this becomes the very reason for the outrage in the community which lynches and castrates him: "He never acted like either a nigger or a white man. That was it. That was what made the folks so mad." *Absalom, Absalom!* is considered to be one of the most complex interpretations of the racial underside of Southern history. In this novel, Faulkner gathers some of the earlier figures of the Yoknapatawpha saga to disclose the demonic assumptions behind Miss Rosa's question, "Why God let us lose the War?" Quentin returns to unearth the causes for the rise of Thomas Sutpen, the progenitor of "Sutpen's hundred", and, later, the Compsons, only to discover a tale of treachery, miscegenation and incest. Yet, much of the moral implications of this tale, which also includes the murder of a half-brother, are undermined by the interpretations ascribed to the events by the various narrators. Denied their true origins, the family's fate is thus dismissed as the workings of "Fate, destiny, retribution, irony – the stage manager, call him what you will", who is now considered the author of the forces of history. Thus, by being absolved of responsibility, history is emptied of its meanings. Though Quentin tells Shreve, his Canadian roommate, that he does not hate the South, five months after this admission, he commits suicide.

This moral uncertainty is also true in the case of the Snopes trilogy, albeit a comic treatment of this crisis. The Snopes represent the "poor whites" in Yoknapatawpha. The epithet "poor" is not so much a description of their economic condition as it is a reference to the poverty of their ethical sense. "Snopesism" thus becomes Faulkner's satire of the philistine deceptions of the rootless Southerner who seized wealth and power in the chaotic Civil War period.

Faulkner's novels are often compared to those of James Joyce to emphasise their modernist character. However, this relationship is not limited merely to Faulkner's use of the interior monologue, but also in the experiments and innovations he introduced in his fiction. For instance, the individual and fragmentary narratives in *The Sound and the Fury, Light in August* and *Absalom, Absalom!* present multiple versions of a history, with the juxtaposing of each version acting as a counterpoint to the others. Thus, not only is Faulkner preoccupied with the aesthetics and language of fiction, his novels also have a self-reflexive quality in which both the story and the act of narration become a central concern. This self-consciousness is also evident in Faulkner's sentence structures, whose length and complexity often bewilders the inattentive reader. Nevertheless, Faulkner's preference for a rhetorical and eloquent style is in keeping with the traditions of oratory in Southern literature and political discourse. Yet, together with these formal concerns, the novels display an equal sense of restraint of authorial control. Characters are portrayed through their speech and action, eliminating authorial commentary. In an interview in 1931, Faulkner had maintained, "In the future novel . . . there will be no straight exposition, but instead presentation, by means of soliloquies or speeches of the characters, those of each character printed in different colored ink. Something of the play technique will eliminate much of the author from the story." Faulkner's novels are, thus, structured by analogy, image clusters, motifs, correlatives and synecdoche. The multiple points of view create alternative interpretations of events and ideas, which finally assume a sense of order that is vindicated in the readers' consciousness. However, the fragmentariness and plurality of the narratives also emphasise the indeterminacy and relativity implicit in these versions of reality. This, in fact, constitutes Faulkner's redefinition of history, which tends to anticipate similar ideas in postmodernism.

Faulkner was awarded the Nobel Prize for Literature in 1950, though most of his major fiction predated this recognition. There are echoes of his earlier achievement in *Intruder in the Dust* (1948), *Requiem for a Nun* (1951) and *The Fable* (1954), the last another attempt to use the setting of World War I for a reassertion of the values Faulkner celebrated in his Nobel address: "courage and honor and hope and pride and compassion and pity and sacrifice." When seen against the occurrence of another World War, this invocation of basic human verities seems to have a note of defeat and despair that characterised his earlier fiction. Thus, in *The Reivers* (1962), his last novel, a comic romance tries to recreate the memories of a lost innocence.

As in the case of the other major American writers of the twentieth century, Faulkner's modernism was defined as much by the traditions of his native soil as by his adaptation of the innovative artistic and literary developments that distinguished the movement in Europe. More important was his contribution to the development of the literature of Southern writers, both contemporary and after the end of his fictional career. American modernism is thus constituted by different, often conflicting, voices – both regional and expatriate.

Ernest Hemingway

War and its physical and emotional afflictions form the theme of Ernest Hemingway's (1899–1961) early fiction. As a volunteer for the Red Cross during the First World War, he had been severely wounded trying to rescue an Italian soldier. In fact, it was during his convalescence, first in Italian hospitals and then at Petoskey, Michigan, that he seriously took up writing. The stories of *In Our Time* (1925), his first important publication, are thus interspersed with brief sketches of his war experiences. Moreover, the distinctive Hemingway world of masculine bonding and an unsentimental acceptance of suffering and death with the courage of "grace under pressure", which characterised the Nick Adams's stories, appear to have been shaped by the writer's ordeal at the Italian Front. Significantly, the war influenced the disillusion and break with earlier traditions which shaped the writing of the post-war American novelists, among whom Hemingway seemed to represent the Lost Generation.

In an important sense, the "unreasonable wound" of war also shapes the world of the narrator, Jake Barnes, in Hemingway's *The Sun Also Rises* (1926), his first novel to receive critical recognition. Though basically a portrayal of the amoral and bohemian expatriate life in Parisian cafes and salons, the novel also attempts to explore a search for meaning in the tenuous relationships between the deliberately careless characters depicted in the novel. Having flitted through several sexual liaisons, Lady Brett Ashley finally chooses Romero, a young Spanish matador. However, at the end of the novel, she gives him up, admittedly for selfish reasons, as she realises that he is too young and that marriage would destroy his career: "You know it makes one feel rather good deciding not to be a bitch," she tells Jake, "It's sort of what we have instead of God." Emasculated physically and psychologically by the war, Jake has to reconcile himself with his isolation. Suspicious of the traditional notions of right and wrong, he can only find a separate peace by accepting a life whose codes of conduct are discovered in the act of living them: "I did not care what it was all about. All I wanted to know was how to live it. Maybe if you found out how to live in it you learned what it was all about." Jake's wound thus becomes a metaphor suggesting not only the holocaust of war but also a sense of disenchantment which dominated the consciousness of the post-war generation and Hemingway's fiction.

This theme would be reiterated in the stories of *Men Without Women* (1927) and *A Farewell to Arms* (1929), the war novel which grew out of his experiences on the Italian Front. Hemingway was convinced that war reduced humans to the condition of cattle in the Chicago stockyards; consequently it became necessary "to expose the romantic, heroic values and language" which were usually used to disguise this senseless violence. Lieutenant Frederic Henry, the novel's protagonist, represents Hemingway's opinion when he says,

> I was always embarrassed by the words sacred, glorious, and sacrifice and their expression in vain. We had heard them . . . and had read them on proclamations that were slapped up by bill posters over other proclamations, now for a long time, and I had seen nothing sacred, and things that were glorious had no glory and the sacrifices were like stockyards at Chicago if nothing was done with the meat but to bury it. . . . Abstract words such as glory, honor, courage, or hallow were obscene beside the concrete names of villages, and the numbers of roads, and the names of rivers, the numbers of regiments and the dates.

This tension between the concrete and the abstract contributes significantly to the formation of Hemingway's style in his novels. For Hemingway, one of the preconditions of writing was to be able to write a "true sentence": "A writer's job is to tell the truth. . . . All you have to do is to write a true sentence. Write the truest sentence you know." Hemingway's fiction, thus, abandons descriptive summaries, the insistent use of adjectives, or rhetorical exaggeration, to create a spare, laconic narrative style which attempted to signify wider meanings by its very taciturnity and omissions. In his 1964 memoir, *A Moveable Feast*, Hemingway observes: "You could omit anything if you knew what you omitted and the omitted part would strengthen the story and make people feel something more than they understood." One of the origins of this tendency is the journalistic precision that he emulated from his days as a reporter for the *Kansas City Star* and his later work as a war correspondent. This involved a continuous insistence on objectivity, relying on the facts of the situation or, what he termed, "the real thing . . . something I was working very hard to try to get". This evident factual emphasis on things corroborates the attitude adopted by most of his protagonists who prefer to depend on their own observations and experiences, rather than readily accept any given opinion regarding the real. In fact, it has also been suggested that the minimalist simplicity and clarity of Hemingway's language and narrative style is also derived from Ezra Pound's theories of Imagist poetry. In "Soldier's Home" (*In Our Time*), for instance, following Pound's advice, Hemingway juxtaposes the reactions of the soldier Harold Krebs with the platitudes of his mother, to evoke multiple implications. In an interview in 1963, Hemingway stated, "I sometimes think my style is suggestive rather than direct. The reader must often use his imagination or lose the most subtle part of my thought."

However, the cynicism which followed the tragic end of the love between Frederic and Catherine Barkley in *A Farewell to Arms*, is reversed in *For Whom the Bell Tolls* (1940), where Hemingway's use of a line from John Donne's poetry, "No man is an island", finds a purpose in Robert Jordan's commitment to the cause of the Spanish Republicans fighting against Franco's fascist forces. Jordan is a typical Hemingway protagonist who has no illusions about the romantic myths of war: "Don't lie to yourself. Nor make up literature about it." Nevertheless, he is also aware that his commitment is "as authentic as the feeling you had when you heard Bach, or stood in the Chartres Cathedral. . . . It gave you a part in something that you could believe in wholly and completely and in which you felt an absolute brotherhood with the others engaged in it." A major aspect of this involvement with the Republican cause subsequently grows out of his love for Maria and, in the treatment of this relationship, Hemingway seems to forsake his characteristic stylistic restraint: "'I love thee'", Jordan tells Maria, "'as I love all that we fought for. I love thee as I love liberty and dignity and the rights for all men to work and not be hungry. I love thee as I love Madrid that we have defended and as I love all my comrades that have died.'" Though an anti-fascist, Hemingway was basically a conservative humanist – an attitude which also influenced his treatment of the Spanish Civil War in his play, *The Fifth Column* (1938). Most of his war novels, thus, tend towards a tragic end, as is also true in the relationship between Robert and Maria.

In his later writing, Hemingway seems to confront the sense of nihilism that is pervasive in his war fiction, by investing in the theme of the active life in the figure of Colonel Richard Cantwell in *Across the River and into the Trees* (1950). This became a culmination of his earlier interest in bullfighting and big-game hunting depicted in *Death in the Afternoon* (1932) and *Green Hills of Africa* (1935). However, there is also the suggestion that, in trying to find an alternative to a sense of alienation, the novelist was equating himself with his protagonists and using his fiction to create a myth of Hemingway the man, the hunter, fisherman and lover, who often superseded the writer and came to be celebrated as "Papa Hemingway". This also involved an assertion of "masculine" values, implicit in the tension between action and contemplation which is basic to American life and culture, which the novelist tried to sublimate in his Nobel Prize-winning novel, *The Old Man and the Sea* (1952), where the archetypal conflict between man and nature is given a Christian resolution: "A man can be destroyed but not defeated." Though this forms the basis of the "Hemingway code", it was not sufficient enough to prevent his suicide on 2 July 1961. His memoir, *A Moveable Feast*, was, therefore, a nostalgic return to the "wonderful" 1920s, as were the last two novels published posthumously – *Islands in the Stream* (1970) and *The Garden of Eden* (1986). Consequently, there is a tendency to find in Hemingway's fiction of the twenties, the qualities which distinguish him as one of America's most notable modernists.

Modernist Poetry

Robert Frost

The inclusion of Robert Frost (1874–1963) among the poets who represent modern American poetry is usually qualified with several reservations. Frost was himself reluctant to use the experimental and untraditional thematic and formal features which became definitive preconditions of modernist writing. In fact, he is said to have remarked that he would rather play tennis without a net than write in free verse. Having spent much of his life working in a mill and in farming, Frost's poetry relies on the familiar and common concerns and rhythms of rural New England life, which found constant expression in his poems. As he told a friend, "I dropped to an everyday level of diction that even Wordsworth kept above." When Frost published his first two volumes of verse, *A Boy's Will* (1913) and *North of Boston* (1914), American poetry was undergoing a transition from the late Romanticism of Edward Arlington Robinson's poetry to the intimations of modernism in the writings of Vachel Lindsay, Carl Sandburg of the Chicago group and of Edgar Lee Masters. Yet, most of their poetry remained within a dominant American tradition that invoked Emerson, Whitman and Dickinson as the sources of their thought and language. Moreover, following his stay in England between 1912 and 1915, Frost's poetry also acquired influences of the British Georgian school of poetry, particularly that of Edward Thomas.

Frost's poetry has often been described as an intersection of self and place. The basic theme in his poems, thus, constitutes an encounter with, and a movement of, the self across a landscape, usually New England, whose best expression is in the lyric, "Two Look at Two". This emphasis on nature gives Frost his Romantic lineage; yet, this does not imply a belief in the Emersonian benignity of nature. As in most of his poetry, Frost's perception of nature is scored with a strong sense of ambivalence. In "Design", the work of the "dimpled spider" which has sucked a moth into "a white piece of rigid satin cloth" and placed it on a "white heal-all" is part of "What but design of darkness to appall?– / If design govern in a thing so small." The sense of doubt, implicit in the interrogative, gives Frost's apprehension of the created world a dualism which undermines the simplistic meanings of these natural details. Frost's relationship with nature had thus been characterised by his notion of "emblemism", which he explained as, "If my poetry has to have a name, I'd prefer to call it Emblemism – it's the viable emblem of things I'm after." In fact, it is this intriguing structure of Frost's poetry, which disguises complex meanings within a disarmingly simple rhetorical surface, that has brought him close to the modernists. His poetry is thus characterised by three contradictory impulses: detachment, irony and commitment. Having presented what he considers an ambiguity in a human situation, he is unable to reconcile the contrast between expectation and reality, and refrains from commitment. At other times, he is able to reasonably explain the irony and transcend the ambiguity into a relative sense of faith, as is evident in "The Birches":

> I'd like to get away from earth awhile
> And then come back to it and begin over.
> May no fate willfully misunderstand me
> And half grant what I wish and snatch me away
> Not to return. Earth's the right place for love:
> I don't know where it's likely to go better.

Defining "the figure a poem makes", Frost had said, "It begins in delight and ends in wisdom". In this sense, his poems involve a continuous process of discovery, both of the natural and human worlds. However, this quest for meaning involves a tension between that which is perceived and much that evades definition. This element of uncertainty permeates many of his poems, as in "For Once, Then, Something", where the speaker trying to find what is at the bottom of a well sees

> something more of the depths—and then I lost it
> . . . .
> . . . What was that whiteness?
> Truth? A pebble of quartz? For once, then, something.

Nevertheless, Frost considered poetry to be a momentary stay against the confusions of the world. The aesthetic that went into his poetry was a self-conscious recreation of what he called the "sound of sense": "I alone of English writers have consciously set myself to make music out of what I may call the sound of sense." He explained this sound of sense as the "living part of the poem", evident in the "intonation entangled somehow in the syntax idiom and meaning of a sentence". Therefore, a poem became a synthesis of verbal music and meaning, form and feeling, where the eye, but more the ear, was needed: "It is so and not otherwise that we get the variety that makes it fun to write and read. *The ear does it*. The ear is the only true writer and the only true reader."

Frost's modernism was as much a part of the incipient complexity in the simple surfaces of sense in sound, as it was in the conscious use of the traditional poetics of syntax, rhythm and rhyme which created a distinctive poetic experience. This often involved a sense of verbal play where Frost uses stanza, metre and rhyme to reinforce the irony of a dramatic situation presented in a poem. Many of his poems literally deal with play as in "The Birches"; but more important is the play that is expressed in Frost's metaphors in "The Road Not Taken" and "Mending Wall":

> He is all pines and I am apple orchard.
> My apple trees will never get across
> And eat the cones under his pines, I tell him.
> He only says, 'Good fences make good neighbors.' ("Mending Wall")

The portable wisdom that made Frost quite a celebrity in his later career, earning him several prizes and a notable performance at President John F. Kennedy's inauguration, thus requires an awareness of this aspect of the poems. Many of his most popular lyrics – such as "The Road Not Taken", "Two Tramps in Mud Time", "The Death of a Hired Man", "The Hill Wife" and"Home Burial" – display a duplicity of meaning, a gap between sense and sound. Frost's poetry thus evokes multiple interpretations – for instance, "Stopping by the Woods on a Snowy Evening" is seen as a death wish, an ethical statement involving social obligations, a record of a religious experience, and a symbol interrogating an existential crisis. This seems to justify his assertion to his friend

Thomas Mosher: "You are not going to make the mistake that Pound makes of assuming that my simplicity is that of an untutored child. I am not undesigning."

Ironically, therefore, it is Frost's deceptive simplicity that makes him a modernist. There is a Janus aspect in his poetry that looks before and after, drawing from nineteenth-century poetic idioms to announce the contraries that would redefine modern poetry in the twentieth. Though Frost was not an innovator, he believed that the demands of poetry inspired the poet to create "his own words as he goes". For him, these words were part of the life from which a poem drew its sustenance and value: "We write of things we see and we write in accents we hear. Thus we gather both our material and our technique with the imagination from life; and our technique becomes as much material as material itself." This has given to his poems their enduring quality, which makes Frost, even today, one of the most respected poets of America.

William Carlos Williams

Along with Frost, modern American poetry is represented by Wallace Stevens (1879–1955) and William Carlos Williams (1883–1963). In fact, Williams was probably one of the most self-consciously American among his compatriot modernist writers, emphasising the importance of national and cultural roots as the basis of the individual in poetry: "Place is the only reality, the true core of the individual. We live in one place and one time, but . . . only if we make ourselves sufficiently aware of it, do we join with others in other places." Williams was evidently referring to the expatriate American writer whose contribution to American modernism remained both significant and exilic. For Williams, the only means of speaking of oneself is to "return to the ground" of the "new locality" of America, as "place is the only universal".

Born in Rutherford, New Jersey, Williams, as a doctor, had travelled wide over Europe and the United States, and was influenced by European art and literary movements. However, an allegiance to the local and an indigenous idiom gave his writing a specific sense of place and time. Thus, he found inspiration in

American modernist painters and photographers such as Charles Demuth, Marsden Hartley, Alfred Stieglitz and Charles Sheeler. Like Wallace Stevens, Marianne Moore and the Objectivist poets, Williams sought to assimilate European modernism within an American context. Therefore, Williams's poems often tend to rest in the familiar and the homely, as in the lyric addressed to his wife, "This Is Just to Say". Poems with similar subjects include, "The Red Wheelbarrow", "Spring and All", "Between Walls" and many others published in his early volumes, *The Tempers* (1913) and *Al Que Quiere!* (1917), and also in a later work, *Pictures from Brueghel and Other Poems* (1962).

Williams's preoccupation with place gives his poetry a significant sense of history. This defines his attempt to write a national epic, *Paterson* (published in five volumes as it evolved from 1946 to 1958, and published in its final but incomplete form in 1963) in the tradition of Whitman. Paterson is an industrial city, beside the "filthy Passaic" and near Rutherford; it is also the name given to the representative American, the protagonist of the poem, who is both the poet and the democratic individual. As in his other poems, the universal is figured in the particular, as the poet mentions in the "Preface":

> To make a start,
> out of particulars
> and make them general.

The myth of Paterson is built through a series of improvisations involving history, folklore, letters, portraits of the people encountered around the city, and even meditations on poetry and slogans – a poetic exercise contemplated and enacted in the mind. Williams's poem, thus, uses a variety of expressive forms – verse, prose, drama, dialogue, anecdotes, interviews, excerpts from books and meditative passages which contain responses from a re-reading of the poem itself. "Unless there is / a new mind there cannot be a new line", became Williams's description of this endeavor in *Book Two*, attesting to the experimental nature of the poem which combined the traditions of the American epic and imagism.

Though he was mainly known as a poet, Williams was also a writer of short stories, novels, plays and influential literary criticism. His short stories were collected in *The Farmer's Daughter* (1961); his plays were also published in 1961 in *Many Loves and Other Plays*; and the trilogy of novels on his wife's family history, *White Mule*, *In the Money* and *The Build-Up* were published in 1937, 1940 and 1952. Towards the end of his career, Williams also devised a new verse form which he termed the "triadic" or "step-down line". This notion of the structured yet "variable foot" is used in the poems of *Pictures from Brueghel*, notably in "Asphodel, That Greeny Flower". Williams defined poetry as "a machine made of words"; yet, in spite of the technological metaphor, what he seems to imply is the belief that, in poetry, words become moments of revelation and discovery of the "thing" or "it". This "it" is variably defined as "beautiful thing!", "radiant gist", "luminous background", or "that secret and sacred presence". This presence underlies most things – from an individual's self to the most trivial objects like the plums which his wife had been saving for another meal in "'This is just to Say"'. Important to this awareness is the fact that language, the word, which by itself is senseless and ambiguous, becomes in the organised poëtic expression, a visionary gleam, as in these lines on the poet's desire to withhold his imminent moment of death, from "Asphodel, That Greeny Flower":

> There is something
> something urgent
> I have to say to you
> and you alone
> but it must wait
> while I drink in
> the joy of your approach
> perhaps for the last time.

Wallace Stevens

"Poetry", Wallace Stevens had said, "is the statement of a relation between a man and the world." In Stevens's poems, though this relationship, like that of William Carlos Williams, includes references to several places, it was more concerned with the mind's conception and interpretation of the world. Thus, throughout his poetic career, from *Harmonium* (1923) to his late poems such as "An Ordinary Evening in New Haven", Stevens considered poetry to be a continuous interaction of the mind and the world – what he termed as "imagination" and "reality". For, as he was to add in the collection of his aphorisms in *Adagia* (1957), he believed that "imagination is the only genius".

In this sense, there is a general consensus about reading Stevens's poetry as one which develops upon Romantic aesthetic preoccupations. This gives credence to his conviction that art and poetry were the only means of understanding reality – "a feeling about the world which nothing satisfies but poetry." However, the novelty and comic flamboyance of this early verse, collected in *Harmonium*, often anticipates the consciously abstract and philosophical meditations of his mature poems in *Ideas of Order* (1936), *The Man with the Blue Guitar and Other Poems* (1937), *Parts of a World* (1942), *Notes Towards a Supreme Fiction* (1942), *Esthétique du Mal* (1944), *The Auroras of Autumn* (1950), *Collected Poems* (1954) and *Opus Posthumous* (1957). Stevens's later poetry, therefore, displays features of Objectivist poetry. "Objectivist" was an epithet coined by Louis Zukofsky in 1930, to describe a school of contemporary poets whose writing paid scrupulous attention to both objects and events and also to the language of the poem, which was seen to be an "objectification" – implying that a poet's words create a new reality that is "an object consonant with his day". Yet, simultaneously, this poetry involves a "decreation" which undermines the materiality of the world and its expressive forms, and transforms it into a "supreme fiction". In *Notes Towards a Supreme Fiction*, Stevens thus presents a strange, illogical and unpredictable world – his "mundo" – which enables the reader to rediscover the originary one through "The imagination, the one reality / In this imagined world."

"We live in the mind", Stevens had written in a 1949 essay, "Imagination as Value". Most of Stevens's notable poems – "The Comedian as the Letter C", "The Man with the Blue Guitar", "Sunday Morning", "Thirteen Ways of Looking at a Blackbird",

"The Auroras of Autumn", "The Owl in the Sarcophagus" and "The Idea of Order at Key West" – are, primarily, meditations on the contemplative mind and the function of poetry. These consist of a concentrated series of meditative reflections, often so complex and obscure that they resist explanation. In fact, they endorse the poet's observation that "a poem need not have a meaning and like most things in nature often does not have"; thus, "Poetry must be irrational." This sense of irrationality involves a deliberate tendency to disrupt syntax and the logical structure of the sentences, as evident in "The Snow Man",

> For the listener, who listens in the snow
> And nothing himself beholds
> Nothing that is not there and the nothing that is.

At other times, Stevens gives precedence to the aural, rather than the grammatical, arrangement of the words by resorting to the use of alliteration and assonance, as in this example from "The Owl in the Sarcophagus":

> And she that in the syllable between life
> And death cries quickly, in a flash of voice,
> Keep you, keep you, I am gone, oh keep you as,
> My memory, is the mother of us all.

The world of Stevens's poetry is, therefore, a universe of literary tropes, whose self-reflexive nature is the basis of an autotelic significance of poetry necessary to the idea of modernism. The textual nature of poetry, this self-contained network of language, is thus a value unto itself. "Words are everything else in the world", writes Stevens, for "metaphor creates a new reality from which the original appears to be unreal." This substitution of the real by the fictional which is, in turn, renominated as the real, is a characteristic investment of the emerging theories of postmodernism, which Stevens anticipates in his poetry. Moreover, it resurrects the nineteenth-century debate of poetry and belief, which is fundamental to the poet's writing. "Poetry", Stevens had written in "The Man with the Blue Guitar", ". . . must take the place / Of empty heaven and its hymns." The traditional figure of the poet as priest is thus given a new valence in this liturgy of art, for "the great poems of heaven and hell had been written," he had observed, "and the great poem of earth remains to be written." Stevens envisages this poem as a dialogue between the Christian idea of redemption and the vision of an earthly paradise: "The greatest poverty is not to live / In a physical world." Though this material earth, which Stevens calls the "fat girl", is a universe of change and death, it is possible to transform it with the imagination to yield a sense of order and meaning: ". . . my green, my fluent mundo . . . will have stopped revolving except in crystal." This crystalline imaginative conception of the earth, which Stevens calls "the essential poem at the center of things", in "A Primitive Like an Orb", thus becomes the trope which holds the promise of an alternative form of redemption. Though in "The American Sublime", Stevens found it to be "The empty spirit / In vacant space", he was later to realise that it was "like / A new knowledge of reality", in "Not Ideas About the Thing but the Thing Itself" (1954).

◆ ◆ ◆

Thus, modern American poetry in the first fifty years of the twentieth century is characterised by a remarkable variety. While the poetry of Frost served as a bridge linking older traditions to the search for newness, while retaining its distinctive regional American identity, the poetry of Williams and Stevens drew from the dominant influences of the poetry of Ezra Pound, T. S. Eliot and the European intellectual developments during this period, to fashion an individual perception and understanding of their time and place. Williams's *Paterson* is thus often compared to Pound's *The Cantos* and Eliot's *The Waste Land* as an interpretation of modern life. With Stevens, however, after the echoes in his early verse, there was an admitted denial of Eliot: "Eliot and I are dead opposites and I have been doing about everything that he would not be likely to do." Yet, no other American modernist has expressed the need to understand the "chaos of life today and at the bottom of all disintegrations". Modern American poetry thus often expresses itself through its opposition to the ostensible signs of modernism, to find a means for, what Stevens calls, an "insight of a special kind into reality".

Modernist Drama

Eugene O'Neill

The growth of modern American drama in the early years of the twentieth century was a result of the history of resistance against the dominance of commercial theatre and entertainment of Broadway in New York. During the last years of the nineteenth century, Jane Addams and Ellen Gates formed the Hull-House Players (1897–1941) and the Chicago Hull-House Theater was established in 1901, initiating the Little Theater Movement across the United States. The theatre groups which made a significant contribution to the revival of modern drama in America during this time were Chicago's Little Theater, Provincetown, Massachusetts' (later New York's) Provincetown Players, founded in 1915, and the Group Theater formed in 1931. In fact, Eugene O'Neill's (1888–1953) first play, the one-act *Bound East for Cardiff* (1916), was produced by the Provincetown Players. In 1916, this group relocated to New York's Greenwich Village and, subsequently, two more plays by O'Neill, *Beyond the Horizon* (1920) and *The Emperor Jones* (1920), were staged. Writing in *Theater U.S.A.* (1959), Bernard Hewitt observed that with these plays, American drama had finally "come of age": "No longer need Americans look abroad for the best in contemporary drama; the native product could stand comparison with the finest Europe could offer."

O'Neill was born into a family of stage performers. His father James O'Neill had become a wealthy matinee idol playing the lead in nearly five thousand performances of *The Count of Monte Cristo*. Confined to a sanatorium for tuberculosis in 1912, O'Neill discovered the writings of Henrik Ibsen, August Strindberg and the Greek tragic playwrights, and finally decided, "I want to be an artist or nothing." O'Neill's *Bound East for Cardiff* earned him a place as a special student in a drama workshop, George Baker's 47 Workshop in Harvard, and this encouraged the publication of *Thirst and Other One-Act Plays* (1914). There followed *Before Breakfast* (1916), *The Moon of the Caribbees and Six Other Plays of the Sea* (1919), and *Beyond the* Horizon (1920) for which he was awarded a Pulitzer Prize that year. In a characteristic American manner, O'Neill admitted to "always trying to do the big thing", wanting to create a "big work" dealing with a "big Subject". This was not simply a desire for success but the expression of his faith in the fact that, ". . . I know I have most to give to a theater." He thus attempted to adapt various forms of drama in his repertoire, which included classical Greek tragedy, Ibsen's social plays, Strindberg's domestic drama, examples of German expressionist theatre and even local melodrama. In an important sense, O'Neill undertook the task of reinventing American drama to give it a legitimate place in world theatre.

O'Neill's career can be divided into two phases. The first phase includes the plays of the 1920s and 30s – *The Emperor Jones, The Hairy Ape* (1922), *All God's Chillun Got Wings* (1924), *Desire Under the Elms* (1924), *The Great God Brown* (1926), *Lazarus Laughed* (1927), *Strange Interlude* (1928) and *Mourning Becomes Electra* (1931). Thus, most of his major plays preceded the Nobel Prize awarded to him in 1936. *Ah Wilderness!* (1933), a comedy, and *Days Without End* (1934) were the last two plays he wrote before he suffered a nervous breakdown and retreated from the stage for over a decade. However, he returned in 1946 with *The Iceman Cometh* and *Long Day's Journey into Night* – written in 1941 but produced posthumously in 1956. This second phase also comprises *A Moon for the Misbegotten* (1947), considered his last play, and those staged after his death – *Hughie* (1958) and two others from an eleven-play cycle he had planned, *A Tale of Possessors Self-dispossessed: A Touch of the Poet* (1957) and its sequel, *More Stately Mansions* (1964).

O'Neill's beginnings in drama suggested an Ibsenian lineage with plays on the conflict between the individual and society rendered in broad realist lines of delineation. However, this conventional mode of dramatic expression also chose to practice distinctive variations of form that turned the plays into profound explorations of suppressed desires and anxieties. In a 1932 essay, O'Neill had thus stated that he wanted "to express those profound hidden conflicts of the mind which the probing of psychology continued to disclose. . . . For what, at bottom, is the new psychological insight into human cause and effect but a study in masks, an exercise in unmasking?" In *The Emperor Jones*, *Desire Under the Elms*, *Strange Interlude* and *Mourning Becomes Electra*, O'Neill is committed to this examination of persons and interpersonal relationships in psychological terms. This concern, therefore, leads him to constant experimentation and innovation of dramatic language and form, which constitutes his contribution to modernist American drama. O'Neill's use of techniques from expressionist drama involved not only the literal adaptation of masks in *The Great God Brown* and in *Lazarus Laughed*, but also influenced a rewriting of Sophocles's tragedy against the historical context of the American Civil war in *Mourning Becomes Electra*. The dramatist thus admitted to a shift in method, but justified this as necessary for a deeper understanding of human experiences. Commenting on his play, *Welded* (1923), O'Neill had said,

> I want to write a play that is truly realistic. The term is used loosely on the stage, where most of the so-called plays deal with what might be called the soul of the character. It deals with a thing that makes the character that person and no other. Strindberg's *Dance of Death* is an example of that real realism.

Though O'Neill's plays have a factual coherence, there is an increasing turn towards abandoning given events and circumstances in order to study past transgressions and secret guilt. Thus, the dramatist's sense of "real realism" is a means to explore forms of spiritual quest or a tragic acceptance of alienation and loss. This is amply demonstrated in *Dynamo* (1929), *The Hairy Ape*, *The Emperor Jones* and *Desire Under the Elms*. Language and dialect are important elements in these plays in defining characters and dramatic tensions. In his use of poetic symbolism, interior monologue, the chorus and the choreographed arrangement of scenes (in *Lazarus Laughed* and *All God's Chillun Got Wings*), together with his experiments in stage lighting and sound design (in *The Emperor Jones* and *The Great God Brown*), O'Neill was able to develop a dramatic experience which is often termed "total theatre".

Like the Italian playwright Luigi Pirandello, O'Neill was obsessed with the idea of the illusions of theatre being a reflection of the shifting realities of life. *The Iceman Cometh* deals with the attempt of a group of men to confront the truth about their lives. However, this turns out to be ironical when it is revealed that it is the illusion – the "pipe dream" – which sustains most people in the world. As Larry Slade, one of the inmates of the boarding-house where the play is set, confirms, "To hell with the truth. . . . As the history of the world proves, the truth has no bearing on anything. It is irrelevant and immaterial, as the lawyers say." The play thus involves the various games and stories that the characters create to withdraw from the real, or to keep truth at bay. This is similar to the tragedy of Mary Tyrone in *Long Day's Journey into Night*. Based on the playwright's own life, this play is not only O'Neill's attempt to come to terms with his experiences as a youth, but the fortunes of the Tyrone family are representative of the loss of faith which characterised what could be considered an "American tragedy". In fact, towards the end of his career, O'Neill became increasingly preoccupied with the past – both his own and that of the nation. In 1946, the dramatist observed, "I do not think you can write anything of value or understanding about the present. You can only write about life if it is far enough in the past. The present is too mixed up with superficial values; you can't know what is important and what is not. The past which I have chosen is one I know."

During the Harvard workshop on drama, George Baker, the supervising professor, is believed to have asked O'Neill why he preferred "grim and depressing subjects". The young writer's reply was candid and simple: "Life looked that way." The dramatist's inclination for tragedy should not be used to obscure his skill in the comic interludes of his plays; yet, despite the variety, his drama reiterates his tragic vision, which remains a significant commentary on human desire and defeat.

Tennessee Williams

Tennessee Williams (1911–83) began his career as a dramatist with a small political theatre group in St Louis called the Mummers, writing a series of protest plays. These were often developed out of his short stories and were critical of industrialists, war profiteers, prison officials and bureaucrats. Williams believed that art should be a "criticism of things as they exist", and in some of these, largely unknown, early plays – *Not About Nightingales*, *Fugitive Kind*, *Candles to the Sun* and *Stairway to the Sky* – he attacked the political and economic system responsible for the degradation of the lives of individuals. He was to insist, "My interest in social problems is as great as my interest in the theatre. . . . I try to write all my plays so that they carry some social message along with the story." In fact, he pointed out that he preferred the one-act form during this time as he "found it easier to get across a message and with more impact if I made it brief". However, this is not to imply that Williams's later work moved away from social concerns. Though there seems to be a general opinion that his major work retreated into the sexual and psychological tensions of isolated and frustrated individuals, he continued to comment on contemporary political issues and injustices. In 1950, he observed, "Our contemporary American society seems no longer inclined to hold itself open to very explicit criticism from within." Speaking against the State Department for impounding Arthur Miller's passport in 1957, he felt that "no man has a monopoly of right or virtue any more than a man has a corner on duplicity and evil and so forth". Repeatedly emerging as an oppositional voice, Williams believed that "the moral decay of America" began with the Korean War but updated this opinion to the Vietnam War which he described as an "incomprehensible evil", which seemed to prove that "this once great and beautiful democracy" had become "the death merchant of the world". This goes to justify Miller's defense of Williams's work:

> Certainly I never regarded him as a sealed-off aesthete he was thought to be. There is a radical politics of the soul as well as that of the ballot box and the picket line. If he was not an activist, it was not for lack of desire for justice, nor did he consider a theatre profoundly involved in society and politics . . . somehow unaesthetic or beyond his interest.

The Depression had a profound influence on Williams's plays; complementary to this was the fact that he was deeply involved in a contemplation of the consequences of the Reconstruction of the American South. In both *The Glass Menagerie* (1945) and *A Streetcar Named Desire* (1947) a consciousness of time and change is a predominant anxiety. This is clearly emphasised by the central role played by memory in *The Glass Menagerie*: "Being a memory play, it is dimly lighted, it is sentimental, it is not realistic", Tom Wingfield, the narrator, states at the play's beginning. Tom's memories involve his mother, Amanda, a Southern belle who clings to the faded illusions of the past, and his sister, Laura, a crippled and shy young woman, who has retreated into a private world symbolised by the menagerie of small glass animal figures she has collected and preserved over the years. The play consists of a series of scenes in which Tom attempts to engage his family with "an emissary from a world that we were somehow set apart from". The experience ends in disaster. Williams's play is about this alienation of the family from the "so called world of ours"; yet, this failure, Tom realises as he leaves, gives the two women an alternative refuge, which is equally seductive and valuable as their sanctuary of glass animals. Significantly, Williams explained his involvement in the theatre as an attempt to create "imaginary worlds into which I can retreat from the real world because . . . I've never made any kind of adjustment to the real world." This statement seems to identify the two main thematic directions of his plays – a psychological neurosis, on the one hand, and art on the other. While Amanda's obsessive chatter is her means of using language in her compulsive struggle to survive the loss of her past, Laura's menagerie is an art work which shields her from "Knowledge! . . . Money! . . . Power!", identified by the gentleman caller as the necessary means of existence. In Tom, Williams also dramatises the aspirations of freedom required for his development as an artist, but which are inevitably weighed down by the guilt of betrayal. In an important sense, *The Glass Menagerie* seems to reflect Williams's own life. His plays thus tend to deal with characters who are symbolic or literal writers or artists; hence, the theatre is a central metaphor in his drama – for theatre or art implies a desire to overcome the ravages of time: "It is this continual rush of time . . . ," Williams writes, "that deprives our actual lives of so much dignity and meaning, and it is, perhaps more than anything else, the *arrest of time* which has taken place in a completed work of art that gives certain plays their feeling of depth and significance . . ." (Italics Williams).

Set in New Orleans, the title of *A Streetcar Named Desire* was actually prompted by "two streetcars, one named DESIRE and the other named CEMETERY". For Williams, the regular service of these vehicles seemed to have "some symbolic bearing", bringing the two opposing verities of experience into a dramatic relationship with each other. This is the conflict which ultimately destroys Blanche Dubois who is caught between death and desire in her "long parade to the graveyard". The play, thus, deals with her conflict with Stanley Kowalski, her brother-in-law, which forces her to confront her own sexual repressions and anxieties. Blanche, whose name itself suggests whiteness and virginity, is a Southern lady in a world which has no place for such ladies; hers is, therefore, a struggle for survival using the redundant means of language and theatricality to recover her self-respect in a dominantly male environ. Thus, in spite of her purity, culture, idealism and the romance of the past, she represents illusions, which Stanley exposes as "lies": "I've been on to you from the start! . . . Not once did you pull the wool over this boy's eyes!" In fact, it is this mutual antagonism which defines the fascination between the two: "We've had this date with each other from the beginning!" says Stanley to Blanche before he rapes her. *A Streetcar Named Desire,* therefore, has to be understood on multiple levels of signification. It has a fairytale pattern of the beauty and the beast, expressing the brutality and mystery in sexuality. It regrets the loss of a dead world and the inability to accept the one that is emergent. It expresses the archetypal conflict of the female and male principles, and yet, finally, it remains a tragedy of two strongly individualised characters engaged in destroying each other.

Williams's plays, therefore, tend to avoid the formal terms of a traditional realistic mode of representation. In fact, he admits his distaste for "the straight realist play with its genuine Frigidaire and authentic ice cubes, its characters that speak exactly as the audience speaks". This would imply that in his plays, the plot or, for that matter, the sets are not there only to provide a context for the action; everything contributes to the psychological exploration of the relationships and the emotional conflicts which form the basis of his drama. Williams once observed that "poetry doesn't have to be words. . . . In the theatre it can be situations, it can be silences." This would justify his preference for the graphic and appropriate metaphor, either as an object or as a gesture, which almost serves as a motif – much in the manner used in Symbolist theatre where the play becomes an explanation of a particular poetic image which attempts to express a feeling or a state of consciousness. However, Williams's theatre does not present the subtle tones and rhythms of poetry found in Stéphane Mallarmé, Paul Verlaine or W. B. Yeats; the poetic in Williams often undermines conventional idioms and images in the shocking devices of the sensational, the violent or the absurd. In his plays, the characters deal in ambivalent and allusive metaphors sometimes unrelated to the immediate moment in which language itself becomes a means of defence against the harsh realities of the world.

In his later plays, Williams was not able to achieve the emotional and formal consistency of *A Streetcar Named Desire. Cat on a Hot Tin Roof* (1955) presents a dual narrative dealing with the relative value of two sons being considered by Big Daddy Pollitt for the inheritance of his estate. This new responsibility becomes an opportunity for Maggie, the "cat" of the title, to revalue her own relationship with her husband. While in *Orpheus Descending* (1957) Williams tried to explore the absurd politics of the South, *The Night of the Iguana* (1961) uses several narratives to understand the sense of loss suffered by individuals whose youth and options have run out and have left them to prepare for a final performance to rediscover meaning in their lives. During this phase, many of Williams's plays resort to weak sentimental solutions, as in the minor comedies – *Rose Tattoo* (1951) and *Period of Adjustment* (1961). *Suddenly Last Summer* (1958) tends towards sensationalism and the others, *Camino Real* (1953), *Sweet Bird of Youth* (1959) and *Summer and Smoke* (1968), do not achieve the same dramatic balance between experience and emotion, which marked his earlier plays. Williams's last years were plagued by alcoholism, addiction to drugs and depression. Though the plays of this period of decline – *The Milk Train Doesn't Stop Here Anymore* (1963), *In the Bar of a Tokyo Hotel* (1969) and *Clothes for a Summer Hotel* (1980) – recall the pathos and intensity of the earlier plays, they tend to become repetitive and obsessed with the personal confessions of a failed artist.

Against the social changes in America of the 1940s and 50s, Williams's plays, with their emphasis on sexual and psychological conflicts, seemed to be rather unfamiliar and subversive. This was partly due to the fact that they were sceptical of conventional morality, thus substituting familiar pieties with an appeal for greater human compassion and understanding. Williams recognised the inexorable waste brought about by time; yet, he denied the possible consolations offered by the past. This contingent view of existence also explains his early dismissal of realism as a relevant mode for his drama, preferring a more complex language of the imagination and its aesthetic figures to revalue the real and, thereby, find an acceptable meaning for the experiences that are portrayed in the plays.

Arthur Miller

The Depression was one of the most significant historical events which shaped modern American drama. The stock market crash in 1929 reduced the American economy to a state of bankruptcy and destroyed the lives of innumerable people. Not only was it the inevitable consequence of a post-war boom, but it also became an implicit criticism of an irresponsible financial system which was the basis of the growth of the nation. Arthur Miller (1915–2005), whose own family was nearly destroyed by the Depression, was to return to this event repeatedly in his plays. The Depression, he felt, was one of the two major catastrophes in American history – the other being the Civil War. For Miller, it seemed that America's past was avenging itself, and he considered the Crash a form of moral judgment: "America has been on some kind of obscene trip, looking to get rich at any cost right through the 20s, at any cost to the spirit, and had elevated into power the men who could most easily lead that kind of quest. And that aggrandizement is what led to the disaster of '29 and the Crash." Together with *Death of a Salesman* (1949), the plays which revolved around this economic meltdown were *The Man Who Had All the Luck* (1944), *After the Fall* (1964), *The Price* (1968) and *The American Clock* (1980).

Therefore, a definitive aspect of Miller's drama is its element of social protest. The protagonist of *All My Sons* (1947) is made to learn that the "consequences of actions are as real as the actions themselves". Joe Keller, who became rich supplying defective airplane parts during the war, has to confront the truth that he was responsible for the deaths of several young airmen, including the suicide of his own son, who was forced into it by the knowledge of his father's guilt. In the play, Miller emphasised the links between the individual and the society, the past and the present, actions and their consequences, for he believed that, "Society is inside man and man is inside society." This Ibsenian and naturalist assumption became, for Miller, the grounds for an examination of the themes of guilt and innocence, which he identified in a preview note to this play, "In all plays and books I try to take settings and dramatic situations from life which involves real questions of right and wrong. Then I set out rather implacably and in the utmost situations I can find, the moral dilemma and try to point a real, though hard, path out." Miller's social criticism, thus, evolves from a recognition that the private and the public are inseparable, and the tragic circumstances in his plays are implicitly structured by this implacable causal justification. Joe can, therefore, only find redemption by pursuing his son's action and this moral emphasis is the true end of art: ". . . there could be no aesthetic form without a moral world, only notes without a staff."

Miller described *Death of a Salesman* as "a love story between a man and his son and, in a crazy way between both of them and America". Thus, as in *All My Sons*, the family is central in Miller's drama and, by extension, the nation is imbricated in its fortunes. Willy Loman, the protagonist in the play, is often seen as a victim of the remorseless forces of capitalism which only recognises his economic value. Miller's play, therefore, attempts to find a justification for the aspirations and sense of dignity of ordinary individuals as implied in Willy's name:

> How may a man make of the outside world a home? How and in what ways must he struggle, what must he strive to

> change and overcome within himself and outside himself if he is to find safety, the surrounding of love, the ease of the soul, the sense of identity and honor which, evidently, all men have connected in their memories with the idea of family?

Referring to the status of a salesman in earlier times, Willy tells Howard, "In those days there was personality in it, Howard. There was respect and comradeship, and gratitude in it. Today, it's all cut and dried, and there's no chance for bringing friendship to bear – or personality."

Willy's tragedy lies in the fact that he invests his faith completely in this illusion of success that his trade symbolises and which is promoted as a national myth – the American Dream. In Miller's drama, the past impinges and is simultaneous with the present; this involves a play where "instead of one incident in one time frame succeeding another" it would "display past and present concurrently with neither one ever coming to a stop". Thus, the past became "a formality, a dimmer present, for everything we are is at every moment alive in us". Miller had initially thought of calling the play "The Inside of His Head", underscoring the development of his dramatic method from an earlier naturalism towards a psychological inquiry in a play

> . . . that did not still the mind's simultaneity, did not allow a man to 'forget' and turned him to see present through past and the past through present, a form that in itself, quite apart from the content and meaning, would be inescapable as a psychological process and as a collecting point for all that his life in society had poured into him.

Therefore, Miller frequently resorts to experimentation with dramatic techniques in his use of variations in lighting and the fluidity of stage-space: "Whenever the action is in the present the actors observe the imaginary wall-lines, entering the house through its door at the left. But in the scenes of the past these boundaries are broken, and characters enter or leave a room by stepping 'through' a wall onto the forestage."

Having discovered the empty rhetoric of the dream of success he had imbued in his sons, Willy's failure is denied any redemption except that of suicide. However, this finality has an ironical consolation in the fact that his son had forgiven his weakness as only human; that Charley had upheld the validity of the fact that "a salesman's got to dream"; and that the playwright had also admitted that

> . . . there is a nobility. . . in Willy's struggle. Maybe it comes from refusal ever to relent, to give up. . . . People who are able to accept their frustrated lives do not change conditions. . . . You must look behind his ludicrousness to what he is actually confronting and that is as serious a business as anyone can imagine.

Miller's next important play, *The Crucible* (1953), based on the infamous Salem witch trials of 1692, was an indictment of what he considered a notoriously similar dragnet of the US Congress's House Un-American Activities Committee (HUAC) led by Senator Joseph McCarthy. The Committee was formed in May 1938 to weed out communists and communist sympathisers in America. Miller's first reaction was an adaptation of Ibsen's *An Enemy of the People* (1950) which, he felt, expressed "the central theme of our social life today . . . the question of whether the democratic vision of the truth ought to be a source of guilt at a time when the mass of men condemn it as a dangerous and devilish lie." *The Crucible* recreates the mass hysteria about witches in seventeenth-century New England, in which John Proctor, the protagonist, and his wife, Elizabeth, become implicated. Proctor can save his wife if he admits his infidelity – a confession, ironically dismissed by Elizabeth's refusal to betray him. Proctor is promised exoneration provided he publicly recanted his earlier opposition of the authorities and revealed more names of such deviants. Though tempted, he ultimately refuses to compromise, invoking the same image of hell-fire that is used by the judges to damn the victims, "A fire, a fire is burning! I hear the boot of Lucifer! I see his filthy face! . . . God damns our kind especially, and we will burn, we will burn together." Though dissimilar to the earlier plays, *The Crucible* has several thematic links with them, particularly in the iteration of the issue of guilt and the implacable nature of the past. Moreover,

Miller was able to give his play a distinctive meaning by comparing it with an example from Greek tragedy:

> Take a play like *Oedipus*, it's not just a personal, psychological or psychiatric story; it is also a story of the legitimacy of authority and the irony of authority seeing evil outside of itself when evil is right in it, in the authority. These are political ideas *par excellence*. . . . I think I go further back than the recent bourgeois tragedies which are deep, personal, psychological works exclusively . . . and have no reference beyond the world that they present.

In 1956, Miller was summoned to testify before the HUAC and was convicted of contempt of Congress as he refused to divulge the names of his friends and fellow writers who were allegedly communists. This was also a period of personal turmoil: he divorced Mary Slattery to wed the celebrity Marilyn Monroe, but this marriage too ended in 1961. These tensions seem to percolate into the plays of this period. Though *A View from the Bridge* (1956) actually deals with the problems of illegal immigration, Miller's treatment of Eddie Carbonne's desperate and unrequited love for his niece assumes a complexity of meaning not to be simply understood as duty. Similarly, in *After the Fall* (1964) and *Incident at Vichy* (1964), the dramatist tries to examine the issues of loyalty and betrayal which dominated his life in the recent past. *The Price* (1968), however, was an attempt to revive a comic treatment of the reunion of two brothers in order to sell the dead father's furniture; yet, this ordinary duty becomes fraught with guilt, frustrations and accusations regarding family disloyalty and irresponsibility. While *The Archbishop's Ceiling* (1977) is a reiteration of the author's criticism of the state control of individual freedom, *The American Clock* (1980) returns to the Depression Era in order to rewind "the American clock . . . in search of those feelings that once ruled our lives and were stolen from us all by time".

Among the last plays that Miller wrote, *The Ride Down Mount Morgan* (1991) remains important for its attack on the cynical self-sufficiency that had become pervasive in America in the seventies and eighties of the previous century. However, the playwright's final comment about these times is recorded in his last play, *Mr. Peters' Connections* (1998), where the old Mr Peters fails to find a coherent meaning in the experiences, events, people and places that have now been irretrievably lost in the flow of time. For Miller, however, this sense of loss and despair would constitute one version of the truth. Committed to an awareness of the relative meanings of the real, the dramatist admitted that though, "I can't say I believe you can ascertain the real, I do believe in the obligations of trying to do so." Ironically, while this obligation involved an acceptance of the facts of failure, it was also an equal assertion of the necessity of a continuing struggle, reaffirmed in Happy's words at the end of *Death of a Salesman*: "All right, boy. I'm gonna show you and everybody else that Willy Loman did not die in vain. He had a good dream. It's the only dream you can have – to come out number-one man. He fought it out here, and this is where I'm gonna win it for him."

♦ ♦ ♦

As is quite evident from the works of the major writers of this period, American modernism was defined by a conjunction of the artistically experimental and the international with a spirit of the local and the native. This duality involved a conflict between the American notion of the "usable past" and that of the modernist idea of tradition which, according to Pound and Eliot, was to be wholly European. However, this tension was resolved to some extent by the contribution of the immigrants to America such as Alfred Stieglitz who had introduced, between 1907 and 1912, the modern European masters of art in his small New York gallery called "291", before their official exhibition at the Armory Show in 1913. Yet, as Van Wyck Brooks (1886–1963) and other critics who visited his salon noted, Stieglitz's own work as a noted photographer was marked by an evocation of America, as he had admitted that he was "trying to establish for myself an America in which I could breathe as a free man".

In fact, the technological, economic and social energies that would shape modernist writing had already made an impact on American poetry and the novel by the end of the nineteenth and early twentieth centuries. American modernism is, therefore, distinguished by an egalitarian cultural inclusiveness which accommodates the "higher" literary forms of poetry, drama and the novel and those of popular culture, Hollywood cinema and the visual techniques of advertising. It is often argued that the "avant garde" also had an American origin precisely in this fusion of the experimental and the popular and commercial. An understanding of American modernism, therefore, remains incomplete without a consideration of the contribution of the Harlem Renaissance and the notable African American writers. The vital connection of African American vernacular culture and jazz with modernism is evident in Scott Fitzgerald's *Tales of a Jazz Age* (1922). In fact, the syncopated rhythms and the formal variations in jazz also contributed to the formal experiments in literary modernism.

CHAPTER 5

From the Beat Generation to American Postmodernism

Anglocentric American Literature from World War II to the Present

Krishna Sen

Although ethnic (African American, Native American and Chicano) as well as multicultural diasporic writing had been produced before the Second World War, it was only in the decades after that War that Anglocentric and non-Anglocentric American literatures developed widely divergent trajectories. To do both these streams of literature full justice, it is necessary to deal with them separately from this point onwards. The decades from the end of the Second World War in 1945 to the twenty-first century have been tumultuous times for the United States. It emerged from the War as the strongest power in the world – politically, militarily, economically, technologically, culturally (in the resurgence of the Hollywood film and popular culture), and in outer space. Further, the US cast itself as the self-styled protector of liberal democracy, a role it professes even today. Under this vaunted aegis, the US not only got embroiled in the near-nuclear Cold War with the former Soviet Union, but also fought wars in Korea, Vietnam, Afghanistan and the Middle East, and "proxy wars" in Central America. The Vietnam War sparked massive protests among American youth, while attempts to suppress militant Islamic movements led to the apocalyptic destruction of the World Trade Center in New York on "9/11" (11 September 2001). At home, the US witnessed an unprecedented social churning that challenged its dominant WASP (that is, white, Anglo-Saxon, Protestant) culture. The 1960s saw successful Civil Rights campaigns by African Americans, Native Americans and Mexican Americans, while liberalised immigration laws enabled large Asian diasporas to settle in the US. Conservative resistance to this so-called undermining of "white" America generated virulent right-wing ethnic and political opposition. All this, plus technological competition from Japan and South Korea, and the repeated global economic downturns that impacted America, somewhat dimmed the post-war elation. Playwright Sam Shepard said, in a September 2014 interview, "We are on our way out as a culture. America doesn't make anything any more! The Chinese make it!"

This is, of course, an overstatement. However, it is literature and the arts that responded most acutely to these events in terms of critique, soul-searching, and the quest for alternative values. Thus, America's role in the Second World War was trenchantly critiqued by realists like James Jones (1921–77) in *From Here to Eternity* (1951) and *The Thin Red Line* (1962), and Norman Mailer (1923–2007) in *The Naked and the Dead* (1948), in the black comedy of *Catch-22* (1961) by Joseph Heller (1923–99), and the surreal absurdity of Kurt Vonnegut (1922–2007) in *Slaughterhouse-Five* (1969) and Thomas Pynchon (b.1937) in *Gravity's Rainbow* (1973). The alienation of American youth was memorably captured by J. D. Salinger (1919–2010) through the character of Holden Caulfield in *The Catcher in the Rye* (1951), while the unsettling eruption of free-wheeling social and sexual mores in small-town white America was chronicled by John Updike (1932–2009) in his Rabbit series about the middle-class American Everyman Harry "Rabbit" Angstrom, and in other novels like *Couples* (1961). Powerful ethnocentric writing by America's ethnic and diasporic minorities challenged the supremacy of "white" American literature – this large body of significantly influential countercultural writing will be discussed in Chapters 6 and 7. Yet, mainstream white authors did not lag behind in innovative experimentation and counter-discursive themes. This was an era of exciting artistic cross-fertilisation between print and other media, with most leading authors working also in film and television or being involved with the visual media, in that their novels and plays were being made into (often very successful) films. Exceptional examples of these new trends in American literature from the mid-twentieth century to the early twenty-first century are the concurrent productions of the Beat Generation, American neo-realism, Jewish American writing (in its delineation of a *white* minority culture), and American postmodernism. What is most interesting in this body of experimental Anglocentric writing (running parallel to strong minority literatures with authors like Maxine Hong Kingston, Toni Morrison and Leslie Marmon Silko) is the veritable tug-of-war between realism and hyperrealism, the normative and the non-normative, and even the literary and the non-literary, as authors strained form and content to articulate unimaginable experiences from the moon landing to "9/11".

The Beat Generation

Writers belonging to what came to be known as the "Beat Generation" (also called "the Beats") are not the same as the "beatniks" (a synonym for hippies). The phrase "Beat Generation" emerged in 1952, while the derogatory word "beatnik" was invented by San Francisco journalist Herb Caen in 1958 to denote the pot-smoking, sexually permissive, hedonistic bohemians who frequented California's beaches. This was not the worldview of the Beats, although their uninhibited lifestyles (political dissent, proximity to Black intellectuals, dabbling in oriental religions, drugs, homosexuality, etc.) provoked considerable negative media coverage and frequent confusion with the beatniks.

The term "Beat Generation" was coined by Jack Kerouac, who co-founded the movement with Allen Ginsberg and other like-minded young writers in New York in the early 1950s. The phrase was modelled on the "Lost Generation" (a common term for the post–World War I generation), and sought to fuse the connotations of "dead beat" ("exhausted" [by capitalist America's moral decline]), "beaten down" ("underprivileged") and "beatitude", thus conveying the range of their social, philosophical and spiritual concerns. It was first used in Kerouac's interview with John Clellon Holmes (author of the 1952 Beat novel *Go*) that appeared under the title "This is the Beat Generation" in the *New York Times Magazine* on 16 November 1952. Holmes wrote: "It involves a nakedness of mind, and ultimately, of soul . . . needing no bohemianism or imposed eccentricity to express it." In his 1958 essay, "Aftermath: The Philosophy of the Beat Generation", Kerouac spelt out the mix of underground and existential elements that inspired their debunking of the "freedom machines" that America was purported to be:

> The Beat Generation, that was a vision that we had . . . ragged, beatific, beautiful in an ugly gracious new way . . . full of intense conviction . . . taking drugs, digging bop, having flashes of insight, experiencing the 'derangement of the senses,' talking strange, being poor and glad, prophesying a new style for American culture. . . . We had our mystic heroes and wrote, nay sung novels about them, erected long poems celebrating the new 'angels' of the American underground . . . [but] the generation itself was short-lived and small in number.

Short-lived or not, the Beat Generation had an enormous impact, not only on America, but also on global literature, popular culture and cinema.

The prominent members of the Beat Generation were William S. Burroughs (1914–97), Lawrence Ferlinghetti (b.1919), Jack Kerouac (1922–69), Allen Ginsberg (1926–97), Neal Cassady (1926–68), John Clellon Holmes (1926–88), Gregory Corso (1930–2001), and Gary Snyder (b.1930). They came from middle-class backgrounds, nearly all were graduates from prestigious institutions like Harvard and Columbia, and were involved with music, art and film, as well as print literature. Of these, Kerouac was the main inspiration and theorist, Burroughs the most radically iconoclastic, and Ginsberg the acknowledged icon of the Beat Generation, while Snyder is widely recognised as one of America's greatest living poets.

William S. Burroughs's first two novels were titled *Queer* (1951, published 1985) and *Junkie* (1953). He shot to dubious fame with *Naked Lunch* (1959), which was banned in parts of America because of the alleged obscenity of its content and language. The book was absolved of obscenity charges and the ban lifted in a 1966 trial. This partly surreal, perhaps partly autobiographical, episodic narrative moving fluidly in time and space, follows drug addict and paedophile William Lee (one of Burroughs's several pen names) as he moves from America to Mexico to Tangier to a dream-like "Interzone" under the influence of marijuana. "Interzone" became a cult term, and was also the title of Burroughs's 1969 collection of science fiction and fantasy stories. The random nature of the narrative in *Naked Lunch* is intensified in the next three novels, clustered as *The Nova Trilogy – The Soft Machine* (1961), *The Ticket that Expanded* (1962) and *Nova Express* (1964). Here Burroughs attempted to craft "a new mythology for the Space Age", where technology overpowers humanity. The trilogy became critically infamous for what Burroughs dubbed the "cut-up technique" – using a new invention, the computer, to cut certain sections from a continuous text, and then paste them back arbitrarily to create an inscrutable effect, as in, "They all went away and sent papers . . . The Dead Man write for you like a major . . . Enter *vecinos* . . ." (from *The Soft Machine*). Parts of the trilogy were also designed as collages using "cut-up" print and illustrations. *The Wild Boys, A Book of the Dead* (1971) is a grotesque and violent, partly "cut-up", account of a drug-addicted homosexual commune plotting to overthrow Western civilisation. In 1979, Burroughs was commissioned to write the script for a film based on Alan Nourse's dystopian 1974 science fiction novel, *The Bladerunner* (slang for "black marketeer") and produced what was in effect a fresh sci-fi novel titled *Blade Runner*, which became a cult book in its own right: however, the enormously successful 1982 science fiction cult movie *Blade Runner* did not use either of these sources. Burroughs's last work, just before his memoir titled *My Education: A Book of Dreams* (1995), was *The Red Night Trilogy – Cities of the Red Night* (1981), *The Place of Dead Roads* (1983) and *The Western Lands* (1987). This trilogy once again envisions a dystopian present and a free-wheeling futuristic utopia. Burroughs frequently revised his novels, and the many versions of a single text were part of his strategy of deliberate mystification.

Jack Kerouac, who famously began a poem with "The story of man / makes me sick", wrote fourteen novels of which two became archetypal narratives of the Beat Generation – *On the Road* (1957) and *The Dharma Bums* (1958). *On the Road*, like many of his semi-autobiographical works such as *The Subterraneans* (1958) and *Big Sur* (1962), is a *roman à clef* featuring his Beat colleagues and other literary friends under fictional names. Here, Burroughs is Old Bull Lee and Ginsberg is Carlo Marx, while Kerouac is the narrator Sal Paradise and his friend Dean is Neal Cassady. But this picaresque tale caught the imagination of young America, not because of these insider jokes, but because it was the quintessential American "open road" novel, as Sal hitchhikes across the breadth of the country, stopping and moving as he pleases, in a symbolic gesture of total freedom from all commitments – "on the road map was one long red line called Route 6 that led from the tip of Cape Cod clear down to Ely, Nevada, and then dipped down to Los Angeles. I would just stay on 6, I said to myself." *The Dharma Bums* chronicles a much later phase when Japhy Ryder (Gary Snyder) introduces Ray Smith (Kerouac) to Buddhism. During an idyllic summer of hiking, rock-climbing, jazz evenings and poetry reading sessions (including Ginsberg's celebrated 1955 debut reading of *Howl*, which is called *Wail* in this novel), Ray searches for meaning in his life by exploring the sayings of the Buddha. Once again, this was the era when American youth were embracing Zen Buddhism, yoga and various guru cults, and the book struck a chord with them and became widely popular.

Allen Ginsberg epitomised the Beat Generation, both in his seminal countercultural creative work and in his dissenting activism. Jewish by birth, a practising Buddhist, openly homosexual, he engaged in nonviolent protests for a variety of causes – for minority Civil Rights and the decriminalising of alternative sexualities, and against all forms of American imperialism abroad. Ginsberg made a sensational debut as a poet with the quasi-epical *Howl* (1955), published in 1956 as *Howl and Other Poems*. The poem was charged for its many references to drug abuse and illicit sexual activities in a much-publicised obscenity trial in 1957, before being cleared by a California court. Ginsberg's poetry was strongly influenced by William Blake, Walt Whitman and the American modernists (mainly William Carlos Williams) on the one hand, and on the other, by the rhythms and idioms of African American poetry and music, and the dialects of the American underworld. With these resources, he transformed Whitman's exhortatory long line with a dark and pungent irony, as can be seen in these excerpts from Part I of the two-part *Howl*:

> I saw the best minds of my generation destroyed by madness, starving hysterical naked
> dragging themselves through the negro streets at dawn looking for an angry fix,
> . . . .
> yakketayakking screaming vomiting whispering facts and memories and anecdotes and eyeball kicks and shocks of hospitals and jails and wars,
> . . . .
> who wandered around and around at midnight in railroad yards wondering where to go . . .

The other poems in the *Howl* volume are equally caustic. "America" is an address to his misguided country –

> America stop pushing. I know what I'm doing.
> . . . .
> I smoke marijuana every chance I get . . .
> . . . .
> Are you going to let our emotional lives be run by Time Magazine?

"A Supermarket in California" is a wickedly satirical invocation to Walt Whitman and his effulgent vision of America as the perfect democracy, as Ginsberg strolls through that symbol of American plenitude, the food section of a California supermarket ("Aisles full of husbands! Wives in the avocados, babies in the tomatoes!") –

> What thoughts I have of you tonight Walt Whitman . . .
> I saw you Walt Whitman, childless, lonely old grubber, poking among the meats in the refrigerator and eyeing the grocery boys.
> . . . .

Where are we going Walt Whitman? . . .
. . . .
Will we stroll dreaming of the lost America of love past blue
automobiles on driveways
. . . .
Ah, dear father, graybeard, lonely old courage-teacher, what
America did you have . . .?

Another poem in the same collection, "Sunflower Sutra", laments, in lines that elongate even the Whitmanesque long line, the destruction of nature by technology –

Jack Kerouac sat beside me on a busted rusty iron pole . . .
. . . .
Look at the Sunflower, he said . . .
. . . .
and the gray Sunflower poised against the sunset, crackly
bleak and dusty with the smut and smog and smoke of
olden locomotives in its eye—
corolla of bleary spikes pushed down and broken like a
battered crown . . .

Of his nearly thirty volumes of poetry, Ginsberg is also acclaimed for *Kaddish* (1961), for his multi-genre *The Fall of America: Poems of These States, 1965–1971* (1973) and *Cosmopolitan Greetings* (1994).

Lawrence Ferlinghetti, who published many works by the Beats through his City Lights Bookstore imprint, was a poet whose motto was – "If you would be a poet, create works capable of answering the challenge / of apocalyptic time" ("Poetry as Insurgent Art"). For Ferlinghetti, the symbol of "apocalyptic time" is the soulless suburban America, as in "Wild Dreams of a New Beginning" –

Lives cross lives
Idling at stoplights
Beyond the cloverleaf turnoffs
Souls eat souls in the general emptiness.

Of his several volumes of poetry, *A Coney Island of the Mind* (1958) was the most popular. Ferlinghetti uses Whitman's long line with gentler irony than Ginsberg. Here is an excerpt from a poem by this Beat poet who has lived to see 9/11, "History of the Airplane" –

> And the Wright brothers said they thought they invented
> something that would make peace on earth
> (if the wrong brothers didn't get hold of it)
> . . . .
> And the Wright brothers were long forgotten in the high-flying
> bombers that now began to visit their blessings on various Third Worlds . . .
> . . . .
> . . . the one fine day a Third World struck back
> . . . into the beating heart of
> Skyscraper America . . .

Neal Cassady's literary output was small – he wrote some poetry and essays and an autobiographical novel, *The First Third* (published by Ferlinghetti in 1971). John Clellon Holmes's semi-autobiographical novel, *Go* (1952), tells of the protagonist Paul Hobbes's struggle to preserve his marriage and family while engaging in the dissenting and countercultural lifestyle of the Beats. Gregory Corso, an American of Italian origin, had a difficult adolescence, including a prison term and a brush with the Mafia in prison. After his release, he joined the Beat group as a counter-discursive poet. In "The American Way", he declares, "They are frankensteining Christ in America", while in "The Whole Mess . . . Almost", he says of his country – "First to go, Truth, squealing like a fink."

Gary Snyder, a scholarly and highly awarded poet, was associated in his youth with the Beat Generation and the San Francisco [Literary] Renaissance, and was later a faculty member at the University of California at Davis and a translator of Chinese and Japanese poetry. A practising Zen Buddhist, he is a prominent environmental activist who has been hailed as the Poet Laureate of "Deep Ecology" (the term coined by Norwegian philosopher Arne Næss to describe his influential ecocentric philosophy). Deep Ecology was inspired by the global environmental movement initiated by Rachel Carson's book, *The Silent Spring* (1962), but it goes further than Carson's empirical concern with preservation and conservation in its metaphysical postulate that human life is just one of many equal components of an integrated earth-based ecosystem, and therefore, spiritually bonded with all other living and non-living entities on this earth. It thus challenges the very basis of post-Enlightenment Western individualism where nature is felt to be at the service of superior humanity, and has greater affiliation with holistic Eastern spiritual systems. Snyder's poetry thus combines a cosmic spirituality with very precise observations of nature and a mature poetic technique. In some ways, Snyder enlarges the template of Romantic poetry and its celebration of nature by not only incorporating imagery from geology, zoology and anthropology, but by foregrounding the plight of Native Americans who have been forcibly detached from their natural roots. "Civilization" refers both to the auroch, an extinct species of black ox, and to the uprooted Native American with his feathers and amber beads –

> Those are the people who do complicated things
> they'll grab us by the thousands and put us to work.
> World's going to hell . . .
> . . . .
> Aurochs grow rare.
> Fetch me my feathers and amber.

"Manzanita" remembers the pre-European America and Native-American nature mysticism –

> Before dawn the coyotes
> weave medicine songs
> dream nets – spirit baskets –
> . . . the whirling dance of striped boys.

"Long Hair" is a Deep Ecology poem using the long Whitman line –

> Hunting Season:
> Once every year the Deer catch human beings . . .
> . . . .
> The men who don't have Deer in them will
> also be taken by surprise and everything will change
> some. This is called takeover from inside.

The sinister poem called "this poem is about deer" again imagines this reversal of roles as deer attack a human hunter –

> The white body rolls and twitches
> In the dark ravine
> As we run down the hill to the car.
> deer foot down scree
> Picasso's fawn, Issa's fawn
> . . . .
> Dancing in the headlights on the lonely road.

But Snyder can also write sensitive nature poetry. "Pine Tree Tops" describes

> pine tree tops
> bending snow-blue, fade
> into sky, frost, starlight.

"A Walk" goes –

> Up the rock throat three miles
> Puite Creek
> In steep gorge glacier-slick rattlesnake country
> Jump, land by a pool, trout skutter
> The clear sky. Deer tracks
> . . . .
> Quail chicks freeze underfoot, color of stone
> then run – cheep! – hen quail fussing.

Yet, somewhere, the old Beat irreverence slips in, as in the haiku on a visit to Japan, "Hiking in Totsugawa Gorge" with its tongue-in-cheek juxtaposition of the arching cascade of a thundering waterfall with a viewer urinating on the rocks far below. And "A Heifer Clambers Up" envisages a pure Beat Utopia –

> tonight all the countries
> will get drunk and have a party
> Russia, America, China,
> singing with their poets . . .

In fact, Snyder, as unconventional as his early Beat colleagues in his politics and poetry, has transcended Ginsberg's ultra-provocative

Howl, and with his Deep Ecology vision, has visualised the possibility of a more caring cosmos.

Neo-realism in American Fiction

While the anti-foundationalist Beat writers systematically undermined America's vaunted international supremacy and its mighty "military-industrial combine" (to quote President Dwight Eisenhower) in unsparingly scatological terms, a new wave of withering realism exposing the waning of the American Dream, even for the apparently prosperous white middle class, came to the fore. Its precursor was John Dos Passos (1896–1970), and its main exponents (many of whom were also practitioners of the controversial "New Journalism" using literary techniques) were John Cheever (1912–82), J. D. Salinger (1919–2010), Norman Mailer (1923–2007), Truman Capote (1924–84), Tom Wolfe (b.1931), John Updike (1932–2009), Ken Kesey (1936–2001), Joyce Carol Oates (b.1938) and Raymond Carver (1938–88).

The hiatus between realism and modernism in American literature had never been as pronounced as in British literature – as between, say, John Galsworthy and Virginia Woolf. From Henry James to F. Scott Fitzgerald, Ernest Hemingway and William Faulkner, American modernism was closer to D. H. Lawrence's fictional paradigm of complex psychic states communicated through symbol and myth, and yet situated within recognisably referential locations (James's Boston, Fitzgerald's New York, Faulkner's Deep South). The focus, however, had always been on psychic states rather than on mise-en-scènes. Hence, despite the solidity of the settings, this fiction was modernist in foregrounding private inner spaces rather than socially shared experiences. Nevertheless, American modernism established a trend towards integrating the empirical with the experiential.

Coming after modernism, American neo-realism adapted many of these techniques. The neo-realist movement was "officially" theorised (though several such novels had already been written) by journalist and novelist Tom Wolfe, in his essay "Stalking the Billion-Footed Beast: A Literary Manifesto for the New Social Novel".

Published in *Harper's Magazine* in November 1989, it sparked heated debates in literary circles. The "billion-footed beast" was New York City of the 1960s and 70s – the raucous setting for hippies, drug dealers, racial riots and anti-Vietnam demonstrations, as well as technological marvels, political machinations and an economic boom that eluded the ghetto poor. Wolfe's complaint was that rather than celebrating New York and cities like it in the manner of Balzac, Zola, Dickens and Thackeray, contemporary American novelists were indulging in "[fictional] Magical Realist novels, and [postmodern] novels of Radical Disjunction" – these "Puppet-Masters were in love with the theory that the novel was a literary game". Wolfe concludes, "Reporting is the most valuable and least understood resource available to any writer with exalted ambitions."

Whether or not one agrees with Wolfe, "reporting" external social reality signalled a significant mode in post–World War II American fiction. But it did not always echo the sordid grimness of early-twentieth-century realists like Frank Norris in *The Octopus* (1901) or Upton Sinclair in *The Jungle* (1906). The new realistic fiction, while never turning away from the bustling social milieu, showed a greater tendency than the earlier realists towards exploring the psychological affects triggered by social contingencies.

Mid-twentieth-century neo-realism was anticipated by John Dos Passos's social realism in the heyday of modernism. Of his nearly thirty novels, the most enduring is the quasi-historical trilogy comprising *The 42nd Parallel* (1930), *1919* (1932) and *The Big Money* (1936), which were republished together as the bestselling *U.S.A. Trilogy* in 1938, and several times thereafter. The trilogy traces the growth of America as a capitalist superpower from its victory in the Spanish-American War (1890) that ended Spanish colonisation in Cuba and Central America, to the 1930s, despite the Great (Economic) Depression (1929– c.1932). A large cast of characters profiling the new urban America – from striking workers to film makers, stockbrokers and advertising executives – use a range of American speech locutions, from ghetto slang to financial Wall Street jargon. But the experimental narrative technique of *U.S.A.* is very different from turn-of-the-century realism – for instance, in the abrasive account of immigrant poverty and social neglect through the moral and physical degeneration of the Chicago-based Lithuanian Rudkus family in *The Jungle*. Through separate narratives, *U.S.A.* follows the intertwined destinies of Mac the feckless printer, Charley Anderson the mechanic, the stenographer Janey and her media mogul boss J. Ward Moorehouse, and Eleanor Stoddard the arty socialite. Dos Passos invokes the techniques of the documentary film (a new medium at that time) by using "Newsreel" for "Chapter" in the descriptive sections, and "Camera Eye" for the introspective interludes, and inserting real life biographies (of J. P. Morgan, Henry Ford, etc.) interspersed with iconoclastic jingles. For instance, "Newsreel I" of *The 42nd Parallel* begins,

> It was the emancipated race
> That was chargin' up the hill
> Up to where them insurrectos
> Were a-fighting fit to kill.

The narrative is often interrupted by current newspaper headlines to situate the events – for instance, "BRITISH BEATEN AT MAFEKING" in *The 42nd Parallel*. But the message of *U.S.A.* is as pessimistic as that of Dreiser's generation – the American Dream, it claims, is declining into corrupt crony capitalism.

The journalistic and documentary-oriented narrative style of *U.S.A.* was recuperated by Truman Capote, Norman Mailer and Tom Wolfe. Capote was noticed for *Breakfast at Tiffany's* (1958), a titillating story about a promiscuous socialite, Holly Golightly, whom he called "an American geisha". But Capote's ultimate aim was to forge a new fictional form. He said, in an interview with *The New York Times*, published on 16 January 1966 – "It seemed to me that journalism, reportage, could be forced to yield a serious new art form: the 'nonfictional novel'. . . . journalism is the most underestimated . . . of literary mediums." Capote shot to fame with his "non-fictional novel" *par excellence* – *In Cold Blood: A True Account of a Multiple Murder and Its Consequences* (1965) – based on a newspaper story of a quadruple murder in rural Kansas. With his friend Harper Lee (author of *To Kill a Mockingbird*), Capote visited the site to interview locals, detectives, even the two psychotic killers, during the long trial before they were hanged, and he personally retraced their steps to all the locations where they hid before their arrest. The "Acknowledgments" state: "All the material in this book not derived from my own observation is either taken from official records or is the result of interviews with the persons directly concerned. . . ." The book thus falls into the oxymoronically titled subgenre of "true crime fiction". The descriptions are flat and factual – "Ordinarily, Mr. Clutter's mornings began at six-thirty; clanging milk pails and the whispery chatter of the boys who brought them." But the work has a complex three-strand interlocking narrative comprising the lives and psychologies (this is the fictional part, along with the dialogue) of the two killers, the murdered Clutter family, and the immediate neighbours. The text not only returns repeatedly to the apparently motiveless malignity of the killers, who neither knew the Clutters nor stole anything much, but also portrays the increasing paranoia in the isolated village community. After this book, Capote wrote a number of "straight novels" (as he called them in *The New York Times* interview), but none of them was as explosive or as well-received as *In Cold Blood*.

Norman Mailer, a prolific writer who won a National Book Award for Lifetime Achievement in 2005, came to the fore as a novelist with *The Naked and the Dead* (1948) and *An American Dream* (1965). He received a Pulitzer Prize for *The Executioner's Song* (1979), and Pulitzer and National Book awards for *The Armies of the Night* (1968). Mailer is also notorious for describing the swinging "hipster" of the 1950s, precursor to the "hippie" of the 1970s, as "The White Negro" in a 1957 essay. Mailer is concerned with the apocalyptic dynamics of good and evil in a fast-changing America – with issues of power, violence, greed, sexuality and libertarianism – and his style is resonant and boldly physical to match. *The Naked and the Dead*, an anti-war novel set on a war-torn fictional South Pacific island modelled on America's World War II Philippines campaign of 1944–45 (in which Mailer's cavalry regiment took part), shows the influence of the new medium of film. It is an intersecting four-part montage of events and characters – symbolically titled "Wave", "Argil and Mold", "Plant and Phantom" and "Wake" – punctuated by "Chorus" sections of psychologically revealing dialogue and "Time

Machine" sections with biographical or historical summaries in fast-forward or flashback. The novel highlights the existential loneliness of human beings in an uncaring power-hungry world. The luridly dystopian *An American Dream* subverts America's success myth by portraying the alcoholism and moral decline of a much fêted World War II hero, Stephen Rojack, who murders his estranged wife in a fit of alcohol-fuelled rage. *The Executioner's Song*, considered one of Mailer's best works, is a "non-fiction novel", like *In Cold Blood*, about the kleptomaniac and psychopath Gary Gilmore who was executed in 1977 for murdering two men. This novel too is based entirely on interviews and legal documents, but delves into the psychology of the characters, although, as with Capote, even this is in the form of reportage – "Gary had been put in Reform School . . . he sure didn't like it in Reform School. His dream when he came out, he wrote, was to be a mobster and push people around." Mailer's second major success in this subgenre, well described in the full title, is *The Armies of the Night: History as a Novel/The Novel as History*. Continuing his anti-war stance, the factual point of departure for this semi-fictional narrative was the sensational "March on the Pentagon" in October 1967, when an estimated crowd of 100,000 gathered around the Lincoln Memorial demanding an end to the Vietnam War. A striking feature of the novel is that, contrary to Capote's dictum in *The New York Times* interview – "for the nonfictional novel form to be entirely successful, the author should not appear in the work" – *The Armies of the Night* is part-autobiographical with Mailer's own participation, his arrest and days in prison being part of the book (and the cause of a lifelong friction between Mailer and Capote). However, the narration is in the third person with "Norman Mailer" appearing as a named character. The narrative is iconoclastic in several other ways. Part 1 ("History as a Novel") begins with *Time* magazine's account of the March and its critique of Mailer's role, and then follows this up with Mailer's refutation, personal observations, snippets from his own interviews with journalists, and legal material from his trial and acquittal. But the core of Part 1 is a long and factual disquisition titled "Why are We in Vietnam?" that is presented as a dream sequence. The shorter Part 2 ("The Novel as History") is an account of the failed negotiations between the protesters and the government, and of the March itself, with forays into the mindsets of the main personae. *The New York Times* review fittingly sums up the thrust of this radically experimental work: "The book cracks open the hard nut of American authority at the center, the uncertainty of our power – and above all the bad conscience that now afflicts so many Americans [over the Vietnam War]."

Tom Wolfe is well known for his tart articles on American politics and culture written in the flamboyant and abrasive style of New Journalism – catchy phrases such as "radical chic" and "the Me Generation" are his coinages. He has over ten book-length "part-fictional" nonfiction narratives – presented either as imaginary "first person" reports or with "appropriately invented" situations – in the New Journalism template. The best known is *The Electric Kool-Aid Acid Test* (1968), a fictitious first-person account of author Ken Kesey and his friends ("The Merry Pranksters") and their hazardous dabbling in LSD and other banned psychedelic drugs. Of Wolfe's four nonfictional novels, the most successful is *The Bonfire of the Vanities* (1987). The title refers to the 1497 bonfire of "vanities" in Florence under the austere Savonarola when citizens were forced to burn their luxury items, art objects and books – and it probably signals Wolfe's views on the shallow sophistication of high-flying New Yorkers. It is a thinly fictionalised scandal story of a Wall Street financier with political ambitions who had a car accident involving two African American boys while out with his mistress, and is a graphic behind-the-scenes exposé by a seasoned journalist of political corruption and skullduggery.

Joyce Carol Oates has, to date, written forty novels and several volumes of short stories, many of which were Pulitzer Prize for Fiction finalists, with the novel *them* (1969) winning a National Book Award. In addition, she has published many plays and collections of essays and poetry. Oates began writing in the accepted neo-realist mode by basing her short stories on sensational incidents or real persons like the serial killer Charles Schmid. Oates's fictional space ranged from the Great Depression to the Vietnam War, a period that saw the US embroiled in several wars across the world, and their shattering effects on American society, especially the minorities and the poor. The novel *them* is set in the African American ghettos in

Detroit during these decades and unflinchingly portrays the harsh realities of drugs, crime, poverty, and sexual and racial abuse in these communities. Unfortunately, much of Oates's prodigious output is now out of print.

A different vein of neo-realism, centred not on scandals and celebrities but on the trials and tribulations of ordinary middle-class America, is seen in the novels of John Cheever, J. D. Salinger and John Updike. Cheever – winner of a Pulitzer Prize, a National Book Award, the National Medal for Literature and many other recognitions – chronicles the unravelling of America's lofty ideal of being a shining beacon to the world, through self-indulgence, commercialism, drugs and sexual permissiveness. *The Wapshot Chronicle* (1957) and *The Wapshot Scandal* (1964), set "in a world of much change", are simultaneously tragic and ribald as they dive below surface appearance to uncover a society "dominated by unscrupulous people". *Bullet Park* (1969) is a dark and troubled novel about the American predicament of psychopathic killers lurking in bright and "normal" neighbourhoods; *Falconer* (1977) plays on the duality of appearance and reality in smug middle-class America, as Ezekiel Farragut, a university professor, finds himself in Falconer State Prison for murdering his brother; and Cheever's last and for many his best work, the novella *Oh What a Paradise It Seems* (1982), is again, as the ironic title suggests, an exploration of the slippage of values in successful America. It is indeed notable how Cheever's muscular social realism is shot through with a modernist sense of psychological displacement.

J. D. Salinger wrote several sensitive short stories – such as "A Perfect Day for Bananafish", "For Esmé – With Love and Squalor" and "Franny" – and three novellas – *Zooey*, *Raise High the Roof Beam, Carpenters* and *Seymour: An Introduction* – but is most renowned for his only novel, *The Catcher in the Rye* (1951), which has been translated into numerous languages. The story is told from the perspective of sixteen-year-old Holden Caulfield who is the archetypal modern teenager – alienated, rebellious, sexually inquisitive, yet confused about his identity and unable to cope with life. The narration is a detailed first-person reminiscence about Holden's inability to adjust and to apply himself to his studies, his unsatisfactory relations with girlfriends and other women who do not take him seriously, and his failure to realise his fantasies of self-sufficiency and autonomy. The myriad inconsequential details of everyday life shape into the pattern of Holden's hesitant personality. The novel's title, taken from Robert Burns's poem "Coming Thro' the Rye" (1796) celebrating the freedom to love, ironically underscores Holden's incapacity to be a "catcher" and connect with others, leaving him lonely and emotionally disjointed.

John Updike wrote thirty novels, including the bestselling *Couples* (1968), several volumes of short stories, poetry and non-fiction. But it is the exponentially popular Rabbit series (winner of two Pulitzer Prizes for Fiction) that established him as one of the most perceptive analysts of small-town America, far from the glamour of New York and California. The series is an extended *bildungsroman* that traces the frustratingly uneventful life of an American Everyman, the kitchen-gadget salesman Harry "Rabbit" Angstrom, from his mid-twenties till death: the main quartet comprises *Rabbit, Run* (1960), *Rabbit Redux* (1971; "redux" means "restored"), *Rabbit is Rich* (1981) and *Rabbit at Rest* (1990), with a concluding novella, *Rabbit Remembered* (2001). It is an emotionally restricted life with limited horizons – "Rabbit" Angstrom is a conservative Republican (*Rabbit is Rich*), full of trepidation about Black people (*Rabbit Redux*). Like *Couples*, the Rabbit series examines the urge among ordinary people to realise the aspirational American Dream in "this land of constant sunshine and eternal youth" (*Rabbit at Rest*), resulting in identity crises as they get caught among the available options – money, sex and power, or a return to the stern Puritan values of an older American Dream.

Ken Kesey and Raymond Carver gave yet another turn to neo-realism with subtle hints of uncanny undercurrents traversing quotidian reality. In his youth, Kesey had an illustrious university career, but also joined the Beat movement and afterwards, formed a hippie group (including Beat writer Neal Cassady) named The Merry Pranksters, which became the subject of Tom Wolfe's non-fictional *The Electric Kool-Aid Acid Test*. Their lifestyle was countercultural, they used illegal hallucinatory drugs, and Kesey was arrested for possessing marijuana. His fascination with psycho-neurotic states later led him to volunteer as a medical guinea pig for a top-secret CIA-funded 1950s US military project, MK-ULTRA, that tested the effects of psychoactive drugs on human beings; and for a while in the late 1950s, Kesey also worked at the Menlo Park mental hospital in California and interacted with the patients there. His best novel, *One Flew over the Cuckoo's Nest* (1962; the 1975 film version won all five major Academy Awards or Oscars), draws on these experiences. The title echoes a nursery rhyme, but since "cuckoo" is slang for a mentally deranged person, "cuckoo's nest" clearly signifies a mental hospital. As a radical freethinker, Kesey exposes how rigorous and unfeeling state-sponsored institutionalisation – symbolised by the domineering Nurse Ratched with her contempt for her mentally unstable patients – actually does more harm than good. In a *Paris Review* interview, Kesey had said, "In my novels and stories evil is always the thing that seems to control. In *Cuckoo's Nest* it's the [state-run] combine." An example of this is the gratuitous lobotomy performed on a violent patient, McMurphy, turning him into a vegetable. The first-person narrative in *Cuckoo's Nest* of a mental hospital inmate, "Chief" Bromden, demonstrates the unnerving twist Kesey gives to neo-realist factuality:

> He [the doctor] checked back every forty minutes to see if I was still alive. . . . The rest of the time I spent studying the inside of my forehead or looking out the one little window in the door. It was six inches wide and eight inches high, and it had heavy chicken wire inside the glass. You get your visions through whatever gate you're granted. Patients straggled by in the hall outside, their faces all ghastly confessions. . . . More is revealed in a human face than a human being can bear, face to face.

Kesey wrote a number of other novels including his favourite, *Sometimes a Great Notion* (1964), that chronicles the social conflicts in rural Oregon where he lived, but none could match the searing emotional impact of *Cuckoo's Nest*.

Raymond Carver wrote only short stories and is one of America's most illustrious exponents of this genre. His detailed delineations of setting in the neo-realist style, enveloped in an atmosphere of emotional suggestiveness that is almost modernist, can best be illustrated through a brief analysis of one of his most famous stories, "Why Don't You Dance?" The opening scene is a yard sale of neatly arranged goods – "The chiffonnier stood a few feet from the foot of the bed. . . . A portable heater was next to the chiffonnier. . . . The buffed aluminum kitchen set took up a part of the driveway", and so on. But the objects are stacked in such a way as to suggest a divorce, or breaking up of the home, indicated tersely by, "His side, her side." A young unnamed couple, obviously seeking to furnish their new home inexpensively with second-hand furniture, stops by and tests out everything. The unnamed middle-aged owner, who seems to be alone, offers them drinks till they are dizzy. It is dusk by the time the couple checks out the record-player and begins to dance. And suddenly, the girl finds herself dancing with the unnamed man on the driveway. The story ends with the inexplicable undergirding the empirical: "Weeks later, she said: '. . . Look at this record-player. The old guy gave it to us and all these crappy records. Will you look at this shit?' She kept talking. She told everyone. There was more to it, and she was trying to get it talked out. After a time, she quit trying."

Jewish American Literature

Small communities of Jewish people from Western Europe had begun to migrate to the thirteen British-controlled American colonies from the seventeenth century. The largest influxes, however, were of poor Jewish agricultural labourers from Eastern Europe in search of better opportunities in the late nineteenth century, German and Eastern European Jews fleeing the Nazi Holocaust during the Second World War, and of Russian Jews from the former Soviet Union after the Second World War. According to the 2010 US census, around six million Jewish Americans constitute just 2.2 per cent of the population, and even this is dwindling due to the increasing number of interfaith marriages.

Yet, Jewish Americans are far more influential than these numbers suggest. Jewish Americans of European origin assimilated more easily into "white" America than other ethnic minorities. Now they are mostly affluent and educated and have formed powerful

"Jewish lobbies" in American business and politics. Many high-profile Americans are Jewish. To name a few – the world of business has the cosmetic tycoons Max Factor and Estée Lauder, fashion king Calvin Klein, Mark Zuckerberg of Facebook, and Google co-founders Sergei Brin and Larry Page; from the entertainment industry, the legendary magician Harry Houdini, William Fox of Twentieth Century Fox, many famous actors and directors including Woody Allen, and Al Capp of the *L'il Abner* comic strip; music icons include Irving Berlin, George Gershwin, Phillip Glass, Paul Simon, Art Garfunkel and Bob Dylan; notable feminists are Betty Friedan and Gloria Steinem, while eminent literary critics include Richard Ellmann, Harry Levin and Harold Bloom; and there are several famous politicians such as President Nixon's Secretary of State Henry Kissinger.

Jewish American literature is a major component of mainstream American literature, having produced four Nobel Laureates – Saul Bellow (1976), Isaac Bashevis Singer (1978), Czesław Miłosz (1980) and Joseph Brodsky (1987). Others have won prestigious national awards and several Jewish American novels have been made into successful Hollywood films. Yet, not all US writers of Jewish origin are classified as Jewish American authors. Emma Lazarus, who wrote the iconic poem "The New Colossus" (1883) on the Statues of Liberty, and Israel Zangwill, who conceptualised an American cultural paradigm in his play *The Melting Pot* (1908), are not categorised as Jewish. Denise Levertov and Arthur Miller, Clifford Odets and Norman Mailer, Isaac Asimov, Allen Ginsberg, Joseph Heller and Tony Kushner are identified with American modernism, American realism, science fiction, the Beats, and American postmodernism respectively, since they do not focus specifically on Jewish issues. In contrast, although all major Jewish American authors move from the particular to the universal, ethnic Jewish identity, lifestyles and concerns, and re-interpretations of controversial episodes from Jewish history are the markers of their oeuvre.

Some of the significant Jewish American writers in English include novelists Bernard Malamud (1914–86), Nobel Laureate Saul Bellow (1915–2005), Cynthia Ozick (b.1928), E. L. Doctorow (b.1931) and Philip Roth (b.1933). However, Nobel Laureates

Isaac Bashevis Singer (1902–91) wrote fiction only in the Yiddish language, Czesław Miłosz (1911–2004) wrote poetry only in Polish, and Joseph Brodsky (1940–96) wrote poetry only in Russian: both Milosz and Brodsky self-translated much of their work into English, while Singer closely supervised his translators (his most famous short story, "Gimpel the Fool", was translated by Saul Bellow) to produce what he called "second originals".

Fiction

As well-known for his four collections of short stories as for his eight novels – notably *The Natural* (1952), *The Assistant* (1957), *The Fixer* (1967) and *Dubin's Lives* (1979) – Bernard Malamud uses the historic Jewish predicament of exile, suffering, anti-Semitism and trauma as a trope for the human condition itself. Equating his alienated Jewish heroes with the modern syndromes of rootlessness and isolation, Malamud says, "All men are Jews, though few men know it." *The Natural* takes the American subgenre of the "baseball novel" to metaphysical heights, as it deploys the myth of the Waste Land to fictionalise the true story of a Jewish baseball prodigy's struggle to regain his former glory after a random act of violence nearly cripples him. *The Assistant* is an introspective story about a simple Jewish store-keeper grappling with his traditional values that are constantly challenged by his sceptical young assistant. *The Fixer*, Malamud's best work, re-inscribes from a Jewish perspective the notorious anti-Semitic Beilis trial in Tsarist Russia. In *Dubin's Lives,* a sophisticated metanarrative on fictionality, a Jewish scholar, William Dubin, writes a biography of D. H. Lawrence that gets entangled with his own life as he begins to re-enact Lawrence's tortuous relationships with men and women in ways that are both angst-ridden and comic, and problematise his Jewish subjectivity.

Saul Bellow has been described by J. M. Coetzee, the 2003 Nobel Laureate in literature, as "one of the giants, perhaps *the* giant" among American novelists. A deeply philosophical and densely intertextual author who said that "we live much more among ideas than we live in nature", Bellow wrote four volumes of short stories and thirteen novels in a rich variety of modes from picaresque and parody to tragedy and myth. His most acclaimed books are *Dangling Man* (1944), *The Adventures of Augie March* (1953), *Henderson the Rain King* (1959), *Herzog* (1964) and *Mr. Sammler's Planet* (1970). Bellow's marginalised, yet unvanquished, Jewish heroes symbolise both the flaws and the strengths of modern Western civilisation. Joseph, the "Dangling Man" of this novella, leads a vacuous life in a seedy suburb of Chicago in 1942, while waiting to be called up for his military draft in an America struggling between the aftereffects of the Great Depression and the trauma of World War II. He is desperately seeking emotional stability as he writes his journal, since he can no longer relate to his own youth when he loved philosophy and dreamed of founding an Utopia: now he is frustrated ("What would Goethe say if he saw the view from this window?") and angry ("a sort of human grenade whose pin has been withdrawn"). The feared draft call ironically comes as a relief: "Hurray for regular hours! And for the supervision of the spirit!" Augie March, hailing from "the bottomside skepticism of West-Side Chicago", is handsome and intelligent but with "a weak sense of consequence" and unable "to stand up to flattery": his picaresque adventures range from smuggling drugs and immigrants to guarding Trotsky in Mexico, as he contests the hegemonic American dream of success: "But then how does anybody form a decision. . . . When does he choose and when is he chosen instead?" In the grotesquely comic and picaresque *Henderson*, the narrator, a swaggering but troubled multimillionaire named L. Eugene Henderson, goes off to Central Africa following a mid-life crisis, in search of adventure – many "Africa novels" are recalled and subverted as Henderson is finally named the "Rain King" of the Wariri tribe, but loses his nerve and flees home to America instead. In *Herzog*, middle-aged Moses Herzog suffers a nervous breakdown after his traumatic second divorce. The novel comprises mental "letters" he "writes' to acquaintances and unknown others, some dead, attempting to examine and explain his failed life. But he finally finds resolution in not needing to "write" any more "letters". In *Mr. Sammler's Planet*, the metaphysically minded seventy-plus Arthur Sammler, "sorry for all and sore at heart", decides to devote the rest of his life to understanding the apocalyptic abysses of contemporary civilisation, including the Holocaust, on his "planet". The novel moves beyond the individual consciousness (Joseph or Herzog) to speak for humanity at large, with Bellow's brooding philosophical style a perfect vehicle for these meditations.

Cynthia Ozick began as a poet but is always remembered for her chilling short story on the Holocaust, "The Shawl" (1989), though she was never in Nazi Germany. But she did grow up in an intensely anti-Semitic neighbourhood in New York, and this is reflected in her first major novel, *The Cannibal Galaxy* (1983). An astronomical term for a galaxy that devours smaller ones around it, it becomes a metaphor for Euro-American culture destroying Jewish culture. Yet, *The Messiah of Stockholm* (1987) whimsically problematises Jewishness itself – if the Ten Commandments forbade untruths and image-making (or idol worship), should a Jewish writer indulge in the imaginary and the fictional? *The Puttermesser Papers* (1997) attempts an intriguing technical resolution for this artistic-ethical dilemma – the "story" of Ruth Puttermesser is a hybrid narrative that claims to be neither fiction nor biography nor memoir. *Foreign Bodies* (2010) is based on Henry James's *The Ambassadors,* with a similar plot moving between New York and Paris, but the characters are Jewish and find themselves to be as much "foreign bodies" in the New World as in the Old.

E. L. (Edgar Lawrence) Doctorow, a chronicler of New York life *par excellence,* authored four books of short stories and twelve novels. His first major work is *The Book of Daniel* (1971) that employs the favoured device of retelling contested Jewish history – in this case, the sensational 1953 trial and execution of Julius and Ethel Rosenberg for allegedly selling American nuclear secrets to the Soviet Union. Their fictional son, Daniel, who seeks the "truth" about his parents, is modelled on the biblical Daniel who was an interpreter of dreams – thus signifying that "truth" is possibly subjective, even ambivalent. In the next work, the highly acclaimed *Ragtime* (1975), set in New York in the first two decades of the twentieth century, a wealthy but emotionally disturbed white family is drawn into an unusual but warm relationship with a talented African American pianist of ragtime music, and gets fatally involved while protesting against his racist persecution. The novel is enriched by its detailed historical background, including several real personalities. In *World's Fair* (1985), a narration in retrospect, Doctorow's childhood alter ego, Edgar, gives a penetrating child's-eye-view of New York, from the Depression of the 1920s to the renewed confidence signalled by the New York World's Fair of 1939, while being tragically unaware of the cataclysm ahead – the Second World War. *Billy Bathgate* (1989) is a graphic account of the gangster-ridden underworld of New York, narrated by an impoverished fifteen-year-old Irish American ghetto boy, Billy "Bathgate" Behan, who joins a notorious mobster, simply to survive.

Philip Roth is a prolific writer with four books in the Zuckerman Bound series, three in the Kepesh series, and twenty stand-alone novels. Of these, the novella *Goodbye, Columbus* (1959), and the novels *Portnoy's Complaint* (1969) and *American Pastoral* (1997), have won major national awards, while many other works have won important literary prizes. Roth's candid exposés of the apparently well-assimilated American Jewish community, in his muscular and exuberant style, have provoked considerable controversy. *Goodbye, Columbus* bares the rigid class divisions *within* American Jewish society through the working-class Neil Klugman's sincere but failed courtship of Brenda from the wealthy Patimkin family. The title ironically underlines the way the American Dream eludes the marginalised and the poor. *Portnoy's Complaint* – the explicitly psychopathological and often coarse and autoerotic monologue of Alexander Portnoy, "a lust-ridden, mother-addicted young Jewish bachelor" – received both high praise and vehement censure for revealing the insecurities of American Jews: "Jew Jew Jew Jew Jew Jew! . . . I happen also to be a human being!" The sardonically titled *American Pastoral* shows how the comfortable life of the affluent Jewish businessman Seymour 'Swede' Levov totally unravels when his idealistic daughter Merry hurls a bomb to protest against the Vietnam War and kills an innocent bystander, even as the myth of America's "Manifest Destiny" disintegrates under the onslaughts of Vietnam abroad and Watergate at home.

Isaac Bashevis Singer, a Jewish American refugee from Poland, wrote nineteen novels, twelve short story collections, twenty children's books and several memoirs. He wrote only in Yiddish to keep alive the historic language of his community, the Ashkenazi

Jews – although in his personal life, he moved away from orthodox Judaism to "personal mysticism". He was awarded the Nobel Prize "for his impassioned narrative art which, with roots in a Polish-Jewish cultural tradition, brings universal human conditions to life."

Poetry

Czesław Miłosz, of Lithuanian origin, defected to the US when he was posted there as a diplomat from the then Communist Poland, and published his famous anti-Stalinist treatise, *The Captive Mind* (1953). Yet his exilic condition always troubled him. Here is an excerpt from a poem dedicated to his diasporic friend, Raja Rao:

> We need God loving us in our weakness
> And not in the glory of beatitude.
> No help, Raja, my part is agony . . . .

The Nobel citation proclaimed that Miłosz "with uncompromising clear-sightedness voices man's exposed condition in a world of severe conflicts".

Russian-born Joseph Brodsky was expelled from the Soviet Union in 1972 for his political views and came to the US aided by W. H. Auden. His self-translated poetry is celebrated for its technical mastery and range of forms. His poems express his pain as a "refujew" (in "Letter to an Archaeologist"). Here are a few lines from "Dutch Mistress", describing his life in exile:

> A hotel in whose ledgers departures are more prominent than
> arrivals.
> With wet Koh-i-noors the October rain
> strokes what's left of the naked brain. . . .

He received the Nobel Prize in Literature "for an all-embracing authorship, imbued with clarity of thought and poetic intensity".

Postmodern American Literature

American postmodernism evolved between the 1960s and the 80s – decades that witnessed the traumatic Vietnam War, the paranoid fear of nuclear attack during the Cold War, global US dominance even as ethnic minorities at home struggled for civil rights, and the exponential growth of new technologies that changed old ways of living forever. In his 1986 travelogue, *America*, French philosopher Jean Baudrillard observed that America had forged a new paradigm of existence that rejected deep-rooted cultures and traditions in favour of novelty, mobility and a virtual reality engendered by the electronic media. Baudrillard described "astral America" as the natural home of the postmodern: "America is neither dream nor reality. . . . It is a hyperreality because it is a Utopia. . . . America is a giant hologram."

Art and literature now needed to find fresh ways of coping with these vertiginous new epistemologies. In his poem "Connoisseur of Chaos", American modernist Wallace Stevens had already hinted at the impossibility of articulating them in conventional terms: "The squirming facts exceed the squamous mind / If I may say so." In the giant strides made by American technology post–World War II, fact was indeed, in some sense, exceeding fiction. Further, the upsurge of non-white minority rights movements and of ethnic American literatures were leading to a disturbing loss of cultural authority by the Anglocentric literary centre. In looking for alternative terminologies and literary terrains, American postmodernism invoked the new surreal hyperrealities of the electronic and social media to subvert established genres and norms. In his essay entitled "The Literature of Exhaustion" (1984), John Barth (b.1930) rejected realism as an exhausted or "used up" tradition and described his own work as "novels that imitate the form of the novel, by an author who imitates the role of an Author". In his polemical critique titled *Surfiction: Fiction Now and Tomorrow* (1975), Raymond Federman (1928–2009) described his meandering self-reflexive anti-narratives as "surfiction" (or "surreal fiction") that destabilised the readers' expectations through the use of textuality and pastiche in order to "unmask its own fictionality . . . and not pretend any longer to pass for reality." Similarly, in his subversion of canonical forms of narration in the essay "Unwriting" in R. L. Williams's edited collection *The Novel in the Americas* (1993), Ronald Sukenick (1932–2004) defined the new narrative practices as modes of "unwriting" – "Every such act unwrites what has been formulated as experience to allow a new sense of experience to evolve. Which once assimilated, will itself need to be unwritten."

The postmodern violation of literary, social and sexual norms in terms of parody, profanity, paranoia, pastiche and defamiliarisation had already been anticipated by the American modernist Henry Miller (1891–1980) in *Tropic of Cancer* (1934), *Black Spring* (1936) and *Tropic of Capricorn* (1939). But his was a lone voice in the great eras of realism and modernism. The outstanding American postmodernists – selected from a large body of notable authors – are, for fiction, Russian-born Vladimir Nabokov (1899–1977), Kurt Vonnegut (1922–2007), Joseph Heller (1923–99), John Barth (b.1930), Richard Brautigan (1935–84), Don DeLillo (b.1936) and Thomas Pynchon (b.1937); William H. Gass (b.1924), Donald Barthelme (1931–89) and Robert Coover (b. 1932) for short fiction; poets Charles Olson (1910–70), John Berryman (1914–72), Denise Levertov (1923–97), John Ashbery (b.1927), Anne Sexton (1928–74), Adrienne Rich (1929–2012) and Sylvia Plath (1932–63); and radically experimental dramatists like Edward Albee (1928 2016), Jack Gelber (1932–2003), Arthur Kopit (b.1937), David Rabe (b.1940), Sam Shepard (b.1943) and Tony Kushner (b.1956). These writers engage in what French theorist Roland Barthes called "[literary] semioclasty", or the overt dislocation of existing literary norms and forms – specifically the notion that art reflects "reality", the use of discontinuous narrative, and the displacement of genre differences and hierarchies (as between literature, history and science, or between high culture and popular culture). They produce sharply satirical, metafictional, multi-genre works that project a dysfunctional and dystopian America.

Fiction

Vladimir Nabokov, a trained lepidopterist and serious chess player, had to flee his native Russia with his family because of his democrat father's anti-Tsarist and anti-communist politics – he became an American citizen in 1945. His first ten novels were in Russian, and he then mastered English to become an influential early postmodernist. Of his nine English novels, his debut novel, which is referenced later in Pynchon's novel *V.*, is *The Real Life of Sebastian Knight* (1941), an elaborate mystification in which a narrator named "V" writes the biography of an elusive Russian-born English novelist, now called Sebastian Knight, whom the narrator has to track down. Nabokov's most sensational and sexually controversial work was *Lolita* (1955) about the nymphomaniac Humbert Humbert's affair with the girl-child Lolita. *Pnin* (1957) is a semi-autobiographical novel recounting many episodes from Nabokov's life. The last major English fiction, *Pale Fire* (1962), is structured as a digressive and preternatural 999-line autobiographical poem entitled "Pale Fire" by a fictitious poet, along with a long autobiographical "Introduction" and a tortuous "Commentary" by a friend who turns out to be someone else.

Kurt Vonnegut's disenchantment with contemporary civilisation stemmed from his traumatic experiences as an American soldier fighting in Germany during the Second World War. An anthropologist and the author of fourteen novels, sixteen short story collections and some poems and plays, Vonnegut blends black comedy and slapstick with ethics and science fiction to create alternative worlds that interrogate a late-capitalist culture. He was also an artist who illustrated his own books. His classic postmodern novels are *Cat's Cradle* (1963), *God Bless You, Mr. Rosewater, or Pearls Before Swine* (1965), *Slaughterhouse-Five, or The Children's Crusade: A Duty-Dance with Death* (1969), *Breakfast of Champions, or Goodbye Blue Monday* (1973) and *Hocus Pocus, or What's the Hurry, Son?* (1990). *Cat's Cradle,* written in 127 discrete sections, foregrounds the total indifference of American scientists to the ethical implications and genocidal possibilities of their inventions, through the career of Felix Hoenikker, an imaginary co-inventor of the atom bomb that pulverised Hiroshima and Nagasaki. With blistering irony, the narrator speaks of how he had planned a book celebrating America's nuclear prowess by interviewing Hoenikker's team ("The book was to be factual. . . . It was to be a Christian book. I was a Christian then."), and found himself engulfed in a monstrously amoral world of "pure research." In *Bless You, Mr. Rosewater*, Vonnegut's fictional alter ego Kilgore Trout exposes the venal hypocrisy of capitalist humanism through millionaire Senator Eliot Rosewater's "Rosewater Foundation", which apparently is set up to help the underprivileged but actually helps him exploit tax loopholes and avoid heavy taxes. The non-linear structure of *Slaughterhouse-Five* fluidly recounts the "time travels" of a World War II American soldier, Billy Pilgrim, who slips into a disoriented dream during the ferocious Allied bombing of Dresden (in which Vonnegut was also caught): Billy "meets" both Kilgore Trout and the two-feet high alien Tralfamadorians (who appear in several Vonnegut novels) and learns from them the true values in life. *Breakfast of Champions* is about "two lonesome, skinny, fairly old white men [Dwayne Hoover and Kilgore Trout] on a planet [earth] which was dying fast" – where people are really robots manipulated by various kinds of unethical propaganda that very few have the free will to resist. *Hocus Pocus* is structured as though scribbled on many scraps of paper, sometimes apparently incoherently assembled by the narrator, a Vietnam war veteran and college professor: he is dismissed from his job for impropriety and starts teaching convicts at an overcrowded American prison maintained by a Japanese conglomerate (a satire on the global economy), where he learns many lessons in survival.

It is difficult to position Joseph Heller. He was Jewish by birth and wrote some pessimistic novels on American life, including *Portrait of an Artist as an Old Man* (2000). But the work for which he will be remembered is his debut novel, *Catch-22* (1963), which is neither particularly Jewish nor realistic, but wickedly parodic in a postmodern vein. The title has become a byword in the English language for an unresolvable situation, especially legal, administrative or bureaucratic, because of crass regulations, as with the fighter pilot Orr's predicament – willfully putting his life in danger would normally be considered crazy; but as a soldier, he would be considered crazy (and punished accordingly) if he did not. All such rules, says the novel, are enshrined in a military memorandum named "Catch-22" and the protagonist Yossarian steers a maniacal course through its many pitfalls. The novel is one of the best satires written on America's war effort during the Second World War (in which Heller himself participated), and the non-chronological narrative from shifting points of view mirrors the existential confusion of ordinary soldiers fighting a war of which they cannot make any sense.

John Barth began his career with two realistic novellas but then radically changed direction with *The Sot-Weed Factor* (1960), and continued in the postmodern vein in his next sixteen books. The title, *The Sot-Weed Factor,* is a partial quotation from the title of a long 1708 satirical poem by a little-known British colonist, Ebenezer Cooke (c.1665–c.1732), and is a sprawling fictive account of Cooke's wanderings – the numerous digressions, lists, flashbacks, stories within stories and black humour recall Laurence Sterne's *Tristram Shandy*. The next work, an unexpected bestseller despite critical scepticism, is the 800-page *Giles Goat-Boy* (1966) that is staged as a "found manuscript" containing textual hyperlinks and a hypertext encyclopaedia in different fonts, written long before the Internet was invented. A mythic fantasy-cum-parody of the messianic cults sweeping America in the 1960s, it tells of a human boy brought up close to nature as a goat, who believes that he is destined to save the world from the Cold War. To this end, he performs all the tasks befitting a hero in Joseph Campbell's Jungian *The Hero with a Thousand Faces* (1949) and finally arrives at the spectral wisdom that "[The] project . . . is to learn where to go by discovering where I am by reviewing where I've been." *Lost in the Funhouse* (1968) is a collection of self-reflexive short stories on the paradoxes of existence. *Chimera* (1972), which explores fictionality in multiple cultures, has three linked novellas titled *Dunyazadiad* (named after Duniyazade, the younger sister of Scheherazade who narrates *The Thousand and One Nights*), *Perseid* and *Bellerophoniad* (which has question and answer sessions with the reader and "mystic" diagrams). The other notable work is the epistolary *LETTERS* (1979), where Barth interacts with the fictional characters of his novels as to their opinion on their roles.

Richard Brautigan has published several novels and volumes of poetry. He is best known for *Trout Fishing in America* (1967) that seeks to defamiliarise the notion of narrative itself through a profusion of anecdotes about trout fishing and other such things that have no central character or incident to bind them together. The book is a comic spoof on American materialism, with occasional comments from a persona named Trout Fishing in America.

Don DeLillo states in a 2005 interview that these are "dangerous times" when a creative artist must resist all forms of power and control. Of his fifteen novels so far, the postmodern classic is *White Noise* (1985) about "the radiance of dailiness" despite rampant consumerism and intrusive technology, as articulated in its three sections – "Waves and Radiation", "The Airborne Toxic Event" and "Dylarama" – by the narrator who is Chair of the Department of Hitler Studies in a provincial university.

As an undergraduate, Thomas Pynchon studied engineering with physics and mathematics before switching to literature and history; and he deploys material from all these diverse fields, as well as from popular culture, the criminal underworld and the drug scene. Anticipating the fiction of Umberto Eco, Pynchon's lengthy, intricate and densely allusive novels, with their playfully convoluted plots, curiously named characters and syntax-bending Joycean diction, are all historical, psychological, anthropological, and ultimately metaphysical thrillers about the contemporary human condition. His debut novel, *V.* (1963), spanning many countries and historical events, revolves around the search for the mysterious "V" (perhaps a person or a place or an icon) by Herbert Stencil, assisted by Benny Profane and his bohemian friends. The many transcultural identities conferred on this enigmatic entity by various personae gesture towards the slippery hyperreality of life in the late-capitalist Western world. In *The Crying of Lot 49* (1966), the heroine, Oedipa Maas, accidentally discovers documents pertaining to an ancient feud between Thurn und Taxis, the official postal service of the Holy Roman Empire since the sixteenth century, and its clandestine rival Tristero (a Pynchon invention). The novel ends by problematising recorded history as Oedipa watches an auctioneer calling or "crying" for bids from collectors for a "lot" (Lot No. 49; hence the title, *The Crying of Lot 49*) that she is convinced contains the postage stamps used by Tristero, thus erasing this underground history from public knowledge. In Pynchon's third and most acclaimed work, the erudite *Gravity's Rainbow* (1973), the main plot, complicated by numerous intersecting stories, concerns the search by many characters for a deadly secret device (the "Schwarzgerät" or "black object") that the Germans plan to install on their V-2 rocket No. 00000 towards the end of the Second World War. The novel is considered a postmodern classic that breaks all boundaries between science and art, history and metaphysics, high culture and popular culture – while its oxymoronic title indicates the eternal conflict between determinism/totalitarianism and the freedom of beauty and creativity. *Vineland* (1990) is set in an imaginary titular town in California, which is the locale for the recording, replete with popular culture motifs of those times, of the cultural, mental and moral transformation of America from the free-thinking "flower power" generation of the 1960s to the paranoia of the 80s, generated by the Cold War. *Mason and Dixon* (1997) is a scrupulously detailed, yet subversively postmodern, retelling of American history in terms of the Mason–Dixon Line demarcating the boundaries of four states in colonial America. Drawn by surveyors Charles Mason and Jeremiah Dixon between 1763 and 1767, the Line became a cultural borderline separating the slave-owning agricultural South from the industrial North during the Civil War. Set within a frame narrative of reminiscence and storytelling that highlights the subjective nature (or even fictionality) of official history, the story focuses on the occluded minority histories of slaves, women and Native Americans; its cast of characters ranges from historical figures (George Washington, Benjamin Franklin) to robots and possible aliens; and the labyrinthine plot with no identifiable centre deftly undermines the selective and inexact accounts of so-called authentic history. *Against the Day* (2006; the title quotes an apocalyptic biblical reference to the end of the world) is a sprawling historical metafiction of over one thousand pages and more than a hundred characters operating in real and imaginary locations. The book is partly about two feuding families at the turn of the twentieth century, and the deliberate randomness of its phantasmagoric plot simulates the disorientation of modern man. The title of the next novel, *Inherent Vice* (2009), is a scientific, technical and also legal term referring to an intrinsic instability or flaw in an entity or argument that renders it innately untenable. This story of a drug-addicted private investigator's failed detective missions, set against the infamous 1970 trial of the criminal cult guru Charles Manson, is a fable about the average man's helplessness against the many shadowy power centres in society – politicians, bureaucrats, the police, business cartels and criminals: in fact, the "inherent vice" is in society itself. Pynchon's latest book, *Bleeding Edge* (2014), is his 9/11 novel, taking as its points of departure the Al Qaeda attack on New York's World Trade Centre, and the equally calamitous global domination of the Internet, to fashion a modern whodunit about the stealing and planting of sensitive or misleading information. Pynchon's novels deconstruct what we call "reality", in the way suggested by Jacques Derrida in "Structure, Sign and Play in the Discourse of the Human Sciences" – "the center had no natural site, [. . .] it was not a fixed locus but . . . a sort of non-locus in which an infinite number of sign-substitutions came into play." While Pynchon has been criticised for being unnecessarily opaque and complicated, many consider him to be the most challenging of American postmodernists. Of his eight novels to date, Don DeLillo has said, "With every book, he is raising the stakes."

Another major facet of American postmodernism is its use of forms and motifs from popular culture to explore serious ontological questions of life and death, good and evil, salvation and damnation. Two of the most highly regarded and highly awarded contemporary American novelists, both with international cult followings, are little known or read outside their circle of committed aficionados, despite the fact that some of their works have been made into successful Hollywood films. These novelists are Cormac McCarthy (b.1934) and Stephen King (b.1947). Like their fellow American postmodernists, they, too, use dislocated narration and multiple voices to decentre the monologic "grand narratives" (to use Jean-François Lyotard's seminal phrase from his Preface to *The Postmodern Condition: A Report on Knowledge*) of American history, politics and culture, and are ultimately apocalyptic in their dark vision of a disintegrating Euro-American ethos, just as Vonnegut is in *Slaughterhouse-Five* or Pynchon in *Gravity's Rainbow*. But theirs is a postmodernism with a difference, because of their distinctive narrative strategies and singular thematic focus. Eschewing postmodern parody, pastiche and iconoclastic play, both McCarthy and King reinvent well-established American popular culture genres such as the Western, the Mexican American *corrido,* the Southern Gothic, horror, science fiction and the crime thriller. By foregrounding the gratuitous violence, destruction and death, and the eschatological resonances that permeate these narratives, the novelists strip them of their patina of heroism and thrill, and transform them into vehicles for an exploration, almost biblical in its intensity, of the ubiquity of sin and evil in this world.

Cormac McCarthy, who hails from the north of America but chose to settle in the American South, fully exploits the dire historical legacy of that region. He locates his meditations on the pervasiveness of evil in the human soul in the restive borderlands between America and Mexico, and the still semi-mythical Wild West of the arid deserts of Nevada and Utah. In an interview with Leonard Pierce, dated 15 June 2009, noted literary critic Harold Bloom places McCarthy in the same league as Faulkner and Pynchon. McCarthy's first novel, the darkly Faulkneresque *The Orchard Keeper* (1965), features murderers and neurotic bootleggers in an isolated corner of Tennessee and projects the loss of innocence through exposure to evil, while *Outer Dark* (1968) and *Child of God* (1973) expose the psychoses, perversities and apostasies that lurk beneath the same seemingly idyllic rural landscape, like the serpent skulking in the Garden of Eden. *Suttree* (1979) puns on the surname of Cornelius Suttree who abandons his luxurious Southern mansion to live like a vagrant with social outcasts after discovering that he had a stillborn twin – his is a spiritual self-immolation or "sati" to absolve himself of the "guilt" of outliving (that is, metaphorically "killing") his "other". Through these early novels, McCarthy honed his starkly minimal language with practically no punctuation except full stops, unidentified speakers and untranslated chunks of Spanish spoken by his Chicano characters. These typical themes and styles coalesced powerfully in *Blood Meridian or the Evening Redness in the West* (1985), perhaps McCarthy's goriest novel about murder, marauding and mayhem along the long Southern border during the bitterly fought Mexican–American War (1846–48), with the sinister Judge Holden disseminating his diabolical "gospel" that "War is God". *Blood Meridian* is a gruesome cult novel that Harold Bloom lauded in his aforementioned interview as "the ultimate Western". The most successful work in McCarthy's tempestuous *Border Trilogy*

(1992–98) that fuses the *corrido* with the Western and Gothic is *All the Pretty Horses* (1992). *No Country For Old Men* (2005), a fast-paced Western-cum-thriller about a good sheriff battling hired killers and ruthless scalp-hunters across Southern borders, was made into a 2007 Hollywood film of the same name and won four Academy Awards including the one for the best picture. *The Road* (2006), a sombre post-apocalyptic tale set in some unspecified future time when an unnamed cataclysm has devastated this ungodly world, is the only McCarthy novel to feature slavery. A *New York Times* review of the novel, dated 25 September 2006, said, "This is an exquisitely bleak incantation – pure poetic brimstone. . . . a terse cautionary tale . . . [of] stupefying ravages . . . [and] almost biblical fury." McCarthy's brutally realistic stories are ominous allegories of good and evil where, unlike the traditional theodicy, the power of evil almost outweighs the good in a searing comment on modern life.

Like McCarthy, Stephen King has won several literary awards. A prolific writer, he has so far published nearly two hundred short stories, online horror fiction, and fifty-four print novels (seven under the pen name of Richard Bachman), many of which are cult bestsellers. The forms he reworks are horror, fantasy, the supernatural and the weird, science fiction and the crime thriller and, again like McCarthy, he makes no secret of his profound concern with evil in today's world. With such a huge oeuvre (including several series of which the "Dark Tower" books are the most popular), much of which has been described as "terrifying" by a devoted readership, only key novels can be discussed. King's debut novel, *Carrie* (1975), one of the most frequently banned books in American school libraries because of its raw horror, is about a well-intentioned school girl who wreaks havoc in her community through her uncontrollable telekinetic powers. In *Salem's Lot* (1975), the narrator returns to his isolated childhood hometown to discover that its remaining inhabitants, still comfortably human-looking, have become vampires. *The Shining* (1977), King's first bestseller, features uncanny psychic events in a dilapidated hotel on a deserted Colorado mountaintop. His other bestseller in the same vein is *Cujo* (1981) that blends psychological horror with the fantastic and the weird. The Dark Tower series (1982–2004) comprising eight novels and a short story collection, that King considers his magnum opus, deftly weaves several popular culture forms together to deploy time/space/perception shifts, such as combining the Western with science fiction and the thriller with post-apocalypse (a narrative set after the end of the world). As the series title indicates, the saga was inspired by several canonical quest narratives from various Arthurian quest fables such as *Sir Gawain and the Green Knight*, the medieval *Song of Roland* (*Chanson de Roland*), Robert Browning's "Childe Roland to the Dark Tower Came" and T. S. Eliot's *The Waste Land* (Dark Tower III [1991] is titled *The Waste Lands*), as well as popular culture quest myths such as *The Wizard of Oz* (Dark Tower IV [1997] is *Wizard and Glass*). However, the traditional quest myth ultimately demonstrates the triumph of positive forces. King's protagonist Roland Deschain, the last survivor of a Western-oriented knightly order known as "The Gunslingers", travels through decaying or spooky urban and rural landscapes blighted by both technology and moral decay, as he searches for the meaning of life in this postmodern era, which remains elusive even in the last volume to date. Finally, a landmark King novel (reminiscent of William Golding's *Lord of the Flies*) is *It* (1986) that rewrites the popular modes of the school story and the boys' adventure story. A monstrous shape-changing entity, known only as "It", that lives in the sewers under the bucolic fictional town of Derry, preys on young and innocent school children who turn catatonic with terror. However, two intrepid boys, Ben and Richie, resolve to hunt it down and, after many gruesome adventures, Ben crushes It's heart with his bare hands. Expectedly, a raging controversy among Stephen King fans is the negative critique, or even the censoring, of a number of his novels by what they dub the "American moral police".

A group of younger white American postmodern novelists is currently making headlines and winning awards. One of the best is Jonathan Franzen (b.1959) who constructs plots with multiple interlocking strands that problematise the celebratory myths of America – he blends postmodern parody with gritty realism to articulate these paradoxes. His debut novel, *The Twenty-Seventh City* (1988), is a complicated cross-genre satirical-cum-political/

financial thriller, while *Strong Motion* (1992) was positively reviewed for its pro-feminist and anti-capitalist thrusts. Franzen's *The Corrections* (2001) won the National Book Award and was shortlisted for other prestigious nominations including the Pulitzer Prize for Fiction. It follows the conservative Midwestern Lambert family and its rebellious younger generation as they grapple with the pervasive angst of a politically and economically challenged America. (The book was published just ten days before 9/11.) *Freedom* (2010), which won major awards and was ranked as one of the best books of the year, once again follows a large cast of family and friends attempting to come to terms with the implosion of the American Dream after the Iraq misadventures and 9/11. *Purity* (2015), which had a less enthusiastic reception, has an unusual structure of apparently unrelated parallel stories, set in different continents, that merge and intersect at the end; but the inconclusive open-ended denouement leaves the future of the characters, and that of contemporary America, in doubt.

Other strong and acclaimed voices in this new cluster of postmodern novelists include Jeffrey Eugenides (b.1960), David Foster Wallace (1962–2008), Chuck Palahniuk (b.1962), Michael Chabon (b.1963) and Dennis Lehane (b.1965). Eugenides has three novels to date – *The Virgin Suicides* (1993), *Middlesex* (2002) and *The Marriage Plot* (2011). The bestselling *Middlesex*, about a genetically challenged Greek American family in frantic pursuit of the American Dream that is compared to the Chimera in Greek mythology, received the Pulitzer Prize for Fiction in 2003 and was a finalist for several other awards. David Foster Wallace is as intellectually complex as Pynchon and has been cited as a literary influence by authors from Jonathan Franzen to Zadie Smith. His Derridean and partly metafictional debut novel, *The Broom of the System* (1987), about a neurotic telephone switchboard operator who questions her own reality, metaphorically subverts the triumphal American "presence". Chuck Palahniuk writes "transgressive fiction" that questions and destabilises accepted social norms. Most of his eighteen novels to date – the best known being *Fight Club* (1996; republished as a graphic novel titled *Fight Club 2* in 2015) and *Lullaby* (2002) – were initially rejected by publishers for excessive violence and sexual perversion. Michael Chabon's third novel, *The Amazing Adventure of Kavalier and Clay* (2000), won the 2001 Pulitzer Prize for Fiction, while his fantasy novel, *Summerland* (2002), won the 2003 Mythopoeic Fantasy Award. The densely packed *Kavalier and Clay* follows two young Jewish refugees in America during and after the Second World War, with America emerging a world power while marginalising many of its own citizens. Dennis Lehane has written six novels in the Kenzie-Gennaro series, three in the Coughlin series, and four other individual novels, besides writing the scripts for, and directing, several films, especially for television.

The Short Story

A major mode in American postmodern fiction is the short story. The aim of the postmodern story is to delve beneath surfaces to expose the rot eating away at the capitalist West and decentre its illusions of superiority. This is intimated in the title of Ronald Sukenick's (1932–2004) "Ecco" (Italian for "here") about the scenes an unnamed narrator witnesses in Venice, where the "here" is not the "here and now" but its "moldering" substratum – "There seems to be an otherworldly concern here for the spirit. It is a practical town, but the unworldly, not the pragmatic, seems fundamental, and the pragmatic in any case is founded on the visible ongoing decay of this world. . . ."

Robert Coover (b.1932), William H. Gass (b.1924) and Donald Barthelme (1931–89) are better known for their short stories than for their novels, and write discontinuous narratives where nothing really happens, to evoke the darker underside, the fragmentation and ennui of contemporary American life. A segment from Robert Coover's long story "The Babysitter", for example, collates snatches of experience – songs, actions, feelings – to project the veiled lust with which the man of the house regards their young babysitter:

> That's My Desire? I'll Be Around? He smiles toothily, beckons faintly with his head, rubs his fast balding pate. Bewitched, maybe? Or, What's the Reason? He pulls on his shorts, gives his hips a slap. The baby goes silent in mid-scream. Isn't this

> [this babysitter] the one that used their tub last time? Who's Sorry Now, that's it.

William H. Gass's "In the Heart of the Heart of the Country" is a rambling and episodic story without a story, about a small town in the American Midwest where life is equated with lifestyle and community with clubs: "The IOOF, FFF, VFW, WCTU . . . the Let's Help Our Town Club, the No-Name Club, the Forget-me-not Club, the Merry-go-round Club. . . ." The unnamed narrator says of this meaningless whirligig, "I must pull myself together, get a grip, just as they say, but I feel spilled, bewildered, quite mislaid." This story by Gass is structured as a chain of several subtitled and apparently unrelated events or descriptions or meditations or lists or literary discussions.

Donald Barthelme adopts this seemingly discontinuous structure in the lengthy story, "Robert Kennedy Saved from Drowning", about President John F. Kennedy's brother, the influential politician Robert Kennedy. The disjunctive sections have telling subtitles – "A Friend Comments K's Aloneness", "K Puzzled by His Children", and so on. The story ends with a ferocious satire on America's propensity to mythicise its heroes. The final section ("K Saved from Drowning") portrays Robert Kennedy as a drowning Superman bereft of magic powers – "K in the water. His flat black hat, his black cape, his sword are on the shore. He retains his mask. His hands beat the surface of the water which rips and tears about him." In the bathetic conclusion, the American Hero is saved by the American Everyman in the shape of the nameless narrator – "His right hand (sword arm) grasps the line that I have thrown him. . . . I pull him out of the water. He stands now on the bank, gasping 'Thank you'."

Barthelme also foregrounds the grotesque and the fantastic. In "The Balloon", this child's toy becomes a sinister gargantuan entity suffocating an entire city, a signifier of the unimaginable unknown lurking beneath the smooth surface of life: "The balloon, beginning at a point on Fourteenth Street, the exact location of which I cannot reveal, expanded northward all one night, while people were sleeping, until it reached the Park. . . . The balloon then covered forty-five blocks north-south, and an irregular area east-west. . . .

That was the situation, then." Moreover, Barthelme frequently mimics and subverts realism with devastating effect to expose the materialistic trivia that clogs quotidian American life. Here are the opening lines of "The New Music" that comprises several pages of terse dialogue between two unnamed speakers:

> – What did you do today?
> – Went to the grocery store and Xeroxed a box of English muffins, two pounds of ground veal and an apple. In flagrant violation of the Copyright Act.

Nearly every postmodern novelist, too, copiously wrote short stories. Analyses of two of these stories – Thomas Pynchon's "Entropy" (1960) and John Barth's "Lost in the Funhouse" (1968) – will illustrate the degree of complexity that the short story form can sustain. In his Introduction to his story collection, *Slow Learner* (1980), Pynchon criticised "Entropy" for belabouring its thesis at the expense of plot and characterisation. "Entropy" is a term used both in thermodynamics and information theory. In thermodynamics entropy refers to the "heat death" or loss of vitality that occurs within a closed system when equalisation of energy among its component particles leads to absolute stasis – this equalisation can be thought of in terms of totally controlled organisation or total disorganisation. In information theory, entropy broadly relates to the expected value of a transmitted message, and particularly to the loss of value when the ratio between successful communication and loss in communication becomes absolutely even and cancel each other out. Pynchon has transferred these connotations of entropy to social systems, one anarchic and the other totalitarian. The story, set in 1957 during the Cold War when unchecked capitalist individualism confronted totalitarianism, explores these two dysfunctional social states in terms of diametrically opposed lifestyles in two apartments located one above the other. In the lower apartment belonging to Meatball Mulligan, a noisily chaotic and occasionally violent weekend party with "simultaneous conversations in three or four languages", attended by Meatball's acquaintances as well as perfect strangers who drift in and out (even entering through the window), has entered its fortieth frenetic hour. By contrast, the apartment above was "hermetically sealed . . . a tiny enclave of regularity in the city's chaos. . . ." The names of the occupants, the man Callisto (a nymph ravaged by Jupiter in mythology, and now the name of one of Jupiter's moons) and the woman Aubade (meaning "morning song" as opposed to "serenade" or "evening song") are sharply opposed to the crudity of "Meatball". Callisto has been holding a sick bird against his chest for three days to revive it by equalising the heat in their two bodies. When the bird nevertheless dies, Aubade breaks open the sealed window to recalibrate the ecosystem of the room. Simultaneously, Meatball's party peters out in total confusion. Neither excessive order nor excessive disorder (i.e., absolute sameness within a system) can be creative. The unrelated halves of the story make it abstruse despite the apparently vivid realism of its descriptions and dialogue, and to that extent it is not an aesthetic whole. Yet "Entropy" remains a bold postmodern experiment. It is not just a fusion of art and science as in science fiction, but an attempt to fashion a literary template to serve as an objective correlative, as it were, for scientific concepts.

John Barth's "Lost in the Funhouse" is a self-reflexive story about writing a story. The operative trope is the "funhouse" which is a darkened structure in an amusement park full of trick mirrors and startling objects and featuring weird sounds to entertain or frighten the visitor. Visitors are well aware of the artificiality of these "ghostly" devices that bright lights would instantly expose, but still "allow" themselves to be duped or get "lost" in the funhouse. From the self-reflexive perspective of postmodernism, realism constitutes a similar strategy of duping the reader into forgetting the fictionality of fiction and believing in the so-called "truth" of the realist narrative. So on one level, the author-narrator of this story acts like a literary editor who lays bare the structural devices shaping a narrative:

> A single straight underline is the manuscript mark for italic type which in turn is the printed equivalent to oral emphasis. . . . Description of physical appearance and mannerisms is one of several standard methods of characterization. . . . The more closely an author identifies with the narrator, literally or metaphorically, the less advisable it is, as a rule, to use the first-person narrative viewpoint.

At another level, the author-narrator tells the story of a gawky teenager, Ambrose, who, like the protagonist of Joyce's "Araby", comes to a painful realisation of his own inadequacy when his older brother Peter coolly takes Magda, whom Ambrose admires, into the funhouse which for Ambrose is "*a place of fear and confusion*" (italics in the original). Despite Ambrose's story being realistically narrated ("The fragrance of the ocean came strong to the picnic ground where they always stopped for lunch, two miles inland from Ocean City"), the author-narrator deliberately undercuts this effect of verisimilitude from time to time, thereby inviting the reader to stand back and assess the storyteller's art or artifice. In fact, the postmodern American short story, like the postmodern American novel, is structured to expose the discordant elements of life in the late capitalist era.

Poetry

Postmodern American poetry is as playfully subversive as contemporary fiction and drama, but sometimes, more overtly engaged with political, social and feminist issues. This group comprises several poets, among them Frank O'Hara (1926–66), Charles Bernstein (b.1950), Susan Howe (b.1937) and the deconstructionist Jackson MacLow (1922–2004). MacLow's 1989 poem "Words nd Ends from Ez" unravels Ezra Pound's "Hugh Selwyn Mauberley". However, for lack of space, only the most influential practitioners will be discussed.

Charles Olson (1910–70), best known for his epical *The Maximus Poems* (1953 and 1956) on American culture and history, anticipated postmodern practice in the dislocated diction, startling juxtapositions, and political critique in his long and complex poems. In "The Kingfishers" (1949), the poet's reflections on the brilliance and energy of the birds are interspersed with quotations from Mao Tse-tung (in French translation) to contrast two different kinds of power: "I, Maximus of Gloucester, To You" (from *The Maximus Poems*) rejects "any old romantic thing" to ponder upon power and domination in society –

> . . . I, Maximus
> a metal hot from boiling water, tell you
> what is a lance, who obeys the figures of
> the present dance

John Berryman's (1914–72) nonconformist diction in his confessional anti-epic, *The Dream Songs* (1964 and 1968), about a commonplace American named Henry, undercuts the gravitas of Romantic and modernist poetry, as in "Dream Song 1" –

> Huffy Henry hid the day
> unappeasable Henry sulked.
> I see his point – a trying to put things over.
> It was the thought that they thought
> they could *do* it that made Henry wicked and away.
> But he should have come out and talked.

Denise Levertov's (1923–97) powerful poetry is politically dissident and formally iconoclastic, as in this mordant poem on indiscriminate American bombing in Vietnam, "Advent 1966" ("advent" is the month before Christmas and the birth of Christ) that cites sixteenth-century Jesuit Robert Southwell's poem "The Burning Babe", where the new-born Christ burns in agony for "men's defiled souls"–

> Because in Vietnam the vision of the Burning Babe
> is multiplied, multiplied
> the flesh on fire
> not Christ's, as Southwell saw it, . . .
> . . . .
> but wholly human, and repeated, repeated
> infant after infant, their names forgotten. . . .

Levertov also anticipates the feminist concerns of Adrienne Rich and Sylvia Plath in poems such as "A Woman Alone". Her poetry, she says in "Illustrious Ancestors", must be

> direct as what the birds say
> Hard as a floor, sound as a bench
> And mysterious. . . .

John Ashbery (b.1927) articulates traditional poetic themes and forms in avant-garde ways. "Farm Implements and Rutabagas [a kind of turnip] in a Landscape" parodies the high pastoral mode through cartoon characters –

> The first of the undecoded messages read: 'Popeye sits in thunder
> Unthought of . . .
> . . . .
> Meanwhile the Sea Hag was relaxing on a green couch ...
> . . . .
> . . . Popeye chuckled and scratched
> His balls: it sure was pleasant to spend a day in the country.

The same irreverent deconstruction is seen in a poem apparently on the Holy Land, which is Christ's birthplace, and where the title runs into the opening line – "'As You Came from the Holy Land' / of western New York state" (that being Ashbery's birthplace). Ashbery's quizzical approach to life is perfectly expressed in "My Philosophy of Life" –

> . . . I had this great idea—
> . . . Briefly,
> it involved living the way philosophers live
> according to a set of principles. Ok, but which ones?

Anne Sexton (1928–74), like Sylvia Plath, was a confessional poet who battled depression, and wrote unusually tender poems (again like Plath) about parents and their infants, including her own daughter, such as "Little Girl, My String Bean, My Lovely Woman" and many others. She also wrote strong political poems such as "After Auschwitz" –

> Anger
> as black as a hook
> overtakes me.
> . . . .
> And Death looks on with a casual eye
> and picks at the dirt under his fingernails.

Yet, her troubled mind breaks through in a poem like "Anna who was Mad" –

> Did I make you go insane?
> . . . .
> Did I tell you to climb out the window?
> Forgive. Forgive.
> Say not I did.
> Say not.
> Say.

Adrienne Rich (1929–2012), like Denise Levertov and Sylvia Plath, is a towering figure in the postmodern poetic scene – and as a Jewish lesbian, she is as concerned as African American lesbian poet Audre Lorde with the harrowing identity politics of American society. In the much-anthologised "Diving into the Wreck" ("wreck" being the metaphor for society) she writes –

> We are, I am, you are
> by cowardice or courage
> the ones who find our way
> back to the scene
> carrying a knife, a camera
> a book of myths
> in which
> our names do not appear.

In "Snapshots of a Daughter-in-Law", Rich explodes the myth that marriage is *nirvana* for woman –

> You, once the belle in Shreveport,
> . . . .
> Your mind now, moldering like wedding-cake,
> heavy with useless experience . . .

She constantly urges female bonding in an insensitive world. "Coast to Coast" ends with the italicised verse –

> *If you can read and understand this poem*
> *send something back, a burning strand of hair*

a still-warm, still-liquid drop of blood

. . . . .

send something back.

The poem "France" again, asserts her dissident, deviant identity in the final italicised lines –

What I am telling you
is told by a white woman who they will say
was never there. I say I am there.

Sylvia Plath (1932–63) is perhaps the most internationally famous of this group of poets, as much for her poignantly confessional poetry and single novel, *The Bell Jar* (1963), as for her tragic marriage with British poet Ted Hughes. Like Adrienne Rich, she uses irregular stanzas and unusual line breaks to signify the discontinuities and disharmonies in women's lives. Poems such as "The Egg", "Nick and the Candlestick" and "Mirror" evoke the various stages in a woman's life – youth and sexuality, the perturbations of motherhood and the agony of ageing.

Drama

Postmodern American drama, like other similar Eurocentric practices, dispenses with traditional plot and characterisation, privileges theatricality in place of dramatic narrative, destabilises representational stage space, uses performative rather than communicative dialogue (that is, self-reflexive rather than self-expressive speech), and often deploys audiovisual media and multicultural theatre conventions. Some of these strategies had already been used earlier by Eugene O'Neill, and W. B. Yeats had appropriated Japanese Noh drama; but they had still maintained the basics of plot, character and scene. Postmodern American theatre was also energised by avant-garde theatre directors like Richard Schechner, with his fluid multimedia stage spectacles such as *Dionysus in '69*, which he called "Happenings". However, no American postmodern playwright has overturned the norms of dramatic representation as completely as Samuel Beckett and Tom Stoppard.

The best known American exponent of postmodern drama is Edward Albee (1928–2016). He explored mid-century American angst at the failure of the American Dream for the average American in nearly thirty plays, some of which are postmodern classics. His first work was a one-act play, *The Zoo Story* (1958), in which Jerry, an alienated social dropout, forces the affluent and established Peter to listen to a long rambling story about his visit to the zoo, and then commits suicide in front of Peter. The next one-act play, *The Death of Bessie Smith* (1959), blasts American racism in the (now disproved) story of the famous African American blues singer Bessie Smith's death without medical attention. The one-act *The Sandbox* (1959) is an allegory on the disintegration of the American family due to excessive individualism. All these motifs recur in the next one-acter, *The American Dream* (1960). Albee's first full-length three-act play is the celebrated *Who's Afraid of Virginia Woolf?* (1962), that plays on the dichotomy of illusion and reality ending in tragic self-realisation as two couples fabricate identities in order to live up to social expectations or to their own image of themselves. A relevant excerpt from the dialogue goes –

> Martha: Truth or illusion, George? You don't know the difference.
> George: No, but we must carry on as though we did.
> Martha: Amen.

The controversial three-act *Tiny Alice* (1964) examines the corrupt liaison between big business, politics and religion in contemporary America. Another three-act play, *A Delicate Balance* (1966), once again reverts to the strain of upper-class Americans striving to maintain the balance between individualism, and family and community commitments. *At Home in the Zoo* (2004) is an amplified version of *The Zoo Story*. Albee's last play, *Me, Myself and I* (2007), about two brothers named "OTTO" and "otto" (who may or may not be alter egos of each other), is an absurd drama about the fundamental irrationality of life. Like Arthur Miller, who in his best plays anatomised American values, American society and the American family in the post–World War II decades, Albee revisits these same themes in the Cold War era, using the postmodern techniques of dislocation, absurdity and performativity as his tools.

Jack Gelber (1932–2003) wrote fourteen plays, but is best known for his debut production, *The Connection* (1959). In this highly awarded and much performed play-within-a-play, the characters of the "producer", "writer" and "photographer" are staging a play about drug-addicted jazz musicians who perform live jazz on stage while they wait, and fight over, their drug supplier or "connection". Arthur Kopit (b.1937) became famous for *Oh Dad, Poor Dad, Mamma's Hung You in the Closet and I'm Feeling So Sad: A Pseudoclassical Tragifarce in the Bastard French Tradition* (1962), where the characters include mad men and the dead. David Rabe (b.1940), who is also a screenplay writer and novelist, is praised for his forceful dramas with their surreal split-level staging. His first acclaimed play, *Sticks and Bones* (1971; also televised), is about David Nelson, a Vietnam War veteran unable to accept his so-called "honourable" role in that conflict. The play scathingly exposes the jingoism and xenophobia of the "average American" Nelson family. Rabe's *In the Boom-Boom Room* (1973) portrays a generational conflict between mainstream American parents and their "flower power" children. *Streamers* (1976) – US army slang for parachutes that fail to open – delineates the many responses to Vietnam in a multicultural group of American soldiers from various social backgrounds as they wait to be shipped out. *An Early History of Fire* (2012) goes back to the volatile and idealistic generation of the 1960s and 70s.

Versatile Sam Shepard (b.1943) – a dramatist with over fifteen plays to date, a successful stage and screen actor, and theatre director – is best known for the award-winning *Family Trilogy* (black comedies on American family life) comprising three full-length plays – *Curse of the Starving Class* (1976), *Buried Child* (1978) and *True West* (1980). Two later plays, *Fools for Love* (1983) and *A Lie of the Mind* (1985), are often regarded as extensions of *Family Trilogy*. The trilogy focuses the grim plight of the American lower middle class struck by inflation and high unemployment during the global economic recession of the 1970s. In *Curse*, the Tate family – frustrated father, exhausted mother, rebellious daughter and idealistic son – scrabble to find the American Dream on their shabby California farm during the Vietnam War years, while trying hard to hold together as a family. This is the "curse" that afflicts the poor in the land of plenty – a character named Weston calls it the "poison" he has inherited from his father which he carries around in his body, and will ultimately bequeath to his son. *Buried Child* is, again, set on a failed farm, this time in Illinois, housing a psychotic family given to depression, crime and incest. (The "buried child" is the offspring of such an incestuous relationship.) *True West*, set in a middle-class suburb, is about the clash between two brothers, one a failure and the other a success, and the way individualism and competitiveness destroy family bonding. *Fools for Love* examines infidelity and failed relationships in both older and younger generations, while *A Lie of the Mind* exposes severe spousal abuse due to financial frustrations. Shepard's dramatic milieu is the dark underside of the American Dream. His settings and dialogues are apparently realistic, but the structural logic is repeatedly disrupted to signal the disharmony in the lives of the characters – the random reactions, hallucinations, incoherence and incoherent interventions create a dystopian obverse of the American Dream.

Tony Kushner (b.1956), playwright, and film and television scriptwriter, is of Jewish parentage and has faced considerable vilification from his own community for his declared homosexuality and strong anti-Israel views. He won the prestigious Pulitzer Prize for Drama, for his seven-hour-long counter-discursive 1993 play *Angels in America: A Gay Fantasia on National Themes* – its two parts being titled *Millennium Approaches* and *Perestroika*. The play foregrounds the marginalisation, even rejection, of alternative sexualities and mental illness in America, and focuses on the emotional instabilities and shattered lives of characters who are homosexuals, queer, drug addicts, drag queens, AIDS patients, and a victim of depression who "sees" the ghost of Ethel Rosenberg (who was executed for treason in 1953). The play uses multimedia and other special effects such as a voyage to heaven, and the cast play multiple roles to signify that no one who is labelled a deviant by the codes of society is ever again treated as a worthwhile individual. Kushner's other plays are either adaptations or co-authored.

♦ ♦ ♦

American postmodernism is often thought to be an Anglocentric phenomenon. This is far from being the case. As will be seen in Chapters 6 and 7, several African American, Native American, Mexican American and diasporic authors wrote radically postmodern works – one has only to think of Amiri Baraka, Toni Morrison, Sherman Alexie, Gloria Anzaldúa or Maxine Hong Kingston, to name only a few. But their dislocations of content, form and theme are in some ways different from the techniques of Anglocentric American postmodernism, since they deploy their own ethnic narrative structures and strategies to subvert established Western literary norms and genres. Chinese American novelist Maxine Hong Kingston, for instance, tells her tales using the format of the rural Chinese "talk story". In other words, postmodern authors who do not belong to the American Anglocentric/Eurocentric tradition are strikingly experimental, but in several different veins.

CHAPTER 6

African American Literature

Krishna Sen

THE POLITICS OF IDENTITY: FROM "NEGRO" TO "COLORED" TO "BLACK" TO "AFRICAN AMERICAN"

The history of Black people in the United States falls into distinct segments. The early phase covers the antebellum (pre–Civil War; "bellum" means "war" in Latin) and postbellum (post–Civil War) periods, or the era of slavery. This is followed by the era of Emancipation and Reconstruction. The post-Reconstruction years saw the institution of slavery being replaced by the equally oppressive social stigma of racism throughout the nation, and efforts by Black leaders to combat it. Till the early twentieth century, people of African origin were called "negroes" even by themselves ("negro" means "black" in Spanish and Portuguese), but with the rise of community consciousness the less offensive designation was "colored people" as opposed to "white people". The next stage occurred in the late 1950s and 60s, and featured diametrically opposed ideologies – the eruption of the radical and aggressive Black Power movement promoted by the Black Panther Party, and simultaneously, the successful nonviolent campaign for full civil rights led by Martin Luther King Jr. (1929–68), culminating in the Civil Rights Act of 1964 (the year King received the Nobel Peace Prize) and the Voting Rights Act of 1965. But it was Black Power, with its provocative slogan "Black is Beautiful" that rendered "negro" and "colored" politically incorrect and "Black" the sign of a proudly assertive racial identity. Much later in 1988, the fiery Black preacher and leader Reverend Jesse Jackson announced at a press conference that his community would henceforth be known by his own coinage, "African-American" (Jackson used the hyphen), to indicate both its past heritage and its present integration into American society. Since then, "African American", usually without the hyphen (and more rarely its hyphenated synonym, "Afro-American"), has been the appellation of choice, although those who prefer "Black" question why white citizens are simply called "Americans" and not "English Americans" or "German Americans". Nonetheless, the successive changes in nomenclature – from "negro" to "African American" – clearly signify progressive levels of empowerment, much as the transition from "sudra" to "Dalit" does in India.

The History that Shaped African American Literature

The Journey to America or "The Middle Passage"

From the fifteenth to well into the nineteenth century, ships engaged in the Atlantic slave trade (colloquially called "slavers" in English) sailed from Western European countries – Spain, Portugal, Britain, France, Holland, and to a lesser extent, Denmark and Sweden – carrying manufactured goods for sale to the West African kingdoms bordering the Atlantic, roughly from modern Senegal to Namibia. The bulk of the payment was in slaves culled from the impoverished peasantry – either kidnapped by European or Arab slave traders or sold by their own African rulers. The slavers then sailed across the Atlantic to the Americas, initially to the Spanish and Portuguese colonies in South America, but increasingly from the mid-seventeenth century onwards, to the plantation colonies of the American South. The slaves were exchanged for agricultural produce – cotton, rice, tobacco and indigo – which was carried back across the Atlantic to Western Europe. The second or middle leg of this triangular journey, involving transportation of slaves from West Africa to the Americas, came to be known as the infamous "Middle Passage".

Historians estimate that ten to twelve million African slaves were forcibly carried to the New World in what was then one of the most lucrative international businesses involving huge monetary investments. Portugal dominated the trade till the mid-seventeenth century when Britain took the lead, until the British Parliament banned British slavers in 1807 – and slavery was abolished in all British colonies in 1833. In March 1807, the US Congress, too, passed the "Act Prohibiting Importation of Slaves" which became effective from 1808; but it was not rigorously enforced and American ports continued to receive slave ships. In the Americas, the trade was handled by slave buyers in Brazil for South America and in all the thirteen colonies for North America. Some amount of slavery existed in the American North till Emancipation, but these were house servants and factory workers rather than field labour, and were comparatively better treated. In fact, the Black poet Phillis Wheatley, who was transported as a seven-year-old to become a house maid with a Northern white family that converted and educated her, hailed her domicile in America as infinitely superior to the poverty and starvation in Africa.

But life was much harsher, and even hellish, for the plantation slaves in the American South, and their agony began with the Middle Passage. In the early days, the voyage across the stormy Atlantic took over six months, and the human cargo of hundreds of captives per ship was packed tightly together in the holds – shackled, and fed one meal a day. The horrors of the Middle Passage are graphically described in Toni Morrison's watershed novel *Beloved* (1987), and its psychological trauma is portrayed in Charles R. Johnson's award-winning novel *Middle Passage* (1990). The death rate aboard the slavers was high due to malnutrition, disease and suicides, while rebellious captives were killed. The massacre of over a hundred Africans on the British slaver *Zong* in 1781 when it ran out of provisions, and the brutal suppression of an African revolt aboard the Spanish slaver *La Amistad* in 1839, greatly spurred the cause of the Abolitionists who wished to eradicate slavery in the US.

Slavery and Its Aftermath

The very first ship to carry Africans to North America, a Dutch slaver, arrived at Jamestown, Virginia, in 1619. But those Africans had already been forcibly baptised and British law, which prevailed in colonial America, exempted Christians from slavery. So they were categorised as "bonded labour" and allowed some human rights. The solution was to bring non-baptised Africans to the US and convert them there, usually after Anglicising their names. "Chattel slavery" or the absolute ownership of slaves, who were treated as chattels or objects with no human rights whatsoever, soon became legal in the American South. This meant that even their offspring, whether born of miscegenation (these were children of enslaved women raped by white masters) or not, were the property of the owners. Thus, slave holdings increased through procreation as much as through transportation. The horrific brutality inflicted on Southern slaves can be gauged from the judgment in the celebrated Dred Scott case (1846–53). Dred Scott was a slave who sued for his freedom when his master relocated from a "slave state" to a "free state", and the case passed through several levels of the judiciary. Denying Scott his liberty at his final appeal, the then Chief Justice of the US Supreme Court, Southerner Roger B. Taney declared, "[Negroes are] beings of an inferior order, and altogether unfit to associate with the white race, either in social or political relations, and so far inferior that they had no rights which the white man was bound to respect."

In 1817, wealthy white Abolitionists promoted the American Colonization Society and actually founded a new state in West Africa named Liberia (from Latin "liber" meaning "free" – now known as the Republic of Liberia) for the settlement of escaped and freed slaves. Later, some ex-slaves were also repatriated to Sierra Leone. But this "Back to Africa" movement did not yield the anticipated result of solving the slavery issue. Ideological and commercial conflicts between the Southern slave states and the Northern "free" states led to the American Civil War (1861–65), during which President Abraham Lincoln officially abolished slavery in the US through the Emancipation Proclamation of 1 January 1863. The period of Reconstruction – from January 1863 to March 1867 – saw the American government attempting, not altogether successfully, to rehabilitate the slaves who had been liberated. In promoting education and job skills it did create the foundation for a better future. Between Reconstruction and the gaining of civil rights in 1964–65, 106 all-Black institutions of higher education, including universities and medical and law colleges, were established, mostly through the efforts of the Black community.

But socio-political integration proved a tougher task. The South retaliated violently against Emancipation by passing the notorious "Black Codes" that curtailed Black people's freedom of movement and congregation. The South's defeat in the Civil War in 1865 triggered the creation, in the same year. of the rabidly racist and fearsome Southern cabal, the Ku Klux Klan, that methodically lynched Southern Blacks and torched their homes till well into the 1960s during Martin Luther King's Civil Rights movement. In 1867, the Republican-dominated US Congress sought to concretise Lincoln's dream of an egalitarian society by granting the vote to adult Black males. Black franchise sparked political pandemonium. Not just the South but also reactionary district administrations in the North promulgated a swathe of discriminatory legislation dubbed the "Jim Crow Laws" ("Jim Crow" being derogatory slang for Black men). The final strike against Black liberty was by Woodrow Wilson, the first Southern President (1913–21) since the Civil War. Though internationally renowned for promoting the post–World War I League of Nations – the predecessor to the UNO – nationally Wilson defranchised Black males in 1913 and legalised racial discrimination and segregation through laws that debarred Blacks from mingling with whites, even to the extent of sharing a bus seat or drinking from the same water fountain. As many African American leaders commented, this was very like the Indian caste system with which they were familiar through their acquaintance with B. R. Ambedkar, who was doing his PhD in Economics at Columbia University in New York between 1913 and 1916.

The African American leadership was not inactive during this period of regression. Booker T. Washington (1856–1915), one of the last of the generations born in slavery, led the movement from 1890 till his death. Politically moderate despite several racist threats, his "Atlanta Compromise" (1895) advocated Black self-sufficiency using the community's own resources in place of confrontation with whites. To this end, he established the famous Tuskegee Normal and Industrial School in the Southern state of Alabama in 1881 and remained its lifelong principal – the first batches of Black polytechnic students literally learnt on the job by building their own schoolhouse due to lack of funds. In 1898, Washington initiated the National Afro-American Council, the first nation-wide Black civil rights group that lobbied actively against discriminatory laws. The most inspiring of his five books was his second autobiography, *Up from Slavery* (1901). A motivational discourse on aspiration and self-help that, though written by a former slave, echoed the national ethos of the Puritan work ethic and the American Dream, it exhorted African Americans to claim rather than grab their political rights through "the possession of property, intelligence, and high character". This was also why he founded the National Negro Business League in 1900, for as he pragmatically observed, "No race that has anything to contribute to the markets of the world is long in any degree ostracized."

Washington's approach was soon rejected as unacceptably conciliatory by younger African American leaders. The "anti-Bookerite" Niagara Movement, an alternative Black civil rights group, was started in 1905 by twenty-nine thinkers and activists led by the acclaimed W. E. B. Du Bois (1868–1963). After outlining the usual "Bookerite" schemes for community development, the "Declaration of Principles" of the Niagara Movement added some important new dimensions: "Protest" ("We refuse to allow the impression to remain that the Negro-American assents to inferiority."); "Agitation" ("Persistent manly agitation is the way to liberty."); and a catchy new phrase, "The Color Line" ("caste distinctions based simply on race and color"). The Niagara Movement ultimately disintegrated due to internal dissensions. Yet, both Washington and Du Bois, in their own ways, gave a voice to their voiceless compatriots that enabled and empowered them, and also provided the impetus for the landmark Black literary and cultural nationalist movement known as the Harlem Renaissance.

Racism, however, was not dead. The violent 1908 race riots in Lincoln's hometown of Springfield, Illinois, where white supremacist mobs destroyed entire Black "ghettos" or urban slums, prompted Black leaders to join hands for the first time with white liberals and Jewish leaders to broaden their support base. The year 1909 saw the formation of the National Association for the Advancement of Colored People (NAACP) that is still active today. Du Bois was a member of its first Board. Its charter outlined its mission statement: "To promote equality of rights and to eradicate caste or race prejudice among the citizens of the United States." Apart from supporting victims of racism and promoting Black self-sufficiency, the NAACP regularly contested discriminatory statutes in the law courts, wrested the right of Black soldiers to become officers in the US army during the First World War, and blocked the release in many cities of D. W. Griffith's epical silent film, *The Birth of a Nation* (1915), for allegedly glamourising the Ku Klux Klan – all this during Woodrow Wilson's tenure. The inter-war years were devoted to a series of unsuccessful court cases seeking to criminalise the lynching of Black men. Post–World War II, NAACP challenged the segregation of Blacks through several law suits. Its first clear victory came only in 1954 with a unanimous US Supreme Court decision that segregation in primary schools was unconstitutional.

The Civil Rights Movement (1954–68)

Martin Luther King Jr. joined the Executive Committee of a Southern branch of the NAACP in Alabama in the early 1950s and soon became its most inspirational leader. He activated a Gandhian programme of peaceful civil disobedience through marches, sit-ins and boycotts, and initiated vigorous drives to register potential Black voters. But the movement took off in right earnest on a cold December evening in 1955 in Montgomery, Alabama, when a tired Black woman named Rosa Parks (1913–2005) refused to vacate a bus seat for a white passenger, and was arrested and fined for her defiance. The NAACP organised a 381-day total Black boycott of Montgomery's buses that were used mainly by Blacks who rarely owned cars. It also successfully desegregated some Southern secondary schools. On 28 August 1963, the King-led NAACP organised the mammoth "March on Washington for Jobs and Freedom", which prompted President John F. Kennedy to send a

Civil Rights Bill to the US Congress, just before he was assassinated on 22 November. But his successor, President Lyndon B. Johnson, persuaded Congress to promulgate a series of pro-Black laws culminating in the Fair Housing Act of 1968 that permitted African Americans to reside in white neighbourhoods – it was passed the week after King's assassination on 4 April. The NAACP lost its centrality with the advent of better times for the Black community, for which it can claim credit. In the long run, it was the NAACP's great fight for civil rights that enabled the election, in 2009, of America's first African American President, Barack Obama.

"Black is Beautiful": The Black Panther Party (1966–82)

The chief ideological opponent of King's and the NAACP's moderate politics in the struggle for civil rights was the bellicose Black Panther Party for Self-Defense (BPP), with a snarling black panther as its logo. Though not the only Black militant group at that time, it was undoubtedly the most influential. The Black Panther Party was founded in October 1966 by Huey P. Newton and Bobby Seale in Oakland, California. Point 10 of its "Ten-Point Program" outlined the basic demands: "We want land, bread, housing, education, clothes, justice and peace." The initial intention was to protect Black people from police brutality by organising gun-toting vigilante groups sporting Afro hairdos. It also aimed to uplift the Black ghetto youth through a nation-wide social service wing that remained active till the dissolution of the party in 1982. But the agenda quickly widened to embrace direct action in politics ("Black Power") and a pan-Africanist Black cultural nationalism in aesthetics ("Black Arts"). The phrase "Black Power" was taken by activist Stokely Carmichael from the title of Richard Wright's 1954 book celebrating African nationalism; the Panthers revived the nineteenth-century Black Abolitionist John S. Rock's emotive rallying cry, "Black is Beautiful", as their slogan; and "Black Arts" was the title of an ideology-defining poem by author-activist LeRoi Jones, who later took the African Swahili name Amiri Baraka, meaning "Prince of Peace".

Numerous Panther leaders were soon jailed for sedition or on criminal charges, many of which were true – some like Eldridge Cleaver fled to long exiles in Cuba or Africa. But the iconoclastic Panther credo attracted millions. The BPP was supported by Hollywood celebrities including white film stars. Two African American medalists raised the Panther salute of clenched fists held aloft, during the American national anthem at the 1968 Olympic Games and were banned for life. The BPP became an international role model for radical groups and inspired the formation of India's Dalit Panther Party in 1972. However, several Panther activists were gunned down in violent police encounters. The leadership changed frequently as earlier leaders were imprisoned or killed, and a distinctly Marxist orientation emerged that was considered renegade in the Cold War era. The 1989 New Black Panther Manifesto dubbed the US as a "black colony" and openly incited Blacks to rebel and secede. The then FBI Director, J. Edgar Hoover, described the BPP as a "Black nationalist hate group" and "the greatest threat to the internal security of the country". The BPP was disbanded in 1982, and supporters claim that this was due to police repression. But it left a lasting literary legacy – the dynamic Black Arts movement of the 1960s.

Black Self-fashioning: The Nation of Islam

The long struggle for Black resurgence involved many lesser stakeholders as well. The most prominent of the smaller Black resistance groups was the Nation of Islam. Its main objectives were to erase the historical taint of African slaves being forcibly converted to Christianity and given Anglicised names by their white masters, and to set "the downtrodden and depressed Black people . . . on the road to Self-Independence", to free them from white "devils". Arguing that Islam was one of the religions of Africa, the Nation's founder Wallace D. Fard evolved his own syncretic brand of Black Islam, added "Muhammad" to his name, and started this quasi-religious organisation in July 1930 at Detroit, Michigan, with himself as its "Black Messiah". After Fard Muhammad's mysterious disappearance in June 1934, the Nation of Islam faced a lot of State harassment and imprisonment of its leaders. Yet, although it remains a minority movement, since the majority of African Americans are staunchly Christian, at its peak in 1964, it had over 30,000 members, including the famous heavyweight boxing champion Cassius Clay, who took the name Muhammad Ali. The most charismatic and controversial Black Muslim leader was actually recruited from inside a prison where he was serving a six-year sentence for burglary, by another jailed Nation activist. This new recruit was Malcolm Little (1925–65), who changed his name to Malcolm X.

Malcolm X rivals Martin Luther King in pan-African and African American hagiography, although his message was confrontation whereas King's was passive resistance. While Nelsón Mandela acknowledged Gandhi and King as his models, Malcolm X was hailed as an inspiration by the cultural nationalist pan-African Négritude movement. In West Indian author and Négritude leader Aimé Césaire's *Une Tempête* (*A Tempest*, 1969), a revisionary rereading of Shakespeare's *The Tempest*, a revolutionary Black Caliban rejects the name given to him by a reactionary white Prospero and cries out – "Call me X !" Malcolm X was famed for his incendiary oratory. "The Black Revolution" (16 June 1963) exhorted Blacks to secede from the US rather than integrate, while "God's Judgment of White America" (2 December 1963) thundered, "If God's unchanging laws of justice caught up with every one of the slave empires of the past, how dare you think White America can escape . . . ?" Such extremism caused friction in the Nation of Islam. He quit it in 1964, became a Sunni Muslim and travelled to Mecca and Europe, only to be assassinated in New York in February 1965. The posthumously published *The Autobiography of Malcolm X* is a twentieth-century bestseller.

The present Nation of Islam national leader, Louis Farrakhan Muhammad (born Louis Wolcott in May 1933), founded the Nation's weekly journal, *The Final Call*, and is famous for organising the "Million Man March" of Black Americans (even beyond the Nation members) to the national capital on 16 October 1995. Its purpose was to galvanise the community and demand greater opportunities since it is still among the poorest group of people in the country. The Nation of Islam has been somewhat on the defensive since 9/11 and Farrakhan has been at pains to establish his group's patriotism, as in this September 2012 article of his on the anniversary of 9/11 in *The Final Call*: "I, on behalf of all the members of the Nation of Islam . . . lift our voices to condemn this vicious and atrocious attack on the United States." But the Nation's membership, though not huge, remains constant, since Black Islam offers an alternative to Christianity and Judaism for African Americans.

The Culture that Shaped African American Literature

The United States twice voted an African American President (Barack Obama) to the White House, and several African Americans now hold important positions in government, education, sports, the performing arts and the media. Yet as cultural artifacts such as literature, films and song lyrics demonstrate, the psychological scars from the ordeals summarised above still lacerate the community. Nobel Laureate Toni Morrison insisted, in a March 1988 interview with *Women's Review of Books*, that it is important to remember that past rather than bury its pain: "The collective sharing of that information heals the individual – and the collective." Clearly, a defining Black cultural experience is the searing trauma of the Middle Passage, slavery, racism, brutality, humiliation and marginalisation: its obverse is a deep-seated suspicion of white America, evident even in Toni Morrison's work. The anger was heightened by the vicious white parody of Black people in vaudeville and broad comedy where white actors were made up as "blackface" characters with shoe polish and portrayed slaves as bestial or boorish creatures.

The regenerative counterpoint of this agony and anger was the memory of Africa and its oral and musical traditions that sustained the slaves, and were later carefully nurtured by cultural nationalist movements such as the Harlem Renaissance and Black Arts. Surprisingly, another invigorating force was Christianity to which the slaves had been forcibly converted – Christ's pledge to succour the poor and the weak and destroy the wicked and the proud was for the slaves then, and for ghetto Blacks now, a testament of hope. Additionally, some of the cultural myths of America as a whole, such as Puritan self-sufficiency and the American Dream, have had a strong impact. Nevertheless, African American culture still remains very different from the European American culture. This relates not just to culinary traditions such as soul food, or to the African "look" with Afros and hair-braiding and dashiki tunics, but to a gamut of aesthetic articulations. In fact, a lot of what captivates the world as "American" popular culture is actually of African American provenance.

Significant markers of the African heritage from the slave era are the various forms of vibrantly rhythmic music and dance with swinging syncopated beats, performed to the heady sound of hand-clapping and African-origin stringed instruments and drums, and with very non-European riffs and improvisations (European music has fixed notation) – jazz, blues, bebop, swing, boogie-woogie, rock 'n' roll, hip hop, and the rhythmic "fast talk" patter that resurfaced in the "rap" music of the 1980s. Christianity blended with slave "rhythm and blues" to produce soul music, gospel songs, Negro spirituals and vigorous metrical chants. Since a normal life was forbidden to the slaves, music and dance helped them endure their tribulations. Other cathartic avenues for self-expression were the strong African oral traditions replete with sly, subversive humour – embodied in folk tales, animal stories, proverbs, word play, and later, the thundering consciousness-raising sermons in Southern Black churches. Verbal artistry based on indirection and nuance and known as "signifying" was perfected by a people denied freedom of expression. The Black community drew inspiration for its long struggle for social justice from its African-origin rituals, its music and dance, and especially "Black writing". Indeed, African American writing, literary as well as discursive, was a key factor in helping the community articulate its aspirations and demands.

Oral Traditions

The Blues

Since the slaves in the American South, with the exception of house slaves, were denied education, they spontaneously created a vibrant oral culture based on African paradigms of storytelling, songs and chants, but these were permeated with a strong Christian content that set them apart from African oral practices. Another significant aspect of slave orality was the development of a distinctive dialect mixing American English with patterns of African syntax, and pronunciation that syncopated words and dropped the final consonant – a Southern Black "language" that resonates through African American writing. Thus a typical expression of suffering in the vocal music of the slaves was the "blues", so called from the Southern Black idiomatic expression, "I'm feelin' blue" (i.e., "miserable"). The themes of the blues were deprivation, depression, and unrequited love. The refrain of "Downhearted Blues" goes,

> Trouble, trouble, I've had it all my days
> Trouble, trouble, I've had it all my days
> Seems trouble's gonna [going to] follow me to my grave.

Here are some lines from "Trouble in My Mind":

> Trouble in my mind, that's true,
> I've almost lost my mind.
> Life ain't [isn't] worth livin', feel like I could die. . . .
> Trouble in my mind, I'm blue,
> My poor heart is beatin' slow.
> Never had so much trouble in my life before.

But other blues songs reveal the secret strength of this troubled mind:

> He call me low-down an' I jus' laugh;
> He kick me in the pants, an' that ain't half.
> He don't know, he don't know my mind.
> When he sees me laughin'
> I'm jus' laughin' to keep from cryin'.

Spirituals and Gospels

"Spirituals" and "gospels" comprise the Christian slave songs. They reveal a more sophisticated verbal art than the colloquial blues with their litanies of woes, and were obviously composed by educated

Black people. The first and last stanzas of an early Negro spiritual, "City Called Heaven", are as follows:

I'm a poor pilgrim of sorrow,
I'm in this wide world alone.
No hope in this world for tomorrow.
I'm tryin' to make Heaven my home.
. . . .
Sometimes I'm toss'd and driven,
Sometimes I don't know where to roam.
But I've heard of a city called Heaven,
And I've started to make it my home.

A well-known early spiritual is "Go Down Moses", in which the slaves are compared to God's chosen people, the Israelites, who were delivered from captivity under the Egyptian Pharaoh (i.e., monarch) by God's prophet Moses – the refrain here is clearly wish-fulfilment:

Go down, Moses
Way down to Egyptland.
Tell ol' [old] Pharaoh,
'Let my people go!'
When Israel was in Egyptland,
'Let my people go!'
Oppressed so hard they could not stand.
'Let my people go!' . . .

Whereas spirituals could be sung anywhere, gospels were essentially hymns sung in "Negro" prayer congregations, and after Emancipation, in segregated Black churches. Here is a complete short hymn with a typical slave theme:

Over my head I see freedom in the air,
Over my head, O Lord, I see freedom in the air.
Over my head I see freedom in the air,
There must be a God somewhere.

The first stanza of a famous gospel song, "Precious Lord, take my hand", goes:

Precious Lord, take my hand,
Lead me on, let me stand.
I am tired, I am weak, I am worn.
Through the storm, through the night,
Lead me on to the Light.
Take my hand, precious Lord,
Lead me home. . . .

The spiritual and gospel genres underlay powerful new songs composed during the Civil Rights movement. "Lift Every Voice and Sing", composed in 1899–1900, was declared the "Negro" national anthem by the NAACP, and is still sung at African American gatherings just after, or even instead of, the official American national anthem "Stars and Stripes":

Lift every voice and sing till earth and heaven ring. . . .
Facing the rising sun of our new day begun
Let us march on till victory is won.

These genres also inspired the well-known Black Panther "prison hymn", spontaneously ad-libbed by Stokely Carmichael to the tune of "Go Down Moses" when he and jailed fellow activists were being beaten by prison guards – "I'm gonna tell God how you treated me. . . . Let my people go!"

Storytelling

Folk tales and animal stories, as with this genre all over the world, were vehicles for propagating social norms and for critiquing the proud and the powerful. Unlike the songs, which have been handed down through generations, these oral tales are mostly lost. One that has survived in various forms – including a 1924 dramatisation by Eugene O'Neill – is "All God's Chillun [Children] had Wings". It is about how, once upon a time, all Africans had wings and could fly because they were God's children. They lost this power due to their transgressions and were cast into slavery. But one day, a very old storyteller reminded them of this miraculous power, and they all gave a great shout and flapped their arms and flew away, escaping slavery forever. The trickster-genre animal stories of the wily Brer (brother) Rabbit who, though small and weak, always outwits the larger and ferocious Brer Fox, Brer Wolf and Brer Bear, have been retold in various media including Walt Disney cartoons. The best known collection in the Southern Black dialect, as told by a fictional character named Uncle Remus, was compiled in 1881 by the white American journalist and folklorist Joel Chandler Harris.

Contesting Slavery through Writing: Slave Narratives and Creative Writing

Slave Narratives

Slave narratives, a distinct literary category comprising autobiographies and memoirs, had been produced by enslaved Africans in the Caribbean islands and South America, but the largest corpus came from the American South and included Abolitionist tracts and sermons. It is estimated that over 6000 Southern slaves, fugitive slaves and ex-slaves wrote or dictated (if they were illiterate) their appalling experiences, of which around 150 were published – about 65 before Emancipation – mostly from England. At that time, they were dismissed by Southerners as concocted, but subsequent historical research has validated their authenticity. Further, in the 1930s, a government-funded initiative known as the Works Progress Administration (WPA) tape-recorded the first-hand testimonies of about 2300 ex-slaves, to compile a historical archive of verbal slave narratives. It is now housed at the Library of Congress in the American capital, Washington DC. In this excerpt in the Southern slave dialect, Andy Anderson, an ex-slave from Texas born in 1843 and interviewed at age ninety-four, remembers Emancipation: "De Marster finished his statement asayin', 'All yous niggers can stay wid me'. I's says to myse'f, not loud 'nough fo' anyone to heah, I's thinks, but de Marster heahs me w'en I's says, 'Lak hell I's will."

The major published slave narratives and tracts had as great an impact on the Abolitionist cause, as the white Abolitionist author Harriet Beecher Stowe's *Uncle Tom's Cabin* (1852). But unlike Stowe's novel that mainly highlighted the horrors of slavery, these narratives demonstrate other significant dimensions as well – they are psychological *bildungsromans* illuminating the struggle for selfhood as much as for physical freedom, and many of them are deeply religious in their quest for spiritual transcendence of their agony through Christian redemption. *The Interesting Narrative of the Life of Olaudah Eqiano, or Gustavus Vassa, the African, Written by Himself* (1789) by Olaudah Equiano (c.1745–97) is the first such published autobiographical narrative to be personally written and not dictated. It was prototypical both for its Abolitionist importance and psychological complexity. Born in an Igbo village in southern Nigeria, Equiano was kidnapped by slave traders as a child, and spent a miserable time in bondage in the West Indies and Virginia till he was sold to a captain in the British Navy and taken to London at the age of twelve, where he managed to buy his freedom in exchange for work. He converted to Christianity at fourteen and his faith was the source of his moral strength. He educated himself, married an English woman and joined the British merchant navy, travelling to the Americas and even the Arctic. He publicly spoke out in Britain against slavery and was influential in creating the climate for the banning of slavery in all British colonies in 1833. The autobiography is written in an extremely erudite style. It begins, "I believe it is difficult for those who publish their own memoirs to escape the imputation of vanity. . . ." Then follow vivid descriptions of the life and culture of his native African village. In outlining his struggle to educate himself, Equiano creates the famous trope of the "talking book" – books "talked" to his master but not to him, and thus he realised the importance of education. He goes on to portray himself as a great sea-faring adventurer and achiever, marked by rationality, courage and skill – Western virtues, but in a Black man. Indeed, a major contribution of *The Interesting Narrative* lay in changing the stereotype of Africans as savages in the minds of white Western readers.

Not all Black slave writers were so moderate. The fiery fugitive David Walker (1785–1830), who sought to incite slave rebellions through his militant tracts, had a price put on his head by Southern states after the publication (in the North at his own expense) of his *Appeal in Four Articles, Together with a Preamble, to the Colonized Citizens of the World* (1829).

There were many others like Walker, but the ex-slave who rivalled Equiano in the power and impact of his writings was Frederick Douglass (c.1818–95), also ultimately a political moderate. Born a plantation slave in Maryland, Douglass educated himself secretly, for, as he later wrote (like Equiano), "knowledge is the pathway from slavery to freedom". In September 1838, he escaped to New York in the free North, where he joined Abolitionist coalitions and became a brilliant anti-slavery orator. From 1845 to 1847, he lectured in England and raised enough money to purchase his freedom and be legally free; and back in America he published the famous Abolitionist newspaper *The North Star,* lectured for the cause, lobbied with American Presidents, and campaigned for women's rights. Douglass's memoirs appeared in three versions of which the first was the most influential, namely *Narrative of the Life of Frederick Douglass, An American Slave, Written by Himself*, published by the Anti-Slavery Office in Boston in 1845. The other two are *My Bondage and My Freedom* (1855) and *The Life and Times of Frederick Douglass* (1881, expanded in 1892). It is in the *Narrative* that he makes the most perceptive comment on the morally degrading effect of slavery on both the slaveholder and the slave: "In entering upon the duties of a slaveholder, she [his mistress] did not perceive that I sustained to her the relation of a mere chattel, and that for her to treat me as a human being was not only wrong but dangerously so. Slavery proved as injurious to her as it did to me." One of Douglass's most famous speeches was "What to the Slave is the Fourth of July [America's Independence Day]?" (1852). It is nevertheless of interest to note that horrifying as many of Equiano's and Douglass's experiences as slaves were, their determination to rise above them and make something of themselves instead of giving way to despair, in some way reflects the core American values of self-sufficiency and the American Dream.

Slave narratives were written also by enslaved Black women. Female slaves suffered special injustices – over and above the brutality inflicted on all slaves, they endured sexual onslaughts from their white masters and mandatory separation from their infants in order not to be distracted from work. A powerful voice against such injustice was that of Isabella Baumfree (1797–1883), who took the name of Sojourner Truth after she escaped from slavery in a northern slave state to New York City with her infant daughter and dedicated herself to fighting for Abolition and women's rights. She was the first Black woman to win a legal battle against a white slaveholder and get back her five-year-old son. Sojourner was an impassioned orator and author of Abolitionist tracts and *The Narrative of Sojourner Truth, A Northern Slave* (1850). But perhaps the best known of the female slave narratives was *Incidents in the Life of a Slave Girl* (1861) by the fugitive slave Harriet Jacobs (1813–97). As a house slave, Jacobs gained some basic education, and her narrative not only highlights the physical victimisation but also the resistance put up by women slaves. She recounts how her spirited grandmother, also a slave, "once chased a white gentleman with a loaded pistol because he insulted one of her daughters". Jacobs herself was ceaselessly harassed. After escaping to the North, and like Frederick Douglass in his early years of freedom, always fearful of being captured under the southern Fugitive Slaves Act, she says, "Only by experience can anyone realize how deep and dark and foul is that pit of abominations."

Creative Writing

William Wells Brown (1814–84), a mixed-race fugitive slave whose *Narrative of William W. Brown, A Fugitive Slave* (c.1848) was eclipsed in sales figures only by Frederick Douglass's first autobiography, soon emerged as the earliest African American creative writer, living in exile in England and returning to the US only after purchasing his freedom in 1857. In the history of Black writing, his *Clotel; or, the President's Daughter* (1853) is the first novel, and *The Escape; or, A Leap for Freedom* (1858) the first drama. He also composed *belles-lettres* and poetry, and in other genres – *Three Years in Europe* (1852) is the first Black travelogue, the two volumes of *The Black Man: His Antecedents, His Genius, and His Achievements* (1863) the first history of the African Americans, and *The Negro in the American Rebellion* (1867) the first Black military history. Clotel and her sister Althesa are the fictional daughters of Thomas Jefferson by one of his female slaves. The novel portrays the special disadvantages of miscegenated or mixed-race people like Clotel (and Brown himself). Clotel's escape mirrors Brown's own, except that she is trapped by slave catchers when she returns for her daughter Mary and commits suicide. The novel then charts Mary's harrowing life until, on being sold to a Frenchman, she meets her Black love in France by chance and they marry there. Brown's caustic humour permeates *Clotel* and its vivid vignettes of the American South "whose ministers [priests] preach that slavery is a God-ordained institution".

Another popular novel by Harriet Wilson (1828–63) – *Our Nig; or, Sketches from the Life of a Free Black in a Two-Story White House, North* (1859) – narrated the racist humiliation suffered even by free-born Black women who worked as maids in white households in the free North. "Nig" is an abbreviation of "nigger", the insulting slang term for "negro" – the young housemaid is simply called "Our Nig" by the family she works for, and not by her given name. As a working-class free Black woman herself, Wilson wrote the first realistic African American novel on the plight of poor Blacks in the North.

The published African American poets of the antebellum and postbellum years are Phillis Wheatley (1753–84), George Moses Horton (1797–1883) and Frances Harper (1825–1911). Wheatley, a Northern house slave educated by her enlightened owners, purchased her freedom using her earnings from the exponential sales of her *Poems on Various Subjects* (1773), the first published book by an American slave. Hers is the ornate style of seventeenth-century British poetry, as in "On Imagination" – "From Helicon's refulgent heights attend / Ye sacred choir, and my attempts befriend" – and her unusual poem of thanksgiving, "On Being Brought from Africa to America":

> 'Twas mercy brought me from my pagan land
> Taught my benighted soul to understand
> That there's a God, that there's a Saviour too.

Horton's poetry is different and quite psychological – his salient theme is the gulf between his condition as a slave and his aspirations as a poet – and has a blues touch. As he says in "George Moses Horton, Myself",

My genius from a boy
Has fluttered like a bird within my heart
But could not, thus confined, her powers employ.

Frances Harper was a free but poor Black with some education and wrote four novels, many short stories and seven volumes of poetry for which she was best known. Her poem "The Slave Mother" describes the moment when the female slave's child is taken away to be sold:

Heard you that shriek? It rose
So wildly on the air,
It seem'd as if a burden'd heart
Were breaking in despair.

It is poignant and also somewhat bizarre to remember that the decades 1830–60, that witnessed some of the most harrowing slave writing, were also the decades of Romanticism and Transcendentalism in white American literature ("Anglo-American literature" in African American terminology) – the era of Poe, Hawthorne, Melville, Emerson and Thoreau that has been hailed as the American Literary Renaissance. The two literatures, written contemporaneously, occupy two diametrically different worlds.

Contesting Racism: The Harlem Renaissance and the "New Negro"

Harlem is, till today, one of the most disadvantaged Black neighbourhoods in New York City; but from the 1920s, it witnessed a remarkable efflorescence of African American thought, literature, art and journalism (with dynamic literary journals such as *Crisis*) that erased the caricatured "Black Sambo" images of African Americans in white racist art. Usually dated 1919–40, the Harlem Renaissance drew its inspiration from the radical socio-political and cultural nationalist thought of predecessors like Booker T. Washington, W. E. B. Du Bois and Hubert Harrison (1883–1927), who coined the term "New Negro", and contemporaries like Arthur Schomburg (1874–1938), Alain Locke (1886–1954) and Marcus

Garvey (1887–1940). Also influential were the post-Reconstruction poets James Weldon Johnson (1871–1938) who composed "Lift Every Voice and Sing" (set to music by his brother), and Paul Laurence Dunbar (1872–1906). Besides his own creative writing, Weldon Johnson did important cultural work for his community by compiling *The Book of American Negro Spirituals* (1925) and *The Book of American Negro Poetry* (1931), with their long archival introductions. Dunbar's parents were slaves and he commemorated that generation by using the Southern Negro dialect for formal literature, anticipating the Harlem Renaissance.

From Du Bois onwards, the Harlem Renaissance intelligentsia was born *after* Emancipation, and some of them were fairly well settled. For instance, Weldon Johnson, a prominent NAACP activist and office-bearer, worked in the American Foreign Service, was the first African American Professor at New York University, and later held the Chair of Literature and Creative Writing at Fisk University in Tennessee in the American South. But they still had to abide by rigid segregation laws and use separate facilities from whites, and they bitterly resented what Du Bois always called a caste system.

Possibly the greatest impact on the Harlem Renaissance was Du Bois's treatise, *The Souls of Black Folk* (1903), a phrase that became synonymous with Black consciousness. He maintained that "a concrete test of the underlying principles of the great republic [the US] is the Negro problem. . . . the Nation has not yet found peace for its sins." His celebrated image of the Black person's "double-consciousness" adroitly identified the fault line in the Black psyche – "It is a peculiar sensation, this double-consciousness, this sense of always looking at one's self through the eyes . . . of a world that looks on with amused contempt and pity." The motif of double-consciousness runs through global Black writing till today.

To overcome this insecurity, Harlem ideologues advocated pride in, and in-depth knowledge of, the originary African homeland. New York City was at this time the hub of a cosmopolitan Black diaspora – not just African Americans, but also Blacks from the Caribbean and Central America. The "claiming Africa" movement reached out to all of these. Schomburg, a Black Puerto Rican migrant in New York, co-founded the Negro Society for Historical

Research in 1911. In "The Negro Digs Up his Past", he held that "the remote racial origins of the Negro . . . offer a record of credible group achievement when scientifically viewed". He then anticipated the postmodern deconstruction of official history by contending that "the first true writing of Negro history [would involve] the re-writing of . . . our common American history".

The most charismatic leader of the "Back to Africa" enterprise was Marcus Garvey, a Jamaican in New York, whose Universal Negro Improvement Association (founded in 1920) attracted crowds of more than 25,000 Blacks chanting Garvey's slogan, "Africa for the Africans". Alain Locke, a Harvard graduate and the first Black Rhodes scholar, edited the anthology *The New Negro* (1925) that became the Bible of the Harlem Renaissance with its gospel of transformation. Locke's premise was that "the younger generation is vibrant with a new psychology; the new spirit is awake in the masses and . . . is transforming . . . into the progressive phase of contemporary Negro life". With socio-political liberation still unimaginable, the New Negro generation turned to the arts as a domain of possibility. The Harlem Renaissance sought to articulate an ethical ethnicity to counter unethical ethnic oppression.

The "Alternative" African American Modernism of the Harlem Renaissance (1919–40)

The Harlem Renaissance produced some of the strongest literature of the modernist era that till today remains overshadowed by European "high modernism". The Black Arts guru LeRoi Jones's (Amiri Baraka's) poem "Return of the Native" begins:

> Harlem is vicious Modernism
> BangClash
> Vicious the way it's made.
> Can you stand such Beauty?
> So violent and transforming.

One hardly associates "BangClash" with W. B. Yeats, T. S. Eliot, James Joyce and Virginia Woolf, or their American contemporaries Robert Frost and William Carlos Williams – even Hemingway is less vehement. Though just as introspective and experimental as "high modernism", Harlem modernism was informed by an intense race consciousness that rejected European cultural tropes and recuperated Africa, the Southern Black vernacular, and the rhythms of blues, jazz and spirituals. The archetypal modernist quest motif is found here in the search for a spiritual self within the racialised and repressed Black body. The project was to fashion a unique Black subjectivity and an African American aesthetic by discovering, to quote Harlem novelist Jessie Fauset's *Plum Bun: A Novel without a Moral* (1928), "the possibilities for joy and freedom that seemed . . . inherent in mere whiteness".

Of the many writers from this exciting phase of Black creativity the major names are: Claude McKay (1889–1948), Zora Neale Hurston (1891–1960), Nella Larsen (1891–1964), Jean Toomer (1894–1967), Langston Hughes (1902–67) and Countee Cullen (1903–46). McKay was of Jamaican origin, widely travelled and with Marxist leanings. Of his five books of poetry, *Harlem Shadows* (1922) won instant fame with its incisive "BangClash" poems that tore apart the façade of Eurocentric culture – "America" ("I love this cultured hell that tests my youth"), "To the White Fiends" ("Think you I am not fiend and savage too?") or "If We Must Die" ("If we must die let it not be like hogs / Hunted and penned in an inglorious spot"). Of his seven prose works, including short stories and travel writing, the novels *Home to Harlem* (1928) and its sequel *Banjo* (1929) became national bestsellers with their raw accounts of Harlem ghetto life – impoverished, violent, yet capable of friendship and love.

Hurston, an anthropologist and folklorist, authored essays, plays, ethnographic narratives, over fifty short stories and four novels. Her most notable works are *Mules and Men* (1935), a lyrical oral history of her Southern hometown in Florida, and *Their Eyes were Watching God* (1937) about a Southern Black woman's search for self-fulfilment, a new theme in this literature. Hurston's major achievement lay in her innovative transformation of a fictional genre much used by Poe and Hawthorne, the Gothic, to convey the Southern Black experience: the horror and terror generated by the use of the supernatural by white novelists become the monstrosity of Black life under the Jim Crow laws. She also re-imagines Eurocentric traditions from an African perspective. In her rewriting of the biblical book of *Exodus* in *Moses, Man of the Mountain* (1939), a Black Moses who is also a voodoo "power doctor" liberates his people from Egyptian bondage. Hurston's works look back to the blues and gospels, and forward to similar narrative strategies in Toni Morrison, Alice Walker and Gloria Naylor, all of whom acknowledged her as a formative influence.

In Nella Larsen's first and best novel, *Quicksand* (1928), the mixed-race heroine Helga Crane lives out a precarious emotional existence on the borderland between Black and white societies, both of which reject her. This and her second novel, *Passing* (1929) – "passing" is a Black idiom for a light-skinned mixed-race African American who tries to "pass" as a white American – are sensitively psychological, not in Freudian or Jungian ways as in Eurocentric modernism, but in their exploration of the "quicksand" of race identity.

A more audacious "alternative" modernism is Jean Toomer's mixed-genre novel *Cane* (1923). Through a lyrical non-linear plot-less mélange of narrative, vignettes of Black rural and urban life, poetry, dialogue, diagrams and songs, Toomer suggests that even if the whole universe seems to repudiate Black people ("Red nigger moon! Sinner!"), that is no reason to despair:

> God's body's got a soul
> Bodies like to roll the souls
> Can't blame God if we don't roll
> Come brother, roll, roll.

Cane does not tell a Black story but invokes the Black soul through traditional oral and narrative modes.

A popular – but now forgotten – Harlem poet is Countee Cullen who mused, in "Yet Do I Marvel",

> I doubt not God is good, well-meaning, kind,
>
> . . . .
> Yet do I marvel at this curious thing:
> To make a poet black, and bid him sing!

But the poet most representative of the Harlem Renaissance, and still widely admired, is Langston Hughes. The complexity of Hughes's poetry derives, on the one hand, from his acknowledged masters – Walt Whitman and Carl Sandburg – and from blues and jazz, on the other. Whitman's meditative long line and dense free verse reverberate through "The Negro Speaks of Rivers", where Hughes draws together all the strands of his Afrocentric heritage in terms of the rivers of Africa and the American South – Euphrates, Congo, Nile and Mississippi. Different from the Whitmanesque sonorousness is the poetry of blues in "Mother to Son" –"Well son, I'll tell you / Life for me ain't been no crystal stair" – and the swing of jazz in "Jazzonia" –

> In a Harlem cabaret
> Six long-heard jazzers play.
> . . . .
> In a whirling cabaret!

– or the refrain of "Dream Boogie" ("Hey pop / Re-bop"). In his "Harlem", Hughes brutally deconstructs the American Dream with the jagged realism of Carl Sandburg: "Maybe it just sags like a heavy load. / *Or does it explode?*" Hughes's prose essay "The Negro Artist and the Racial Mountain" articulates core Harlem values: "If white people are pleased, we are glad. If they are not, it doesn't matter. We know we are beautiful. . . . and we stand on top of the mountain, free within ourselves."

Modern cultural historians, including African Americans, consider the Harlem Renaissance a failure, since the New Negro ideology did not solve the Negro Question, and cite the violent Harlem Riot of 1935 as proof. However, the Harlem Renaissance was not only a seminal moment in Black cultural and intellectual history, but laid the foundation for a distinctive African American aesthetic.

African American Literary Realism (1940–60)

The Harlem Riot of 18–19 March 1935, in which property worth $2 million was vandalised, was sparked off by a combination of circumstances – the rising anger of African American urban masses at continuing marginalisation and police brutality, compounded by spiralling inflation and unemployment following the severe economic crisis that began in 1929 and continued through the Second World War (the Great Depression). Under these circumstances, the celebration of the uniqueness of Black experience by the writers of the Harlem Renaissance seemed both euphemistic and isolationist. The next generation opted for a gritty urban realism and social protest that focused on the frustrated Black populations in the ghettos of Chicago, Boston and New York, far removed from the rural American South. The major names among a large body of authors are the novelists Richard Wright (1908–60), Ralph Ellison (1914–94) and James Baldwin (1924–87), the poet Gwendolyn Brooks (1917–2000) and the dramatist Lorraine Hansberry (1930–65). Some critics describe this phase as African American naturalism. Naturalistic writing, however, implies a scientific detachment and analysis, whereas Wright and Ellison are vehement in their protest and every writer in this movement is indignant about the worsening conditions in Black ghettoes.

Richard Wright, a prolific novelist and essayist, is credited with initiating the trend with his *Native Son* (1940; dramatised with a collaborator in 1941). *Native Son* exposed the evils of racism as forcefully as *Uncle Tom's Cabin* had exposed the evils of slavery. It chronicled the dismal life of young Bigger Thomas in a Chicago slum. Wright vividly describes the deprivation of the Thomas family, cramped in a single grimy rat-infested room, and the psychological impact on Bigger: "He [Bigger] knew that the moment he allowed himself to feel to its fullness how they lived, the shame and the misery of their lives, he would be swept out of himself with fear and despair." Bigger is imprisoned and sentenced to death for inadvertently killing a white woman – his helpless rage against society ultimately consumes him. In his memoir, *Black Boy* (1945), that traces his own life from the South to Chicago, membership in the Communist Party and literary fame, Wright records the suffering of ghetto Blacks during the Depression: "on some days I witnessed as many as five thousand jobless Negroes, led by Communists, surging through the streets." Expectedly, in his essay "Blueprint for Negro Writing", Wright argues for the Black writer's social involvement and responsibility as against a quest for aesthetic satisfaction (which was his charge against the Harlem Renaissance): "If his conception of the life of his people is broad and deep enough . . . then his writing will embrace all those social, political and economic forms under which the life of his people is manifest."

Ralph Ellison concurred with Wright – "I recognize no dichotomy between art and protest," he said in his 1955 *Paris Review* interview. His *Invisible Man* (1952), a graphic account of Black America's nightmares with echoes of Wright's short story "The Man Who Lived Underground", is an acknowledged classic of twentieth-century fiction. It is a *bildungsroman* of an unnamed Black narrator's transition from his small Southern hometown where he is humiliated by white men, via a prestigious liberal arts college that unjustly expels him, to Harlem. There he gets embroiled in the confrontational race politics of the "Brotherhood" (as Ellison dubs the Communist Party) that he joins, versus Ras the Exhorter and his cohorts (Black extremists), both of whom manipulate the deprived masses for their own gain. Caught in a full-fledged riot and fleeing his Black adversaries and the police, the narrator falls into a manhole. Totally disillusioned with the neglect and insignificance of the Black person in 1950s America, he decides to withdraw from life and live anonymously in a basement "damp and cold like a grave": "I am invisible, understand, simply because people refuse to see me. . . . You wonder whether you are simply a phantom in other people's minds. Say, a figure in a nightmare. . . ." In the epiphanic denouement that many critics find implausible, the narrator finally emerges from his self-imposed hibernation and engages with life, "since there's a possibility that even an invisible man has a socially responsible role to play" – though the story remains open-ended as this new avatar is not delineated. *Invisible Man* is an episodic novel in which several segments seem lurid and grotesque, but for the fact that they portray the grim realities of contemporary Harlem life. But whereas Wright's Bigger is so subjugated as to be incapable of introspection, the better educated and articulate Invisible Man has a complex mind. It is in his evocation of the atmospherics of this mind – as when the protagonist meditates on the "visibility" of Blacks to white people in the crowded streets – that Ellison is paradoxically called a modernist as well as a realist: "Do the others see them, think about them, even those standing close enough to speak? And if they spoke back . . . what would they say? For they were outside in the dark with Sambo."

The comparatively younger James Baldwin attempted a different kind of realism. In his essay "Everybody's Protest Novel", he took issue especially with Wright for depicting Black life in terms of white stereotypes of non-intellectual pursuits, anger, alcoholism, violence and total lack of agency. As he said elsewhere, he hoped "to prevent" himself "from becoming merely a Negro, or even merely a Negro writer". A prolific writer, Baldwin is best remembered for his semi-autobiographical first novel, *Go Tell it on the Mountain* (1953), a later novel, *Giovanni's Room* (1956), and two volumes of autobiographical essays, *Notes of a Native Son* (1955) and *Nobody Knows My Name: More Notes of a Native Son* (1961). The theme of *Mountain* is the crucial role of the Christian Church among the Southern Blacks, as a source both of social repression and spiritual regeneration. In *Giovanni's Room* (1956), a white protagonist enters into a homosexual relationship with an Italian bartender named Giovanni, in Paris, making Baldwin the first African American writer to feature white characters in sympathetic central roles.

Gwendolyn Brooks desired to "call . . . all Black people" through her poetry, as she stated in her 1972 autobiography. Yet she is recognised today, not just as a Black poet, but as one of America's foremost women poets, because of her powerful lines and perfect control over rhythm – such as in "Mother" ("Abortion will not let you forget / You remember the children you got that you did not get"), "The Children of the Poor" ("People who have no children can be hard: / . . . What shall I give my children? who are poor . . ."), "Malcolm X" ("a sorcery devout and vertical / beguiled the world"), and her bittersweet ballad for poor misguided ghetto boys like Bigger Thomas, "We Real Cool": "We real cool. We / Left school. . . ."

Another strong woman writer is Lorraine Hansberry who was the first Black dramatist to have a play produced in one of New York's prestigious Broadway theatres. *A Raisin in the Sun* (1956), now a classic work, sketches a range of Black attitudes in the 1950s. It tells of the poor Black Younger family from Chicago's seedy South Side who come into money and buy a white house in a respectable white locality – the fulfilment of their American Dream. While the white neighbours oppose their moving in, offer to buy them out and threaten a law suit, the daughter, Benatha Younger, is caught between two Black suitors – the upwardly mobile and assimilationist George who rejects his African heritage, and Joseph who glories in it. The Youngers finally shift to their dream house and an uncertain future. The play echoes the real-life experience of the Hansberry family in the days preceding the Civil Rights-inspired legislation giving Blacks the right to reside in white localities. The play's title, a line from Langston Hughes's "Harlem", not only gestures forcefully towards the implosion of the American Dream for African Americans, but is significant in demonstrating the way Black writers from the Harlem Renaissance onwards consciously and habitually quote their predecessors in order to construct an integrated African American literary tradition.

The "Black Arts" Movement (1960–70)

In his poem "We are Unfair", LeRoi Jones (Amiri Baraka) potently invoked the magical strength claimed by the Black Power movement: "We are black magicians. / Black Arts we make ..." The poem gave the movement its provocatively punning name – Black Arts. Panther journalist Larry Neal spelt out the symbiotic relationship between politics and art in his 1968 essay "The Black Arts Movement": "Black Art is the aesthetic and spiritual sister of the Black Power concept. . . . It presupposes a separate symbolism, mythology, critique and iconology [as compared to white America]." In "Towards a Black Aesthetic", Hoyt Fuller declared, "The Black revolt is as palpable in letters as it is in the streets." Thus Panther ideologue Addison Gayle claimed that "the de-Americanization of the Black people lies at the heart of the Black Aesthetic", and Panther's cult guru Maulana Karenga stressed the social responsibility of Black Arts to endow "mute matter" (i.e., the ghetto Black) with "force and function". Author Ishmael Reed, who was *not* a Black Panther, hailed the empowerment of the Black writer through a unique Black iconography: "Black gave the example that you don't have to assimilate. . . . the challenge is for cultural sovereignty and Black Arts struck a blow for that."

The result of this dynamic political-creative agenda was the exponential flowering of Black writing of course, but also painting (the "Black Realist" school, for example, and the monumental Black figures of Barkley L. Hendricks), music (the birth of urban blues and Rap), cinema (the raging "Blaxploitation" films of Melvin Van Peebles and others), and journalism (not just the commercially successful *Jet* and *Ebony,* and the *Reader's Digest* clone *Negro Digest*, later renamed *Black World,* but also *Black Dialogue*, *Black Scholar*, and *The Journal of Black Poetry*). The decade produced powerful prose outside of the Black Arts movement in Martin Luther King's mesmerising speeches and sermons, Malcolm X's *Autobiography*, and John A. Williams's (1925–2015) *The Man Who Cried I Am* (1967), a fictional *bildungsroman* based on Richard Wright. It also saw Panther Eldridge Cleaver's (1935–1998) *Soul on Ice* (written in prison in 1965 and published in 1968), projecting the Black quest for identity in white America. Yet, perhaps poetry was the major genre of the Black Arts movement just as fiction had been for the realists earlier – especially the poetry of Amiri Baraka (1934–2014), who also wrote politically charged plays and essays, Sonia Sanchez (b.1934) and Nikki Giovanni (b.1943).

Amiri Baraka was not just a Black Panther ideologue and Black Arts practitioner but a revolutionary on many fronts. His poem "January 1, 1959: Fidel Castro" (1959) and his prose polemic *Cuba Libre* (Free Cuba, 1961) started a pro-Communist Cuba wave that was considered seditious by the American government in the context of both the Vietnam War and the Cold War with Soviet Russia. But his main preoccupation was with the aesthetics of the Black Arts. "Wise I" echoes the blues to spell out Black troubles –

> WHYS *(Nobody Knows*
> *The Trouble I Seen)*
> Traditional.

So in "Ka'Ba" he says –

We need magic.
Now we need the spells to raise up
return, destroy, create.

"Black Art" begins, "Poems are bullshit unless they are / teeth", and calls for "Poems that wrestle cops into alleys / and take their weapons leaving them dead". "Notes for a Speech" conjures up "something locked in / hate, of hate, of hate", and provides a good transition to Baraka's volatile and violent play *Dutchman* (1964). Clay, a Black man whose name conveys the malleability and assimilationist tendencies in Black people that Baraka hated, meets a white woman named Lula eating an apple (the sign of Eve) as they ride a subway train in New York City. Lula alternately mocks, manipulates and maddens Clay with her flirtatious talk. Clay slaps her and launches into an acrid monologue on white people's perversity towards Blacks, whereupon Lula, the archetypal white predator, stabs Clay and then coolly turns her attention to another young Black man who has just entered the compartment. *Dutchman* represents what Baraka called in an essay titled "The Revolutionary Theatre", "black nigger magic": "The Revolutionary Theatre should force change; it must *be* change. . . . The Revolutionary Theatre must EXPOSE!"

Sonia Sanchez, who was greatly influenced by Malcolm X, is a prolific and much awarded poet and author of seven plays and numerous essays, besides being a respected academic. She is one of the architects of the Black Arts movement, as is evident from her first two collections of poems, *Homecoming* (1969) and *We Are BaddDDD People* (1970), and in the sinister free-flowing enchantment of her long poem "A Blue Book for Blue Black Magical Women". Sanchez is a poet of haunting metaphors and unusual rhythms and rhymes. "Blues", an early poem recollecting the panic of slavery, goes –

. . . in my half hour
negro dreams
i hear voices knocking at the door
i see walls dripping screams

The eponymous title poem of her latest collection to date, *under a soprano sky* (1987), has less rage but still her blue-black tone –

> the woods, tall as waves, sang in mixed
> tongues that loosened the scalp
> . . . .
> under a soprano sky a woman sings
> lovely as chandeliers.

Nikki Giovanni demonstrated her Black Power and Black Arts affiliations in her early volumes of poetry, *Black Feeling, Black Talk* (1967), *Black Judgment* (1968) and *Re:Creation* (1970). Her nineteenth collection, *Chasing Utopia: A Hybrid*, appeared in 2013. Giovanni is concerned with the interface of gender and race – not just Black womanhood but also Black motherhood that is central to the stability of the Black family. In "Nikki-Rosa", she says –

> and I really hope no white person ever has
> cause to write about me
> because they never understand
> Black love is Black wealth and they'll
> probably talk about my hard childhood
> and never understand that
> all the while I was quite happy

Indeed, the Black Arts women poets – Sanchez, Giovanni and others – not only transcended the masculinist and misogynist thrust of Black Power, but added range, depth and subtlety of tone to the screaming aggression of Baraka. Their complex blend of power, passion and politics paved the way for the great African American women writers of the succeeding decades.

From the 1970s: The Efflorescence of African American Literature

The long gestation period of African American literature – from simple orality to the more assured art of Hurston, Hughes, Ellison and Sanchez – flowered in the 1970s with a resonant roll call of names that made African American writing one of the foremost Anglophone literatures of the world – in fiction, among others, Paule Marshall (b.1929), Nobel Laureate Toni Morrison (b.1931), Alice Walker (b.1944), Gayl Jones (b.1949), Gloria Naylor (1950–2016), and science fiction author Octavia E. Butler (1947–2006); and in poetry, among others, the widely read and anthologised Maya Angelou (1928–2014), Audre Lorde (1934–1992), Ntozake Shange (b.1949) and America's first African American poet laureate Rita Dove (b.1952). This galaxy of distinguished women has outshone the talented and award-winning African American male authors of this era – among others, in fiction Ishmael Reed (b.1938), John Wideman (b.1941) and Charles R. Johnson (b.1948), poet Yusef Komunyakaa (b.1947) and playwright August Wilson (1945–2005). Having transited through self-discovery, protest and politics, African American literature from the 1970s onwards is both local and universal, and able to portray the past suffering of Black people, which is still the dominant theme, as emblematic of the suffering of humanity in general.

Fiction

The theme of Paule Marshall's work – seven novels, a volume of short stories and a memoir – is the difficulty of remaining true to her Afrocentric heritage and Black American culture while trying to gain a foothold in the cosmopolitan world of white America. This is a new phenomenon in contemporary Black life. Her semi-personal first book, *Brown Girl, Brownstones* (1959), is acclaimed as the earliest Black feminist novel. *Soul Clap Hands and Sing* (1961), recuperating the title of a slave-era Gospel song, comprises novellas about aged Black men condemned to spiritual sterility for abjuring their culture and people for fame and power in the white world. Another well-received novel is *Daughter*s (1991), about a successful but conflicted Black woman attempting to reconcile her rural Black Caribbean upbringing with the bright lights of New York.

Toni Morrison, born Chloe Ardelia Wofford, received the Nobel Prize for Literature in 1993, America's Presidential Medal of Freedom in 2001, and several literary awards for her watershed novel *Beloved* (1988). Her first novel, *The Bluest Eye* (1970), about the sordid ghetto life of young Pecola who is raped by her drunken father, is a classic example of Du Bois's "double-consciousness" – one of the other reasons for Pecola's mental imbalance at the end is her desperate craving to be a pretty white girl with blue eyes. *Sula* (1973) spans a long period from the slave era to around 1840 and explores the ways in which Black society sought to imitate white norms of decorum through its rejection of the nonconformist young girl, Sula. *Song of Solomon* (1977), which is a *bildungsroman* of a Black boy growing up in the North, and *Tar Baby* (1981), about the love affair between a privileged and highly educated Black girl and an impoverished Black man, are analyses of the many new strata in Black society and their interactions, showing that Black social dynamics have become more varied and complex. *Beloved* (1988) is a haunting novel based on a true story of a slave mother who killed her own girl child to prevent her from growing up as a sexually violated slave woman, and vividly reveals the psychological trauma of slavery. The language of *Jazz* (1992) follows the rhythms and cadences of that musical form in the psychological exploration of an exploited Black man. *Paradise* (1997) is a complex novel about the distorted psyches of a people with a long history of being exploited. *Beloved*, *Jazz* and *Paradise* are often grouped together as Morrison's subversive Dantesque trilogy (after Dante's *Divine* Comedy), where, however, the inhabitants of the ironically named town "Paradise" are as damned as those in the Hell of *Beloved*. Morrison's last four novels till date are *Love* (2003), *A Mercy* (2008), *Home* (2012), and *God Help the Child* (2015). Her perception of how "blackness" is actually a damaging cultural construct is powerfully communicated in her non-fictional essay *Playing in the Dark: Whiteness and the Literary Imagination* (1992). Morrison's strength lies in her ability to both sensitively critique and condole her emotionally destabilised characters in a language that is unmistakably African American, without seeming strange.

Alice Walker – a much awarded novelist, but also a poet with nine volumes of poetry and a prolific essayist – is in many ways an overtly radical author, but not always in the manner that Black Arts was. Like Toni Morrison, she both empathises with and critiques her own suffering people, but sometimes her critique is too near the bone. *The Third Life of Grange Copeland* (1970), the first of her thirteen novels to date, tells the harrowing story of a freed slave unable to establish himself anywhere during Reconstruction. *Meridian* (1976) focuses the experiences of a Black woman activist in the Civil Rights movement, Walker's opinion being that the contribution of women in the movement had been occluded. Walker's most famous novel, *The Color Purple* (1982), won the 1983 Pulitzer Prize and National Book Award, but it also launched Walker's reputation as a controversial writer – not only for its explicit violence and suggestions of lesbianism, but because it is a scathing exposure of the subordinate position of women in Southern Black rural society. By this time, Walker was active in the Black Feminist movement known as "womanism" (Walker's coinage) – Walker's *In Search of Our Mothers' Gardens: Womanist Prose* (1993) is a definitive theoretical work of this particular movement. Womanism is reflected in *You Can't Keep a Good Woman Down: Stories* (1982) and *The Temple of My Familiar* (1989). Further controversy was stirred by *Possessing the Secret of Joy* (1992) where Walker made the nonconformist assertion that Africa could no longer be considered the originary homeland of American Blacks after so many centuries of separation – her all-American but Black heroine Tashi takes a sentimental journey back to her ancestral village and submits to her ancient heritage by undergoing the African rural practice of cliterodectomy, but the trauma almost destroys her mind. Walker has been greatly reviled within her own community for this "dishonouring" of Africa.

Gayl Jones is a chronicler of the strange and fascinating aspects of Southern Black life. Her first and best known novel, *Corregidora* (1975), poignantly archives a Southern Black tradition of music and of "bearing witness" to the community's suffering through the life of a blues singer, Ursa Corregidora, whose grandmother was a violated slave. *Eva's Man* (1976) ignited controversy for its graphic accounts of sexual and psychological abuse. *The Healing* (1998) deploys oral storytelling techniques to recount the career of an itinerant Southern faith healer.

Gloria Naylor is justly famed for her extremely detailed and perceptive accounts of the family life and social interactions of poorer African Americans. She especially foregrounds the role of the mother in holding together Black families where the men are too often given to heavy drinking and desertion, in novels such as *The Women of Brewster Place* (1982), *Linden Hills* (1985), *Mama Day* (1988), *Bailey's Café* (1992) and *The Men of Brewster Place* (1999).

Octavia Butler's science fiction constitutes a departure from the usual themes of the genre. She followed in the footsteps of an acclaimed Black science fiction writer, Samuel R. Delany (b.1942), whose work largely went unnoticed by the general public during the raucous Black Arts era. However, he did win many esteemed science fiction awards – Nebula Awards for *Babel – 17* (1966) and *The Einstein Intersection* (1967), and a Hugo for *The Motion of Light in Water* (1988). He was inducted into the Science Fiction and Fantasy Hall of Fame in 2002. Butler has written the dystopian Patternist and Parable science fiction series, and several individual science fiction novels and short stories. She has won both a Hugo and a Nebula for her 1984 short story "Bloodchild".

The male novelists of this period are naturally less concerned with the issues and traumas specific to Black women. John Wideman has worked in several prose genres and written ten well-received novels, all revolving around the vicissitudes and moral victories of Black life in the North – beginning from the era of his great-great-grandmother who was a fugitive slave, right down to life in the Black localities of modern Pittsburgh and Philadelphia. Yet, perhaps his most admired work is his frank, gripping and sensitive autobiography, *Brothers and Keepers: A Memoir* (1984), written in many voices, about how, by God's grace, he escaped the ghetto to become a respected novelist and university professor while his younger brother Robby was sucked into ghetto gangs despite the family's best efforts and was condemned to life in prison for armed robbery and murder.

Charles R. Johnson began his career as an influential journalist, cartoonist, screen and television script writer and winner of many media awards before going on to do a PhD from the State University of New York at Stony Brook. He then wrote several short stories and novels, of which *Faith and the Good Thing* (1974) is recognised as the first African American philosophical novel. But Johnson's fame chiefly rests on *Middle Passage* (1990), a turbulent story of a freed slave who unwittingly stowed away on an illegal slave ship in New Orleans on its final voyage for human cargo, in order to escape a compromising situation, and became embroiled in a mutiny on board. The novel won the 1990 US National Book Award for Fiction not only for its fast-paced action and graphic account of conditions aboard a slaver, but also for its gallery of weird or colourful characters engaged in this gruesome trade.

Ishmael Reed – author of ten novels, plays and over twenty collections of poetry and songs, till date – is noted for his wide ranging and iconoclastic talent. Many of his contentious novels, which tend to be both temporally and spatially fluid, have either been shortlisted for or awarded National Book Awards. *Mumbo Jumbo* (1972) is a non-narrative tale that charts a metaphysical plague striking the United States in the 1920s; *The Last Days of Louisiana Red* (1974) draws on Greek myth and American popular culture to explore Black political and cultural nationalism; *Flight to Canada* (1976) is a controversial "post-racial" parody of the slave narrative and audaciously telescopes time; while *Juice!* (2011) is a volatile semi-fictional account of the sensational trial for murder of a Black man named O. J. Simpson. Reed uniquely received two National Book Awards in the same year, 1972, for his novel *Mumbo Jumbo* and his poetry collection *Conjure*.

Poetry

The decades from the 1970s onwards saw some of the greatest poetry in the African American literary canon, written by a bevy of superb women poets. Maya Angelou, born Marguerite Anne Johnson, was nicknamed "Maya" by her brother, and went through a disastrous childhood and adolescence till her shortlived interracial marriage in 1951 to a Greek American musician, Tosh Angelos, that also launched her stage, television and film career. Her life was always unconventional and tempestuous. In 1969, she wrote the first of her seven autobiographies, *I Know Why the Caged Bird Sings*, chronicling her life up to age seven and gaining widespread international acclaim. Angelou's memoirs are among her best works and reverberate with the spirit of her dictum expressed in an interview: "You may face many defeats but you must never *be* defeated." Her poem on this theme, titled "Still I Rise", is celebrated as a modern African American statement of cultural identity:

> You may write me down in history
> . . . .
> You may trod me in the very dirt
> But still, like dust, I'll rise.
> . . . .
> Bringing the gifts that my ancestors gave,
> I am the dream and the hope of the slave,
> I rise

In "A Brave and Startling Truth" she declares for her race – "We must confess that we are the possible." "On the Pulse of Morning" calls for the acceptance of all races and sectors ("the Gay and the Straight") that constitute the nation –

> Here on the pulse of this new day
> You may have the grace to look up and out
> And into your sister's eye, into
> Your brother's face, your country

"The Million Man March Poem", commemorating Louis Farrakhan's historic rally in 1995, contends – "The hells we have lived through and live through still / Have sharpened our senses and toughened our will." In "Caged Bird", the caged bird "sings of freedom" precisely because it cannot freely float in the air, and this is the theme of her first autobiographical volume. Angelou was inspirational, not only for her community, but for all marginalised minorities in the US – a fact recognised when President Bill Clinton invited her to recite "On the Pulse of Morning" at his inauguration in 1993, making her only the second American poet to be so honoured after Robert Frost read his "Dedication" at President Kennedy's inauguration in 1961.

Audre Lorde, of Caribbean descent, was a highly regarded, unconventional and controversial poet, an outspoken advocate of lesbian feminism and a Civil Rights activist. Neither in her life nor in her work did she distinguish between the personal (her lesbianism), the political and the poetical. The essays collected in *Sister Outsider* (1984) are some of the foremost documents in contemporary alternative sexuality theory – she proudly claims her many identities as "Black, lesbian, feminist, mother, lover, poet". Her two memoirs – the personal/theoretical *Uses of the Erotic: The Erotic as Power* (1981) and the semi-mystical *Zami: A New Spelling of My Name* (1983) where she identifies with the African warrior goddess Afrikete – range through all these personas. Lorde is best known for the five volumes of poetry published in the 1970s, often reminiscent of the Black Arts poetic but largely focused on women – *From a Land Where Other People Live* (1973), *New York Head Shop and Museum* (1974), *Coal* and *Between Ourselves* (both 1976) and *The Black Unicorn* (1978). Her "A Litany for Survival" speaks

> For those of us who live at the edge of the shoreline
> standing upon the constant edge of decision
> crucial and alone

"The Winds of Orisha" (the Orisha are goddesses of the Nigerian Yoruba tribe imagined as a divine sisterhood) asserts –

> This land will not always be foreign.
> How many of its women ache to bear their stories
> robust and screaming like the earth erupting grain

Lorde responded to Black repression everywhere. "The Evening News" begins with a mother speaking to another mother – "I am kneading my bread, Winnie Mandela / while children who sing in the streets of Soweto are jailed. ..." Lorde wrote in the essay "Poetry is Not a Luxury", "For each of us as women there is a dark place within where hidden and growing our true spirit rises." Lorde is a poet of this dark place.

Feminist activist Ntozake Shange – who hails from a poor Southern background – has, to date, written fifteen plays, six novels and five books for children, but is better known for her eighteen volumes of experimental poetry. However, her 1975 poetic drama, sometimes also called a long poem in dialogue (originally written as separate poems), *for colored girls who have considered suicide / when the rainbow is enuf*, won the prestigious Oboe Award, and became the second play by an African American woman to reach Broadway, after Hansberry's *A Raisin in the Sun*. Besides *for colored girls*, Shange is well known for another long and complex choreopoem (a form which combines poetry, dance, music and song) in many voices, *a nite with beau willie brown*.

The rich and varied poetry of Rita Dove is difficult to confine to a particular theme or practice. Though she has also published short stories, essays, a novel (*Through the Ivory Gate*, 1992), and a verse play (*The Darker Face of the Earth*, 1994), she is greatly acclaimed for her many collection of poems – especially *Thomas and Beulah* (1986), *Grace Notes* (1989), the song cycle *Seven for Luck,* premiered by the Boston Symphony Orchestra in 1998, and the historically sweeping 200-page *Sonata Mulattica* (2009). Dove is masterly in expressing deep emotions in the simplest language, as in her sketches of a mother's life in "Motherhood" ("She dreams the baby's so small she keeps / misplacing it") and "Daystar":

> She wanted a little room for thinking:
> but she saw diapers steaming on the line
> a doll slumped behind the door.

The *Thomas and Beulah* poems are written in the lilting swaying rhythms of Negro boat songs on the Mississippi and slave ballads. She uses Greek myths in "Demeter Mourning" and "Persephone Abducted" to remember the forcible separation of slave mothers and daughters. And this is her message to the white people who encounter poor Blacks on the street, in the ironically titled "Lady Freedom among Us" –

> Don't lower your eyes,
> or stare straight ahead to where
> you think you ought to be going
> don't mutter oh no
> not another one

Finally, here is "I Have Been a Stranger in a Strange Land" to summarise the past centuries of Black experience in America – "It wasn't bliss. What was bliss / but the ordinary life? . . ."

Yusef Komunyakaa, who won the Pulitzer Prize for Poetry in 1993 for his poetry collection *Neon Vernacular*, takes most of his subject matter from his Southern Louisiana milieu. "Facing It" states –

> My black face fades
> hiding inside the black granite.
> I said I wouldn't
> dammit: No tears.
> I'm stone. I'm flesh.

The "Banking Potatoes" poems are about the small pleasures of a deprived people. Another series of poems evokes the swing and rhythm of jazz. Komunyakaa's later poems record his experiences as a Black American soldier in the Vietnam War, feeling emotionally closer to the deprived people he was supposed to kill because of his own marginalised background.

Drama

Several African American novelists wrote plays and the poets Sonia Sanchez, Maya Angelou, Ntozake Shange and Rita Dove wrote poetic drama, operas and dramatic song cycles. August Wilson is known mainly as a playwright. He received two Pulitzer Prizes for his series of ten plays, *The Pittsburgh Cycle*, of which the best known is *Fences* (1987). It tells of the difficult days and many emotional turmoils of a lower-middle-class Black family in a big Northern city, sometime in the twentieth century – the "fences" are both real and metaphorical, signifying simple physical boundaries, but also the mental ghettos in which some of the characters lock themselves.

African American Intellectual Movements

No account of African American literary developments can be complete without mentioning the exponential growth, from the

1960s, of African American Studies as a serious branch of cultural studies in the US. The first Black Studies department was started by the Black Arts poet Sonia Sanchez, while she was teaching in a California college. Though it was soon shut down by the college president, it planted a seed that has matured into a full-fledged academic discipline in all leading American universities. Many major Black writers were also college and university professors, and their work was valuably complemented by a new generation of African American scholars, like Henry Louis Gates Jr., who now hold high positions in prestigious universities such as Harvard and Cornell. The second major intellectual development was the emergence of the radical Black feminism, Alice Walker's "womanism", and Black alternative sexuality studies, all of which are now integral components of the American feminist discourse. The African American discursive corpus is now as extensive and vibrant as the African American literary corpus.

♦ ♦ ♦

Each generation of African American writers habitually recalls and subtly cites the traditions and writings of their predecessors so as to construct an integrated literary canon of their own. The tragedies, traumas and hard-won triumphs of Black history in the US remain the overriding themes, and the oral traditions that were enshrined in them remain powerful expressive inspirations. Yet, it is still a history fraught with paradox. Even as the African American Barack Obama held office for a second term as President, an indigent Black peddler named Eric Garner was ruthlessly beaten to death by a white policeman in New York for not having a licence, on 14 July 2014, leading Alice Walker to call for a massive protest meeting through her website. Despite the best of laws, mindsets persist and racism dies hard. So, though much has been achieved, much still remains to be done to fulfil Martin Luther King's dream – and African American literature continues to lead the way.

CHAPTER 7

Native American, Mexican American and Multicultural American Literatures

Krishna Sen

NATIVE AMERICAN LITERATURE

When Christopher Columbus, the Italian explorer funded by Spain to discover a sea route from Europe to Asia, landed on a Caribbean island in 1492 and imagined that he had reached India, he mistakenly named the people he found there "Indians". Thus the indigenous inhabitants of America were called "American Indians" by Europeans – the derogatory terms "Red Indian" and "Redskin" to describe their coppery complexion were also used. It was not until the Black Civil Rights movement in the 1960s that American Indians were motivated to assert their identity. Inspired by Black cultural nationalism, which shed the racist term "Negro" and adopted "African American" to signify both their African and American heritages, the indigenous peoples replaced the colonial misnomer "Indian" by "Native American" to denote that they were the original inhabitants of North America. The Canadian "Eskimos" – an allied ethnic group – opted for "Inuit", meaning "the (original) people" in their language. Native Americans are not a homogeneous populace – they comprise distinct tribes or "nations", each with its own language and culture. Currently the US government recognises 562 separate Native nations. Hence some of them chose the rubric "First Nations". But "Native American" is the preferred appellation, though "American Indian" is still used officially, as in the naming of the National Museum of the American Indian inaugurated in 2004.

Historians concur that these erstwhile nomadic hunter-gatherers came to North America from Central Asia via a land bridge that connected Siberia to Alaska, some 60,000 years ago. After a large-scale melting of the glacial ice around 12,000 years back, the land bridge was submerged by the body of water now known as the Bering Strait. So the latest that Central Asian tribes could come to North America is about 12,000 years ago, giving them a very long history there. Native American historian Vine Deloria Jr. says that their indigenous word for North America is simply "ours". This is reflected in the geography – names of America's rivers ("Mississippi", "Missouri", etc.) and states ("Nebraska", "Dakota", "Massachusetts", etc.) that are not of European origin (as with "Maryland", "Virginia", "Louisiana", etc.) are all of Native American provenance. This is also true for Canada.

Over time, the nations ceased to be nomadic, fostered settled agriculture, and evolved complex social structures, political systems and defence pacts such as the Five Nations Iroquois League. But European contact from the sixteenth century onwards proved disastrous. The fertile lands that Europeans coveted had to be wrested from their original owners. The nations fiercely resisted this encroachment. A series of conflicts, collectively called the Indian Wars, extended from King Philip's War (1675–78) to the 1890 massacre of the Lakota people performing the Ghost Dance at Wounded Knee Creek in South Dakota. The Ghost Dance was a widely practised quasi-religious Native movement following the 1889 prophecy of a Paiute leader that this ritual community dance could call up the spirits of ancestors to exterminate the whites. But rituals and poisoned arrows were no match for guns, though the nations quickly learnt to use horses from the Spanish and gunpowder from the British. Often they willy-nilly allied with one or the other European invader to protect themselves, and fought on both sides in the American War of Independence (1775–83) and the American Civil War (1861–65).

These wars and massacres massively depopulated the nations. But even deadlier were the infectious diseases brought by Europeans against which they had no immunity – chicken pox, measles, and above all, smallpox. Historians estimate that nearly 18 million Natives perished in smallpox epidemics alone. Presently, Native Americans comprise only 0.9 per cent of the American population, according to the US Census of 2010.

After American independence in 1776, Native Americans, who were regarded as "aboriginals", were as victimised racially as African slaves, except that they were never enslaved. Their customs (buffalo hunts and ritual powwows) and costumes (feathered headdresses, leather moccasins and tomahawks) were derided and caricatured. Christian missionaries were already converting them from the seventeenth century, and in 1824 the Bureau of Indian Affairs (BIA) was founded to "civilise" them. By now the slogans of Manifest Destiny and the Frontier were spurring white settlers to occupy the entire continent, and to facilitate this, President Andrew Jackson passed the Indian Removal Act of 1830. The tribes were coerced into leaving their ancestral lands, which they held to be sacred, and force-marched to distant and infertile "Indian Territories". The most violent of these relocations was the "Trail of Tears" of the Choctaw and Cherokee nations from 1831 to1833, after gold was discovered in their territories. But soon there was no land left even for relocation. In 1851, the Indian Appropriation Act decreed that the nations were to be penned up in "reservations", their movements curtailed, and their children compelled to attend BIA-run "Indian" boarding schools to become forcibly Americanised.

Some public awareness and empathy followed the white activist Helen Hunt Jackson's (1830–85) crusading *A Century of Dishonor* (1881), and the distressing three-part memoir of an Indian boarding school by a Sioux woman, Zitkala-Sa, in *The Atlantic Monthly* (January–March 1900) – *Impressions of an Indian Childhood, The School Days of an Indian Girl* and *An Indian Teacher among Indians.* On 2 June 1924, the Indian Citizenship Act formally conferred

American citizenship on all tribes that had not yet voluntarily accepted it. The reservations were encouraged to be financially independent by running craft centres, casinos and liquor stores for tourists. Native leaders used the extra income to found their own schools and colleges, and a cultural revival gradually began.

The next watershed moment was the Second World War. Thousands of Native American soldiers travelled abroad for the first time, widening their horizons. But post-war unemployment and continuing prejudice drove many to drink and drugs. Following the granting of Black Civil Rights in 1964, President Lyndon B. Johnson signed the Indian Civil Rights Act of 1968 that, among other things, allowed them to leave the reservations. Today, many live in cities and have married into other communities. Also, in 1968, the activist American Indian Movement (AIM) was formed. The AIM persuaded major universities to launch Native American Studies courses, and occupied and shut down Wounded Knee town, the site of the 1890 massacre, for seventy-one days in 1973 to highlight their demands. Yet, Native Americans as a whole still have a long way to go. In 1974, the Canadian Inuit leader George Manuel coined the term "Fourth World" for indigenous peoples of North and South America, to denote that they are even more deprived than the Third World.

Representation of Native Americans in White American Literature and Media

Europeans in colonial America represented the Native American either as the diabolical savage or as the noble savage – but always as savage, the quintessential Other, the target of venom, condescension or ridicule. William Bradford dubbed them "wild men" inhabiting "a hideous and desolate wilderness" in his journal, *Of Plymouth Plantation* (1630–51). Even Benjamin Franklin, who appreciated their social system, titled his treatise *Remarks Concerning the Savages of North America* (1782). "Captivity narratives", a major early American prose genre composed by white captives in the Indian Wars, propagated their demonic image. The archetypal captivity narrative by Mary Rowlandson (1637–1711) – *The Sovereignty and*

Goodness of God: Being a Narrative of the Captivity and Restoration of Mrs. Mary Rowlandson (1682) – was written six years after her eleven-week ordeal during the King Philip's War, before being ransomed. It created a quasi-biblical template for all later captivity narratives from the seventeenth to the mid-nineteenth centuries: the pious Christian captive is rescued by the grace of God from the devilish pagan captor. Rowlandson wrote, "Thus these murderous wretches went on, burning and destroying . . . Oh the roaring, and singing and dancing, and yelling of those black creatures . . . which made the place a lively resemblance of hell." But the most vitriolic attack on "Injuns" (Indians) was Robert Montgomery Bird's (1804–54) *Nick of the Woods* (1837), a saga about the settlement of Kentucky in the 1780s that raucously commended the "justified bloodshed" of "ignorant, violent, debased, brutal natives". From the 1860s the Bird-inspired Beadle Dime Novels series widely circulated negative images of "howling savages made for biting the dust".

Conversely, the romantic noble savage, the innocent child of nature, featured in John Augustus Stone's (1801–34) play *Metamora; or, The Last of the Wampanoags* (1829); in novels like Lydia Maria Child's (1802–80) *Hobomok, A Tale of Early Times* (1824), James Fenimore Cooper's (1789–1851) *The Last of the Mohicans* (1826) and *The Deerslayer* (1841), Catharine Maria Sedgwick's (1789–1867) *Hope Leslie* (1827), and Helen Hunt Jackson's iconoclastic *Ramona* (1884) about the love of a white woman for a Native man; and in Henry Wadsworth Longfellow's (1807–82) epical poem "The Song of Hiawatha" (1855). Cooper's and Longfellow's popularity sparked a wave of pulp literature romanticising the American Indian. But this noble savage was actually ignoble since he was portrayed as honourable but too naïve to cope with the white man's wiles. The portrayals smacked of primitivism since the Native was always seen as wild, free and natural, as compared to the "civilised" white man.

These two stereotypes of the Native American – the quaint noble savage and the vicious bloodthirsty savage scalping his victims – continued in the emerging genres of American children's literature, American "Old West" adventure stories and the American Western. Works of children's fiction writers like Laura Ingalls Wilder (1867–1957) and Walter D. Edmonds (1903–98), illustrated with idyllic but illusory pictures of heroic or simple natives, reinforced these notions, while "Old West" adventures mainly centred around a masked gunman named The Lone Ranger and his slow-witted, comic, caricatured Native companion Tonto. The cliché of the vicious Native was largely fabricated by the genre of the Western that encompassed fiction (especially by Zane Grey [1872–1939] and Louis L'Amour [1908–88]), theatre (notably the Buffalo Bill Wild West troupe), numerous Western serials on television, and action-packed Hollywood films primarily starring John Wayne and Clint Eastwood – though Hollywood did try to make amends with a sympathetic but exoticised portrayal of Native Americans (speaking pidgin English) in *Dances with Wolves* (1990), that won several Academy Awards or Oscars. The other phenomenon of white authors composing "insider information" accounts of Native life has produced acclaimed and well-researched works such as Joseph Epes Brown's *The Gift of the Sacred Pipe* (1982) on the Oglala Sioux sage Black Elk. But some of these were proven fabrications such as Ruth Beebe Hill's *Hanta Yo: An American Saga* (1980) on the Lakota. Native Americans, like other minorities, remain perennial outsiders in white America and misrepresentations of their cultures severely alienate the community.

Native American Oral Culture: Myths, Legends and Traditional Tales

Native American oral traditions exist in around fifty language families comprising hundreds of distinct languages. Each nation had its own oral heritage that structured its moral and social organisation. The oral pieces were translated in the early seventeenth century by Jesuit missionaries and later by white anthropologists and litterateurs, but were often doctored to suit European moral and literary tastes. They were originally not intended to be literary pieces, as for example this Papago invocation to the eagle:

> The eagle sings:
> The sun's rays lie along *my wings*
> And stretch beyond their tips . . . [emphasis added]

This is not a celebration of a majestic bird as in Hopkins's "The Windhover" – the speaker literally identified himself with the eagle to share its power through sympathetic magic.

The oral canons of all Native nations fall into five clusters – originary or creation myths, legends of culture heroes/heroines, animal trickster tales, mythico-historical narratives, and chants, riddles and prayers. Creation myths, which envisaged a pantheistic and spiritual universe and (as in all tribal cultures) a ritual bond between a sacred landscape and its inhabitants, come in two categories that may differ in detail from nation to nation – the "Emergence stories" and the "Earth-Diver stories" – and both include post-creation migration narratives from the Spirit World to its American homeland.

In Emergence myths, the people emerge from the womb of Great Mother Earth and pass through various stages of evolution till they finally arrive at their homeland appointed by Great Father Sun. The translated Pima Emergence hymn goes –

> This is the White [i.e., sunny] Land! We have arrived singing
> Headdresses waving in the breeze
> We have come! We have come!
> The land trembles with our dancing and singing.

Earth-Diver stories tell of a great flood (like the biblical Flood) that imperilled the universe till the tribe's totem animal dived in and brought up enough mud to create the earth. For the Arapaho, this totem animal is the turtle. Some myths include a Creator (the Iroquois call him "Everything Maker"), but never the Fall of Man or Hell as in Christianity.

Cultural legends projected named mythological personages like the Seneca hero Gagka, or generic saviour figures like the White Buffalo Calf Pipe Woman of the Lakota and the Spider Woman of the Laguna Pueblo and Navajo. They either saved their tribes from perdition or initiated some core cultural practice. Trickster tales featuring animals like Coyote, Raven and Hare performed crucial social functions – the equivocal actions of the tricksters constitute moral fables that distinguish between good and evil or socially acceptable and unacceptable behaviour. But the wily trickster was also a survivor against all odds through a capacity for rapid identity transformation, and this facet was frequently invoked by Native American leaders during their traumatic encounters with Europeans.

Mythico-historical narratives interpreted real events in indigenous terms. An apt example is "The Tale of How America was Discovered", attributed to the Cayuga leader Handsome Lake (1735–1815). A Native youth craved for glory by discovering a new land: he sought it in vain till a Stranger (i.e. Christopher Columbus) offered help, but with five "gifts" – cards, money, whiskey, a fiddle and poisoned (i.e., infected) blood. Sorely tempted, the youth agreed, but the new land was soon taken by the Stranger's men and all its wealth ravished by the "gifts". Another (anachronistic) version goes that the youth was a converted Christian who mistook the Stranger for the Lord but found him to be the Devil. The story critiques both European guile and Native gullibility. Lastly, chants, riddles and prayers, set to music and ritual movements, were for healing, alleviating natural disasters, absorbing nature's power, performing ceremonies, and bringing good harvests and good luck. The aim was to integrate human, natural and spirit worlds. A Navajo healing chant goes – "House made of Dawn . . . Male deity, your offering I make . . . Restore my body for me . . . Happily with abundant plants may I walk . . . May it be beautiful all around me . . ."

Native American Writing in English: The Early Phase

Autobiography

Early Native writing in English was a product of English education at the Indian boarding schools or after conversion to Christianity. Autobiography was the genre of choice to project the suppressed Native voice and challenge white stereotypes. *Native American Autobiography: An Anthology*, edited by Arnold Krupat, features fifteen Native autobiographies in English from the eighteenth and nineteenth centuries – additionally, there are many letters and shorter journals in archives.

The earliest Native autobiography in English, that of the Sauk chief Black Hawk who fought the Black Hawk War of 1832 against British colonists, was actually dictated by Black Hawk, during the imprisonment following his defeat, to an English interpreter, and published in 1833. Subsequent autobiographies were written by the authors themselves. The Reverend Samson Occom (1723–92), a converted Christian minister from the Mohegan nation, wrote an undated account, *A Short Narrative of My Life*, that is thought to be one of the earliest personally written memoirs. In *A Short Narrative*, Occom vividly recorded not only his spiritual awakening through the Bible, but also the treachery of his English mentor, Eleazar Wheelock, who promised to care for Occom's family during the latter's trip to England to raise money for Wheelock's school, but left them starving and destitute.

The best-known early Native autobiographer in English is William Apess (1798–1839) of the Pequot nation who became a Methodist minister and Native activist. In 1829, he published *A Son of the Forest: The Experience of William Apess, A Native of the Forest, Comprising a Notice of the Pequot Tribe of Indians, Written by Himself.* While giving a detailed account of his life and his serious engagement with Christianity, Apess also documented the social marginalisation of Natives:

> I thought it disgraceful to be called an Indian; it was considered as a slur upon an oppressed and scattered nation, and I have often been led to inquire where the whites received this word, which they so often threw as an opprobrious epithet at the sons of the forest. I could not find it in the Bible and therefore concluded that it was a word imported for the special purpose of degrading us. . . . The proper term which ought to be applied to our nation . . . is that of *Natives* . . .

Another notable autobiographer was George Copway (1818–69) of the Ojebwa (or Ojibwa) nation and a Methodist preacher. In 1847, he published a memoir about his life and times using his given Native name – *The Life, History and Travels of Kah-ge-ga-gah-Bowh, Written by Himself*, and subtitled *With a Sketch of the Present State of the Ojebwa Nation.* While giving many personal details, including his travels in Europe, Copway is especially valuable for his careful chronicling of the crafts, customs and ceremonies of the Ojebwa in the first six chapters. A similar personal and community history was the Paiute Sarah Winnemucca's (1844–91) *Life among the Piutes [sic]: Their Wrongs and Claims* (1883).

Political Discourse

In his Preface to *The Life, History and Travels*, Copway voices his concern for "the present state and prospects of my poor countrymen . . . those who were once lords of the land". This fear is reflected in numerous political tracts, though responses varied from appeasement to resistance. The Cherokee Trail of Tears prompted Cherokee journalist Elias Boudinot (1802–39), who edited the *Cherokee Phoenix*, to advocate acculturating to white norms as the only way to survive. In his "Address to the Whites" in Philadelphia in 1826 he said, "We have seen everywhere the poor aborigines melt away before the white population . . . until only a few solitary creatures are left to tell the sad story of extinction. . . . They hang upon your mercy as to a garment. Will you push them from you or will you save them? Let humanity answer." Boudinot was killed by fellow Cherokees for supporting the Indian Removal Act. Very different was William Apess in his "An Indian Looking-Glass for the White Man" (1833): "Now I ask if degradation has not been heaped long enough upon the Indians? . . . is it right to hold and promote prejudices?" Apess concluded that only when "the mantle of prejudice [is] torn from every American heart – then shall peace pervade the Union."

Fiction

The first Native American novel was *The Life and Adventures of Joaquin Murieta: The Celebrated California Bandit* (1854) by the Cherokee John Rolling Ridge (1827–67). It portrayed the California gold rush in the Cherokee territory. The first Native American woman novelist was S. Alice Callahan (1864–94) with *Wynema: A Child of the Forest* (1891) about a cross-cultural friendship between a white teacher (Genevieve) and her Native student (Wynema).

Sioux author Charles Eastman (1858–1939) vividly portrayed the Sioux culture in popular short story collections such as *Red Hunters and Animal People* (1904), *Old Indian Days* (1907) and *Smoky Days, Wigwam Evenings* (1910). Noted activist and anthropologist D'Arcy McNickle (1904–77) of the Salish Kootenai nation also wrote fiction and is best known for *The Surrounded* (1936) that anticipated later fictional themes of Native American alienation and identity formation.

Post-1960s: The Native American Literary "Renaissance"

Native American Renaissance is the title of a 1983 book by Kenneth Lincoln on post-1960s Native American literature. Though criticised for downplaying oral traditions and early writing, it highlights a remarkable efflorescence of acclaimed work by authors hailing from the emerging urban educated middle class. N. Scott Momaday (b.1934), whose *House Made of Dawn* won the Pulitzer Prize in 1969 and initiated the Renaissance, is a PhD from Stanford University and a lawyer by profession – others are university professors. So their negotiation of their community's predicament differs from that of their forbears.

Lincoln divides the Renaissance into two phases. The first features novelists N. Scott Momaday (Kiowa), Gerald Vizenor (b.1934; Ojibwa), James Welch (1940–2003; Blackfeet) and Leslie Marmon Silko (b.1948; Laguna Pueblo); and poets Paula Gunn Allen (1939–2008; mixed Lebanese/Laguna) and Simon J. Ortiz (b.1941; Acoma Pueblo). The second phase has younger writers – novelists Louise Erdrich (b.1954; mixed German/Ojibwe) and Sherman Alexie (b.1966; Spokane/Coeur D'Alene), and poet Joy Harjo (b.1951; Creek). All are activists, all have won prestigious literary awards, many teach at leading universities, and some have received national honours.

In his theoretical work, *Manifest Manners* (1994), Vizenor describes the common theme of Native American writing as "Postindian survivance" – "Postindian" in transcending white stereotypes, and "survivance" or "trickster hermeneutics" to subvert white dominance. Survivance also involves recuperating the originary culture. As LaVonne Ruoff says, in *Native American Literatures*, "Although individual Indians today vary in the extent to which they follow tribal traditions, their worldview and values continue to reflect those of their ancestors." This is contrary to Western thinking but akin to traditional Asian and African societies.

The protagonists of all the debut novels of Lincoln's first phase move from intense alienation, sparked by social prejudice, to spiritual recovery through a return to their roots – Abel in Momaday's *House Made of Dawn* (1968), the unnamed narrator of Welch's *Winter in the Blood* (1974), Tayo in Silko's *Ceremony* (1977), and the travellers in Vizenor's *Darkness in St. Louis Bearheart* (1978; revised in 1990 as *Bearheart: The Heirship Chronicles*). Mirroring the Native American's location at the edge of American society, Abel and Tayo, both of them confused and self-destructive World War II returnees, are illegitimate and mixed-blood *mestizo* respectively, while Welch's hero is an alcoholic. They get involved in brawls and are jailed, or escape like tricksters. Abel is redeemed by re-embracing his Native culture, signalled by his singing the Navajo healing song "House Made of Dawn". Tayo is reintegrated with restorative nature by the old Navajo healer Betonie and the medicine woman T'seh. Welch's feckless narrator finally realises that he must look inward to resolve his identity crisis: aided by Yellow Calf, a wise community elder, he learns to accept his origin and memories, and thaw the "ice" in his blood.

Not only thematically but narratologically also, Renaissance authors merge past and present by drawing on their inherited cultural traditions to articulate contemporary concerns, much like African American authors. It is this remembering and reinventing the community's defamed past that makes minority literature both spiritual and political. Momaday's *House Made of Dawn* engages with the Native trope of healing in its very title, while *The Way to Rainy Mountain* (1969), an account of his Kiowa people, is a blend of history, folklore and ritual verse. Silko uses a story-based plot and the stream of consciousness technique for Tayo's delusional moments in *Ceremony*, but the novel proceeds thematically through successive Laguna Pueblo chants – the opening Creation chant on

Thought-Woman ("as she named them / they appeared") and her panacea ("the only cure I know / is a good ceremony") prefigure Tayo's spiritual salvation through Native means rather than psychiatric counselling (that failed), and the interspersed chants mark the way forward. Vizenor's *Bearheart* is radical in interweaving science fiction with Blackfeet trickster myths in an oxymoronic mode he calls "mythic verism" (i.e., mythic verisimilitude), rather like "magical realism".

Paula Gunn Allen, author of a well-received novel on the "marginal of the marginal", or the mixed-blood *mestizo*, in *The Woman who Owned the Shadows* (1983) as well as *The Sacred Hoop: Recovering the Feminine in American Indian Traditions* (1986), expressed the conflict between Native and white ways in her poetry. In "The Blind Lion" she says – "The silence I have grown carefully through the day / Slides away from me … I fall into noisy abstraction . . .". "Coda" uses the Whitmanesque long line to fuse together mythic and modern perceptions –

> . . . if I'd had
> the flames of melted streets and lived in laughter sharp
> as August grass …

The stress of Native American existence surfaces again in "The Derner Report on Camp Creek Road" where the community's history is compared to "a journey as long as a night of rot".

Simon J. Ortiz is widely hailed as the most significant contemporary Native American poet. Like his fellow authors, he contrasts the materialistic life of America with the earth-oriented life of "the People". In "From Sand Creek" he contrasts an America "of steel and mad death" with the neglected beauty of nature as flowers bloom and a spring wind rises from Sand Creek. The two worldviews clash with each other. In 'Spreading Wings in the Wind" Ortiz observes –

> I must remember
> that I am only one
> among many parts . . .

"Morning Star" is about the sacred space of the union between the human, the natural and the spiritual –

> the center of all spaces
> looking out
> and always.

The elemental Native spirit reverberates in the closing lines of "Grand Canyon, Christmas Eve 1969" –

> I lie down on my earth bed ...
> Here it is possible
> to believe eternity.

The later work of the first-phase Renaissance novelists, like that of the younger second-phase writers Louise Erdrich and Sherman Alexie, shifts the gaze to present-day Native American urban experience. In Momaday's *Ancient Child* (1989), Locke Setman or Set, a Kiowa artist and urbane yuppie, exhibits his paintings in New York and Paris; in Welch's *The Indian Lawyer* (1990), thc Blackfeet hero Sylvester Yellow Calf is a corporate lawyer seeking election to the US Congress; Vizenor's Griever de Hocus, in *Griever: An American Monkey King in China* (1986), is a middle-class teacher. Yet, there are strong mythic undertones. "Set" is the Kiowa word for "bear", and Momaday's enigmatic Set transits between human and animal intuitions (as when he "hears" the hawk ruffling its feathers in the wind), pointing to the cosmic union of all beings. The aptly named Griever de Hocus is a protean trickster figure, and Welch's Sylvester Yellow Calf is torn between the two worlds signified by his name.

Prolific and acclaimed author Louise Erdrich has fourteen novels and a short story collection till date besides children's literature, poetry, anthologies and non-fiction, and is the founder of Birchbark Books and Wigwam Press. She employs postmodern techniques like fluid time shifts, multiple narrators, plural perspectives, defamiliarisation and mystification, intersected by Native myths, storytelling and animal and trickster lore, to project Native experiences of racism, violence and insecurity in past and present times. Her first novel, *Love Medicine* (1984; revised and expanded versions in 1993 and 2009), mixes first and third person narration to highlight Erdrich's recurrent themes of personal tragedy and loss of cultural and spiritual identity due to white hostility and insensitive government legislation. *The Beet Queen* (1986) focuses on the predicament of mixed-bloods, and *Tracks* (1988) shows the alleviating impact of the elder-cum-trickster figure Nanapush on the miseries of life in the reservation. *The Plague of Doves* (2008) and *The Round House* (2012) demonstrate how Native Americans can be murdered and raped with impunity by outsiders using loopholes in the laws governing the reservations.

The novels and short stories of Sherman Alexie – who also writes poetry, non-fiction and screenplays and directs films – are replete with black comedy and Native American Gothic. In his acerbic 1996 essay, "How to Write the Great American Indian Novel", Alexie problematises white responses even today to "the [Indian] savage in blue jeans and T-shirt" and concludes darkly: "In the Great American Indian novel when it is finally written all of the white people will be Indians and all of the Indians will be ghosts." This is exactly what happens in his fiction. Racially prejudiced and vengeful whites are the real savages in blue jeans and T-shirts. But there is a mordant pun on "ghosts". Alexie's Native characters are not the triumphant ghosts of the Ghost Dance but ordinary folk confused at being stereotyped as arcane "earth people" or cartoon characters or menacing savages, who become "ghosts" unable to forge authentic selves.

Alexie is not afraid of controversy. The problem, he says in "A Drug Called Tradition" in his first book, a story collection titled *The Lone Ranger and Tonto Fistfight in Heaven* (1993), is that "Although it is the twentieth century and planes are passing overhead, the Indian boys have decided to be real Indians." Yet as the boy Thomas discovers, "Your past is a skeleton walking one step behind you, and your future is a skeleton walking one step in front of you." Both *Lone Ranger* and Alexie's second book and first novel, *Reservation Blues* (1995), chart the dislocation of Native youth as a traditional culture clashes with a late capitalist consumer culture. In his second novel, the macabre Gothic *Indian Killer* (1996), a Seattle-based

American Indian named John Smith decides to "fulfil" his "destiny" as a savage by serially killing whites: undetected till the end, he dances the Ghost Dance in the final chapter caustically captioned "A Creation Story". The novel critiques the destructive nature of both white and Native mythologies. Of the two novels published in 2007, *The Absolutely True Diary of a Part-Time Indian* tracks the violence encountered by a teenager when he enrols in a white high school to realise the American Dream, and *Flight* uses the "trickster transformation" motif and fantasy to reveal the vulnerability of a deprived Native adolescent killer, Zits. Of four story collections after *Lone Ranger*, black comedy permeates accounts of alcoholism, failure and hate crimes in *War Dances* (2009) and *Blasphemy* (2012).

Joy Harjo, a widely praised poet, has published seven volumes of poetry, besides other work. Harjo's ethnic roots are very strong, as in "Remember" – "Remember the sky that you were born under . . . Remember the moon, who she is . . . Remember the wind . . . I hear her singing Kiowa war dance songs at the corner of Fourth and Central." But she also speaks for all voiceless people in a racially hostile world. In "Anchorage" she writes –

> And I think of the 6th Avenue jail, of mostly Native
> and Black men . . .
> . . . .
> . . . who would believe
> the fantastic and terrible story of all of our survival . . .

Like her peers in the Native American Renaissance, Joy Harjo has put Native American creative writing on the literary map of America.

Mexican American or Chicano/Chicana Literature

"Chicano" (feminine "Chicana") is an abbreviation of Spanish "Mexicano" (sixteenth-century pronunciation – "Mechicano") or "Mexican", and is applied to American citizens of Mexican origin. Chicanos were initially not immigrants. Mexico, a Spanish colony since 1521, gained its independence in 1821 and immediately faced border conflicts with an expansionist US. The skirmishes escalated into the Mexican-American War (1846–48) that ended in a decisive American victory. With the Treaty of Guadalupe Hidalgo, signed on 2 February 1848, Mexico ceded its entire northern portion that either enlarged existing American states or created new states in what is called the "American Southwest" – Texas, New Mexico, Arizona, Nevada, Utah, Wyoming, Colorado and California. Mexicans residing in these areas willy-nilly became a marginalised American ethnic minority. Later Mexican entrants, mostly illegal immigrants in search of a better life, are also called Chicanos – a very large influx of such immigrants occurred during the Mexican Revolution and Civil War (1910–20).

The Second World War had the same impact on Chicano army recruits as on African Americans and Native Americans – the new cosmopolitanism made white racism more insufferable. The Civil Rights ferment of the 1960s inspired the Chicano labour leader Cesar Chavez (1927–93) to unionise impoverished Chicano agricultural labourers in the United Farm Workers Association (UFWA). Chavez promoted Chicano labour rights through lengthy strikes and Gandhian fasts and died during one such fast. Chavez's movement also catalysed Chicano cultural nationalism or "chicanista" that led to a major artistic revival.

Chicanos have retained their Mexican-Spanish identity. They have Spanish names and speak Spanish (making Spanish the second language in the US after English), are Roman Catholics rather than Protestants, and identify with Spanish and Latin American culture. So along with Cuban and Puerto Rican immigrants, they are classed as Hispanics (colloquially "Latinos") – culturally closer to South America than to the US where even African Americans and Native Americans speak English and are Protestants.

Nineteenth-century Chicano literature was written in Spanish and used genres common to Spain – romance, picaresque novella, "decinas" (a ten-line poem with a fixed rhyme scheme), "historia" (a blend of history and personal memoir) and "corrido" (a melancholy narrative ballad on social injustice, much like the slave-era blues). Notable *historias* (histories) in Spanish were by Juan Seguin

(1806–90) and Mariano Vallejo (1807–90) on the conquest of Texas and California respectively. Other *historias* recorded vanishing lifestyles under American occupation. English works were fewer. The old Spanish West was chronicled in the memoirs *Tough Trip through Paradise 1878–1879* by Andrew Garcia and the multi-volume *My Life on the Frontier* (published in 1935) by Antonio Miguel Otero (1859–1944). The interwar years saw the emergence of several literary journals that encouraged Chicano poetry, short fiction and folklore, mostly in Spanish, and after the Second World War, "Tejano" (i.e., Texan) Spanish literature flourished.

The Chicano cultural renaissance from the 1960s witnessed more writing in English, and the emergence of a hybrid "Spanglish", or fluid mix of Spanish and English. In a 1994 interview, Chicana novelist Sandra Cisneros described Spanglish as an asset that gave her "twice as many words to pick from . . . two ways [i.e., Anglo and Chicano] of looking at the world". Another aspect was the recuperation of the ancient Mexican-Aztec inheritance to complement the Mexican-Spanish heritage. The two pasts coalesced in the fusion of two iconic figures – the Virgin of Guadalupe (i.e. the Virgin Mary) who was said to have appeared five times to believers in the Mexican town of Guadalupe in December 1531, and La Llorona or the Weeping Woman from a famous Mexican folktale. The composite Catholic-cum-folk mother figure became a symbol of the lost Aztlán, the legendary homeland of the Aztecs, in the Chicano creative imagination.

The cultural revival emanated from several sources in the Southwest. In 1965, Chicano dramatist Luis Valdez (b.1940) launched the proletarian El Teatro Campesino (The Farm Workers' Theatre) that initially performed plays on social issues with untrained actors atop flatbed trucks in the fields, but soon became so famous that the renowned British theatre director Peter Brooks came as Guest Director in 1973, and the US government sponsored a tour of Europe in 1976. Another major inspiration was Americo Paredes (1915–99) whose voluminous research on Chicano folkways consolidated Chicano literary culture. Paredes was also famous for two very different works. *With His Pistol in His Hand: A Border Ballad and Its Hero* (1958) is his account of the Chicano protagonist of a famous *corrido*, the indigent ranch-hand Gregorio Cortez, who successfully challenged a brutal white Texas sheriff to a duel. Paredes's very popular novel, *George Washington Gomez* (1990), signalled the fractured Chicano identity through the hero's Anglo-Mexican name.

A crucial literary milestone was the corrosive 1969 poetry collection in English by Abelardo ("Lalo") Delgado (1931–2004), *Chicano: 25 Pieces of a Chicano Mind.* The poem "stupid America" goes –

> stupid america, hear that
> chicano
> shouting curses on the street
> he is a poet ...

Equally important are two novelists who wrote in Spanish about the harsh destiny of Chicanos in America – Rolando Hinojosa-Smith (b.1929) and Tomás Rivera (1935–1984).

The 1970s saw a number of major authors in English/Spanglish who popularised Chicano literature in the US and who, like their peers in other American ethnic minorities, have won major literary honours and are noted academics in leading universities – novelists Rudolfo Anaya (b.1937), Francisco Jiménez (b.1943), Helena Maria Viramontes (b.1954), Sandra Cisneros (b.1954) and Ana Castillo (b.1953); playwright Luis Valdez (b.1940); poet Gary Soto (b.1952); and influential feminist essayists Cherríe Moraga (b.1952), and Gloria Anzaldúa (1942–2004) who introduced the seminal "border theory" in ethnicity and race studies.

The quintessential and most acclaimed Chicano novel is Rudolfo Anaya's lyrical multi-layered *bildungsroman*, *Bless Me, Ultima* (1972). The book is rooted in Chicano culture symbolised by the seven-year-old protagonist Antonio's grandmother Ultima, who is a "curandera" or traditional healer. The story swings between two opposed worlds on the US–Mexico border during the Second World War – the myth and magic of a vanishing past and the bitter experiences of a violent present. The past is figured through Ultima's arcane knowledge of curative herbs and waters, the earth-oriented life of Antonio's mother's "pueblo" or village, and the unfettered cowboy culture of his father's clan from the "llano" or plains of Las Pasturas. The bitter present is the rustic town of Guadalupe where the Virgin's worship is marred by the railway bringing noisy American tourists, and Los Alamos where the atomic bomb was developed. The testing of the bomb near Antonio's home, showering radiation on an area classified as "empty" by the government, since only Chicanos and the Native American Comanche lived there, is the cataclysmic event of the novel. A confused Antonio, by now an adolescent, finally seeks solace in his grandmother's myths and the lives and beliefs of his parents, as opposed to a menacing Anglo modernity. Anaya said of the novel in a 1995 interview: "What I've wanted to do is compose the Chicano worldview—the synthesis that shows our true mestizo [i.e., mixed Spanish-Mexican] identity—and clarify it for my community and myself."

Ultima is the first of a trilogy and is followed by *Heart of Aztlán* (1976) and *Tortuga* (1979). Both novels feature visionary healers (Crispin and Benjie/Tortuga respectively) and supernatural out-of-body experiences that transport characters away from the sordid present to the mythic Chicano spiritual abode of Aztlán. Among Anaya's several other works of fiction and poetry, the critically acclaimed novel is *Albuquerque* (1992). Abran Gonzalez, a proud Chicano intensely antipathetic to the "Anglos", accidentally discovers that he is half-white and has to come to terms with his distressing new mixed-blood identity. This late novel looks at the relatively recent phenomenon of Chicano-Anglo parentage and calls for a broader spirit of cultural tolerance.

Francisco Jiménez illegally emigrated from Mexico, with his peasant family, as a child. *The Circuit: Stories from the Life of a Migrant Child* (1997) is a vivid account of those hard-scrabble days of poverty and prejudice from a child's point of view. *Breaking Through* (2001) recounts how the family is caught by the police and flees into hiding and back-breaking labour in Arizona to escape deportation. *Reaching Out* (2008) narrates how he worked to pay for his education and became a university professor, and the emotional complexities that attend becoming successful from a penniless background. These autobiographical narratives in Spanglish, in effect, constitute a modern Chicano fable that both problematises and asserts the American Dream.

Helena Maria Viramontes began her writing career with *The Moth and Other Stories* (1985). Her *Under the Feet of Jesus* (1994) moves fluidly back and forth in time and between first and third person narratives, to track a group of starving migrant Chicano children doing underpaid work in California's lush vineyards and orchards. In following the main character Petra's journey into womanhood and her incredible strength in both surviving and caring for others, the novel reveals a strong element of Chicana feminism. Feminist protest recurs in *Their Dogs Came with Them* (2007), which is about the interconnected lives of four young Chicana women during the rebellious "chicanista" era of the 1960s in a "barrio" (i.e. Chicano ghetto) in Los Angeles.

Sandra Cisneros's family transited between Chicago and Mexico City all through her formative years, making border crossings the marker of her fiction in a variety of senses – literal, metaphorical, psychological and philosophical. Cisneros is the first Chicana novelist to be published by mainstream publishers like Vintage and Random House. Her first major novel, *The House on Mango Street* (1984), a semi-autobiographical *bildungsroman*, tells of a young Chicana, Esperanza Cordera, grappling with issues of race, class and gender while growing up in Chicago – the unusual narrative format uses poetic first-person vignettes in the present tense or linked mini-stories without a formal plot. *Woman Hollering Creek and Other Stories* (1991), which includes the well-known "Eyes of Zapata", contains thirteen stories exploring social roles and relationships in border country in three sections with a quasi-*bildungsroman* structure of childhood, adolescence and adulthood. *Have You Seen Marie?* (2012) is a lyrical narrative of a woman's search for a missing cat as a way to cope with the trauma of her mother's death. Cisneros also has two well-regarded volumes of poetry, *My Wicked, Wicked Ways* (1987) and *Loose Woman: Poems* (1994), again following the *bildungsroman* mode.

A prolific author in several genres, Ana Castillo is best known for her "Border novels", written in the Spanglish of northern New Mexico, that explore the problematics of race and gender in the border country between Mexico and America. Castillo's epistolary first novel, *The Mixquiahuala Letters* (1986), in which two Chicanas correspond about their fate as outsiders in both

America and Mexico, established her as a leading Chicana feminist. In fact, Castillo coined the popular term for Chicana feminism – "chicanisma". Her artistic project in fiction and poetry is to demonstrate the inner strength and survival skills of the apparently docile Chicana reared in conservative rural and Catholic Mexican traditions. *So Far from God* (1993) is about a middle-aged single mother and her four daughters combating the perpetually marginalised Chicana condition. *The Guardians* (2007) recounts the violence and instability of border life with its human traffickers, illegal immigrants and "disappeared" migrants and returnees to Mexico. *Give It to Me* (2014) portrays changing times through an unusually assertive middle-aged Chicana.

The creator of Chicano theatre and founder, in 1965, of the still flourishing El Teatro Campesino that premiered his plays, Luis Valdez writes what he terms "theatre of reality". The author of over thirty plays, tele-scripts and film scripts in Spanish and Spanglish, Valdez writes about grim Chicano realities as farmhands and urban barrio dwellers, but he also projects Chicano role models – the successful Hollywood film *La Bamba* (1987) on the sensational Chicano rock 'n' roll star Ritchie Valens was scripted and directed by Valdez. Of the Spanglish works, Valdez's first full-length play, *The Shrunken Head of Pancho Villa* (1964), is a searing black-comedy-cum-absurd-drama that rips through Anglo stereotypes of Chicanos. The1979 musical stage play *Zoot Suit* (later made into a film), about social prejudice and police brutality against Chicano barrio youth in Los Angeles during the Zoot Suit Riots of 1943, won several national awards and was the first Spanglish play to be performed in New York's prestigious Broadway theatre district. *Corridos: Tales of Passion and Revolution* (1983) is a consciousness-raising drama on Chicano folk heroes, while *I Don't Have to Show You No Stinking Badges* (1986) probes the effects of poverty and prejudice on Chicano family and social dynamics. *Mundo Mata* (*The World Kills*, 2001) is an epical drama about the exploited Chicano farm workers' agitation, with a parallel plot on Chicano soldiers sacrificing their lives for America in Vietnam. The radical theme of *Mummified Deer* (2000) is the Chicano's rarely acknowledged ethnic affinity with Native Americans. Valdez has recently begun to speak for all minorities. For instance, *Valley of the Heart* (2014) traces the rocky relationship between Japanese-American and Chicano neighbours in the wake of the Pearl Harbor attack when even the marginalised Chicano displayed racial prejudice against the Japanese-Americans.

Gary Soto has written memoirs and several novels for young adults but is best known as one of the foremost poets in America today. Unlike Valdez whose revisionary theatre often verges on "agitprop", Soto's tone is quieter and more measured though he is equally trenchant about the Chicano condition. Soto is the poet of everyday Chicano life. "A Red Palm" describes the bleeding palm of an underpaid Chicano cotton-picker who is paid by the number of lengthy rows of cotton he can pick –

> . . . The sun is a red blister
> Coming up in your palm . . .
> . . . .
> . . . by the end of the first row
> You can buy one splendid fish . . .
> . . . Another row, another fish,
> . . . .
> . . . Ten hours and the cupboards creak.

"Saturday Night at the Canal" is set in a dismal Chicano school – "The hallways / Stank of poor grades and unwashed hair" – where frustrated teenagers dreaming of escape are "feeling awful because San Francisco was a postcard / On a bedroom wall." "Braly Street" recounts the clearing of Chicano slums –

> It's sixteen years since our house
> Was bulldozed, and my father
> Stunned into a coma . . .

But it is not all misery, and "Kearney Park" records the fleeting joys of Chicano life –

> True Mexicans or not, let's open our shirts
> And dance, a spark of heels
> Chipping at the dusty cement.

"Forget the room of one's own – write in the kitchen,"[7] declare Cherrie Moraga and Gloria Anzaldúa in their jointly edited Chicana feminist classic, *This Bridge Called My Back: Writings by Radical Women of Color* (1981; "women of color" is the American term for non-white American women). This volume virtually inserted the occluded Chicana voice into American (largely white) feminist discourses. Playwright, poet, essayist and influential lesbian feminist theorist, Moraga's *Loving in the War Years: Lo que nunca pasó por sus labios* (1983) and *A Xicana* (i.e., Chicana) *Codex of Changing Consciousness: Writings 2000–2010* (2011) foreground the Chicana subjectivity and its resistance against stereotyping and marginalisation.

The most crucial intervention in Chicano identity politics, Chicana feminism, and ethnicity and race studies is Gloria Anzaldúa's *Borderlands/La Frontera: The New Mestiza* (1987; "mestizo"/"mestiza" are Mexican terms for a mixed-blood man/woman). This multi-genre (prose, poetry, myth, history, cultural memory and autobiography) Spanglish work also initiated a new form of the Latin American narrative mode of "testimonio" (i.e., recording the trauma of race, class and gender bias towards a whole community from a personal perspective) that Anzaldúa calls "autohistorias" (i.e., revising mainstream history as written by the dominant majority in terms of minority personal and community experience). The title signifies the empowerment of the marginalised. While the English/Anglo word "borderlands" implies a peripheral location, its Spanish/Chicano equivalent, "la frontera" or "the frontier", signals the beginning of a new land. So every border is also the frontier of a new domain that the de-privileged (minorities, women) can claim for themselves. As a result, all boundaries are destabilised and established norms and hierarchies subverted by the newly self-assertive subaltern ("the new mestiza"):

> The US-Mexican border es una herida abierta [i.e. 'is an open wound'] where the Third World grates against the First and bleeds . . . the life-blood of two worlds merging to form a third country – a border culture. . . . A borderland is a vague and undetermined place created by . . . an unnatural boundary. It is in a constant state of transition. The prohibited and the forbidden are its inhabitants. Los atravesados (i.e. 'those who traverse boundaries') live here . . . Ambivalence and unrest reside there.

Ranging imaginatively from Aztlán to America, Anzaldúa declares on behalf of all "border people", "Waging war [against hegemonic hierarchies] is my cosmic duty." Of all Chicano writers and thinkers, Anzaldúa is the best known internationally for her interdisciplinary theoretical contribution to the study of subaltern cultures.

MULTICULTURAL/DIASPORIC AMERICAN LITERATURES

The American multicultural and diasporic literary corpus primarily comprises Asian American literature and Arab American literature. Some histories of American literature written by white American scholars include Native American, Chicano and African American writing as part of multicultural American literature. These communities oppose this approach since it assumes the primacy of white European (especially British) culture in the US. Native Americans and the early Chicanos were indigenous to the places in which they originally lived, while African Americans have been domiciled in the US for nearly as long as the white people. They regard their cultures as integral to American culture. Hence other scholars maintain that multiculturalism refers specifically to the large body of Asian and Arab immigrants who have taken American citizenship. Apart from literature, these diasporas have made major contributions to American literary and cultural theory. Edward Said (1935–2003), a Palestinian, galvanised postcolonial studies with his *Orientalism* (1978) and *Culture and Imperialism* (1993); Homi K. Bhabha (b.1949), from India, strongly impacted diaspora theory with *The Location of Culture* (1994); and both postcolonialism and postcolonial feminism gained in depth and complexity from the work of Gayatri Chakravorty Spivak (b.1942) and Chandra Talpade Mohanty (b.1955) from India and Trinh T. Minh-ha (b.1952) of Vietnam.

The word "diaspora" referred to the tragic dispersion of the Jews from their homeland in Palestine and what is now Israel, following successive waves of conquests from the sixth century before Christ. Today, however, this forced removal from the homeland due to adverse political or military circumstances is described as "exile", while "diaspora" is reserved for voluntary relocation from the homeland to what is called the "hostland" for better economic prospects. To understand the changing contours of multicultural diasporic literature in the US, it is necessary to track the transitions in diasporic experience from the late nineteenth century to the present day.

The early diasporas were made up of impoverished rural manual labourers, mainly from China and Punjab, who helped build the transcontinental railway systems in both the US and Canada – they came without their families and were illiterate, overworked and underpaid by local standards, but still earned enough to send money home. By contrast, diasporas from the mid-twentieth century onwards were largely educated middle-class professionals in better-paid jobs, though the manual labour component still exists. The issues common to both categories were their nostalgia for home, and the difficulty of being accepted in a culturally different hostland that privileged its white citizens. The situation is even more acute for second-generation diasporans born in the US, who feel, but do not look, American – and this is true of the second generation in all hostlands. Homi K. Bhabha has theorised these agonising psychological conflicts surrounding cultural hybridity as the problem of being caught between two cultures. Shirley Geok-lin Lim, an American diaspora theorist and author from Hong Kong, has traced mood swings from an intense desire to replicate the homeland in the foreign home by clinging to homeland customs, rituals and cuisine, to an intense desire to acculturate in the hostland and be accepted by it. Most diasporic writing describes these feelings of alienation, rejection and frustration in the hostland, whether among the privileged or the subaltern.

With the onset of globalisation and modern communication and transportation facilities, diasporas can keep in touch with the homeland through electronic media; and for the privileged, home is just a swift jet ride away. Recent diasporic American literature mirroring this shift is thus both transnational as well as multicultural. Though life is still exilic for the poor who cannot afford the journey home and whose native villages are not yet computer accessible, affluent diasporans now maintain homes and businesses in both homeland and hostland. Hence, twenty-first-century diasporic writing in the US and elsewhere has developed new transnational themes about straddling the two cultures of "home" and "away", and is more of a search for roots rather than a lament for lost roots. It also confronts the issue of "reverse acculturation" or the difficulties of adjusting to the *homeland* for those returning after a long time or for second-generation diasporans accustomed to the hostland environments. Bhabha describes this phenomenon as the uncanny sensation of being not at home at home.

South Asian American Literature

Writers of Indian origin dominate the South Asian diasporic corpus in the US. There is a distinction between American citizens regarded as diasporic authors and those classed under Indian Writing in English (IWE). While those classed as diasporic authors mainly project the problematic experiences of Indians living in the US, Amitav Ghosh and Kiran Desai, like Salman Rushdie (who is a British citizen), have written on subcontinental themes and fall under the IWE corpus. Bapsi Sidhwa from Pakistan (who wrote the famous *Ice Candy Man*), now an American citizen, also foregrounds subcontinental issues. With globalisation, though, diasporic fiction has begun to use homeland locations, but the perspective remains diasporic. The literary stalwarts of the South Asian Indian diaspora are Agha Shahid Ali (1949–2001), Bharati Mukherjee (b.1940), Meena Alexander (b.1951), Chitra Banerjee Divakaruni (b.1956) and Jhumpa Lahiri (b.1967).

Agha Shahid Ali, who was born and brought up in Srinagar, Kashmir, before moving to the US, is the poet par excellence of the nostalgia for home. In "Snowmen" he reflects –

> My ancestor, a man
> Of Himalayan snow,
> Came to Kashmir from Samarkand . . .

"The Prayer Rug" evokes every-day life in Kashmir –

> the women of the house
> pulling thick threads
> through vegetables

rosaries of ginger
of rustling peppers
in autumn drying for winter

"Tonight" figures Ali as the archetypal exile from his strife-torn homeland – "And I, Shahid, only am escaped to tell thee— / God sobs in my arms. Call me Ishmael tonight." In "Of Light", it seems that even "Manhattan, a bride in diamonds", exudes fathomless loneliness as though "a djinn has deprived even Aladin of light". "In Search of Evanescence", from the 1991 collection, *A Nostalgist's Map of America*, sketches a surreal cartography of diasporic loss, and has been quoted by both Amitav Ghosh and Salman Rushdie –

India always exists
off the turnpikes
of America.

Calcutta-born Bharati Mukherjee's experience as an expatriate, first in Canada and then permanently in the US, transited from alienation to assimilation to an assertion of her migrant identity. Her outburst in *Days and Nights in Calcutta* (1977) regarding "the impossibility of ever having a home" in an alien land alters to the reluctant admission that America induces "unpredictable transformations on its latest newcomers"; in the essay "Immigrant Writers: Give Us Your Maximalists!" (1988), this is modulated to the exultant "I am one of you now!"; and in a 2001 article, "On Being an American Writer", she defines her unique project as demonstrating "the sometimes painful realization on the part of America's native sons and daughters that *their* identity has been changed by these 'exotic' immigrants." Her literary career, spanning over three decades, traces these transitions in diasporic sensibility. *Wife* (1975) and the short story collections entitled *Darkness* (1985) and *The Middleman and Other Stories* (1988) recount the difficulties of adapting to America. *Jasmine* (1989), that brought Mukherjee instant fame, moves from an aspiration for America to the alienation in America to a total acculturation, as the rustic Punjabi heroine metamorphoses from Jyoti to Jasmine to Jassy to Jane. The fictional trajectory shifts and becomes more India-focused from *The Holder of the World* (1993), a cross-genre mythico-historical saga. Partly set in the opulent and powerful India of the seventeenth-century Emperor Aurangzeb, its corresponding American location, in a startling reversal of the present, is the poor and backward colony of Massachusetts that garnered most of its revenue from trade with India. In *Leave It to Me* (1997), the consciously bi-cultural heroine Devi/Debbie's hope is to balance "American wants with Indian needs". Another shift occurs with the bestselling *Desirable Daughters* (2002) that foregrounds the, by now, well-established Bengali community in Silicon Valley that is no longer an immigrant underclass, and tracks three sisters and their often conflicted engagements with their hybrid Bengali-American identities. *The Tree Bride* (2004) is atypical in being set almost entirely in colonial East Bengal as Tara, one of the three sisters, seeks to recuperate the history of her rebellious ancestor Tara Lata. With the advantages of globalisation, the immigrant is concerned to retrieve her lost past in the homeland than to wrestle with her American present in which she is now comfortably ensconced. Yet another fictional mutation occurs in *Miss New India* (2011), following a trend that is increasingly being seen in diaspora fiction. Set entirely in India, the novel aims to portray twenty-first-century aspiring Indian youth through the character of the small-town heroine Anjali "Angie" Bose, who escapes from an overly moribund Bihar to an overly lurid Bangalore in search of a more exciting life. Mukherjee's forte is her strong narrative lines and her intuitive perception of the diasporic psyche. However, she tends to sensationalism as in the Half-face sequence in *Jasmine* – and she is not on sure ground when experimenting with forms as with the science fiction episodes in *Holder*, and especially when she ventures outside the ambit of diaspora experiences.

Meena Alexander is best known as a poet, but she has written a strong and lyrical novel, *Nampally Road* (1991; reissued 2013), based partly on her own temporary return to Hyderabad in the 1970s to teach and write. Though narrated through Mira Kannadical, who is attempting "to stitch together" her conflicting Indian and expatriate selves, the real protagonist is the titular road. It is the turbulent scene of police brutality, communal riots and political chicanery, but also of Durgabai's care for the poor and the spirituality of Swami Chari – in short, all the contradictions of modern India encapsulated in a pulsating Bakhtinian chronotope. Her other novel, *Manhattan Music* (1997), is unduly schematic in describing the diasporic dilemmas of Sandhya Rosenblum, an Indian migrant with an American Jewish husband, and her friend with the culturally loaded name, Draupadi. Far more gripping in grappling with these issues is her autobiography, *Fault Lines: A Memoir* (1993), the title starkly projecting the dislocations of diaspora that contrast with her secure childhood in her grandmother's ancient house in Kerala. Alexander has written ten books of poetry to date. Her poems are intensely lyrical and evocative of home, with short stanza clusters building up into long meditations. "Fragile Places", from the collection *Raw Silk* (2004), invokes ancient India –

> The world is a forest on fire
> Sankara
> Rain blazed on Tiruvella – the red gorge.
> Sankara speaks to me.

"Migrant Memories", from *Birthplace with Buried Stones* (2013), is laden with nostalgia for the bygone aura of home –

> A lifetime ago grandmother Eli wore gold
> Stepped off a boat into a paddy field and vanished.
> . . . .
> Turmeric pounded on stone, crushed fenugreek
> She kept in a jar by her bedside. Why, no one knew.

But "Sidi Syed's Architecture" from an early volume, *House of a Thousand Doors* (1988), depicts migrancy as a positive and perennial phenomenon and migrants as cultural catalysts, while reflecting on the famous Sidi Sayyed Mosque in Ahmedabad –

> I sometimes wonder what he was like,
> Sidi Syed, a small man
> come all the way from Abyssinia,
> . . . .
> It was Ahmed's city then, in the year 1500.

Chitra Banerjee Divakaruni's central theme is the psycho-drama of women's lives as they transit from Divakaruni's native Calcutta (now Kolkata) to the US. The author of eight novels and two volumes of short stories, besides poetry and young adult fiction, Divakaruni has an acute sense of the nuances of female desire and interaction, though her narrative voice is at times melodramatic or banal. *Arranged Marriages* (1995) is misleadingly titled, since its eleven sensitive stories delineate problems that can befall any marriage. Divakaruni suggests (like Bharati Mukherjee) that America is a unique crucible of identity formation with its opportunities and mobility inciting profound attitudinal changes in docile Indian wives, goading them to interrogate and subvert traditional marital roles – but similar situations occur in rapidly modernising urban India as well. The second story collection, *The Unknown Errors of Our Lives* (2001), contains the award-winning "Mrs. Dutta Writes a Letter" about the mortification of an elderly Bengali widow living with her California-based son who discovers that her old-fashioned ways embarrass her daughter-in-law. Divakaruni's best-known novel (also filmed, starring Aishwarya Rai Bachchan) is *The Mistress of Spices* (1997). In this magical realist fable about the problematic nature of cultural authenticity, Tilo, a clairvoyant Indian immigrant and acolyte of the mysterious First Mother, sells, in her California store, Indian spices that miraculously heal the mind and body and help solve problems. She loses her powers and nearly dies when she falls in love with Doug, an American, but is restored to him on proving her loyalty to the Mother. By contrast, the realistic *Sister of My Heart* (1999) and its sequel, *The Vine of Desire* (2002), follow two cousins through a network of intricate relationships from Calcutta to America – the long sections in Calcutta are vibrant with the author's first-hand knowledge of the city. *Queen of Dreams* (2004) returns to fabulation with the interface between a modern daughter doing research at Berkeley and her psychic "dream-teller" mother. *The Palace of Illusions* (2008) is a radical retelling of much of the *Mahabharata* from the feminist standpoint of Panchaali (Draupadi). *One Amazing Thing* (2010) deviates from the normal pattern of fantasy or diasporic crises and follows the paradigm of *The Canterbury Tales,* arguing for the efficacy of stories as nine stranded survivors of an earthquake tell stories to keep up their spirits. *Oleander Girl* (2013) once again tracks tangled relationships from Calcutta to America.

Jhumpa Lahiri is a second-generation diasporan who has never lived in India, though she has visited her family in Calcutta. Her masterly narrative skill, fine eye for detail reminiscent of the meticulous realism of Balzac and Flaubert, and sensitive evocation of the pain of lost souls, have brought her worldwide fame and major awards with just four books – two volumes of short stories, *Interpreter of Maladies* (1999) and *Unaccustomed Earth* (2008), and two novels, *The Namesake* (2003; filmed by Mira Nair in 2006) and *The Lowland* (2013). The stories in *Interpreter of Maladies* are set in both India and America, and the latter group focuses on first-generation Indian immigrants clinging to their home culture, while the author sets up subtle contrasts with America, as in the different Indian and American concepts of mothering in "Mrs. Sen's". In *The Namesake*, the introspective second-generation diasporan Gogol is caught between his parents' traditional expectations and his own Americanness, but ultimately learns to value his Indian heritage. The stories in *Unaccustomed Earth* (the title quoting Hawthorne's "striking roots in unaccustomed earth" from the first chapter of *The Scarlet Letter*), though located mostly in America, could well have happened in India because of the Indian/Bengali orientations of the characters (even though in "Hell-Heaven" the two children are so Americanised that they "barely looked Bengali") – as in Ruma's choice of family over career in the title story, Aparna's jealousy in "Hell-Heaven", or the conflicted relationship in "Hema and Kaushik". In *The Lowland*, the elder of two brothers marries Gauri, the pregnant and maltreated wife of his Calcutta-based younger brother slain in the Naxalite violence of the 1960s, and takes her away to America. (The knotty social and psychological ramifications of such a move in the strata of Bengali society that Lahiri depicts would surely have constituted the entire novel in the hands of an indigenous Bengali author.) Gauri discovers herself in America and sheds her Bengali identity along with her sari and long hair, in the predictable binary of static and orthodox India versus dynamic and liberal America. Gauri lacks the whimsical charm of

Gogol; and this diffuse novel, spanning continents and cultures, lacks the concentrated emotional charge of the short stories.

It is noteworthy that though South Asian American authors have written about diasporic Indians and Indians in India (as in some of Lahiri's work and Mukherjee's later novels), they have not experimented with Indian narrative forms, preferring to use realism, science fiction or fantasy. Nor, except for some of Alexander's poems and Divakaruni's *The Palace of Illusions*, has much use been made of Indian myths and folktales as discursive paradigms for diasporic experience. Indeed, Mukherjee prefers to identify herself as an American author, and not as a diasporic Indian writing in America.

Chinese American Literature

Nineteenth-century Chinese migrants composed some memoirs in English such as Yung Wing's (1828–1912) *My Life in China and America* (1909). During and after the Second World War, C. Y. Lee (b.1917) produced nine popular novels including *The Flower Drum Song* (1957; later a successful musical and a film) about a generational conflict in a Chinese American family over an arranged marriage. Jade Snow Wong (1922–2006) wrote two memoirs, *Fifth Chinese Daughter* (1945) and *No Chinese Stranger* (1975) about the struggle for acceptance in America, which are now considered diaspora classics. Of first-generation immigrant writers, Malaysian Chinese poet, novelist and critic Shirley Geok-lin Lim (b. 1944) is known for her autobiographical novel *Joss and Gold* (2001). But Chinese American literature really flowered from the 1970s with strong women novelists like Maxine Hong Kingston (b.1940), Amy Tan (b.1952) and Gish Jen (b.1955), and playwright David Henry Hwang (b.1957) – all of them second-generation diasporans born in America of Chinese immigrant parents or of half-Chinese descent. Ed Lin, born in New York, of Chinese-Taiwanese origin, has won major awards for his crime fiction and feature films. Of the Chinese writers who fled to the US after the brutal suppression of pro-democracy protesters by Chinese authorities in Beijing's Tiananmen Square in 1989, Annie Wang has written a popular "bad girl" novel titled *Lili: A Novel of Tiananmen Square* (2001), but the most powerful author in this group is the poet and novelist Ha Jin (b.1956).

Maxine Hong Kingston's sharply gendered vision targets not only American stereotypes about Chinese women (as docile owners of laundries), but also the oppressive Chinese patriarchy. Her best work, *The Woman Warrior: Memoirs of a Girlhood among Ghosts* (1976), has the distinction of being the most widely taught text in the US. Though it has been called "postmodern", it actually deploys a non-European genre – the traditional Chinese "talk-story", which is an episodic narrative moving fluidly in time and space and blending fact, fiction, fable, folklore, oral history, legend and myth. *The Woman Warrior* is an autobiography with a difference about Maxine, her mother with her trove of traditional tales and an aunt in the land of "ghosts" – the mocking Chinese slang for pale-skinned Americans. Despite constant schooling by her anxious mother on the submissiveness expected of women, the defiant Maxine, too often taunted as "nigger yellow", refuses to "cut off her tongue". She takes as her icons a rebellious aunt and the legendary Chinese woman warrior Fa Mu Lan. This aunt polluted the well in their village in China by drowning herself in it after being ostracised for a pregnancy out of wedlock, while the fiery Fa Mu Lan, who killed the Snake Giant and the wicked baron, inspires Maxine: "I would have to grow up a warrior woman." This trope helps Kingston negotiate her diasporic experience in a positive manner instead of bewailing her displacement. She resolves to strengthen her Chinese identity, since "it translates well". The book is as much about the culturally regenerative power of myths and stories as it is about coming of age in an alien land. While *The Woman Warrior* celebrates the women in Kingston's family, *China Men* (1980) extols its adventurous men – her great-grandfather in a sugarcane plantation in Hawaii, her grandfather on the California railroad, her hard-working father, and an unnamed brother fighting in the American army in Vietnam. Kingston depicts her ancestors, not as impoverished migrants, but as actors in a heroic saga of travelling to the "Gold Mountain" (i.e., America) and "claiming America" by assisting in its development. *China Men* is a Chinese American appropriation of American history by filtering it through eighteen talk-stories which mingle family history with national events. Her very different third novel, *Tripmaster Monkey: His Fake Book* (1989), is about a fifth-generation Chinese American who is still "foreign" because of his Chinese appearance. His name, Wittman Ah Sing, both claims and subverts America – "Wittman" recalls Walt Whitman, while "Ah [i.e., "I"] Sing" is a cunning pastiche of Whitman's canonical "I Hear America Singing" and of the African American poet Langston Hughes's bitter parody focusing on America's ethnic prejudice, "I, Too, Sing America". *Tripmaster Monkey* invokes a sixteenth-century Chinese classic, the aptly titled *Journey to the West* by Wu Cheng'en, where a major character is the trickster figure of the Monkey King who foils every attempt to subdue him. Wittman's "fake book" is his pseudo-autobiography – a piquant retelling of three ancient Chinese tales in terms of contemporary American media culture to signal his two interlocking selves, ancient and modern. To delineate the Chinese American identity, Kingston takes China as her prism for viewing and interpreting America.

Amy Tan's over-arching theme, which has produced a series of bestsellers, is the tussle, but also the underlying rapport, between first-generation diasporic Chinese mothers and their second-generation Americanised daughters. In *The Joy Luck Club* (1989), Chinese immigrants in San Francisco – three mother-daughter pairs and a motherless daughter – meet to play *mahjong* (a Chinese game played by four people with 144 tiles) and share stories about their lives in China and America. The book is structured like a *mahjong* game with four four-part sections, each prefaced by a short parable on the realities of diaspora – the first, for instance, is about a Chinese woman travelling to her El Dorado, America, with a duck that imagined it was a swan. *The Kitchen God's Wife* (1991) assails Chinese patriarchy and recuperates a Chinese American female identity by foregrounding the titular figure of the nameless and forgotten wife of Zao Jun, the Chinese Kitchen God – Winnie Louie, who represents this maltreated wife, finally finds peace through a closer relationship with her daughter Pearl, whose American ways she had always censured. *The Hundred Secret Senses* (1995), which verges on magical realism, explores the strength of bonding and sisterhood among Chinese American women. *The Bonesetter's Daughter* (2000) powerfully traces the tortured relationship between Ruth Young, a fully Americanised career woman, and her mercurial and orthodox Chinese mother Lu Ling, the unlikely narrator. *Saving Fish from Drowning* (2005), whose omniscient first-person narrator is a deceased Chinese female tour guide, departs from Tan's norm in its seriocomic depiction of American tourists in Myanmar. *Rules for Virgins* (2012), and *The Valley of Amazement* (2013) into which *Rules* was later incorporated, return to the mother-daughter theme.

As opposed to Kingston's and Tan's evocations of China and the difficulties of finding acceptance in America, Gish Jen's work glories in the freedom and diversity of American life: "In the Old World there was one way of life, or two, maybe ten. Here [in the US] there are dozens, hundreds. . . . We newish Americans leapfrog from world to world, reinventing ourselves *en route*," Jen wrote in the *New York Times Magazine* in 2000. Besides highly regarded short stories, Jen has written four novels celebrating the American Dream. In *Typical American* (1991) Ralph (Yi-feng) Chang, his sister Theresa and future wife Helen move from China to initially turbulent, but ultimately satisfying, lives in America. The heroine of *Mona in the Promised Land* (1996), the maverick teenage daughter of upwardly mobile Ralph and Helen Chang, shocks the Chinese American community with her decision to be a "solo Jew" – as she says, "America means being whatever you want and I happen to pick being Jewish." The multiple narrators of *The Love Wife* (2004) chronicle the richness, but also the tensions, of multi-ethnic America in the interracial family of the Chinese Carnegie Wong – his wife the white American Janie Bailey, their biological son and two adopted daughters of different nationalities, and the Chinese nanny Lan whom Janie fears is Carnegie's "love wife" according to traditional Chinese custom. *World and Town* (2010) explores the complex psychology of Hattie Kong, a retired Chinese American school teacher who has become so acculturated that she is unable to accept the Cambodian refugees fleeing a civil war to settle in her neat New England town because of their alien ways, even though they are Asians just as she is.

David Henry Hwang, a prolific playwright, has written around twenty-five plays, many of them multiple award winners, ten operas, and several film and television scripts. The curious conflict between established Americanised Asian Americans and Southeast Asian refugees flooding America from the mid-twentieth century is repeated in the award-winning *FOB* (i.e., "Fresh Off the Boat"; 1980). *FOB*, *The Dance and the Railroad* (1981), about an impoverished nineteenth-century Chinese opera singer working on the California railroad, and *Family Devotions* (1981), a black comedy about the ambivalent impact of Christianity on Chinese religious practices, constitute Hwang's "Chinese American Trilogy". His successful *M. Butterfly* (1988) is a darkly subversive deconstruction of the stereotypes of China in Puccini's *Madame Butterfly*. *Yellow Face* (2007), *A Very DNA Reunion* (2010) and *Chinglish* (2011) comprise another trilogy about identity crises and cultural confusion in Chinese Americans. Hwang's reworking of C. Y. Lee's *The Flower Drum Song* was distinctive for staging the first all-Asian cast in American theatre. Indeed, Hwang is the first Asian American dramatist to win prestigious American drama awards such as the PEN/Laura Pels International Foundation for Theater Award.

The most hauntingly sensitive novel by Ha Jin (the pen name of Jīn Xuěfēi) is *Waiting* (1999), written in the US but charting the story of an unloved wife against the tumultuous background of Maoist China from the 1960s to the 80s. Most of Jin's novels have epical Chinese contexts, such as *War Trash* (2004) about a volunteer with a conscience in the Chinese People's Volunteer Army during the Korean War of the 1950s. But his recent *A Map of Betrayal* (2014) delves into the psychology of Gary Shang, a Chinese American Communist spy working for the CIA. Jin writes poetry in English in the Chinese "Misty Poetry" tradition, as in "Ways of Talking" about his flight from China –

> We used to like talking about grief
> ....
> After losing a land and then giving up a tongue
> we stopped talking of grief

Chinese American writers have strongly recuperated their ethnicity, their ethnic literary traditions and their own myths and stories in their English writings. Along with South Asian American literature, their writings form the main component of Asian American literature.

Japanese American Literature

Japanese Americans divide themselves into five categories – the first generation born in Japan who later emigrated to America are the *issei*, while the second, third, fourth and fifth generations born in the Americas are the *nisei*, *sansei*, *yonsei* .and *gosei* respectively. Japanese American literature focuses on the cultural frictions between these hierarchical "generations" of migrants, and especially the cultural trauma of the "internment" or the enforced incarceration (euphemistically called "Relocation") of Japanese Americans during the Second World War, when their loyalty became suspect after Japan declared war on America.

Monica Sone (1919–2011), Hisaye Yamamoto (1921–2011) and John Okada (1923–1971) are the early important authors of Japanese American literature. Sone's memoir, *Nisei Daughter* (1953), chronicles her youth in Seattle and the pain of internment, as well as the conflicted relationship between orthodox Japanese culture and American ways. Yamamoto wrote the well-regarded *Seventeen Syllables and Other Stories* (1988), in which she explored the exigencies of being Japanese in the US. Okada's only novel, *No-No Boy* (1956), portrays the psychological scars of internment. Young Ichiro Yamada is provoked into answering "No . . . No" when asked whether he would swear allegiance to the US and fight the Japanese: after a two-year imprisonment for disloyalty, he returns to a hostile American neighbourhood in Seattle and a deranged mother convinced that Japan has won the war.

Another important *nisei* writer is the playwright Hiroshi Kashiwagi (b.1922). His Japanese American theatre troupe, Grateful Crane Ensemble, premiered most of his plays. Kashiwagi's US citizenship was cancelled during the Second World War and restored after a long legal battle, and this experience is his enduring theme in plays like *The Plums Can Wait* (1949) and *Laughter and False Teeth* (1953), all the way to *The Betrayed* (1993). He also wrote a bilingual Japanese-English play, *Mondai wa Akira* (*The Problem is Akira*; 1956).

Garrett Hongo (b.1951), a *yonsei* poet, is the most prominent Japanese American literary voice today. Two of his poetry collections, *Yellow Light* (1980) and *The River of Heaven* (1998), won several awards. Hongo's poems project the uniqueness of Japanese culture even in the US. "Who among You Know the Essence of Garlic" goes –

> Can your foreigner's nose smell mullets
> roasting in a sauce of brown bean paste
> and sprinkled with novas of sea salt?
> . . . .
> Who among you know the essence
> of garlic and black lotus roots
> . . . .
> and pale-blue rice wine simmering
> in the stomach of a big red fish?

"Something Whispered in the Shakuhachi" (i.e., Japanese flute) imagines the internment –

> All through Relocation,
> in the desert where they put us,
> . . . .
> I could hear my flute's
> wail like fists of wind
> whistling through the barracks.

And in "And Your Soul Shall Dance", happiness is walking through

> . . . fields
> of tomato and summer squash,
> alone and humming a Japanese love song.

Filipino American Literature

Filipino American authors, like their Chinese American and Japanese American counterparts, write almost as much about their native land and culture as about the tribulations of immigrant life. The first major Filipino American literary voice is that of Carlos Bulosan (1913–56), who migrated to America in 1930 and became a prominent activist in the anti-racist Filipino American labour movement. His autobiographical *America is in the Heart: A*

Personal History (1946) now ranks as a classic account of migration to America. It is also extremely readable. Here are some of his experiences:

> I found the dark hole of the steerage and lay on my bunk for days without food. . . . Why had I left home? What would I do in America? . . . But somewhere in the room a [Filipino] peasant boy was playing a guitar and someone was strumming a mandolin. . . . There were more than two hundred of us in the steerage. . . . [In America] we were drawn together because the white people of Yakima Valley [in California] were suspicious of us. . . . A small farmer in Wapato who had tried to protect his Filipino workers had had his house burned. So however much we distrusted each other . . . we knew that beyond the walls of our bunkhouse were our real enemies, waiting to drive us out of Yakima Valley.

Among several authors of this generation is Bienvenido Santos (1911–96) whose novel, *The Praying Man* (1982), about corruption in the Philippines, was banned there by President Marcos. Other notable names include the short story writer José Garcia Villa (1908–97); playwright Nick Joaquin (1917–2004), best known for *A Portrait of the Artist as Filipino* (1952) about an ageing Filipino painter whose sole masterpiece comes too late in life to redeem him; and Linda Ty Casper (b.1932) who has written historical novels set in the Philippines, such as *The Peninsulares* (1963) and *The Three-Cornered Sun* (1979).

An acclaimed contemporary author is Jessica Tarahata Hagedorn, a first-generation immigrant born in Manila in 1949. Her best novel is *Dogeaters* (1990), set in the politically volatile but culturally rich Manila of the 1950s. Manila remains Hagedorn's favourite setting – its glitzy beauty and Machiavellian politics recur in *Dream Jungle* (2003), while *The Gangster of Love* (1999) is about a Filipino migrant family's arrival and adventures in California. Peter Bacho (b.1951) has so far written three novels – *Cebu* (1991), *Nelson's Run* (2002) and *Entrys* (2005) – apart from short story collections and non-fiction. *Cebu* is notable for depicting a pro-US Filipino American community in Seattle, and also the effects of globalisation as they revisit their homeland in Cebu Island in the Philippines. R. Zamora Linmark (b.1968) writes about the Filipino-Hawaiian experience in his two novels to date, *Rolling the R's* (1997) and *Leche* (2011), with three books of poetry in between. Poet Eileen Tabios (b.1960), who frequently deploys the long Whitmanesque line, has gained considerable recognition. Here is a single line from "I Do" – "I do know English for I have something to say about this latest peace stirring between a crack that split a sidewalk traversing a dusty border melting at noon beneath an impassive sun."

Korean American Literature

Younghill Kang (1903–72), the first Korean American writer, captured the archetypal immigration story and the problems of acceptance in his autobiographical novel, *East Goes West: The Making of an Oriental Yankee* (1937). Earlier in 1931, he had written about his life in Japanese-occupied Korea (from where he fled to the US in 1921) in *The Grass Roof* (1931).

The first internationally acclaimed Korean American voice was that of the first-generation immigrant author Theresa Hak Kyung Cha (1951–82) – novelist, poet and filmmaker. She is best known for her radical multi-genre feminist narrative *Dictée* (1982), a surreal mélange of prose, poetry, Korean shamanic chants, photographs, sketches and catalogues of subversive women. It begins with a verse epigraph –

> May I write words more naked than flesh
> stronger than bone, more resilient than
> sinews, more sensitive than nerve.

This is surely reminiscent of Hélène Cixous's call in *The Laugh of the Medusa* (1975) for women to write the body. The layered work is structured spatially rather than temporally, with several strata superimposed upon and played off against one another – Sappho, Hesiod, legends of heroic Korean women, Cha's mother's journal, Cha's own story and those of several other characters, such as an unnamed immigrant girl. Cha's project was to configure "the great presence of women, the woman's space".

The well-known contemporary Korean American writers are Linda Sue Park (b.1960) and Chang-rae Lee (b.1965). Park's forte is Korean historical fiction – her first trilogy is set in ancient and medieval Korea, *When My Name was Keoko* (2002) is about the Japanese occupation and the forced prostitution of Korean women, and *Project Mulberry* (2005) is about Korean immigration to the US. Her popular books for young adults depict various aspects of Korean culture – food, pottery, silkworms or kite-flying.

Chang-rae Lee writes spacious, brooding, award-winning novels on the dilemmas of the Korean American diaspora and their complicity in Korea's troubled past under Japanese imperialism, for they left Korea rather than staying on to fight. *Native Speaker* (1994) is about the migrant "emotional alien" Henry Park; *A Gesture Life* (1999) projects, through a series of flashbacks, the past guilt and present alienation of the elderly Doctor Hata; *The Surrendered* (2010) engages the abdication of responsibility during the Korean War; and *On Such a Full Sea* (2014) is a futuristic political novel about the decentred Korean diaspora in a declining America confronted by an irresponsible China.

Arab American Literature

Arab American literature is little noticed but very rich. Its internationally famous pioneers were Ameen Rihani (1876–1940) and Kahlil Gibran (1883–1931), who are rarely recognised as being Arab American authors. Both were Lebanese Maronite Catholic immigrants fleeing persecution by the Ottoman Turks and Lebanon's majority Islamic Druze community. Rihani, who became an American citizen in 1901, was known for espousing Arab nationalism. His English works – comprising fiction, poetry, essays and political tracts – were written by 1922, but much of it was published posthumously even as recently as the 2000s by the Centre for Arab American Studies at the University of Maryland. The only novel published in his lifetime, *The Book of Khalid* (1911), illustrated by his friend Kahlil Gibran, is the first in English by an Arab American. This three-part autobiographical/philosophical work ("To Man", "To Nature" and "To God"), code-switches between Arabic and English words and uses the Arabic literary conventions of the imaginary "found manuscript" and direct address to the reader. It concerns two boys, Khalid and Shakib, who leave Lebanon for America as children and grow up as Westernised bohemians. But Khalid ultimately recuperates his culture and spirituality and, following the eternal migrant's dream, returns to his homeland, albeit in tragic circumstances. Rihani's poetry celebrates his Lebanese heritage even in exile –

> I am the East
> I am the cornerstone
> Of the first Temple of God

and

> And though rootless and friendless and helpless
> And loveless and godless I stand
> the waves of my life shall continue
> to murmur and laugh on the strand.

The impoverished Gibran family came to America when Kahlil was only ten and, at great cost to themselves, nurtured his gifts as an artist and writer. During his meteoric transnational career spanning Paris and New York and blessed with many wealthy patrons who practically venerated him like a sage, Gibran wrote extensively in both Arabic and English. Of his English works, *The Prophet* (1923) has been translated into as many languages and has sold as many copies as the Bible. Gibran brought the solace of Eastern mysticism to a West disillusioned after the First World War, propagating the notion of the spiritual superman that he found in Nietzsche's *Thus Spake Zarathustra.* Almustafa the Prophet is a spiritual superman and so also is Christ in his *Jesus, The Son of Man* (1928). But Gibran's work also reflects the agony of a double exile. He never lived long enough in Lebanon to really be a part of it, and yet always felt alienated in America.

Gibran's English writings begin with *The Madman* (1918) and *The Forerunner* (1920). *The Madman* is a collection of parables projecting a sense of physical and spiritual displacement in a world of fake appearances and is the first stage in Gibran's journey to self-realisation: "And as if in a trance I cried, 'Blessed are the thieves who stole my masks,' Thus I became a madman. And I have found both freedom and safety in my madness." The lurking dangers of life are reflected in the parable "My New Pleasure" when both the angel and the devil claim his new pleasure. *The Forerunner* is a radical claim for human autonomy. The forerunner is one's own spiritual self, "the foundation of your giant-self" – a timely call after the First World War for human beings to take responsibility for their own actions. In Gibran's best-known work, *The Prophet*, the prophet Almustafa is (like Gibran) an exile who yearns to find his true (spiritual) "home" that has no geographical location: "Son of my ancient mother . . . How often have you sailed in my dreams." Western readers identified with Almustafa's cry: "How shall I go in peace and without sorrow?" Almustafa finds peace in his aphoristic "truths" that celebrate human aspiration: "Your children are not your children. / They are the sons and daughters of life's longing for itself"; "self is boundless and measureless"; and "Beauty is eternity gazing at itself in the mirror / But you are eternity and you are the mirror." In *Jesus, The Son of Man* (1928), the man-god Jesus symbolises the paradoxical coexistence of limitation with limitlessness, that is beyond human capability: "The heart of the world quivers with the throbbing of your heart / But it burns not your song"; and "Man would dream your dream but would not wake to your dawn."

A modulation occurred in Gibran's thought after Rabindranath Tagore was awarded the Nobel Prize for Literature in 1913. He began to read Tagore's English works (in translation and in the original) and was drawn to Indian Upanishadic spirituality. Gibran met Tagore several times during the latter's visits to the US, and the new direction is evident in Gibran's *The Earth Gods* (1931), though many feel that it shows a reduction of his poetic power. The title iconoclastically suggests that deities are after all humanly fashioned. Gibran contrasts different sorts of deities and religious orientations – the First and Second Gods are vengeful and absolutist but the Third God is anti-essentialist and signified by the "blue flame" that illuminates but does not burn. Gibran also wrote an English play on the theme of resurrection, *Lazarus and His Beloved* (1933).

Contemporary Arab American literature is concerned with social, political and feminist, rather than spiritual and philosophical, issues, as well as with the problems of acculturation. Thus in the poem "Dying with the Wrong Name", Lebanese American Sam Hamod bewails the exigency of having to Americanise one's Arab name to function in American society. Another powerful exposition of the endangered Arab immigrant identity is Egyptian American Eugene Paul Nassar's (b.1935) memoir *Wind of the Land* (1979). Recent important women authors are Palestinian American poets Naomi Shihab Nye (b.1952) and Lisa Suhair Majaj (b.1960). The contribution of this generation is to revive Arabic literary tropes and folk forms in the English language, but also to write politically sensitive literature. As Nye says of her tragic native Palestine in "Blood" – "Where can the crying heart graze? / What can a true Arab do now?"

The Importance of Anthologies

American literature written by the Chinese, Japanese, Filipino and Korean diasporas, including works published even by small presses, gained wide circulation and became easily accessible for academic courses, through the publication of several well-edited anthologies – a facility not yet accessed to that extent by the South Asian Indian diaspora. The trend was initiated by the 200-page *Aiiieeeee! An Anthology of Asian American Writers* (1974) edited by Frank Chin and other members of the Combined Asian Resources Project (CARP). This was followed in 1991 by *The Big Aiiieeeee! An Anthology of Chinese American and Japanese American Literature* edited by another group from CARP, which now also included major Canadian authors like Japanese Canadian Joy Kogawa. ("Aiiieeeee" is an onomatopoeic neologism for the Chinese exclamation of delight or surprise.) The aim of these inter-ethnic anthologies, as stated in the Preface to the first volume, was to counter the negative white evaluations of these works such as orientalism or "unwholesome [i.e., ethnic] literary devices", and to project what Korean American critic Elaine H. Kim called the "unstereotyped aspects of Asian American experience". Indeed, since the 1970s, nearly twenty other anthologies of Southeast and Northeast Asian American writing have been published, some focusing solely women's writing or gay writing or poetry from this literary corpus. By contrast, only in 2010 was the first widely circulated South Asian American anthology published – *Indivisible: An Anthology of Contemporary South Asian American Poetry*, edited by Neelanjana Banerjee and others.

♦ ♦ ♦

Multicultural American literature comprises works by immigrant authors of several nationalities including the Caribbean islands and Central and South America, but the diasporas analysed above have produced the largest and most significant bodies of literary work. In his essay, "Reflections on Exile", Edward Said had spoken about how exiles and immigrants "cross borders, break barriers of thought and experience". The current wide circulation and academic study of diasporic American literatures are a tribute to the ways in which these authors have enlarged and enriched the predominantly Eurocentric orientation of what President John F. Kennedy had famously described as "a nation of immigrants".

CHAPTER 8

American Popular Literature and Culture

Ashok Sengupta

THE AMERICAN WESTERN

The origins of the popular Western can be traced back to James Fenimore Cooper's (1789–1851) Leatherstocking novels. In fact, Cooper is considered to have given the Western its thematic formula – that of the conflict between wilderness and civilisation and the trials of the Western hero caught between these contending forces. Thus, Cooper's novels provide a dualistic model involving contrasts in setting, characterisation and the use of narrative methods. In *The Deerslayer* (1841), for instance, Natty Bumpo's lake dwelling is surrounded by wild forests, his clothes mix Indian finery with common homespun fabric, and the narrative adapts the frontier experience within the traditional form of the historical romance. Moreover, Natty, the pioneer frontiersman, becomes representative of this foundational phase of American history, illustrating, on one hand, the idea of freedom and individualism implicit in the Frontier myth, and the reaction against organised society which, ironically, threatens this myth. This thematic pattern is repeated in some of the novels by Cooper's contemporaries – such as *Nick of the Woods* (1837) by Robert Montgomery Bird (1806–54), James Kirke

Paulding's (1778–1860) *Westward Ho!* (1832) and *The Yemassee* (1835) by William Gilmore Simms (1806–70). The Westerns were also influenced by the tales of Bret Harte and Washington Irving's stories, and many of them were derived from the Mexican *vaquero* narratives and the South American *gaucho* novel.

The immediate impulse for the growth of the Western was, however, given by the "dime" novel initiated by Erasmus Beadle, who established the Beadle and Adam Publishing Company in New York in 1860. In a period of thirty years, the publishing company produced a phenomenal nine thousand titles by its star writers – Edward Ellis, Prentiss Ingraham, Ned Buntline and Edward Wheeler. Thus, the driving force behind the popular Western was not so much the myth as it was the market. Mass publishing, therefore, created "pulp" fiction which, at the turn of the century, received a smarter showcasing in the appearance of the "slicks" which, finally, culminated in the paperback revolution around 1934 with Robert Graff's Pocket Books. Most of the important writers of the popular Westerns – Owen Wister (1860–1938), Zane Grey (1872–1939), Max Brand (1892–1944), Jack Warner Schaefer (1907–91) and Louis L'Amour (1908–88) – began with the "pulps" and achieved notable commercial success in the industry.

Owen Wister is often considered to be influential in shaping the formula of the Western novel. In his fiction, Wister tends to oppose official history with his personal version of the West. This contributes to the creation of a fiction which, while being romantic and idyllic, also reflects contemporary events and conflicts. Wister's *The Virginian: A Horseman of the Plains* (1902) follows the pattern set in Cooper's novels in its desire to reconcile the East and the West – civilisation and the wild. By telling the story of the Virginian, a handsome cowboy who arrives at Medicine Bow, Wyoming, to become the foreman of a flourishing ranch, Wister's novel establishes the familiar conventions of the genre, weaving a tale of violence, revenge, love and friendship around this basic event. Thus, the masculine theme of conquest, both of the land and the "pretty" school teacher, Molly, becomes one of the basic features of the genre, whose realism involves a continual struggle with a pure yet implacable nature and human greed and treachery. However,

Wister's *Journal* records an implicit hierarchy between the two worlds of community and the wilderness which, in fact, is the basis of the myth of the West: "I feel more certainly than ever," Wister wrote in a Journal entry,

> that no matter how completely the east may be the headwaters from which the West has flown and is flowing, it won't be a century before the West is simply the true America with thought type and life of its own kind. We Atlantic coast people, all vanished with Europe, will vanish from the face of the earth. We're not type—nor race—we're transient. All the patriotism of the war doesn't make us an institution yet. But this West is going to do it.

The myth of the "true America" constitutes the major topos of the nation which these popular novels construct. Ironically, this myth developed under the shadow of the official closing of the Frontier in 1890. Therefore, in an important sense, the myth of the West is an attempt to fill the gap left by the passing of the Frontier. This was singularly achieved by Frederick Jackson Turner's (1861–1932) celebrated work, *The Frontier in American History* (1920). In fact, Wister's argument of the West as the authentic America is central to what is now called the Turner thesis:

> The true point of view in the history of this nation is not the Atlantic coast, it is the great West. . . . The fact is that here is a new product that is American. At first the frontier was the Atlantic coast. It was the frontier of Europe in a very real sense. Moving westward the frontier became more and more American. . . . Thus the advance of the frontier has meant a steady growth of independence on American lines. And to study this advance . . . is to study the really American part of our history.

Thus, not only is the theme of civilising the wilderness Turner's contribution to the popular Western, but the codes which define the hero, such as individualism, love of freedom and the sense of personal honour, is fashioned within a discourse and a narrative of the nation.

In fact, it is this myth of the true America, implicit in Turner, which the formula Western attempts to reaffirm and ratify. An important variation on this project involves an attempt to create an alternative pattern of history which not only recuperates the West but also idealises and protects these popular versions of the actual changes taking place in the Frontier. The myth of the West, thus, acquires a sense of eternity by the fact that it is often corrupted and denied. The incipient tension that characterises it determines the conventions and forms of the popular Western. For instance, Zane Grey's *Riders of the Purple Sage* (1912) presents the heroic resistance of a woman to the designs of a polygamous Mormon church elder. The story uses personal drama to reflect on the evolving social and moral principles of the increasingly transracial and multicultural communities that were defining the West and America.

Though L'Amour considered himself "just a storyteller, a guy with a seat by the campfire", his historical romances have been noted for their authenticity of locale and the history of the West. This is evident in *Westward, the Tide* (1950), his first novel, and *Hondo* (1953), and also in *How the West Was Won* (1963), an epical account of the courage and endurance of those who braved the perils of nature, the Natives and death, to make the West their home. In fact, L'Amour defended his fiction, which was often disparagingly dismissed as "Westerns", by observing, "If you write a book about a bygone period that lies east of the Mississippi River, then it is a historical novel. If it is west of the Mississippi, it's a Western, a different category. There is no sense to it." One feature that was used to overcome this attitude was to endow this fiction with a series of mythic and universalising elements. In the novels of Zane Grey and Max Brand who, incidentally, tried to write classical and epic poetry, there are direct comparisons and allusions to classical myths which give these popular tales a larger significance. There is also the use of the West as a metaphor of traditional mythic archetypes, both Greek pastoral and Christian, or, particularly, Medieval, to give the novels a literary and cultural authority. This is clear in Grey's *The Code of the West* (1934), *Knights of the Range* (1939) and *The Deer Stalker* (1949).

Therefore, one important emphasis in both the literary and the cinematic Western is the landscape of the wide prairies, the majestic mountains and the depthless canyons which itself constitute a geography of breathtaking beauty and humbling magnitude, and distinguish the "real" America of the popular Western. This setting defines the terms of the human drama of heroic struggles and elemental passions reiterated in most of this writing, as in A. B. Guthrie Jr.'s *The Big Sky* (1952) and in L'Amour's novels –*The Man Called Noon* (1970) and *Where the Long Grass Blows* (1976), among many others. The Sackett series of novels by L'Amour – such as, *Sackett* (1961) and *Fair Blows the Wind* (1978) – not only confirm the formulaic nature of this fiction but also testify to the theme of the family as an important aspect of the community values endorsed by this fiction. Central to the popular Westerns is the cowboy or the gunslinger, who is refigured as the knight with a personal sense of honour and duty. He helps restore the community to its sense of harmony but refuses to be bound to its domestic commitments, fading into the wilderness from which he had appeared, as the end of Jack Warner Schaefer's *Shane* (1949) suggests:

> Shane was looking down the road and on to the open plain and the horse was obeying the silent command of the reins. He was riding away, and I knew that no word or thought could hold him. The big horse, patient and powerful, was already settling into the steady pace that had brought him into our valley. There were men in the porch behind me, but I was aware only of that dark shape growing small and indistinct along the far reach of the road. A cloud passed over the moon and he merged into the general shadows and I could not see him and the cloud passed on and the road was a plain thin ribbon to the horizon and he was gone.

This natural setting is, however, often simplified to act as a backdrop to the American narrative of the nation, reproduced and ideologically justified in this popular fiction. Thus, the civilising project that is reenacted in the popular Westerns involves a continuous writing over the wilderness to erase another history peopled by the Native Americans which has been documented in

Dee Brown's *Bury My Heart at Wounded Knee: An Indian History of the American West* (1970), and in such stories as Dorothy Johnson's *A Man Called Horse* (1950) and Walter Van Tilberg Clark's *The Ox-Bow Incident* (1940).

Though based on contemporary history, the popular Westerns did not acquire the nation-building status as some of the Latin American novels did. Schaefer, for example, is concerned not with the conventions of the formula Westerns, but reads into the history on which this West is built, his attempt to understand its failures, its betrayals and its decline. *Shane* is Schaefer's first version of this revisionist history, while in *Company of Cowards* (1957), he attempts to examine the history of the Civil War which, in turn, becomes a critique of the myth of the West. This tendency to confront another "true" West marks many of the later novels in the genre, such as Larry McMurtry's *Lonesome Dove* (1985), John Byrne Cookes's *Snow Blind Moon* (1985), Wallace Stegner's *Angle of Repose* (1971) and the novels of Cormac McCarthy (b.1933). A bleak cynicism is thus pervasive in McCarthy's fiction, as in *All the Pretty Horses* (1992) where the characters are trapped in unforeseen and inescapable evil. In fact, his Border trilogy, which also includes *The Crossing* (1994), *Cities of the Plain* (1998) and his later novel, *No Country for Old Men* (2005), interrogate the tainted legacy of America's Frontier and its violent history. McCarthy's novels deal with an awareness of the darker side of human nature and seem resigned to its inexorable acceptance. In an interview given to the *New York Times* in 1992, McCarthy admitted,

> There is no such thing as life without bloodshed. The notion that the species can be improved in some way, that everyone could live in harmony, is really a dangerous idea. Those who are afflicted with this notion are the first ones to give up their souls, their freedom. Your desire that it be that way will enslave you and make your life vacuous.

There has, however, been a major revision of the myth of the West both in fiction and film. This is primarily a result of the significant recognition and growth of Native American literature involving a rewriting of the relationship between the settlers and the Natives, which had shaped the history of the American West. The simplistic formula Westerns have thus been replaced with revisionist versions or anti-Westerns which not only interrogate the myth but, thereby, announce the passing of the Old West. Yet, ironically, even in its decline, the Old West assumes a residual significance, asserting its mythic stature. This seems to be expressed in a sense of memory and desire in the popular Westerns. For instance, Jake Hamlon, the hero of Schaefer's last novel, *Mavericks* (1967), concludes, "I'u tells you what we can do. We can remember 'em like they once was."

American Science Fiction

There seems to be a common agreement about Edgar Allan Poe (1809–49) being the originator of American science fiction. Brian Aldiss, in his authoritative history of the genre, *A Trillion Year Spree* (1973), cites a 1905 review recognising Poe as "the father of science fiction". In fact, Poe's stories are marked by a balance between science and fantasy, rationalism and mysticism, which is usually considered the definitive formula of science fiction. *Al Aaraaf* (1829), an early poem by Poe, seems to anticipate his later tales of "arabesque" in this category. In a note to the poem, Poe explained that the title of the poem was a reference to a star "discovered by Tycho Brahe which appeared suddenly in the heavens" and then equally "suddenly disappeared". The mysterious romantic predilection of this phenomenon seems also to imply an awareness of the inscrutable nature of the universe, always distant and receding from human grasp. The 1839 story "Conversation of Eiros and Charmion" is, however, about a possible earth disaster from the fires caused by a passing comet. In "The Colloquy of Monos and Una" (1841), Poe foresees another disaster – a consequence of the human misuse of the earth. "The Facts of the Case of M. Valdemar" (1845) reveals the writer's interest in the contemporary pseudo-science of hypnotism and catalepsy when a dead man is made to remain in suspended animation by a hypnotic spell.

Poe's *Eureka: A Prose Poem* (1849) is notable for its references to the French scholar Pierre-Simon Laplace's theories, the German astronomer Johann Madler's belief that the Milky Way had at its core a massive object that attracts all the stars, and also a suggestion of what could be termed the Big Bang Theory. His "Mellonta Tauta" (1849) – Greek for "those things that are to be" – is set in the year 2848 and is a satirical, aerial commentary on the United States. *The Narrative of Gordon Pym* (1838) uses the same formula of exploration and adventure to reflect on the possibility of strange lands and peoples near the South Pole – a conjecture that was first noted in "MS in a Bottle" (1833) which speaks of the notion of a "hollow earth". However, the most famous of Poe's science fiction is evidently *The Unparalleled Adventure of One Hans Pfaall* (1835). Dealing with a balloon journey to the moon, the novel has a characteristic Poe penchant for hoaxes and playfulness. For instance, the balloon's journey to the moon begins on 1 April, All Fools Day; and it is also suggested that Pfaall lifts off into space using the principle of levitation. Nevertheless, this doubtful journey is narrated with all the seriousness and sense of scrupulous scientific facts and details necessary to such accounts.

In fact, Poe seems to have been deeply influenced by another tale of a trip to the moon by George Tucker (1775–1861), writing under the pseudonym Joseph Atterley, whose *Voyage to the Moon* (1827) is made in a craft coated with anti-gravity substance, giving rise to a series of novels using anti-gravitational themes and devices. "Chrysostom" Trueman's *The History of a Voyage to the Moon, With an Account of the Adventures and Subsequent Discoveries* (1864) also speaks of a gravity "repellante" enabling the travellers to reach their destination where they find the Lunarians to be reincarnated human souls, called "Notol", living in a Utopian society. Similarly, John Jacob Astor's (1864–1912) interplanetary adventures are made possible by the use of a concept called "apergy", a propelling principle, for *A Journey to Other Worlds* (1894). Likewise, Frank Stockton's (1834–1902) "A Tale of Negative Gravity" (1886) has a variation of the same anti-gravity device in the form of a backpack used to climb mountains and lift heavy objects.

Edward Bellamy's (1850–98) Utopian novel, *Looking Backward: 2000–1887* (1888), is one of the most notable science fiction works of the turn of the century. Its protagonist, Julian West, time travels to the year 2000 by means of a hypnotic trance, to find a harmonious, technologically advanced, collective society of equal men and women, living according to the principles of the "Religion of Solidarity". When the novel ends with West waking in the poverty and squalor of nineteenth-century America, Bellamy reserves a final optimistic twist when it is revealed that it was the return to 1887 that was the nightmare: West is safe in the Utopia of 2000. Bellamy's novel became a national bestseller inspiring several other versions, such as the dystopian *Caesar's Column, A Story of the Twentieth Century* (1890) by Ignatius Donnelly (1831–1901). Thus, by the 1890s, there was a significant growth of science fiction which would include Milton Ramsay's (1848–1906) *Six Thousand Years Hence* (1891), Addison P. Russell's (1826–1912) *Sub-Coelum: A Sky Human World* (1893) and Robert Braine's (1861–1943) *Messages from Mars by Aid of the Telescope Plant* (1892).

In the twentieth century, as mentioned earlier, the growth of education provided a considerable surge in the reception and writing of popular fiction. This increase in the reading public in the United States was also a consequence of the changes in publishing involving a shift to cheaper production and marketing in the form of "dime" novels and, in the case of science fiction, the "pulps" and magazines in the first two decades of the century. Edward Ellis (1840–1916), one of the major figures behind this history of popular fiction, mainly wrote dime Westerns, but made an interesting departure from the formula in *The Steam Man of the Prairies* (1868). Here, a steam engine, shaped like a giant man, thunders across the Midwest carrying the enthusiastic into various unexpected adventures. Harold Cohen (1854–1927), a prolific hack-writer, adapted this idea in *Frank Reade and His Steam Man of the Plains* (1876). Subsequently, this became the Frank Reade Library with nearly two hundred weekly or bi-weekly titles described as the archetypal pulp and the earliest serial publication solely devoted to science fiction.

"Pulp" is a term denoting a particular type of popular fiction printed on cheap paper manufactured from treated wood pulp and written by hack writers. Its emphasis was on low costs and wide circulation. Therefore, the basis of pulp science fiction was not their magazine format but this inexpensive reach to a wide readership. Consequently, there emerged a narrative formula involving an eventful plot, strong characters, exotic settings and a simple ethical code. Hugo Gernsback (1884–1967) was the most important figure to advance the cause of science fiction in pulp magazines, and this period is sometimes called the Gernsback Era. Gernsback was interested in electric inventions and in 1908 founded a magazine called *Modern Electric* which, apart from having articles on technical subjects, included science fiction such as his own serialised novel, *Ralph 124C41+: A Romance of the Year 2660* (1911–12). However, it is in the role of an editor that Gernsback is remembered in the history of the genre. In 1924, he announced his intention to publish a magazine solely devoted to what he termed "scientifiction"; and in 1926, created *Amazing Stories: the Magazine of Scientifiction.* In the first editorial of this "New Sort of Magazine", Gernsback tried to redefine science fiction as equally entertaining as it was educative: "Not only do these amazing tales make tremendous interesting reading – they are also always instructive. . . . For the best of these modern writers of scientifiction have the knack of imparting knowledge and even inspiration without once making us aware that we are being taught." Gernsback wanted to reshape this writing by purging it of its magic and mysticism and thereby make it more scientific – thus emerged the category that is now termed "Hard SF". Despite his financial failure, Gernsback went on to publish *Astounding Stories of Super Science* in 1930, which later became the standard magazine for this genre, *Astounding Stories,* in 1933. In fact, some scholars consider the pulps to have dominated the whole period of science fiction history between 1926 and 1960, also called the "Magazine Era", which had a considerable influence in the later golden age of the genre.

Two science fiction writers who came into prominence through the Gernsback pulps were Edgar Rice Burroughs (1875–1950) and E. E. "Doc" Smith (1890–1965). Burroughs, who had already achieved success with his *Tarzan of the Apes* (1912) series, had also serialised his first science tale, *Under the Moon of Mars* (1912), whose book form was titled *A Princess of Mars* (1917). The hero, John Carter, simply uses the force of his will to travel to Mars and there battles several foes in the style of the popular Westerns. Several sequels followed –*The Gods of Mars* (1914), *Thuvia, Maid of Mars* (1920), *The Chessmen of Mars* (1922), *Swords of Mars* (1936), to name just a few. He also wrote *At the Earth's Core* (1914) and *Pirates of Venus* (1934) which ran into twenty-six sequels. Dealing mainly with the adventures of the spaceman Carson Napier, Burroughs's fiction, like the popular Westerns, emphasises a masculinist ethic of physical prowess, courage and the will to achieve against all odds, which had, in fact, an American trademark that popular writing valorised. Edward Elmer Smith, writing as E. E. "Doc" Smith, had a doctorate in food science (which earned him the "Doc" in his penname) and was one of the most important pulp science fiction writers. Specialising in "super space operas"– a subgenre in the genus – his *The Skylark of Space* (1910; published 1928) ran into several sequels till *Skylark Du Quesne* in 1965. Among Smith's fiction, the more popular were the novels of the Lensman series, which included *Triplanetary* (1934), *Galactic Patrol* (1937–38), *Second Stage Lensman* (1941–42) and *Children of the Lens* (1947–48). These recount the adventures of a group of humans, endowed with telepathic and telekinetic powers called the "Talents", using a mysterious device, the "lenses", to battle evil forces. In spite of their formulaic and often banal excess, these novels which began in the pulps had a significant influence on the later writers celebrated as the "Golden Age" writers of the genre, who finally conferred on it a seriousness and respectability that would distinguish science fiction as an important literary mode in the later twentieth century.

The Golden Age of science fiction usually acknowledges the contribution of another editor, John W. Campbell (1910–1971) who, in 1938, assumed the custodianship of the *Astounding* (renamed *Analog* in 1961) and encouraged what he called "idea-fictions" with a recognisable element of science or pseudo-science which extrapolated concepts from technology. In 1946, Campbell observed, ". . . to most people science fiction seemed lurid, fantastic and nonsensical trash"; however, the new-age writing in this genre would become "stories of people living in a world where a Great idea or a series of them, and a Machine or machines, form the background. But it is the man, not the idea or the machine, that is the essence." The Golden Age does not, actually, represent a movement in science fiction; rather, it is more a periodising category which began around 1938 and went on to the 1950s, and then had a second spell between 1960 and 1970, when this genre saw an unprecedented growth and cultural impact.

Isaac Asimov (1920–90) was one of the most notable architects of the Golden Age of American science fiction. His early short story, "Nightfall" (1941), considered a classic of this genre, reenacts the Copernican revolution when an orbiting world with multiple suns and, therefore, without the experience of darkness, discovers night and the countless stars in the sky. Asimov's Foundation series – comprising *Foundation* (1951), *Foundation and Empire* (1952), *Second Foundation* (1953), *Foundation's Edge* (1982) and *Foundation and Earth* (1986) – is a recreation of Edward Gibbon's (1737–94) *Decline and Fall of the Roman Empire* (1776–88) on an interplanetary scale. Hari Seldon, a scientist, uses his notion of "psychohistory" to predict the dissolution of the Galactic Empire and the future of the universe through a period of anarchy to an ultimate reestablishment of order. However, before this epic chronicle, Asimov had acquired recognition and success with his first robot novel, *Caves of Steel* (1954). Written in the form of a detective thriller, it notably formulates the "three laws of robotics" which set the terms of this theme in the genre.

Robert A. Heinlein (1907–88) is considered another major figure of this period. Beginning with stories in Campbell's *Astounding,* his "The Roads Must Roll" (1940) is a remarkably innovative story where in a future America, people travel, not in cars on freeways, but on a vast network of rolling roads. These roads are maintained by a collective labour force and thus the notion of "rolling" becomes a metaphor of their power and a symbol of revolution. The "Universe" (1941) and "Commonsense" (1941), two other stories which followed, inspired the novel *Orphans in the Sky* (1964). Apart from *Starship Troopers* (1949), Heinlein is chiefly known for his *Stranger in a Strange Land* (1961). The latter tells the story of Valentine Michael Smith who was raised by Martians. Smith returns to earth with mystical powers to found a religious cult which emphasises an intuitive or empathetic experience of the world, termed "grokking" or "grok" – a term which has subsequently entered the English language. However, in spite of its initial promise, the novel fails to separate the fiction from literal scripture and becomes a parody of religious ideas. Heinlein's novels often involve political satire, as in *The Puppet Masters* (1951) and *Double Star* (1956); whereas, in *Have Space Suit – Will Travel* (1958), he is able to construct a time-travel adventure which was popular with teenage readers.

Among the other writers of the Golden Age Jack Vance (1916–2013) is considered a versatile stylist, not only for the experimental prose that he cultivates but also because of the imaginative range and multiplicity of his narratives. This is evident in *Big Planet* (1957) and *Emphyrio* (1969). His science fiction cycles – such as the Planet of Adventure series (*City of the Chasch*, 1968; *Servants of the Wankh*, 1969; *The Dirdir*, 1969), the Durdane trilogy (*The Anome*,1973; *The Brave Free Men*, 1973; *The Astura*, 1974), and the Demon Princes series (*The Star King*, 1964; *The Palace of Love*, 1967; *The Face*, 1979; and *The Book of Dreams*, 1981) – tend towards a certain repetitiveness but attest to a complex ingenuity in the conception of the tales.

Cleve Cartmill's (1908–64) "Deadline" (1944), a short story, is a remarkable case of science fiction extrapolating information to describe the making of an atom bomb so convincingly that it had the US military security inspect the *Astounding* offices. Another prolific writer was Poul Anderson (1926–2001) whose *Brain Wave* (1954) ascribes the declining intellectual activity on earth to its orbital journey through cosmic radiation. Though most of Anderson's novels are military space operas, in *Tau Zero* (1970) he depicts a damaged spaceship acquiring increased velocity and almost reaching the speed of light. This expansion of time implies that the crew survives the end of the world and flies into a reborn universe. Algis Budrys (1931–2008) was one of the earliest writers to explore cyborg fiction, in his *Who?* (1958), and repeated this concern with the theme of dual identity in *Rogue Moon* (1960). Similarly, Alfred Bester (1913–87) is often considered to have invented "New Wave" and "cyberpunk". While his *The Demolished Man* (1953) is a complex crime mystery, *Tiger! Tiger!* (1956; titled *The Stars My Destination* in the US) is a *bildungsroman* which is based in the twenty-fifth century when teleportation, or what Bester calls "jaunting", is common. Finally, George Stewart's (1895–1980) single post-apocalyptic novel, *Earth Abides* (1949), is an elegiac tribute to that which has passed.

From its inception in the seventeenth century, science fiction has confronted religious and spiritual questions regarding the absence of belief in a god or organized faith in other worlds. The protagonist of James Blish's (1921–75) *A Case of Conscience* (1958) is faced with doubts about the inhabitants of the planet Lithia who have no notion of "God" or the "soul" or, for that matter, have any sense of sin in their paradise. Thus, this fiction involves a radical interrogation of theological verities related to the validity of earthly ideas of divinity and salvation. For instance, Blish's Cities in Flight series – comprising *They Shall Have Stars* (1956), *A Life for the Stars* (1962), *Earthman Come Home* (1955) and *The Triumph of Time* (1958) – is more concerned with spiritual issues with its hero, the mayor of New York, finally deciding on love as the only value to be taken when they transmute into the life of new cosmoi. This preoccupation with the emotional and spiritual consequences of planetary travel and colonisation also characterises the writing of Ray Bradbury (1920–2012). His *The Martian Chronicles* (1950), a collection of linked stories, is nostalgic about the childhood small-town experiences which act as a consolation for the loss in an uncertain future. Bradbury's novels are, thus, marked by a lyricism evident also in *The Illustrated Man* (1951) and *Fahrenheit 451* (1953), which uses this temperature for books to burn as emblematic of totalitarianism.

Literary modernism, with its traditional elitism implicit in its sense of thematic seriousness and formal experimentation, had for a considerable time dismissed science fiction for its mass appeal and market compulsions. Yet, as this genre evolved in the post–World War II period, it attracted the contribution of writers who brought into it the qualities that were usually associated with "high" culture. The 1960s and 70s thus witnessed a resurgence of science fiction by writers acclaimed for endowing the genre with an element of critical and philosophical profundity. This is apparent in Frank Herbert's (1920–86) Dune series (1963–65), John Barth's (b.1930) *Giles Goat-*

Boy, or The Revised New Syllabus of George Giles Our Grand Tutor (1966) and Philip K. Dick's (1928–82) *The Three Stigmata of Palmer Eldritch* (1965), *Do Androids Dream of Electric Sheep?* (1968) and *Ubik* (1969). Herbert's five-part Dune series – containing *Dune Messiah* (1969), *Children of Dune* (1976), *God Emperor of Dune* (1981), *Heretics of Dune* (1984) and *Chapter House Dune* (1985) – may be termed an ecological science fiction adventure based on an anti-technological and mystical society attempting to find a new messiah. This search continues in Barth's *Giles Goat-Boy*, which centres on a human raised as a goat on a farm, who believes he is the messiah. Situated in a location between two campuses, the novel becomes an extravagant parody of the messianic tendency that finally inverts the assumptions of mystical faith.

Philip Dick's novels have been critically acclaimed for their complex explorations of the multiple nature of reality, often determined by illusionary human assumptions. Thus, the "real" is usually veiled by appearances; in fact, it becomes necessary to sift through several realities to find the one relevant to the individual characters in *Eye in the Sky* (1957). Similarly, *The Three Stigmata of Palmer Eldritch* (1965), whose titular protagonist is a messiah-figure, suggests that drugs induce a religious and transcendental reality equally valid for those who are under their spell. *Do Androids Dream of Electric Sheep?*, which was celebrated in a masterful film adaptation, *Blade Runner* by Ridley Scott, in 1982, portrays an abandoned Earth populated mainly with androids who have to be "retired" by the human protagonist, Rick Deckard. Yet, at the end, it is an android who is responsible for exposing the fraud in which most of the humans are involved. *Ubik* can be divided into two parts: the first concerns a category of individuals, the "psi", who undertake espionage for corporations and are "caught" by the "anti-psi"; and the second, derived from Dick's 1964 story, "What the Dead Men Say", dealing with dead people being kept in a state of "half-life" in a cold storage, so that their brain waves can be read and used by the living. However, life seems to be a form of consumption which ultimately leads to entropy and death as *Ubik*'s protagonist admits at the end: "Metabolism, he reflected, is a burning process, an active furnace. When it ceases to function, life is over. They must be wrong about hell, he said to himself. Hell is cold; everything there is cold." Having experienced a series of "visions" or "communications" in 1974, Dick started seeing himself as a reincarnation of several messiahs. This ultimately found expression in a series of novels such as *VALIS* (1981), *The Divine Invasion* (1981) and *The Transmigration of Timothy Archer* (1982).

Ursula Le Guin (b.1929) was one of the foremost writers to succeed Dick in the genre. Her early novels illustrate an equal balance between fantasy and "Hard SF", as in *Rocannon's World* (1966), *Planet of Exile* (1966) and *City of Illusions* (1967). In 1967–68, she admitted to have shifted from this formula: ". . . got my pure fantasy vein separated from my science fiction vein by writing *A Wizard of Earthsea* and then *The Left Hand of Darkness*, and the separation marked a very large advance in both skill and content. Since then I have gone writing, as it were, with both the left and right hands." Thus, her Earthsea series become the "left-handed" fantasy which includes *A Wizard of Earthsea* (1968), *The Tombs of Atuan* (1971), *The Farthest Shore* (1972), *Tehanu* (1990) and *The Other Wind* (2001). Together with these, her other novels dealt with scientific ideas that are complex and far-ranging in their imaginative range and emotional intensity. *The Left Hand Of Darkness* (1969) is considered one of her most notable books and deals with the visit of Genly Ai, a foreign delegate to the icy world of "Winter" on an errand to forge a planetary democratic consortium. "Winter", in fact, is a humanoid collective of no fixed gender, changing from an asexual gender to either male or female according to contingencies. Travelling between the liberal Karhide nation and the totalitarian Orgoreyn, Genly is finally able to convince its people of the need to join the planetary organisation. Le Guin's fiction, thus, has an ideological conflict which shapes the narrative, as in *The Dispossessed: An Ambiguous Utopia* (1974) which is one of the most comprehensive critiques of the Utopian tendency. *The Lathe of Heaven* (1971) is a parable on the power and dangers of the imagination which often substitutes dream for reality; and *Always Coming Home* (1985) shows Le Guin investigating the nature of communication which is central to human communities.

Though the gender ambivalence in Le Guin's *The Left Hand of Darkness* has led many to assume her fiction to be underscored with feminist ideas, it is Joanna Russ (1937–2011) who has been more direct in announcing such an intention in her fiction. *The Female Man* (1975) has four separate narratives by women of their experience of the world and also that of a Utopian planet, Whileaway. Russ's "When It Changed" (1972) had earlier dealt with an all-female society – but one which was aware of their faults and strengths – but in the later novel Russ seems to be more political in its concern with the feminist agenda. There were, however, other women writers in the genre who achieved a measure of commercial success, such as Marion Zimmer Bradley (1930–99). Her Darkover series comprising twenty-six titles – from *The Planet Savers* (1962) to *Traitor's Son* (1999) (*A Flame in Hali* [2004] was left unfinished at her death and was completed by Deborah Ross) – began basically as adventure tales which supported "male" values, and then in the 60s she turned to feminism and, finally in the 80s, she advocated gay rights. Other notable examples of women's science fiction would also include *Woman on the Edge of Time* (1976) by Marge Piercy (b.1936), Alice Sheldon's (1915–87, pseudonym James Tiptree Jr.) collection of stories *Warm Worlds and Otherwise* (1975), and C. J. Cherryh's (b.1942) Arthurian romance in a stranded spaceship, *Port Eternity* (1982), and a more homely world portrayed in *Downbelow Station* (1981).

Among the science fiction writers of the 1980s and 90s, Gene Wolfe's *The Book of the New Sun* (1980–83) has received critical attention. Consisting of four volumes –*The Shadow of the Torturer* (1980), *The Claw of the Conciliator* (1981), *The Sword of the Lictor* (1982) and *The Citadel of the Autarch* (1983) – Wolfe's novel recounts a chronicle of a future "Urth" (Earth) where human society is reconciled to a dying sun and dig into medieval structures with some advanced technological facilities to face an evident inevitability. This series has an indirect link with Wolfe's next project, *The Book of the Long Sun* (1993–96), another collection of four volumes. *The Book of the Short Sun* (1999–2001) – comprising *On Blue's Waters* (1999), *In Green's Jungles* (2000) and *Return to the*

Whorl (2001) – continued following the journey of the Long Sun spaceship. Wolfe's fiction displays the indeterminate complexities associated with a postmodernist novel in which one may discover multiple perspectives with every new reading.

The eighties also saw the development of "cyberpunk", a term coined by Bruce Bethke (b.1955) in a short story, "Cyberpunk" (1983), though the novel which was believed to have used this idiom and form predates the term – Bruce Sterling's (b.1954) *The Artificial Kid* (1980). However, it was William Gibson's (b.1948) debut novel *Neuromancer* (1984) which helped to define and popularise the form – a combination of a computer-generated virtual reality or cyberspace, called the Net or Matrix, and the violent dark world of androids, as in Dick's *Do Androids Dream of Electric Sheep?*. Gibson's hero is a hacker bent on stealing protected information from cyberspace. This leads him to a sentient space computer which finally asserts its supremacy. The sequels to *Neuromancer* – *Count Zero* (1986) and *Mona Lisa Overdrive* (1988) – together with *Virtual Light* (1993) and *Idoru* (1996), do not achieve the same success as his first work, but Gibson remains a pioneer in tracing a new direction that science fiction was to take in the twenty-first century. After Gibson, the most important name in this category is Pat Cadigan (b.1953) whose version of cyberpunk explores the interface between humans and computers, in *Synners* (1991) and *Tea from an Empty Cup* (1998). John Shirley's (b.1953) Eclipse Trilogy, comprising *Eclipse* (1985), *Eclipse Penumbra* (1988) and *Eclipse Corona* (1990), is equally notable. Orson Scott Card's (b.1951) 1985 novel, *Enders Game*, deals with a battle in cyberspace with an alien species called the Buggers but highlights the dangers of children being consumed in such virtual battles – a conclusion which is emphasised in its sequels, *Speaker for the Dead* (1986) and *Xenocide* (1991). The five-volume Homecoming series attempts to rewrite the Bible as science fiction, recounting the Exodus as an interstellar journey.

The more traditional science fiction of the 1990s include the works of Dan Simmons (b.1948) whose *Hyperion* (1989) and *Fall of Hyperion* (1990) are space operas which reflect on the hopes and despairs involved in a religious quest. In the same series – Hyperion

Cantos – *Endymion* (1996) and *The Rise of Endymion* (1997) present a caricature of the Catholic Church becoming a tyrannical power. Kim Stanley Robinson's (b.1952) Mars trilogy (*Red Mars*, 1992; *Green Mars,* 1994; and *Blue Mars*,1996) is another notable work of this period, while David Foster Wallace's (1962–2008) *Infinite Jest* (1996) and Douglas Coupland's (b.1961) *Girlfriend in a Coma* (1998) confront the reality of a world dominated by technology and the possibility of its bringing about the end.

There continues to be an increasing interest in science fiction in the twenty-first century, the regularity with which these novels are published implying a renewed involvement of contemporary writers in the genre. A random survey would, therefore, include Kim Robinson's *2312* (2013), John Scalzi's (b.1969) *Old Man's War* (2005) and *Fuzzy Nation* (2011), Suzanne Collin's (b.1962) *The Hunger Games* trilogy (2008–10), Daniel H. Wilson's (b.1978) *Robopocalypse* (2011), and Robert Charles Wilson's (b.1953) *Burning Paradise* (2013) and *Last Year* (2016). In fact, the history of this genre is a testimony to its gradual development from a form of popular fiction to its present stature as an alternative category of imaginative literature valued for an equally serious and profound examination of the nature of our world and the future of our race.

American Detective Fiction

The beginning of American detective fiction is usually traced to Edgar Allan Poe (1809–49). Though only three of Poe's stories feature his famous detective, Le Chevalier C. Auguste Dupin, the elements of murder, detection and mystery are characteristic of many of his stories published in the 1840 collection titled *Tales of the Grotesque and Arabesque*. Thus, apart from "The Murders in the Rue Morgue" (1841), "The Mystery of Marie Roget" (1842–43) and "The Purloined Letter" (1845), non-Dupin stories such as "Thou Art the Man" (1844) and "The Gold Bug" (1843) are also included – the last for its deciphering of a cryptogram to find a treasure, thus making this a feature of detection, also used later by Arthur Conan Doyle (1859–1930). However, scholars now consider the development of this subgenre as linked to the Gothic tradition, which was a major form of writing in nineteenth-century America. In fact, this element is implicit in the very title of Poe's stories which he had derived from E. T. A. Hoffman, a Prussian Romantic author, whose *Mademoiselle de Scudery* (1820) is identified as an early example of crime fiction. Narratives dealing with crime are also evident in the sermons and didactic writing of the Puritan and colonial period. These were gradually incorporated into secular pamphlets which confront the criminal potential of an unstable American society newly emerging as a nation in the eighteenth century.

However, by linking crime to the Gothic, American crime fiction devised a distinctively national variety first explored in the novels of Charles Brockden Brown (see Chapter 2). As stated earlier, Brown was one of the important predecessors of the American novel and was influenced by the writings of William Godwin (1756–1836). *Arthur Mervyn* (1799–1800), Brown's second novel, developed upon Godwin's *Caleb Williams* (1794) by making the investigator more confident and ultimately successful in his search for the criminal. In fact, *Edgar Huntly* (1799), which has been considered the first detective novel in America, is an account of Huntly's pursuit of Clithero Edny who, Huntly believes, had murdered his friend Waldegrave. Brown had become interested in the developing sciences of the time and applied some of these new scientific theories to unravel the crime, assigning it to a case of sleepwalking and schizophrenia. The elaborate plot includes inheritance puzzles and mysterious characters, but the emphasis is on the psychological tensions often expressed through symbols derived from the wild American landscape and the "savage" natives, suggesting the dark recesses of the individual's mind and the sources of his demented actions.

Poe named the Dupin stories "tales of ratiocination", trying to distinguish them by their intellectual emphasis and the probable scientific influence that shaped them. There is a distinct literary element in these tales – Dupin is widely read in the classics, has a poetic ability and a literary style, and likes to spend his time in the ancient library where the narrator first meets him. Though he does visit the scene of the crime in "The Mystery of Marie Roget", he mostly works out of his armchair, reading the newspapers and thinking. Poe distances the stories from his American readers by locating the first two in Paris, thereby giving them a sense of mystery and excitement associated with the continental city. Yet, this location and the urban experience became generic of crime fiction – as the city itself became a character, as in Doyle's London, Raymond Chandler's Los Angeles and Sara Paretsky's Chicago; and the detective was often viewed as an alienated urban onlooker or the modern "flaneur" as Walter Benjamin, the German critic and theorist, characterised the detective in his essay on another Poe tale, "The Man of the Crowd". However, in "The Mystery of Marie Roget", Poe attempted to solve a mysterious death that had occurred in New York during that time. Referring to newspaper reports, Dupin contemplates the incident and tries to offer a solution which, unfortunately, turns out to be wrong.

In fact, none of the Dupin stories actually involves a crime, in the true sense: the Rue Morgue deaths are caused by a rogue animal, the other is apparently an abortion gone wrong, and the third is the consequence of a court intrigue. Nevertheless, Dupin displays a method of detection which combines analysis and empirical scrutiny – which explains the locked room of the first story to be the result of a window having shut owing to a broken nail, interestingly termed a "*clou*" in French. The same analytical subtlety and simplicity is in evidence in "The Purloined Letter", where Dupin is sure that the letter is "hidden" at an obvious place where no one will be prompted to look for it. "Thou Art a Man", written after Dupin's abilities as a detective had been confirmed in the two earlier stories, thus has most of the motifs of a crime story – such as the innocent suspect condemned on circumstantial evidence, the process of detection, and the use of the red herring of the least likely suspect. Yet, the end resorts to the traditional devices of the Gothic, when the corpse is startingly made to sit up and the ventriloquist's skill is used to pronounce, "Thou art the man", which brings about the final exposure when the killer faints in admission of his crime. Despite its Gothic devices, Poe's stories were the first to study the work of the mind of a master grappling with the inscrutable and the unusual. In this they were able to demonstrate the main directions of the development of crime fiction and its portrayal of the detective.

In the nineteenth century, though there was a basic tendency to adapt the established European patterns of this fiction, elements intrinsic to American culture were also woven into the narratives. Anna Katherine Green's (1846–1935) *The Leavenworth Case* (1878) prepares the terms and features of much future detective fiction in her use of the "whodunit" techniques of the locked room, faked suicide-murder of a millionaire, incriminating letters to be rescued from the post and telegraph department, the plotted movements of the story and the manipulation of the readers' expectations. Her detective, Ebenezer Gryce, anticipating later such figures in this genre, is "a portly, comfortable personage", a less than heroic figure who often leaves the investigation to New York lawyer Everett Raymond, but returns in the final scene to unravel the mystery and compel the murderer's confession. *The Leavenworth Case*, together with Green's next three novels, starting with *That Affair Next Door* (1897), created a model that would be adopted by Agatha Christie and other writers. Incidentally, Green replaced the "paternalistic" Gryce in *That Affair* with Amelia Butterworth, an elderly woman detective who relies on confession and long informative explanations in the final solution of the crime. The closing years of the century saw a significant growth of crime fiction owing to the tremendous success of dime novels, with about 801 titles being produced between 1882 and 1899. An enormous variety of detective figures was displayed in these novels, which seemed to anticipate those who would emerge in later writing – for instance, "Old King Brady" who is the "rugged and durable American", or the popular theatre star "Hankshaw, the Yankee detective", both of whom relied on disguise, physical prowess and a brawling ability, rather than any intellectual skills. A difference from this model was apparent in the accounts written by Allan Pinkerton (1819–84), who was a professional detective and spy and created the Pinkerton National Detective Agency, and wrote of the cases handled by the agency. Pinkerton left behind (or had ghostwritten) at least eighteen accounts of crimes based on real experiences, many of which were published posthumously. These included *The Expressman and the*

Detective (1874), *The Gypsies and the Detective* (1879), *The Spy of the Rebellion* (1883) and *Thirty Years a Detective* (1900). These novels testified to the growing popularity of realistic crime fiction in the last decades of the nineteenth century.

In his essay "The Simple Art of Murder" (1944), Raymond Chandler (1888–1959) redefined American crime fiction by decentering it from the English country house and the library, and returning it to where it actually happened. Speaking of Dashiell Hammett's (1894–1962) writing as the representative pattern, Chandler said,

> Hammett gave murder back to the kind of people that commit it for reasons not just to provide a corpse; and with the means at hand, not with handwrought dueling pistols, curare and tropical fish. He put these people down on paper as they are, and made them talk and think in the language they customarily used for these purposes. . . . [Hammett] was spare, frugal, hard-boiled, but he did over and over again what only the best writers can ever do at all. He wrote scenes that seemed to have never been written before.

Thereby, emerged the distinctive American variety of crime fiction called the "hard-boiled" crime novel, a product of the pulp magazine *Black Mask,* which was edited by Captain John Shaw from 1926 and to which both Hammett and Chandler contributed their writings. "Hard-boiled" primarily referred to a style of writing characterised by brusque colloquial aggression, a spare and unsentimental directness, and linguistic rigour. For instance, in Hammett's *Red Harvest* (1929), when Bill Quint scoffs at Hammett's detective, the Op (short for "Operative"), "So you're the gumshoe?", the Op has a characteristic reply, "That's the bunk. . . . I come all the way down here to rope you, and you're smarted up."

The hard-boiled crime novel was actually a product of the America of the Depression years, reflecting the anxieties about capitalism, economic and political instability, and the nexus between law and crime that became pervasive in its social institutions and policies. Chandler makes this an important aspect of this fiction, in "The Simple Art of Murder":

> The realist in murder writes of a world in which gangsters can rule nations and almost rule cities, in which hotels and apartment houses and celebrated restaurants are owned by rich men who made their money out of brothels, in which . . . the nice man down the hall is a boss of the numbers racket; a world where a judge with a cellar full of bootleg liquor can send a man to jail for having a pint in his pocket.

In Hammett's *Red Harvest* and *The Glass Key* (1931), criminals are the pillars who support the rich and famous, the bold and the beautiful. The irony, however, lies in the fact that having used these equivocal agents to strengthen their position, they have now lost control over them. In fact, the devil's disciples have now started demanding their master's pound of flesh. Thus, the Continental Op is hired to rid Personville, aptly mispronounced Poisonville, of their menace. Similarly, in Chandler's *The Big Sleep* (1939), Carmen Sternwood, the daughter of Philip Marlowe's client, turns out to be the killer, justifying his disgust, "To hell with the rich. They make me sick." Not only does this suggest the radical nature of the social critique implicit in the hard-boiled version of crime fiction, which may have been influenced by Hammett's affiliations to the Communist Party of America, but more significantly, it undermines the centrality of the detective and the success of detection which is basic to traditional crime fiction. "That the law breaker is invariably sooner or later apprehended is probably the least challenged of extant myths," observed Hammett in his "From the Memoirs of a Private Detective". "And yet," he added, "the files of every detective bureau bulge with records of unsolved mysteries and uncaught criminals." In spite of punishing the offenders, many of these novels end only with a provisional solution and often a recognition that the criminal is not fully culpable, deserving a second chance, as in Chandler's *Farewell My Lovely* (1940). In both Hammett and Chandler there is, therefore, and oppressive awareness that crime will return very soon; that even as one particular serpent is scotched, evil has not been destroyed completely. Thus, at the end of *Red Harvest*, the Op ironically tells his client that the city is "all nice and ready to go to the dogs again".

This ambiguity in the resolution of the hard-boiled variety denies official law and the detective any moral authority or dominance. The consequent vulnerability that this confers to the custodians of order and justice gives these novels a strong sense of social criticism. In *Red Harvest*, therefore, a group of criminals is helped in a back-door escape by a section of the very police force conducting the raid on their hideout. Similarly, in Chandler's *Farewell My Lovely* (1940) and *The Lady in the Lake* (1943), Marlowe is savaged by the police for prying into cases which reveal their complicity. This not only implies an alienation of the detective but a complex identification with the criminal. This "double" nature is suggested not merely in the sympathy for the betrayed and desperate but entails the doubtful use of methods strictly defined as "criminal" in detection and punishment. Thus, the Op in *Red Harvest* and Samuel Spade in *The Maltese Falcon* (1930) often resort to deception, bribery and coercion to achieve their ends. In *Farewell My Lovely*, Marlowe uses liberal supplies of whisky to force out of Mrs Florian the real identity of the "Lovely" in the title. Spade is unrepentant about his devious methods and remains inscrutable: "Don't be too sure, I am as crooked as I am supposed to be," he tells Brigid O'Shaunessy. When, at the end of the novel, Brigid argues that he cannot turn her over to the police because he is in love with her, he adds, "But I don't know what that amounts to. Does anyone ever? But suppose I do. What of it? Maybe next month I won't. . . ." Emotion, therefore, is oblique and elided in the gaps of the sentences and the silences implicit in the brevity of the epithet or the phrase. When the huckster, Dinah Brand, is murdered, the Op's hesitations suggest the feelings he is trying to control, "Slowly, gently as if afraid of awakening her, I let go of the ice pick. . . .", the instrument which had been used to kill her. In these novels, therefore, it is not the impersonal and amoral professionalism which concerns Hammett but what he regards as the bewildering predatory struggle beneath civilisation. Everyone, including the detective, seems to be rendered an imposter by civilisation. And this realisation tends to mock the idea of a "just solution" to the crimes, just as the Maltese Falcon mocks the notions of ownership and value. For, the final irony is that this priceless artefact turns out to be a fake like everyone else in the novel. Believed to have gold beneath its feathers, it is revealed to be merely an empty leaden object: the illusory substituting the real becomes the central mystery that the detective has to unravel.

The detective in the hard-boiled form of crime fiction, thus, undergoes a change which not only differentiates him from the traditional prototype but invests the figure with a complex role and responsibility. The private-eye in Hammett and Chandler negotiates a liminal space between the underworld and respectable society. He not only mediates between the criminal and the police but, as the Op complains, the rites of this passage often vitiate his own personality: "It's this damned town," the Op tells Dinah, "Poisonville is right. It's poisoned me. It's what the place has done to me.... I'm going blood-simple." Thus, the myth of the detective's immutability is challenged – here he is tested in more ways than the purely cerebral, and a sense of personal integrity stands as his only defence. In Chandler's *The Big Sleep*, when Carmen tries to seduce Marlowe, he throws her out of his bed and apartment, for as he asserts,

> ... this was the room I had to live in. It is all I had in the way of a home. In it was everything that was mine, that had any association for me, any past, anything that took the place of a family. Not much; a few books, pictures, radio, chessmen, old letters, stuff like that. Nothing. Such as they were they had all my memories.

Unlike Hammett's works, Chandler's fiction has a conscious sense of style which involves the metaphoric and the idiomatic. Moreover, Chandler's detective is sensitive to the nuances of the business of crime and punishment with its disenchantments and defeats. Several studies have, therefore, confirmed a heroic ethic in his novels, which is often undermined by the desire and deceit of this corrupt world. In "The Simple Art of Murder",Chandler tries to conceive his protagonist in terms of the traditional romance: "... down these mean streets a man must go who is not himself mean, who is neither tarnished nor afraid. The detective in this kind of story must be such a man. He is the hero, he is everything. He must be a complete man and a common man and yet an unusual man." A personalised sense of honour often distances the detective in these novels. The detective, like the criminals, occupies a marginal third position – neither of the law nor of the criminal but an alternative sense of justice where the hard-boiled detective is both judge and jury. While the Op organises a gang war which mutually destroys the criminals in *Red Harvest*, Marlowe allows Velma to escape at the end of *Farewell My Lovely*.

A corollary to a refashioned detective is also a transformation of the methods of detection. In fact, the hard-boiled form of this fiction abandons the clue-puzzle formula of the European tradition and, in following the *Black Mask* model, gives more importance to physical action. Though the detectives go through the basic motions of investigation, the solution is not always a result of this exercise. Often, as in the instances of *The Big Sleep* and *The Maltese Falcon*, it is apparent that the culprit has been identified much before the final solution with the detective creating situations to trap his victim into making a confession. Rather than being a linguistic chess game, these novels tend towards an intuitive discovery which is suggested by the word "hunch". Interestingly, "hunch" is an American term without a parallel in standard British English. By undermining the importance of detection, the hard-boiled version reverses the logic of the detective novel by stating that there is first a crime and then a solution.

The covert operations of the detective text are not limited only to its formal structure but also include the relation between language and meaning. Most of these novels draw attention to the ambiguity of the verbal sign. For, as appearances in this world are rarely predicated on the real, language has to perform a complex mediation to separate the false from the true. In the hard-boiled novels, a deliberate simplification and reduction of words to the denotative and the paratactic is basic to the style which emphasises the material, concrete and the colloquial. This is obvious in the use of the American vernacular and also in the creation of what is called a "novel of spoken action". Even the choice of a first-person narrator becomes an indication of the verbal action, by providing a graphic intensity to the depiction of this violent world. For Hammett and Chandler, style is not simply a matter of a verbal choice but also an index of personality and behaviour. The texture and tone of Chandler's prose creates Marlowe's credible individuality, for Marlowe is gifted with a quintessentially American stylistic feature – the wisecrack. The wisecrack marks an aggressive verbal excess of the wise guy who is no respecter of authority and whose irreverent wit is often an effective weapon of defence against the dissembling world. In *Farewell My Lovely*, when Lindsay Marriot finds Marlowe observing an avant-garde figurine in his house, he identifies it as the work of the famous sculptor, Asta Dial's *Spirit of Dawn* he had recently acquired. "'I thought it was Klopstein's, *Two Warts on a Fanny*,'" Marlowe replies, adding, "Mr. Lindsay Marriot's face looked as if he had swallowed a bee. He smoothened it out with an effort. 'You have a peculiar sense of humor', he said. 'Not peculiar,' I said, 'Just uninhibited.'"

In an important sense, the hard-boiled form represented an essentially personal style of writing which assumed a generic signature of American crime fiction in the twentieth century. However, as stated earlier, it also involved a view of the world which was indivisible from the style of this fiction. Though the style went on to influence several writers, both contemporary to and coming after Hammett and Chandler, the vision that they expressed became increasingly redundant in the post–World War II developments in America. Nevertheless, crime fiction after the hard-boiled era never remained quite the same as in the Golden Age examples of this subgenre. While its undoubted romanticism with an individualist conception of action fits into the American tradition, the ambiguity and limitations attendant on this notion of agency undermine the original idealism associated with its hopes of redemption. American historians of crime fiction, therefore, distinguish two broad schools of this literature – the hard-boiled and the more conservative, English convention of the clue-puzzle crime novel.

Willard Huntington Wright (1888–1939) wrote *The Benson Murder Case* (1926) under the pseudonym "S. S. Van Dine", adding ten more titles using a similar formula. His plots dealt with the criminal side of the American acquisitive instinct, insisting that there "simply must be a corpse in a detective novel, and the deader the corpse the better". Van Dine's success with the European version of the American crime novel found several followers. Two cousins, Frederic Dannay (1905–82) and Manfred

B. Lee (1905–71), assumed the name "Ellery Queen" (which was also the name of their detective) to produce *The Roman Hat Mystery* (1929), *The Tragedy of X* (1932) and *The Spanish Cape Mystery* (1935), and continued to write well into the 1970s. Another important contributor to the American variety of the clue-puzzle was Rex Stout (1886–1975) whose detective, Nero Wolfe, never leaves his study, depending for most of his information on a Watson-like assistant, Archie Goodwin, in *The League of Frightened Men* (1935), *Not Quite Dead Enough* (1944), *Murder by the Book* (1951) and *A Family Affair* (1975), among others. Together with these writers, others brought to the methods of detection different ideas such as that of academic psychology by C. Daly King (1895–1963) who was himself a practising psychologist. His "Obelists" (a person who suspects) series, complete with references and footnotes, appear both ingenious and contrived in *Obelists at Sea* (1932) and *Obelists En Route* (1934). A comic treatment of this form is displayed by Craig Rice (1908–57; penname of Georgiana Randolph Rice) whose *My Kingdom for a Hearse* (1957) is set in the 1920s Jazz age. If not for their importance but for their enormous success, one should also include in this list the adventures of the teenage sleuth Nancy Drew, created by Carolyn Keene (also known as Mildred Wirt Benson), whose exploits inevitably assert the values of the dominant, white, bourgeois American.

However, the private-eye model was not the only version that prevailed during these years. Erle Stanley Gardner (1889–1970), a Californian lawyer, made his detective, Perry Mason, a committed defender of people's rights against the equivocal power of the law. Though the novels are not preoccupied with the exercise of investigation, leaving most of this work to Paul Drake, Mason's assistant, the climax is characteristically in a courtroom in most of the novels, beginning with *The Case of the Velvet Claws* (1933) and continuing into as many as eighty-one titles.

The work of Mickey Spillane (Frank Morrison Spillane; 1918–2006) returns to the hard-boiled formula by emphasising sadism and violence for a criticism of the corruptions in New York City. His detective, Mike Hammer, is not inclined to the use of intellectual deductions, depending more on the commitment to the ethics of the vigilante – often for avenging personal betrayal in the early *I, the Jury* (1947) and *Vengeance is Mine* (1950). In Spillane's later novels, a Cold War anxiety and gender prejudice tend to permeate his fiction, as is evident in *One Lonely Night* (1951). They also shift into a mix of the crime and spy thriller, as in *Tomorrow I Die* (1984) and *The Killing Man* (1989). The figure of Chandler's sceptical and self-doubting detective returns in the writing of Ross Macdonald (born Kenneth Millar;1915–83). In *The Moving Target* (1949, published under the name John Macdonald), the detective, Lew Archer, traces the crime in a family to the trauma and the secrets of parenthood. Thus, a Freudian twist is given to the nineteenth-century inheritance narrative and extended to examine a new preoccupation with juvenile delinquency. Macdonald's *The Wycherly Woman* (1961) deals with the tragedy of false identities, while *The Underground Man* (1971) combines the troubles of dysfunctional families with ecological concerns.

Complementing these two major types of detective fiction is a version which is termed the "crime novel" which also seemed to develop first in the 1930s and continued into the twenty-first century. This is mainly focused on the situation of the criminal before, during and after the crime, and thus would more appropriately be termed the novel devoted to the criminal. Therefore, this naturally implies a decentring of crime fiction – from the importance given to detection to that of the psychopathology of crime. It is possible to find its origins in the Newgate and the Gothic novels, but in America the theme was explored in the novels of W. R. Burnett (1899–1982) who as George Grella produced such notable examples as *Little Caesar* (1929), *High Sierra* (1941) and *The Asphalt Jungle* (1949). A remarkable version of this subgenre is James M. Cain's (1892–1977) *The Postman Always Rings Twice* (1934) which, in its inquiry into a convicted man's reminiscences, is a study of obsession and of crime as an existential reality in a world of loss and disillusion. Interestingly, this investigation of criminal psychology became the province of women writers such as Mignon Eberhart (1899–1996) whose *The Patient in Room 18* (1929) and *The Dark Garden* (1933) combine the use of puzzles with richly emotive Gothic settings. Dorothy B. Hughes's (1904–93) *The So Blue Marble* (1940) chooses a male detective to deal with the tragic consequences of the crime in which the wealthy become trapped; whereas, in *In a Lonely Place* (1947), she introduces a new theme by dealing with the problem of a war hero who returns to become a psychotic killer. In fact, this focus on the criminal psyche and the increasing movement towards an urban Gothic is revealed in the writing of Cornell Woolrich (1903–68), whose *The Bride Wore Black* (1940), later made into highly successful film versions, tells the story of a woman widowed on the day of her wedding and her relentless search for the killers to avenge her loss. This turn to the "transgressor centered crime novel", a term coined by Stephen Knight in *Crime Fiction Since 1800: Detection, Death, Diversity*, in fact, became an important aspect of crime fiction in the 1950s, with Jim Thompson's (1906–77) *Nothing More than Murder* (1949) and *The Killer Inside Me* (1952), which in their repeated sadomasochistic portrayal of crime, assume almost a form of a pornography of violence. Thompson, however, pushes this to a surrealist extreme in *The Getaway* (1958). In Thompson's fiction, the unsentimental realism of Hammett and Chandler achieves a conclusive form, though without the justifying values. Although not as important as Thompson, David Goodis (1917–67) also deserves mention for his *Dark Passage* (1946),considered a distinctive example of a crime noir novel. His *Nightfall* (1947) and *Cassidy's Girl* (1951) are also notable for their variant use of the private-eye formula. Goodis's *Down There* (1956) formed the basis of the Francois Truffaut film classic, *Shoot the Piano Player* (1960).

Apart from Pauline Hopkins's (1859–1930) *Hagar's Daughter* (1901–02) and John Edward Bruce's (1856–1924)*The Black Sleuth* (1907–09), which appeared in periodicals, there were few examples of African American detectives or crime novels. An early instance was *The Conjure-Man Dies* (1932) by the Harlem writer Rudolph Fisher (1897–1934), which was a police procedural with elements of a Black modernist sensibility. This prepared the ground for the writing of Chester Himes (1909–84) whose police detectives, "Grave Digger" Jones and "Coffin" Ed Johnson, scour the streets of Harlem using both words and their guns as weapons in *The Five-Cornered Square* (1959) and *Cotton Comes to Harlem* (1965). The incidence of African American crime fiction is paradoxical in America where evil is designated by colour and race. Thus, the preponderant task of this version of writing in this subgenre was first to redefine the racial stereotypes implicit in this fiction and then try to "know the truth", as Himes said in a lecture, for "(if) this plumbing for the truth reveals within the Negro personality . . . homicidal mania, . . . a pathetic sense of inferiority, . . . uncle tomism, hate, fear and self-hate, this then is the effect of oppression on the human personality". The most important contribution that Himes made to crime fiction is to bring racial ideology to the centre of the subgenre. The two "ace detectives" of the white Lieutenant Anderson's team are, thus, caught in an ambivalent double bind: to bring evidently violent African American criminals before the law while simultaneously recognising that these are also victims of a larger crime – the effects of racism on the African American population. When Anderson in *Cotton Comes to Harlem* regrets "to see (Black) people tearing at one another like rapacious animals", Jones is quick to point out, "Hell, what do you expect? . . . As long as there are jungles there'll be rapacious animals." Himes saturates his fiction with a rich profusion of details of African American culture and history. Thus, the "cotton" of the title is linked to America's slave history, the "Return to Africa" and other radical Black movements, and to the Harlem cultural renaissance and, particularly, to the Jazz age. Moreover, as in the hard-boiled version, Himes's detectives are often participants in gratuitous violence which does not bring them any nearer to solving the crime, as in the 1969 novel, *Blind Man with a Pistol.* Distinctive to Himes's fiction is his use of humour sometimes bordering on the absurd, for he believed, "[r]acism introduces absurdity into the human condition". This sense of comic absurdism anticipates the movement of crime fiction towards the postmodern adaptations of this genre.

There were, however, other writers who had made notable contributions to African American crime fiction, such as the white novelist John Ball (1911–88), whose *In the Heat of the Night* (1965) recounts the struggle of an African American detective, Virgil Tibbs, to solve a racial murder against racial attacks in a Southern town. Though not in the same class as the novels of Himes or Ball, Ernest Tidyman's (1928–84) *Shaft* (1970), the film version of which acquired a tremendous success, shows the growing confidence of the African American crime writers, for this novel series, till *The*

Last Shaft in 1975, was almost a Black parody of the dominant white private-eye and spy hero convention. Walter Mosley's (b.1952) work is often compared to that of Chandler. His first novel, *Devil in a Blue Dress* (1990), is set in Los Angeles and has a freelance African American detective, Ezekiel "Easy" Rawlins. Rawlins undertakes cases of crime influenced by issues of class and colour in *A Red Death* (1991), *White Butterfly* (1992), *Black Betty* (1994) and *A Little Yellow Dog* (1996). Recalling the work of Himes, these novels are rich in African American colloquialisms and also reveal an awareness of other oppressed races, particularly the Hispanics and Jews. Mosley's success is also evident in his attempt to venture into other kinds of crime fiction in newer series with novels such as *Always Outnumbered, Always Outgunned* (1997) and *Fearless Jones* (2001).

Significantly, African American crime fiction actually prepared the context for the development of the postmodern crime novel. By undermining the traditional models of the genre and writing against the dominant white racial politics that shaped this type of fiction, the African American crime novel became what one commentator calls the "anti-detective novel". The main contours of this growth became evident in Ishmael Reed's (b.1938) *Mumbo Jumbo* (1972) and Clarence Major's (b.1936) *Reflex and Bone Structure* (1975). Reed's skills as a parodist is clear in the figure of his trickster detective named PaPa LaBas who has an agency called the Neo-HooDoo Kathedral. The novel is an exercise in fantasy, ironically given credibility with a bibliography and details of African American history. Similarly, Major parodies the conventions of white and racially conscious crime fiction, thereby deconstructing the tradition in almost a postmodern rewriting of the crime story. Though Thomas Pynchon's (b.1937) *The Crying of Lot 49* (1966) is sometimes considered to be a postmodernist detective novel because of its unresolved quest theme, Paul Auster's (b.1947) *The New York Trilogy*, comprising *City of Glass* (1985), *Ghosts* (1986) and *The Locked Room* (1986), is usually given a more representative status of this form of fiction in America. The first novel actually introduces the protagonist, a poet and detective writer named Quinn, who impersonates a private eye called Paul Auster and undertakes a quest of a mad scientist who, it is revealed, is also searching throughout New York for the letters and implication of the phrase "The Tower of Babel", apparently used by Jorge Luis Borges. The random nature of knowledge and the indeterminacy of meaning arise as a result of imbricated narratives which interweave the lives of Quinn with that of Blue in *Ghosts* and Fanshawe in *The Locked Room*, where the last becomes a recurrent motif drawn from crime fiction but also suggests the solipsistic imprisonment of the alienated self, which characterises urban existence and its postmodern representations. Auster, thus, recognises the complexity of the nature and meaning of the term "private-eye" and finds a generic association of the detective and writer, in *City of Glass*:

> In effect, the writer and the detective are interchangeable. The reader sees the world through the detective's eyes, experiencing the proliferation of its details as if for the first time. . . . Private eye. The term had a triple meaning for Quinn. Not only was it the letter 'i', standing for 'investigator', it was 'I' in the upper case, the tiny life-bud buried in the body of the breathing self. At the same time, it was also the physical eye of the writer, the eye of the man who looks out from himself into the world and demands that the world reveal itself to him. For five years now, Quinn had been living in the grip if this pun.

Generically, detective fiction, by its very self-consciousness, demonstrates the linguistic nature of the world and an awareness that fiction plays an important role in constructing the real. Language, thus, becomes a site of detection involving the recovery of the true from false stories or versions of the world. The urban underworld, which is largely the domain of crime fiction, metaphorically suggests a linguistic maze from which the detective must free meaning. Ironically, the very physical and material emphasis of this world – often expressed in the sense of detail and the paratactic nature of the style used in this writing – while asserting presence, implies its very opposite in the suppression and absence of meaning. By making language the location for contradictory versions of the real, crime fiction denies the institution of any singular or univocal meaning, encouraging alternative and multiple views of the world. American crime fiction is a continuous quest and reassertion of the validity of this belief.

♦ ♦ ♦

In marked contrast to that of England and Europe, the literature of America has been considerably influenced by the forms and values of popular culture. As it is evident, the writers of its "great" tradition admit to a conscious or, at most, an unconscious debt to the "little" as well. In fact, Nathanael West once considered giving *Miss Lonelyhearts* (1933) the subtitle, "a novel in the form of a comic strip". *Miss Lonelyhearts* is structured as a series of graphic narrative frames dealing with the events and characters of the novel. West justified his intention by adding, "Forget the epic, the master work. . . . Leave slow growth to the reviewers; you only have time to explode. Remember William Carlos Williams's description of the pioneer women who shot their children against the wilderness like cannon balls. Do the same with your novels. A novelist can afford to be everything but dull." Instances suggesting this awareness and assimilation of the popular remains enduring in the work of several writers, from Edgar Allan Poe and Mark Twain to Scott Fitzgerald, and in Horace McCoy's *They Shoot Horses, Don't They?* (1935). Therefore, the divide between the elite, literary culture and the common, mass culture – which had fissured literature since Matthew Arnold – seemed to have been provisionally bridged in what Henry James disparagingly called the "papered democracy" of the United States.

In fact, this anxiety over America's lack of a tradition and culture remained a refrain among many of its writers – notably, Nathaniel Hawthorne, Walt Whitman, William Dean Howells, James and Gertrude Stein. Thus, F. R. Leavis, in his *Mass Civilization and Minority Culture* (1930), chose the American example to warn against the philistine "leveling down" which was almost correlative to the developing technocracy that had come to dominate culture in the twentieth century. For Leavis, the evident lack of a sense of the past and a historical continuity deprived the United States of any notion of tradition and, therefore, of culture, condemning it to, what he termed, an "antihuman reductivism that favours the American neo-imperialism of the computer". Historians and theorists of popular culture, thus, consider this nation a model of homogenised forms and ideological manipulations implicit in popular literature and culture. Since popular culture is directly determined by the forces of urbanisation and industrial capital, it is inexorably bound to the commercial and consumerist values promoted by its economic and political institutions. American mass culture thus became the opiate that is interminably replicated and passively accepted the world over. This actually constitutes a global form of cultural imperialism, disseminated in the iconic American products like Hollywood, Coca-Cola, MTV, Nike and McDonald's.

Ironically, however, by this contentious logic, American popular culture becomes emblematic of the nation. In fact, as observed earlier, many of the foundational myths which are generic to American exceptionalism – such as the Frontier and the American Dream – have been refigured and validated more emphatically in its popular culture, particularly in cinema and the music industry. Nevertheless, the evident recognition of *difference* invested in this formation of a national and cultural identity also suggests an awareness that the tradition of American culture is defined not by its continuities, but by its variations, contestations and its local and regional adaptations. Thus, there seems to be a significant development of this culture, redefining earlier notions of text and tradition in the present century when American difference is rewritten as a vibrant multiculturalism, whose plural voices and forms renegotiate the borders of what can now be clearly seen as American *cultures*. It is, therefore, this heterogeneous and heteroglotic cultural identity that seems to be a rephrased answer to Crèvecoeur's classic question: "What then is the American, this new man?" The Vietnamese, feminist theorist and filmmaker Trinh T. Minh-ha, thus, redefines the contemporary American sense of identity by stating, ". . . identity is a way of re-departing . . . to start again with re-departures, different pauses, different arrivals . . .". It is this distinctive promise of being able to repeat the past that made the African American novelist Ishmael Reed celebrate America's "exciting destiny" – a destiny "to become a place where cultures of the world criss cross . . . because the United States is unique in the world: The world is here."

A Comparative Timeline for American Literature

Krishna Sen

Years	Major Historical and Sociopolitical Events in America	Major Texts and Literary Movements in American Literature	Corresponding British Literary Movements, Texts and Authors
		Early American Literature	
Before recorded American history	North America (US and Canada) settled more than 12000 years ago by about 30000 indigenous tribes	Indigenous Native American oral traditions; no written literature in any language	Old and Middle English literature; Chaucer (c.1343–1400)
1492	Columbus "discovers" America; names the tribes as "American Indians".	No written literature	Morality plays; *Everyman* (written in the late 1400s and premiered in 1510)
1550–1613	1550–90: Two failed attempts to establish English colonies in America 1579: Drake claims New Albion for England 1585: establishment of the Roanoke colony	**Narratives of exploration** 1588: Thomas Harriot, *A Briefe and True Report of the New Found Land of Virginia* in the original Latin 1590: Thomas de Brye releases the same book in four languages including English	[Reigns of Elizabeth I (1558–1603) and James I (1603–25)]

	1598: New Spanish colony, New Mexico – violent resistance leading to massacre of the native inhabitants of the city of Acoma 1605: Weymouth exploration of New England 1607: First English colony at Jamestown, Virginia 1609: Henry Hudson explores the Hudson river	1584: Arthur Barlow, *The First Voyage to Roanoke: The First Voyage made to the Coasts of America with two barks, wherein were Captains M. Philip Amadas, and M. Arthur Barlowe, who discovered part of the countrey now called Virginia anno 1584. Written by one of the said captaines, and sent to Sir Walter Ralegh, Knight, at whose charge and direction, the said voyage was set forth*	**The English Renaissance and Elizabethan literature** – Sidney, Spenser, the University Wits and Marlowe, Shakespeare, Bacon, Ben Jonson, Donne, prose writers; King James Version of the Bible (1611)
1614–39	1619: First enslaved Africans arrive at Jamestown 1620: Puritans arrive on the *Mayflower* and establish Plymouth 1622: Plymouth massacre 1626: Founding of Salem, Massachusetts 1630–43: Another 16000 English colonists establish settlements around Massachusetts Bay	Oral traditions of Negro slaves **Chronicles of colonial settlement** 1616: John Smith, *A Description of New England* 1630: John Winthrop's sermon on the ship *Arbella* – "A Model of Christian Charity" also known as the *City on the Hill* sermon 1630–50: William Bradford, *Of Plymouth Plantation*	**Jacobean Age** Jacobean drama – revenge tragedies, city comedies (Webster, Tourneur, Middleton, Marston, Massinger); tragicomedies of Beaumont and Fletcher; Metaphysical poetry

1640–69	1642: Beginning of English Civil War 1635 and 37: Roger Williams and then Anne Hutchinson ousted from Massachusetts for protesting against Puritan intolerance 1648: Margaret Brent, first colonial woman barrister, denied right to vote in Maryland Assembly 1655–65: Puritans persecute Quakers 1641–61: Maryland and Virginia colonies legalise lifetime servitude for Blacks	1645: John Cotton's *The Way of the Churches of Christ in New England* (justifies colonisation of America) 1656: John Hammond, *Leah and Rachel, or The Two Fruitfull Sisters, Virginia & Mary-land* <u>Poetry</u> 1650: Anne Bradstreet, *The Tenth Muse, lately Sprung up in America* 1662: Bestselling poem by Michael Wigglesworth, "The Day of Doom"	[1642–58: Oliver Cromwell, Puritan Commonwealth and closing of the theatres; 1660:The Restoration of Charles II] Milton, *Paradise Lost* (pub. 1667) **English Neoclassicism** Dryden, *Essay of Dramatic Poesy* (1668)
1670–99	1675–78: First Indian War (King Philip's War) 1681: William Penn receives charter to found Pennsylvania 1689: First rebellion by New England colonists against British Governor in Boston 1692: Salem witchcraft trials begin	**Historical Narratives** 1670: Samuel Danforth, *A Brief Recognition of New-Englands Errand into the Wilderness* 1676: Increase Mather, *A Brief History of the Warr with the Indians in New England* **First Captivity Narrative** 1682: *Narrative of the Captivity and Restoration of Mrs. Mary Rowlandson*	Milton, *Paradise Regained* and *Samson Agonistes* (1671); Dryden's heroic tragedies, *All for Love* (1678), *Absalom and Achitophel* (1681); Bunyan, *The Pilgrim's Progress* (1678); Aphra Behn, *Oroonoko* (1688)

	1688–1763: Colonists battle the French and the Native tribes in prolonged wars ending with the Treaty of Paris	**Puritan Sermons** 1684: Increase Mather, *Remarkable Providences* 1689: Cotton Mather, *Memorable Providences* 1693: Cotton Mather, *The Wonders of the Invisible World*	**Restoration Comedy** Wycherley, *The Plain Dealer* (first performed 1676); Congreve, *The Way of the World* (1700 first performance); **Sentimental Comedy** Colley Cibber, *Love's Last Shift* (1696) [1689–95: political and philosophical works of Locke (published posthumously till 1707)]
1700–49	Number of English colonists c.1700 – about 275000 1710–17: Irish and German immigrants 1712–15: Wars in the Carolinas with Native tribes 1710–24: France and Spain build forts and towns in the southeast 1732: English found southern colony, Georgia	1702: Cotton Mather, *Magnalia Christi Americana* 1708: Ebenezer Cook, "The Sotweed Factor, Or a Voyage to Maryland, A Satyr" (satire) 1719–98: *The Boston Gazette* 1733–58: Benjamin Franklin, *Poor Richard's Almanack*	Addison, *The Spectator* (1711–12) Steele, *Tatler* (1709–11) **The Augustan Age** Swift, *Gulliver's Travels* (1726); Pope, *An Essay on Criticism* (1711), *The Rape of the*

	1734: Jonathan Edwards's fiery sermons spark the "Great Awakening" 1739–42: Wars between British and Spanish colonies	**Historical Narratives** 1705: Robert Beverley, *The History and Present State of Virginia* 1727 and 1747: Cadwallader Colden, *History of the Five Indian Nations* **Captivity Narratives** 1707: John Williams, *The Redeemed Captive* 1728: Elizabeth Hanson, *Gods Mercy Surrounding Man's Cruelty, Exemplified in the Captivity and Redemption of Elizabeth Hanson*	*Lock* (1712), *Dunciad* (1728–43), *An Essay on Man* (1733–34) and *An Epistle to Dr. Arbuthnot* (composed in 1734 and published in 1735) **The Rise of the Novel** Defoe, *Robinson Crusoe* (1719), *Moll Flanders* (1722) Richardson, *Pamela* (1740), *Clarissa* (1748) Fielding, *Joseph Andrews* (1742), *Tom Jones* (1749)
1750–99	1754: Colonies adopt Benjamin Franklin's "Plan of the Union of British Colonies" 1764: James Otis, *Rights of the British Colonies Asserted and Proved* 1765: Colonies oppose England's Stamp Act 1770: English troops open fire on Boston colonists (The Boston Massacre)	1751: Benjamin Franklin, *Experiments and Observations on Electricity* (expanded and reprinted in 1753 and 1754 as parts 2 and 3) 1776: Thomas Paine, *Common Sense* 1782–83: Benjamin Franklin, "Remarks concerning the Savages of North America" **Gendered Writing** 1768: Milcah Martha Moore, *The Female Patriots*	Sterne, *Tristram Shandy* (1759) **End of Neoclassicism** Samuel Johnson, *The Vanity of Human Wishes* (1749), *The Rambler* (1750–52), *A Dictionary of the English Language* (1755), *Rasselas* (1759)

<table>
<tr>
<td></td>
<td>December 1773:
"Boston Tea Party"
1775: Patrick Henry of Virginia, "Give me liberty or give me death."
1775–83: The American War of Independence (from British rule)
4 July 1776: Declaration of Independence
1789–96: George Washington first President of free US
1790: Only adult white male property owners get the right to vote
1793: Draconian Fugitive Slaves Act</td>
<td>1790: Judith Murray, On the Equality of the Sexes

African American Literature
1773: Phillis Wheatley, Poems on Various Subjects, Religious and Moral
1789: First slave narrative by Olaudah Equiano: The Interesting Narrative of the Life of Olaudah Equiano

Native American Literature
1768: Samson Occom, A Short Narrative of My Life (published first in 1982)</td>
<td>The Transition
Blake, Songs of Innocence (1789), The Marriage of Heaven and Hell (1790–93), Songs of Innocence and Experience (1794)

The Gothic Novel
Horace Walpole, The Castle of Otranto (1764), Ann Radcliffe, The Mysteries of Udolpho (1794)

Pre-Romantic Poetry
Thomson, Collins, Cowper, Gray, Goldsmith

Drama
Oliver Goldsmith, She Stoops to Conquer (1773)
Sheridan, The Rivals (1775)

English Romanticism
Wordsworth, Lyrical Ballads (1798)
Coleridge, "The Rime of the Ancient Mariner" (1798)</td>
</tr>
</table>

		The Ninteenth-Century American Literary Renaissance	
1800–29	1800: (a) first census – 5.3 million people (b) Library of Congress established (c) failed slave rebellion in Virginia (d) capital city, Washington DC 1803: "Louisiana Purchase" from France increases territory 1803–05: Cross-country expedition to the Pacific coast; white settlers follow 1805–25: New southwestern slave-holding states formed, despite stiff Native resistance	1828: Noah Webster's *Dictionary* Fiction 1801: Charles Brockden Brown's *Clara Howard* and *Jane Talbot* (epistolary) 1819: Washington Irving, *Rip Van Winkle* 1826: James Fenimore Cooper, *The Last of the Mohicans* **Native American Literature** 1829: William Apess, *A Son of the Forest: The Experience of William Apes, A Native of the Forest, Comprising a Notice of the Pequod Tribe of Indians, Written by Himself*	Wordsworth, *The Prelude* (1850) Coleridge, *Biographia Literaria* (1817) Keats, *Odes* (1819) Shelley, "Ode to the West Wind" (1820), *Prometheus Unbound* (1820) Byron, *Don Juan* (1818–23) Fiction Scott, *Waverley* (1814), *Kenilworth* (1821) Jane Austen, *Pride and Prejudice* (1813), *Emma*(1815) Mary Shelley, *Frankenstein* (1818)
1830–65	1830: Indian Removal Act and "Trail of Tears" 1836: Formation of "Transcendental Club" 1838: Alexis de Tocqueville writes *Democracy in America*	**American Transcendentalism** Emerson: "Nature" (1836), "The American Scholar" (1837), "The Harvard Divinity School Address" (1838), *Essays* 1st Series (1841), *Essays* 2nd Series (1844)	**The Victorian Era** [Reign of Queen Victoria, 1837–1901, as Empress of India 1876–1901; the Industrial Revolution, c.1760–1840; Darwin, *Origin of Species* (1859)]

<table>
<tr>
<td></td>
<td>1846–48: Mexican American War – US victory, annexation of extensive territory
18–20 July 1848: First Women's Rights Convention at Seneca Falls
1849–55: California Gold Rush
1851: Indian Appropriation Act confines all tribes in reservations
1852: Harriet Beecher Stowe, Uncle Tom's Cabin
1860: Lincoln elected 16th US President on anti-slavery platform; South Carolina (slave-holding state) secedes from the Union
12 April 1861: Unionist attack on South Carolina starts the civil war between slave-holding Southern states (the Confederates) and the anti-slavery Northern states (Unionists)</td>
<td>Thoreau: Civil Disobedience (1849), Walden (1854)

American Romanticism
<u>Poetry</u>
1847: Emerson, Poems
1855: Longfellow, Hiawatha
1855: Whitman, Leaves of Grass
1865: Whitman, Drum Taps [Posthumous – 1890, 1891]
1896: Emily Dickinson, Poems [3 Volumes]
<u>Fiction</u>
Hawthorne, Twice-Told Tales (1837), The Scarlet Letter (1850)
Poe, “The Fall of the House of Usher”, Tales of the Grotesque and Arabesque (1839), “The Black Cat” (1843), “The Raven” (poem, 1845), “The Cask of Amontillado” (1846)
Melville, Typee (1846), Moby-Dick (1851)</td>
<td>Carlyle, Sartor Resartus (1833–34), Past and Present (1843)
Dickens, The Pickwick Papers (1836–37), Bleak House (1852–53), Great Expectations (1860–61)
Charlotte Bronte, Jane Eyre (1847)
Emily Bronte, Wuthering Heights (1847)
Thackeray, Vanity Fair (1848), Pendennis (1848–50)
Trollope, Barchester Towers (1857)
Tennyson, In Memoriam (1849)
Browning, Men and Women (1855), Dramatis Personae (1864)
Ruskin, The Stones of Venice (1851)
Arnold, The Scholar Gipsy (1853)</td>
</tr>
</table>

	1861–65: The American Civil War **1 January 1863: Lincoln's Emancipation Proclamation (abolishing slavery)** 19 November 1863: Lincoln's Gettysburg Address (defines democracy – "of the people, by the people, for the people") 9 April 1865: Civil War ends with Unionist victory 15 April 1865: Death of Lincoln after being shot at by a Confederate sympathiser 24 November 1865: Southern state of Mississippi enacts "Black Codes" limiting civil rights of freed slaves. 1866: Formation of rabidly anti-Black Ku Klux Klan	**African American Literature** Slave Narratives 1845: Frederick Douglass, *Narrative of the Life of Frederick Douglass* 1847: William Wells Brown, *Narrative of William W. Brown* 1850: Sojourner Truth, *Narrative of the Life of Sojourner Truth: A Northern Slave* 1855: Frederick Douglass, *My Bondage and My Freedom* 1861: Harriet Jacobs, *Incidents in the Life of a Slave Girl* Fiction 1853: William Wells Brown, *Clotel* 1859: Harriet Wilson, *Our Nig* Drama 1858: William Wells Brown, *A Leap for Freedom* **Native American Literature** 1847: George Copway's Autobiography Fiction 1854: John Rollin Ridge, *The Life and Adventures of Joaquin Murieta*	George Eliot, *Adam Bede* (1859), *The Mill on the Floss* (1860), *Silas Marner* (1861), *Romola* (1863) **Pre-Raphaelite Poetry and Painting** (1848–c.1860) Christina Rossetti, "Goblin Market" (1862) **The 'Condition of England' novels** Gaskell, *Mary Barton* (1848), *North and South* (1854) Charlotte Bronte, *Shirley* (1849) Charles Kingsley, *Yeast* (1848), *Alton Locke* (1850)

1866–79	1865–77: Reconstruction Era for rehabilitating emancipated slaves 1867: Anti-Black Jim Crow Laws 1869: Completion of Transcontinental Railroad across the US using mainly Chinese labour, sparks oil and gold boom 1876–79: Telephone, phonograph, electric bulb invented	**American Realism** Mark Twain, *Tom Sawyer* (1876), *Huckleberry Finn* (1884) 1868: Horatio Alger, *Ragged Dick* 1868: Louisa May Alcott, *Little Women* 1876: Bret Harte, *Gabriel Conroy* 1881: Joel Chandler Harris, *Uncle Remus: His Songs and Sayings*	Arnold, *Culture and Anarchy* (1869) Pater, *Marius the Epicurean* (1885) Hardy, *Far From the Madding Crowd* (1874), *The Return of the Native* (1878) George Eliot, *Middlemarch* (1871–72) Meredith, *The Egoist* (1879) **Literature of the British Empire** Rudyard Kipling H. Rider Haggard
1880–99	1880 census: over 50 million people 1888: Invention of Kodak box camera 1881: Booker T. Washington founds Tuskegee Institute to educate young Blacks 1884: the first skyscraper (10 floors) in Chicago 1886: Statue of Liberty in New York 1889: Oklahoma Land Rush – tribal territory occupied; more tribal land occupied by three new states – North and South Dakota and Washington	**American Realism** 1885: William Dean Howells, *The Rise of Silas Lapham* Stephen Crane, *Maggie, A Girl of the Streets* (1893), *The Red Badge of Courage* (1895) Frank Norris, *McTeague* (1899) **American Modernism** [1890: William James, brother of Henry James, first uses the term "stream of consciousness" in his *The Principles of Psychology*]	Hardy, *The Mayor of Casterbridge* (1886), *Tess of the D'Urbervilles* (1891), *Jude the Obscure* (1895) Oscar Wilde, *The Picture of Dorian Gray* (1890), *Lady Windermere's Fan* (1892) **Science Fiction** H. G. Wells

	29 December 1890: 200 protesters from American Indian Movement (AIM) persecuted/killed in Wounded Knee town, South Dakota 1893: Hawaii monarchy overthrown; annexed in 1898 1898: US overseas imperialism begins with occupation of the Philippines 1899: Thorstein Veblen, *The Theory of the Leisure Class*	Henry James, *The Europeans* (1878), *The Portrait of a Lady* (1881), *The Princess Casamassima* and *The Bostonians* (1886), *The Turn of the Screw* (1898) **African American Literature** 1881/92: Douglass, *Life and Times of Frederick Douglass* 1899: Charles Chesnutt, *The Wife of His Youth and Other Stories of the Color Line* **Gendered Writing** 1892: Charlotte Perkins Gilman, "The Yellow Wallpaper" 1899: Kate Chopin, *The Awakening*	**British Modernism** Conrad, *Almayer's Folly* (1895), *The Nigger of the 'Narcissus'* (1897), *Heart of Darkness* (1899) Yeats, *The Celtic Twilight* (1893), *The Land of Heart's Desire* (1894)
1900–39	Rise of capitalism, industrialisation, urbanisation, slums 1903: First eleven-minute film by Edison; first twelve-second aeroplane flight by Wright brothers	**American Realism** (focusing on growing urban problems) <u>Fiction</u> Theodore Dreiser, *Sister Carrie* (1900), *The Financier* (1912), *An American Tragedy* (1925) Frank Norris, *The Octopus* (1901), *The Pit, A Story of Chicago* (1903)	**British Realism** <u>Drama</u> George Bernard Shaw <u>Fiction</u> John Galsworthy, Arnold Bennett **Edwardian Poetry** Robert Bridges Walter de la Mare

<table>
<tr>
<td></td>
<td>11–13 July 1905: Black leaders from fourteen states meet under DuBois's leadership to form pro-Civil Rights Niagara Movement
1908: Henry Ford launches the Model T Ford motor car
1909: Niagara Movement joins with white liberals to form National Association for the Advancement of Colored People (NAACP); adoption of term "Colored" instead of "Negro"
1912: Arizona joins the Union
6 May 1912: 10000 women march in New York for women's suffrage
1913: Income tax introduced
1913: Violent nation-wide industrial strikes for better pay and work conditions (continues till 1916)
1914: World War I begins
6 April 1917: US enters the War
11 November 1918: World War I ends with Germany signing the Armistice Act</td>
<td>Jack London, The Call of the Wild (1903), Sea Wolf (1904)
Edith Wharton, The House of Mirth (1905)
Upton Sinclair, The Jungle (1906)
O. Henry, Stories Vols. 1–3 (1904, 1909, 1910)
Willa Cather, O Pioneers (1913), My Antonia (1918)
Sinclair Lewis, Main Street (1920)
Steinbeck, Of Mice and Men (1937), The Grapes of Wrath (1939)
<u>Drama</u>
1935: Clifford Odets, Waiting for Lefty, Awake and Sing, Till the Day I Die
1938: Thornton Wilder, Our Town

American Modernism
<u>Fiction</u>
Henry James, The Ambassadors (1903), The Golden Bowl (1904)
F. Scott Fitzgerald, This Side of Paradise (1920), The Great Gatsby (1925), Tender is the Night (1934)
Ernest Hemingway, The Sun Also Rises (1926), A Farewell to Arms (1929)
William Faulkner, The Sound and the Fury (1929), As I Lay Dying (1930)</td>
<td>World War I Poets
Wilfred Owen
Siegfried Sassson

Science Fiction
H. G. Wells

British Modernism
Conrad, Yeats, Synge, Eliot, Pound, Joyce, D. H. Lawrence, E. M. Forster, Dorothy Richardson, Virginia Woolf

The Thirties Poets
Auden, Spender, Isherwood, Dylan Thomas

Novelists of the Thirties
George Orwell, Graham Greene

Prose
Bertrand Russell</td>
</tr>
</table>

<table>
<tr>
<td></td>
<td>28 June 1919: US President Woodrow Wilson convenes the League of Nations
31 August 1919: US Communist Party formed in Chicago
1920: 19th Amendment to the Constitution gives white women the right to vote
1920: Communist party declared a "Red Menace"
10 November 1921: Margaret Sanger forms the American Birth Control League
1924: Harsh new immigration law with strict quotas
1925: John Scopes of Tennessee arrested, tried, fined $1000 for teaching Darwin's theory of evolution
October 1927: The first "talking picture" The Jazz Singer
1929–39: Stock market crash and the Great Depression (25 per cent unemployment)
September 1939: World War II begins</td>
<td><u>Poetry</u>
William Carlos Williams, Poems (1909)
Robert Frost, North of Boston (1914), Mountain Interval (1916, updated 1921), New Hampshire (1923), West-Running Brook (1928)
Carl Sandburg, Chicago Poems (1916)
Wallace Stevens, Harmonium (1923)
<u>Drama</u>
Eugene O'Neill, The Emperor Jones (1920), The Hairy Ape (1922), Desire Under the Elms (1924)
<u>Discursive Writing</u>
Henry Adams, The Education of Henry Adams (1907)

The American Western
Zane Grey, The Heritage of the Desert (1910), Desert Gold (1913), The Light of Western Stars (1914)

African American Literature
<u>Ideological/Aesthetic Writing</u>
Booker T. Washington, Up from Slavery (1901)</td>
<td></td>
</tr>
</table>

	Nobel Laureates in Literature Sinclair Lewis (1930) Eugene O'Neill (1936) Pearl Buck (1938)	W. E. B. DuBois, *The Souls of Black Folk* (1903) Alain Locke, *The New Negro* (1925) **The Harlem Renaissance (1920–37)** Poetry Claude McKay, *Harlem Shadows* (1922), *Home to Harlem* (1928) Countee Cullen, *Color* (1925), *The Black Christ* (1929) Langston Hughes, *The Weary Blues* (1926), *Montage of a Dream Deferred* (published 1951) Modernist Fiction Jean Toomer, *Cane* (1923) Zora Neale Hurston, *Color Struck* (1925), *Their Eyes Were Watching God* (1937) Nella Larsen, *Quicksand* (1928), *Passing* (1929) **Diasporic Writing** Arab American Ameen Rihani, *The Book of Khalid* (1911) Kahlil Gibran, *The Madman* (1918), *The Forerunner* (1920), *The Prophet* (1923), *Jesus, The Son of Man* (1928)	

		Korean American Younghill Kang, *The Grass Roof* (1931), *East Goes West* (1937)	
1940–55	1941: Japan attacks Pearl Harbor; US declares war on Japan; Hitler declares war on the US 1942–46: Internment of Japanese Americans May 1945: World War II ends with German surrender, but Japan continues the war August 1945: US drops atomic bombs on Hiroshima and Nagasaki; Japan surrenders 1946: US withdraws from the Philippines, but occupies Korea 1947–53: Cold War between US and USSR; Senator Joseph McCarthy's anti-Communist crusade in the US 1948: IBM introduces the earliest computer 1949: UNO (founded 1945) HQ in New York	**American Modernism** Fiction Hemingway, *For Whom the Bell Tolls* (1940), *The Old Man and the Sea* (1951) Faulkner, *Sanctuary* (1931), *Light in August* (1932), *Absalom, Absalom!* (1936) Drama Eugene O'Neill, *Mourning Becomes Electra* (1931), *The Iceman Cometh* (1939), *Long Day's Journey into Night* (1956 published, written in 1941–42) Tennessee Williams, *The Glass Menagerie* (1944), *A Streetcar Named Desire* (1947), *Cat on a Hot Tin Roof* (1955) Poetry Wallace Stevens, *Collected Poems* (1954), William Carlos Williams, *The Desert Music* (1954)	**End of Modernism** T. S. Eliot, *Four Quartets* (1945), *The Cocktail Party* (1949), *The Confidential Clerk* (1953), *The Elder Statesman* (1958) Virginia Woolf, *Between the Acts* (1941) **The Absurd** Samuel Beckett, *Waiting for Godot* (1953) **Fiction** George Orwell, Graham Greene, Kingsley Amis

	1954: Historic Brown vs Board of Education law suit challenging racial segregation in schools **Nobel Prize for Literature** William Faulkner (1949) Ernest Hemingway (1954)	**The American Western** Louis L'Amour, *Hondo* (1953), *Crossfire Trail* (1954) **African American Literature** 1940: Richard Wright, *Native Son* Poetry Gwendolyn Brooks, *A Street in Bronzeville* (1945), *Annie Allen* (1949) **Diasporic Writing** Chinese American Jade Snow Wong, *Fifth Chinese Daughter* (1950) Filipino American Carlos Bulosan, *America is in the Heart* (1946) Japanese American Monica Sone, *Nisei Daughter* (1953)	
1956–69	1957: US Congress passes law against racial discrimination in public places; but racism continues in the Southern states 1958: First Xerox machine 1959: Alaska and Hawaii become full-fledged states 1959: Second phase of the Cold War begins	**End of Modernism** Tennessee Williams, *The Night of the Iguana* (1961) Robert Frost, *In the Clearing* (1962) William Carlos Williams, *Pictures from Breughel* (1962) **The Beat Generation/Beats** Poetry 1956: Allen Ginsberg, *Howl*	**Fiction** William Golding Iris Murdoch Margaret Drabble **The Absurd** Samuel Beckett, *Krapp's Last Tape* (1958)

	8 November 1960: Kennedy elected president; space race with USSR begins; protests by the Beats	1960: Gary Snyder, *Myths and Texts* Fiction 1957: Jack Kerouac, *On the Road* 1959: William S. Burroughs, *Naked Lunch*	**The "Angry" Generation** Drama and Fiction Osborne, Arden, Wesker, John Wain, John Braine, Alan Sillitoe **Literature of the British Empire** Paul Scott, *The Raj Quartet* (1966–75)
1956–69 (contd)	1961: Civil Rights Movement begins; separatist "Black Power" units launched; new nomenclature, "African American", replaces "Colored" 1961: US military involvement in Vietnam begins (to prevent Communist takeover) 1 October 1962: Violent anti-Black protests as the first Black students enrolls at the University of Mississippi under heavy police protection 1963: Widespread NAACP protests against racial discrimination; police brutality	**Jewish American Literature** Fiction 1957: Isaac Bashevis Singer [wrote only in Yiddish], *Gimpel the Fool* (collection) 1961: Joseph Heller, *Catch-22* 1964: Saul Bellow, *Herzog* 1966: Bernard Malamud, *The Fixer* Poetry Czeslaw Milosz [wrote only in Polish] Joseph Brodsky [self-translated his Russian Poetry] **American Postmodernism** Fiction Vladimir Nabokov, *Lolita* (1955), *Pnin* (1957), *Pale Fire* (1962)	**The Movement Poets** Philip Larkin, Donald Davie, D. J. Enright, Elizabeth Jennings, Thom Gunn, Robert Conquest

	22 November 1963: President Kennedy assassinated 1964: Escalation of US military involvement in Vietnam 1964: President Lyndon Johnson enacts Civil Rights Act for African Americans 1965: President Lyndon Johnson enacts Voting Rights Act for African Americans 1965–75: The Vietnam War; massive protests by students and liberals 1965–66: Widespread race riots against continuing discrimination; Malcolm X shot, hundreds arrested; Martin Luther King Jr. launches peaceful Gandhian civil disobedience 1966: The first African American member of US parliament	Thomas Pynchon, *V* (1963), *The Crying of Lot 49* (1966) Kurt Vonnegut, *Cat's Cradle* (1963), *Slaughterhouse-Five* (1969) John Barth, *Giles Goat-Boy* (1966) Richard Brautigan, *Trout-Fishing in America* (1967) <u>Short Stories</u> Donald Barthelme William H. Gass <u>Drama</u> Edward Albee, *The Zoo Story* (1959), *The Sandbox* (1960), *Who's Afraid of Virginia Woolf?* (1962) <u>Poetry</u> Sylvia Plath, Denise Levertov, Anne Sexton, Adrienne Rich, Gary Snyder, John Berryman and John Ashberry **Science Fiction** Arthur C. Clarke, *The Sands of Mars* (1951), *Childhood's End* (1953), *The City and the Stars* (1956), *2001: A Space Odyssey* (1968)	

	From 1966: Native Americans and Mexican Americans (Chicanos) begin to agitate for their civil rights and franchise 1962: United Farm Workers led by Cesar Chavez founded for rights of Chicano agricultural labour October 1967: The first Black US Supreme Court judge appointed 4 April 1968: Martin Luther King Jr. is assassinated 8 July 1969: US troops begin to withdraw from Vietnam 20 July 1969: American astronauts first humans to walk on the moon 15 August 1969: 400000 people at Woodstock to protest against Vietnam War – Bob Dylan and Joan Baez sing anti-war songs like "We Shall Overcome" November 1969: Internet invented	**African American Literature** <u>Realism</u> *Fiction* 1952: Ralph Ellison, *Invisible Man* 1956: James Baldwin, *Giovanni's Room* *Drama* Lorraine Hansberry, *Raisin in the Sun* (1959) <u>The Black Arts Movement</u> *Poetry* Nikki Giovanni, *Black Feeling, Black Talk* (1968) Sonia Sanchez, *Homecoming* (1969) Amiri Baraka, *Black Magic* (1969) *Drama* Amiri Baraka, *Dutchman* (1964), *A Black Mass* (1966) *Prose* 1965: *Autobiography of Malcolm X* **Native American Literary Renaissance** <u>Fiction</u> N. Scott Momaday, *The House Made of Dawn* (1968), *The Way to Rainy Mountain* (1969)	

	Nobel Prize for Literature John Steinbeck (1962)	**Diasporic Writing** Japanese American John Okada, *No-No Boy* (1957) Chinese American C. Y. Lee, *The Flower Drum Song* (1957)	
1970–2015	1970: 448 US colleges and universities on strike against Vietnam War 30 April 1975: Vietnam War ends 1980–2003: US at war in Kuwait, Iran and Iraq (1990–91: Gulf War) 1991: Cold War ends with dissolution of USSR 1991–93: Economic recession in the US 4 July 1997: US spacecraft lands on Mars **11 September 2001 (aka 9/11): Two planes hijacked by terrorists crash into the World Trade Center in New York; Taliban claims responsibility** December 2001: US invades Afghanistan December 2003: Iraqi President Saddam Hussein captured and hanged	**American Postmodernism** Thomas Pynchon, *Gravity's Rainbow* (1973), *Mason and Dixon* (1997), *Against the Day* (2006), *Inherent Vice* (2009), *Bleeding Edge* (2013) Don DeLillo, *White Noise* (1985) Cormac McCarthy, *Blood Meridian* (1985), *All the Pretty Horses* (1992), *No Country for Old Men* (2005), *The Road* (2006) Stephen King, *Carrie* (1974), *Salem's Lot* (1975), *The Shining* (1977), *It* (1986) **Jewish American Literature** Saul Bellow, *Mr. Sammler's Planet* (1970) E. L. Doctorow, *Ragtime* (1975) Cynthia Ozick, *The Messiah of Stockholm* (1988) Philip Roth, *American Pastoral* (1997)	**Major Poets** Ted Hughes, Seamus Heaney **Neo-Victorian Fiction** John Fowles, A. S. Byatt, Sarah Waters **Neo-Realist Fiction** Graham Swift, Julian Barnes **Postmodern Drama** Harold Pinter, Tom Stoppard, Edward Bond, Peter Shaffer **Postmodern Fiction** Ian McEwan, Martin Amis, Alan Hollinghurst, Irvine Welsh, Mark Haddon

	2004: Facebook launched November 2008: Barack Obama elected first Black President of the US 2009–10: Economic recession in the US 2011: Osama bin Laden, mastermind of 9/11, killed by US soldiers, in Pakistan November 2012: Obama re-elected 2013: US Supreme Court recognises same-sex marriage, though it is not legal in all fifty states 2015: Same-sex marriage legalised in all fifty states 2015: US battles ISIS in Syria **Nobel Prize for Literature** Saul Bellow (1976) Isaac Bashevis Singer (1978) Czeslaw Milosz (1980) Joseph Brodsky (1987) Toni Morrison (1993)	**The Historical Western** Louis L'Amour, *How the West was Won* (1962) **African American Literary Renaissance** <u>Fiction</u> Toni Morrison, *The Bluest Eye* (1970), *Sula* (1973), *Beloved* (1987), *Jazz* (1992), *Paradise* (1997) Ishmael Reed, *Mumbo Jumbo* (1972) Alice Walker, *Meridian* (1976), *The Color Purple* (1982), *Possessing the Secret of Joy* (1992) Charles Johnson, *Middle Passage* (1990) Gloria Naylor, *The Women of Brewster Place* (1982), *Mama Day* (1988) <u>Poetry</u> Audre Lorde, *Coal* (1976), *The Black Unicorn* (1978) Maya Angelou, *And Still I Rise* (1978), *I Shall Not be Moved* (1990) Rita Dove, *Thomas and Beulah* (1986), *Grace Notes* (1989), *Sonata Mulattica* (2009) Yusef Kommunyakaa, *Copacetic* (1984), *I Apologize for the Eyes in My Head* (1986)	**Black British Literature** Caryl Phillips, Benjamin Zephaniah, Zadie Smith, Linton Kwesi Johnson **Multicultural British Literature** Doris Lessing, Kazuo Ishiguro, Abdulrazak Gurnah, Buchi Emecheta, Hanif Kureishi, Hari Kunzru, Monica Ali, Ayub Khan-Din **Literature of the British Empire** William Dalrymple

		<u>Drama</u> Ntozake Shange, *For Colored Girls who have Considered Suicide/when the rainbow is enuf* (1976) August Wilson, *Fences* (1983) <u>Gendered Writing</u> Maya Angelou, *I Know Why the Caged Bird Sings* (1969) Audre Lord, *Zami, A New Spelling of My Name* (1982), *Sister Outsider* (1984) **Native American Literary Renaissance (contd.)** N. Scott Momaday, *The Ancient Child* (1989), *In the Bear's House* (1999) Leslie Marmon Silko, *Ceremony* (1977), *Almanac of the Dead* (1991) Louise Erdrich, *Love Medicine* (1984), *The Beet Queen* (1986), *Tracks* (1988), *The Round House* (2012) Gerald Vizenor, *Darkness in St. Louis Bearheart* (1978), *Bearheart: The Heirship Chronicles* (1990) Sherman Alexie, *Reservation Blues* (1995), *The Lone Ranger and Tonto Fistfight in Heaven* (1993), *Indian Killer* (1996)	

		Poetry Paula Gunn Allen, *Life is a Fatal Disease: Poems 1962–1966* Joy Harjo, *How We Became Human: Poems 1975–2001* (2002) **Mexican American (Chicano) Literary Renaissance** "Corrido" (Border Ballad) Americo Paredes, *With a Pistol in his Hand* (1958) Fiction Abelardo "Lalo" Delgado, *Chicano: 25 Pieces of a Chicano Mind* (1969) Rudolfo Anaya, *Bless Me, Ultima* (1972), *Heart of Aztlan* (1976), *Tortuga* (1979). *Albuquerque* (1992) Sandra Cisneros, *The House on Mango Street* (1984), *Have You Seen Marie?* (2012) Americo Paredes, *George Washington Gomez* (1990) Ana Castillo, *The Mixquiahuala Letters* (1986), *So Far From God* (1993), *The Guardians* (2007), *Give It to Me* (2014) Helena Maria Viramontes, *Under the Feet of Jesus* (1992), *Their Dogs Came With Them* (2007)		

<u>Drama</u>
Luis Valdez [created Teatro Campesino], *The Shrunken Head of Pancho Villa* (1964), *Corridos* (1987), *Valley of the Heart* (2014)
<u>Poetry</u>
Gary Soto, *New and Selected Poems* (1995)
<u>Gendered Writing</u>
Cherrie Moraga and Gloria Anzaldúa (eds.), *This Bridge Called My Back* (1981)
Gloria Anzaldúa, *Borderlands/La Frontera* (1987)

Diasporic Literature
<u>South Asian American</u>
Fiction
Bharati Mukherjee, *Wife* (1975), *Jasmine* (1989), *Desirable Daughters* (2002), *Miss New India* (2011)
Chitra Banerjee Divakaruni, *Arranged Marriage: Stories* (1995), *The Mistress of Spices* (1997), *The Palace of Illusions* (2008), *Oleander Girl* (2013)
Meena Alexander, *Nampally Road* (1991)

		Jhumpa Lahiri, *Interpreter of Maladies* (1999), *The Namesake* (2003), *Unaccustomed Earth* (2008), *The Lowland* (2013) *Poetry* Agha Shahid Ali Meena Alexander Chinese American *Fiction* Maxine Hong Kingston, *The Woman Warrior* (1976), *China Men* (1980), *Tripmaster Monkey: His Fake Book* (1989) Amy Tan, *The Joy Luck Club* (1989), *The Kitchen God's Wife* (1991), *The Valley of Amazement* (2013) Gish Jen, *Mona in the Promised Land* (1996), The *Love Wife* (2004) Ha Jin, *Waiting* (1999), *War Trash* (2004), *A Map of Betrayal* (2014) *Drama* David Hwang, *FOB* (1980), *Family Devotions* (1981). *M. Butterfly* (1988), *Chinglish* (2011)		

		Japanese American Yoshiko Uchida, *Journey to Topaz* (1971) Cynthia Kadohata, *Weedflower* (2006), *The Thing About Luck* (2013) Korean American Theresa Hak Kyung Cha, *Dictee* (1982) Chang Rae Lee, *A Gesture Life* (1999), *The Surrendered* (2010), *On Such a Full Sea* (2014) Linda Sue Park, *When My Name Was Keoko* (2002), *Project Mulberry* (2005) Filipino American Bienvenido Santos, *The Praying Man* (1982) Jessica Hagedorn, *Dogeaters* (1990)	

Select Bibliography

Histories of American literature (listed according to dates of publication as the later histories offer newer critical perspectives):

Elliott, Emory et al, eds. *The Columbia Literary History of the United States*. New York: Columbia UP, 1988; rev. ed. 2013. Print.

Ford, Boris, ed. *The New Pelican Guide to English Literature. Vol. 9, American Literature.* London and New York: Penguin, 1988; 1991. Print.

Elliott, Emory et al, eds. *The Columbia History of the American Novel.* New York: Columbia UP, 1991. Print.

Bradbury, Malcolm, and R. Ruland. *From Puritanism to Postmodernism: A History of American Literature*. New York and London: Penguin, 1991. Print.

Parini, Jay, ed. *The Columbia History of American Poetry*. New York: Columbia UP, 1993. Print.

Elliott, Emory. *The Cambridge Introduction to Early American Literature*. Cambridge: Cambridge UP, 2002.

Bercovitch, Sacvan, gen. ed. *The Cambridge History of American Literature*. 6 vols. Cambridge: Cambridge UP. Various dates. Print.

Kalaidjian, Walter. *The Cambridge Companion to American Modernism*. Cambridge: Cambridge UP, 2005. Print

Graham, Maryemma, and Jerry W. Ward Jr., eds. *The Cambridge History of African American Literature*. Cambridge: Cambridge UP, 2011. Print.

Gray, Richard. *A Brief History of American Literature*. New Jersey: Wiley-Blackwell, 2014. Print.

American Literature Sites. Web. http://public.wsu.edu/~campbelld/amlit/sites.htm

Key Texts on American culture and literature (available in several editions or online, unless otherwise stated; listed according to dates of publication to locate these crucial concepts in their historical contexts):

Winthrop, John. "A Model of Christian Charity" (1630). [This Puritan sermon was the first to describe America as "a City upon a Hill"]

Crèvecoeur, J. Hector St. John de. *Letters from an American Farmer* (1782). [Highlighted the democratic and entrepreneurial spirit of America as opposed to feudal Europe]

Emerson, Ralph Waldo. "The American Scholar" (1837). [Distinguished between American literature and British literature]

O'Sullivan, John L. "Annexation" in the July–August 1845 issue of *Democratic Review* and a column in *New York Morning News* dated 27 December 1845. [Coined the phrase "Manifest Destiny"]

Lincoln, Abraham. "Emancipation Proclamation" (1 January 1863). [States that "all persons now held as slaves . . . shall henceforward be free"]

———. "Gettysburg Address" (19 November 1863). [Defined American democracy as "government of the people, by the people, for the people"]

Turner, Frederick Jackson. "The Significance of the Frontier in American History" (1893). [Introduced the "Frontier Thesis"]

Adams, James Truslow. *The Epic of America* (1931). [Coined the phrase "The American Dream"]

Washington, Booker T. *Up from Slavery* (1900) [Inspirational anti-racist autobiography]

DuBois, W. E. B. *The Souls of Black Folk* (1903). [Coined the phrase "the color line" that is fracturing American society along racial lines]

King Jr, Martin Luther. "I have a Dream" (28 August 1963). [This speech was a stirring call for an end to racism in the US.]

Kennedy, John F. *A Nation of Immigrants* (1964). [The title has become an iconic definition of the US.]

Anzalduá, Gloria. *Borderlands/La Frontera: The New Mestiza*. 4th ed. San Francisco: Aunt Lute Books, 1987; 2012. [A multi-genre text celebrating the Chicana cultural heritage]

Baudrillard, Jean. *America* (1986). Trans. Chris Turner. London: Verso, 1988. [The noted French philosopher describes the US as the quintessentially postmodern nation.]

Some important critical works on American literature listed according to dates of publication to indicate shifting theoretical concerns:

Matthiessen, F. O. *American Renaissance: Art and Expression in the Age of Emerson and Whitman.* New York: Oxford UP, 1941. Print.

Smith, Henry Nash. *Virgin Land: The American West as Symbol and Myth.* Cambridge, Mass.: Harvard UP, 1950. Print.

Hoffman, F. J. *The Modern Novel in America,1900–1950.* New York: Houghton Mifflin, 1951. Print.

Miller, Perry. *American Thought: Civil War to World War I.* New York: Holt, Rinehart and Winston, 1954. Print.

———. *Errand into the Wilderness.* Cambridge, Mass.: Harvard UP, 1956. Print.

Chase, Richard. *The American Novel and Its Tradition.* Staten Island, New York: The Gordian Press, 1957. Print.

Fiedler, Leslie. *Love and Death in the American Novel.* New York: Stein and Day, 1960. Print.

Marx, Leo. *The Machine in the Garden: Technology and the Pastoral Ideal in America.* New York: Oxford UP, 1964. Print.

Rosenberg, B., and D. M. White, eds. *Mass Culture: The Popular Arts in America.* New York: The Free Press of Glencoe, 1957; rev. ed. 1962. Print.

White, D. M., ed. *Popular Culture in America.* Englewood-Cliffs, New Jersey: Prentice-Hall, 1970. Print.

Slotkin, Richard. *Regeneration through Violence: The Mythology of the American Frontier, 1600–1860.* Middletown, CT: Wesleyan UP, 1973. Print.

Berger, Arthur Asa. *Pop Culture.* Dayton: Ohio UP, 1973. Print.

Bigsby, C. W. E. *Approaches to Popular Culture.* London: Edward Arnold, 1976. Print.

Slotkin, Richard. *The Fatal Environment: The Myth of the Frontier in the Age of Industrialization, 1800–1890.* Norman: U of Oklahoma P, 1985. Print.

Bigsby, C. W. E. *A Critical Introduction to Twentieth Century American Drama: I. 1900–1940; II. Williams, Miller, Albee; III. Beyond Broadway.* New York: Oxford UP, 1982–85. Print.

Bradbury, Malcolm. *The Modern American Novel.* London and New York: Penguin, 1983. Print.

Gates Jr., Henry Louis *The Signifying Monkey: A Theory of African American Literary Criticism.* New York: Oxford UP, 1988. Print.

Fiske, John. *Understanding Popular Culture.* London: Unwin Hyman, 1989. Print.

Winks, R. W., ed. *Mystery and Suspense Writers: The Literature of Crime, Detection and Espionage.* 2 vols. New York: Scribner, 1998. Print.

Singh, Amritjit, and Peter Schmidt, eds. *Postcolonial Theory and the United States: Race, Ethnicity and Literature.* Jackson: UP of Mississippi, 2000. Print.

Campbell, Neil, and Alasdair Kean. *American Cultural Studies.* London and New York: Routledge, 2002. Print.

Lee, Robert A. *Multicultural American Literature: Comparative Black, Native, Latino/a and Asian American Fictions.* Jackson: UP of Mississippi, 2003. Print.

Priestman, Martin, ed. *The Cambridge Companion to Crime Fiction.* Cambridge: Cambridge UP, 2003. Print.

Wirth-Neshr, Hana, and Michael Kramer, eds. *The Cambridge Companion to Jewish American Literature.* Cambridge: Cambridge UP, 2003. Print.

Lloyd-Smith, Allan. *American Gothic Fiction: An Introduction.* New York: Continuum, 2004. Print.

Porter, Joy, and Kenneth M. Roemer, eds. *The Cambridge Companion to Native American Literature.* Cambridge: Cambridge UP, 2005. Print.

Knight, S. *Crime Fiction since 1800.* London and New York: Palgrave Macmillan, 2010. Print

Index